The Gospel of John: Believe and Live

The message of the gospel of John is recapitulated in this verse:

"But these are written, that ye might believe that Jesus is the Christ, the Son of God; and that believing ye might have life through his name."

John 20:31 (KJV)

In *The Gospel of John: Believe and Live*, Elmer Towns thoroughly examines this beloved book. While he focuses on many vital words, Towns places a particular emphasis on two key words: *believe* and *live*. The author explains, "John's ultimate purpose is that his readers will believe the life and death of the Son of God and receive eternal life."

In twenty-four chapters, Christ's ministry unfolds, and the magnitude of His greatness is revealed through the discussion of His many appellations, including: the Word of God, the Saviour, the Good Shepherd, the Bread of Life, the Servant, and the Resurrection. The truths revealed in *The Gospel of John: Believe and Live* will help you to better understand what God wrought through the Saviour.

THE GOSPEL OF JOHN: BELIEVE AND LIVE

BY Elmer Towns:

Understanding the Deeper Life
The Gospel of John: Believe and Live

THE GOSPEL OF JOHN: BELIEVE AND LIVE

ELMER TOWNS

Library of Congress Cataloging-in-Publication Data
Towns, Elmer L.

The gospel of John: believe and live/Elmer Towns
    p. cm.
ISBN 0-8007-1644-2
1. Bible. N.T. John—Commentaries. I. Title.
BS2615.3.T68   1990
226.5'077—dc20   90-34670
                              CIP

CONTENTS

PREFACE

I have had a lifelong love affair with the Gospel of John, and I'm not sure where it began. I think it's the greatest book in the Bible. Right after I received Christ, I read through the Gospel of John. It could have begun there, or it could have started while I was a freshman in college. I taught the Gospel of John to a high school youth group and wrote a series of study lessons for the teens to answer.

While at Dallas Theological Seminary, I heard J. Sidlow Baxter preach a sermon that surveyed the total gospel. If I was not already aware of my love for the Gospel of John, it surely developed during that chapel message. Baxter walked over to the piano and played the seven notes of the scale from do to ti. He told us that seven is the number of perfection and that we would find a repetition of the number seven throughout John. Pointing out that the piano scale was not complete until he played the eighth note, which was do, he had the audience say the notes from do to do. As we repeated the scale, he counted from one to eight. He told us seven is the number of perfection but eight is the number of new beginnings. Also, Baxter told us that eight is the number of the Holy Spirit.

The number eight occurs repeatedly in John. There are seven miracles, plus one more (chapter 21), making eight. The same is true of the "great I am's" and the "eight witnesses."

Dr. John Mitchell, founder of Multnomah School of the Bible, Portland, Oregon, came to Dallas Theological Seminary and lectured on the Gospel of John. The practical insight of his lectures are evident in this manuscript. He taught me how to look for life-related principles in John.

I've taught the Gospel of John at Midwest Bible College, Baptist University of America, and Liberty University and have preached through the gospel at a number of Bible conferences. My first manuscript on John was written for Winnipeg Bible College correspondence courses in 1963. I named the book *The Deity of the Saviour* to reflect the twofold theme of John. This gospel was written, first, to demonstrate the deity of Christ and, second, that those who believe in Him would have eternal life (John 20:31).

In 1973 I made twenty-six television tapes on the Gospel of John at University Baptist Church, Gainesville, Florida, that were eventually aired over the educational network in that state. A number of people helped to perfect the technical presentation of that course, and I am indebted to them for the graphics and student workbook. In 1981, Mr. John Peach, a graduate assistant at Liberty Baptist Seminary, helped edit the videotapes into a learning resource manual.

In 1985, Mr. Doug Porter continued the project by editing the material into lessons for the layman. He helped me research the Greek terms, to make them readable for laymen.

This volume represents so much from so many sources that I cannot take sole credit. Yet it represents my research and class notes which I have reworked in great detail to provide an accurate commentary that is as true to the biblical text as possible. While I cannot take full credit, I do take full responsibility for all the weaknesses and omissions.

May this book accomplish the dreams of the many who have invested so much into its pages.

THE GREATNESS OF JOHN

Last of all, John, perceiving that what had reference to the bodily things of Jesus' ministry had been sufficiently related, and encouraged by his friends, and inspired by the Holy Spirit, wrote a spiritual gospel.

CLEMENT OF ALEXANDRIA

The Gospels are the first fruits of all writings, and the Gospel of John is the first fruits of the Gospels, and no one can receive its meaning who has not lain back on Jesus' breast.

ORIGEN

Here the profoundest mysteries of religion are opened up by a beloved disciple; Christ is lively pointed out, in his person and offices, and in his heart directed in the way of closing with him by faith; and the sure grounds of lost sinners' confidence are clearly demonstrated.

GEORGE HUTCHESON

Here it is that a door is opened in heaven, and the first voice we hear is, Come up hither, come up higher. Some of the ancients, that supposed the four living creatures in John's vision to represent the four evangelists, make John himself to be the flying eagle, so high does he soar, and so clearly does he see into divine and heavenly things.

MATTHEW HENRY

Luther is reported to have said that if a tyrant succeeded in destroying the Holy Scriptures and only a single copy of the Epistle to the Romans and of the Gospel of John escaped him, Christianity would be saved. He spoke truly; for the fourth gospel presents the object of the Christian faith in its most perfect splendor, and the Epistle to the Romans describes the way of faith which leads to this object, with an incomparable clearness. What need of more to preserve Christ to the world and give birth ever anew to the Church?

F. GODET

9

The Gospel of John has a special character, which has struck the minds of all those who will give it a little attention, even though they have not always clearly understood what it was that produced this effect: it not only strikes the mind, but attracts the heart in a way not to be found in any other parts of the holy book.

JOHN NELSON DARBY

For in the whole range of literature, there is not composition which is a more perfect work of art, or which more rigidly excludes whatever does not subserve its main end. From the first word to the last there is not paragraph, sentence, or expression which is out of its place, or with which we could dispense. Part hangs together with part in perfect balance.

MARCUS DODS

The Gospel of John is the most unusual and perhaps the most valuable member of the quartet of canonical gospels. Although it deals with the same broad sequence of events to be found in the pages of the others, it is quite different in structure and style.

MERRILL C. TENNEY

I like the comparison of John's Gospel to a pool in which a child can wade and an elephant can swim. It is both simple and profound. It is for the earliest believer in the faith and for the mature Christian. Its appeal is immediate and never failing.

LEON MORRIS

Of all the books of the New Testament, the one which has commanded the greatest interest and devotional attachment is the Gospel according to John. The scholar may study it chiefly because of its problems, and the ordinary believer because of its power to feed his soul, but in either case the gospel continues to be the center of attention.

EVERETT F. HARRISON

The first chapter of the Fourth Gospel is one of the greatest adventures of religious thought ever achieved by the mind of man.

WILLIAM BARCLAY

The critic may range the gospel with Philo and the Alexandrian philosophers; but, and the question is important, did the poor and ignorant, when they lay a-dying, ever ask their Rabbis to read to them of the voluminous writings of Philo or of those like him?

SIR EDWYN HOSKYNS

John is the greatest book in the Bible. Give it to the new Christian because of its straightforward simplicity. Give it to the scholar because of its deep profound mysteries. Give it to all because its message is Jesus Christ. It is the greatest book in the Bible because, when honestly encountered, the reader will come to realize Jesus as his Lord and God. He will fall to his knees and worship the person of the book—Jesus Christ.

The Gospel of John: Believe and Live

ONE

THE GOSPEL OF JOHN

I. INTRODUCTION

The Gospel of John seems to be the simplest of all books in the Bible to understand. That is why most new Christians are told to begin studying the Bible by reading the book of John. But at the same time, it is the most profound book in the Bible. Scholars have spent many years investigating its terms and their implications. John, the author, paints a comprehensive picture of the Lord Jesus Christ—majestic in His humanity, yet simply presented in His deity. And so, this gospel communicates perhaps the most profound truths about Jesus Christ found anywhere in Scripture. John not only recalls as an eyewitness the events in the life of Christ, he also interprets the meaning behind the miracles. When Jesus reveals Himself as God, the Jews react in violent confrontation, leading ultimately to the crucifixion of Christ. The Gospel of John tells what impact this controversy had on the disciples and, in a broader sense, the implications for people today. John's ultimate purpose is that his readers will believe the life and death of the Son of God and receive eternal life.

II. THE UNIQUE EMPHASIS OF JOHN

The message of the book of John is underlined by the use of two key words, *believe*, used ninety-eight times and *life*, used thirty-six times.

15

KEY WORDS	But these are written, that ye might believe that Jesus is the Christ, the Son of God; and that believing ye might have life through his name. John 20:31
Believe: 98 times *Life:* 36 times	

The Apostle John wrote with a twofold purpose—as noted in 20:31—to communicate Christ through His miracles and teachings so men might, first, believe that Jesus was indeed who He said He was, the Son of God; and second, they might have eternal life because of their belief. John's twofold purpose as seen in John 20:31 is illustrated in Chart 1.

Chart 1

Twofold Purpose	Believe—that Jesus is the Son of God
	Life—personal salvation

The phrase "that ye might continue believing" (*hina pisteuete*) is a purpose clause combining the preposition *hina* with a present active subjunctive. It was not John's objective that the reader merely come to a crisis of faith and know certain facts as a result of reading this gospel, but rather that the reader might "keep on believing." That which he is to believe is perhaps one of the most identifiable statements of Christology—"that Jesus is the Christ, the Son of God." The first letters of the first principal Greek words in this phrase spell *ichthus* (fish). Early Christians often used the sign of a fish to identify themselves as those who believe in the deity of Jesus Christ.

The second part of John's twofold purpose is really a by-product of the first. If the reader "continues to believe," he will "keep on having life." Again John uses a present active subjunctive (*echete*), emphasizing that the Christian life is a continuing adventure in faith. For John, life is more than mere existence. Life is an experience of abundant joy, peace, and victory over sin.

III. THE EIGHT KEY WORDS

John, under the inspiration of the Holy Spirit, uses special words to communicate his unique message. These key words give insight into the unique contribution of this fourth gospel.

> Believe
> Life
> Sign
> I am
> Truth
> Knowing
> Witness
> Father

A. Believe. The word *believe* (*pisteuo*) is the most significant word in the gospel. Often *believe* is accompanied with the preposition *eis* (in, into) and always with an object. Belief is in the active tense and always moves into its object, the Lord Jesus Christ. At the same time, John totally avoids the use of the noun *pistis* (faith). He may have resisted using the noun because it was too static for him. On several occasions the process of believing is preceded by the act of hearing (5:24,25; 6:44,45; 10:3,16,27; see 10:8; 12:46). John uses the verb *orao* (I hear) in contrast with the usual word *blepo* (I see), implying more than physical vision in believing. In the Gospel of John, believing is the total response of the whole person to God as He has revealed Himself through His Son, Jesus Christ. Some argue that John's concept of salvation lacks the doctrine of repentance. Although the word *repentance* is absent from the gospel, it certainly is implied as a part of believing, because John includes obeying in believing; *i.e.*, believing is pictured as drinking (4:14), eating (6:35,51), or walking (8:12,31). Hence when a person believes in Christ, he is in the process of repenting.

B. Life. The second significant word in John is *life.* The Greeks had three words for *life*, each with a different shade of meaning and emphasis. First, the term *psuche* referred to the self who was alive. It was very close to the Hebrew concept of *kardia* (heart) and is translated on occasion "heart"

(Ephesians 6:6) and "mind" (Philippians 1:27). John uses *psuche* as the life laid down by the good shepherd (10:11). Second, the word *zoe* in classical Greek normally referred to the essence or principle of life itself—the existence of life as opposed to death. The third word, *bios*, was used by Greek writers to describe one's manner of life and was almost exclusively used with reference to human life (such as biography). In this gospel, John uses the word *zoe* as spiritual life, often accompanied by the adjective *aionios* (eternal). As *aionios* is also an attribute of God, it has been suggested that eternal life is nothing short of the life of God. John equates eternal life with the knowledge of God in Christ's high priestly prayer (17:3).

C. *Sign.* Five words in the New Testament describe miracles: *terata* (wonders), *erga* (works), *thaumasia* (wonderful things), *dunameis* (powers), and *semeia* (signs). While the synoptic gospels prefer the word *dunameis* (to emphasize the power of Jesus), John employs the word *semeion* some seventeen times to point out the spiritual significance of eight miracles in the gospel. These signs were one way Jesus "manifested . . . his glory" (2:11). This word is used in the Septuagint to convey the idea of a heavenly symbol (Genesis 1:14), a protective mark (Genesis 4:15), a pledge (Genesis 17:11), a miracle (Exodus 7:3,9), a memorial (Exodus 13:9), a

Chart 2

THE EIGHT MIRACLES IN JOHN		
Sign	Reference	Jesus' Power Over
1. Turning of water into wine	2:1–11	Creation
2. Healing of the nobleman's son	4:46–54	Space
3. Healing of the lame man	5:1–9	Time
4. Feeding of the 5,000	6:1–14	Food
5. Jesus walks on the water	6:15–21	Natural laws
6. Healing of the blind man	9:1–12	Physical laws
7. Raising Lazarus from the dead	11:1–44	Death
8. Miraculous catch of fishes	21:1–11	All of the above

sample of divine power (Isaiah 7:11), and a signal (Jeremiah 6:1). Of the eight miracles of Jesus recorded in the gospel (*see* Chart 2), the first seven are in the book of signs (1:19—12:50). Also, following some signs, John records an extended dialogue with Christ providing some clue as to the heavenly meaning behind the sign.

D. I Am. John is the only Gospel which records the "great I am's" of Christ. (*See* Chart 3.) Seven times John records Jesus saying, "I am. . . ," attaching it to a metaphor. These seven statements give special insight into who Christ claimed to be. Christ was stating more than a metaphor, that He was like bread, a light, or a good shepherd. He was identifying Himself with Jehovah of the Old Testament. This emphatic expression had a particular connotation to the Jews. In the Old Testament the term *Lord* is a derivative of the verb *to be.* When Jehovah revealed His name to Moses as "I AM" (Exodus 3:13,14), He was stating, "I AM THAT I AM." Jehovah is the self-existing One. The Jews of Christ's time knew that when He stated, "I am," He was claiming, "I am Jehovah of the Old Testament." No wonder they were angry and on several occasions actually took up stones to kill Him (John 5:17,18; 8:58,59). These seven individual claims of Christ will be discussed further in the subsequent chapters.

Yet, there is an eighth claim that Christ makes that is an even greater statement about Himself. Jesus simply says, "I am" (*ego eimi*). Even though it is counted as an eighth claim, it occurs several times (4:26; 8:24,28,58; 13:13,19; 18:5,6,8). This is a statement of identification with Old Testament deity. Christ is implying "I am . . . I am," the self-existent One. He is claiming to be their God.

E. Truth. A fifth significant word in the message of this gospel is *truth.* John speaks of truth twenty-five times in the gospel and uses the two words for "true" a total of twenty-one times (*alethes,* thirteen times, *alethionos,* eight times). When the word *truth* appears in the other gospels, it always carries the meaning of veracity or dependability, that which is consistent with and corresponds to reality. The word *true* in the other gospels is objective and carries no innate moral quality; it is simply fact. John, however, uses the word in a theological or moral way to show Jesus is the giver, source, and personification of truth (1:14,17; 14:6). Truth, then, is

Chart 3

THE EIGHT GREAT I AM'S	
Metaphor	Reference in John
1. I am the bread of life	6:35
2. I am the light of the world	8:12; 9:5
3. I am the door	10:9
4. I am the good shepherd	10:11
5. I am the resurrection, and the life	11:25
6. I am the way, the truth, and the life	14:6
7. I am the vine	15:5
8. I am . . . I am (Exodus 3:14)	4:26; 8:24,28,58; 13:13,19; 18:5,6,8

the highest revelation of God, for it is God Himself. When Jesus is the truth, He reveals perfectly the Father who has been hidden. Jesus speaks the truth (8:40,45,46; 16:7) which is able to give people moral freedom (8:33–36) and sanctifies the believer to God (17:17,19). Truth is also closely related to John's emphasis on believing. Believing in Jesus Christ is coming to the truth (8:32; 16:13). Also, only John records the twenty-five double verilies (amen, amen) of Christ, an expression which occurs elsewhere only in Numbers 5:22 and Nehemiah 8:6. Some have translated this statement, "Truly, truly." According to Godet, this expression implies a doubt to be overcome in the mind of the hearer.

F. Knowing. The sixth significant word in John is *knowing*. While John uses two words for knowing (*ginoskein*, fifty-six times, and *eidenai*, eighty-five times), he completely avoids the noun meaning "knowledge." He may be reacting to the Gnostics and their improper use of the term. Perhaps John is reminding us that biblical knowledge is not a doctrinal statement to be learned but rather the experience of new life through belief in Jesus Christ. Knowledge is not merely cognitive but has a moral connotation. In John's writings, knowing is closely related to faith. Believing and knowing are interrelated: when one believes, he knows that he has eternal life (*see* 1 John 5:13). According to John, to know and understand a fact and then act upon it amounts to faith.

The two words for knowing imply two different kinds of knowledge. *Ginoskein* means "to acquire knowledge" or "to learn by experience," whereas *eidenai* means "to possess innate knowledge about something" but not to learn it. John uses this latter word to emphasize the omniscience of Christ, the former word to express how a believer may know he is saved.

G. Witness. The term *witness* (*marturia*) is one of John's characteristic words, occurring forty-seven times as both a noun and verb in this gospel. The witness in this gospel is not primarily a verification of the historical facts, but chiefly a testimony to the character and significance of the person of Christ. The attestation of factual history is only a part of John's greater goal. John identifies eight kinds of witnesses to the character of Christ, as illustrated in Chart 4. A rule of Jewish law declares, "At the mouth of two witnesses, or at

Chart 4

EIGHT WITNESSES IN JOHN	
Witness	**Reference**
1. Witness of the Father	5:32,34, 37; 8:18
2. Witness of the Son	3:11; 8:14, 18; 18:37
3. Witness of the Holy Spirit	15:26; 16:13,14
4. Witness of the Scriptures	1:45; 5:39,40,46
5. Witness of the works of Jesus	5:17,36; 10:25; 14:11; 15:24
6. Witness of the Baptist	1:7,8; 5:33–35
7. Witness of the disciples (including John)	15:27; 19:35; 21:24
8. Witness of changed lives	4:39; 9:25, 38; 12:17

the mouth of three witnesses, shall the matter be established" (Deuteronomy 19:15).

As a witness John was most certainly observant. He recorded the emotions and motives of Christ (2:24; 4:1–3; 6:15; 11:33; 13:1,21; 18:4) and reflections of the disciples (2:11,17,22; 12:16). He remembers the very hours of certain events (1:39; 4:6,52; 19:14) and the particular statements of Philip (6:7; 14:8), Andrew (6:9), Thomas (11:16; 14:5), and Judas (14:22). Particularly memorable was the last day he spent with Jesus before the crucifixion. About one-third of the gospel, 237 of 879 verses, deals with that twenty-four hour period.

It is estimated that John was nearly one hundred years old at the time he wrote the gospel which bears his name. As an old man he understands in his heart many of the lessons from the teachings of Jesus that before he may have understood only with his head. Therefore, John writes to communicate the meanings behind the miracles and teachings of Christ. This is, perhaps, another reason why the Gospel of John is so profoundly deep and yet simple enough for men of all ages, education, and backgrounds to understand.

Although the author does not name himself in this book, the early church had no problem identifying him as John the Apostle. The content of the gospel makes it clear the book was written by a close confidant of Jesus. Further, the author uses two phrases to identify himself as one extremely close to Jesus. He is both a witness (19:34,35; 21:24) and the disciple "whom Jesus loved" (13:23–25; 19:25–27; 20:2; 21:20). The other gospels suggest the disciples most intimately associated with Jesus were Peter, James, and John. Peter is referred to in the third person. Neither of the sons of Zebedee are named in the gospel; however, James was martyred far too early to be considered the author of this gospel (Acts 12:2). By process of elimination, it is evident that only John could have written this book.

Early authorities agree that John was the author, including the writer of the Muratorian Fragment (A.D. 170), Clement of Alexandria (A.D. 190), Tertullian (A.D. 200), Origen (A.D. 220), and Hippolytus (A.D. 225). Eusebius claims to have discovered the existence of two Johns in Ephesus, and some modern scholars have used this discovery to argue for a non-apostolic authorship of this gospel. However, Eusebius's discovery is based on an unlikely interpretation of an isolated passage in which the name *John* appears twice. Eusebius argued one was the Apostle John and the other was the elder or presbyter John. A close examination of the original statement made by Papias reveals that neither is called an apostle, both are called elders (presbyters), and both are called disciples of the Lord. In contrast to this weak argument, Irenaeus, a disciple of Polycarp, who was a friend of the Apostle John, claimed the gospel was written by the apostle and further claimed that Johannine authorship was what Polycarp had taught.

H. Father. The phrase *ho pater* (the father, used of God) occurs 121 times, and the phrase *my father* occurs 35 times. These phrases appear more than any other key word because the thrust of Christ's message was to reveal the heavenly Father. The word *Father* was used only a few times of God in the Old Testament, and then it was never His name or title. In the Old Testament the word *Father* was applied to Him metaphorically—God was like a father, or God had the characteristics of a father. The Jews understood that Jesus was telling them God was a Father and that He was the Son who had a special relationship to the Father, with whom He was equal. As a result they tried to kill Him (5.17,18).

The unique revelation of the Father is enhanced by the revelation of Christ as: (1) the only begotten Son of the Father (1:14,18; 3:16,18; *see* 1 John 4:9); (2) the Son of God (3:18); (3) Son (3:17); and (4) the Son of Man (3:14).

I. Other Key Words. John has many other unique words that communicate his particular message. Their numerous occurrences in John as opposed to the few times they appear in the other three gospels signify their importance to John. (*See* Chart 5.)

IV. THE UNIQUENESS OF JOHN'S WRITING STYLE

A. A Climactic Style. John's writing style differs from other biblical writers in that he has a climactic quality in his works—he was concerned with last things. John was probably the last person to write a New Testament book: he was also the author of the last gospel, the last New Testament

Chart 5

Key Word	Greek	Times in John	Times in Synoptics
Abide	meno	41	12
Finish	teleioo	19	2
Flesh	sarx	13	11
Glory	doxa	44	38
The Jews	Ioudaioi	71	17
Light	phos	23	14
Love	agape	57	35
Verily, Verily	amen amen	25	0
Work	ergon	27	9
World	kosmos	79	15

book (Revelation), and the last book added to the canon (Third John). Theologically, John addressed the doctrine of last things (eschatology) and wrote what is considered the last or ultimate word on Christ (1:14).

Within this gospel, the reader is exposed to an adventure in suspense that builds climactically to carefully reveal Christ. In the first chapter, John presents Christ as the Eternal Word of God (1:1) and builds his defense of that statement. Using the teachings of Christ and His miracles to support the claim that Jesus is indeed the Christ, the Son of the Living God, John tries to convince men to believe in His deity that they might have eternal life (20:31). The apex of the book reveals Thomas falling before Christ and confessing Him as "my Lord and my God" (20:28). This statement is the ultimate purpose of the author. He wants each reader to acknowledge Christ as his Lord and his God.

John writes the ultimate and last word on Christology. His simple statement, "The word was made flesh" (1:14), summarizes the supernatural union of the divine and human natures of Christ. Clearly, Jesus is very human in this gospel. He gets angry (2:15), tired (4:6), and could eat (4:31). He identifies with the questioners (6:5,28,29) and experiences grief (11:33,35,38) and human need (19:28). Yet this is the same Christ who is, without doubt, God. The ultimate revelation of Christ is a picture of Him as the God-man.

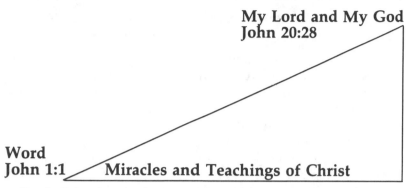

My Lord and My God
John 20:28

Word
John 1:1   Miracles and Teachings of Christ

B. *A Selective Style.* John is selective in both what is included and what is excluded. This gospel contains no account of the birth, baptism, or temptations of Jesus because John emphasizes Christ's deity. However, John describes the Word becoming flesh, the results of the baptism, and the encounter the Jews have with Christ because He claims deity. John also chooses not to refer to demons, the Last Supper, or the agony of Gethsemane.

There is no explicit reference in John to parables. The word translated "parable" in 10:6 is not the usual term *parabole* but rather *paroimian* and literally means "a wayside saying or proverb." It was also used of an allegory but not of a parable in the sense of those which appear in the synoptic gospels. There Jesus is the Son of Man with undebatable wisdom; in John, Jesus is the Son of God who speaks with authority.

Equally interesting is what John does include. Only John identifies a public ministry of Christ prior to John the Baptist's imprisonment. Of the seven key miracles in the life of Christ, five are unknown outside this gospel. While John makes it clear that the ministry of Christ lasted over three years, he chooses to record only twenty days of that period: he omits all the events in the second year (5:1—6:4).

C. *An Extended Narrative Style.* John's use of extended discourses is also unique. Only John includes the conversations with Nicodemus, the Samaritan woman, the father of the sick son, the paralytic at the pool of Bethesda, Mary and Martha, and Peter at the seashore. The gospel is marked by several extended discourses with "the Jews" (those who opposed Him and ultimately were responsible for His death). John records most fully the teaching of Christ in the upper room and immediately preceding his betrayal, including the high priestly prayer of Christ in chapter seventeen.

D. A Style that Features People. Many newspapers and magazines include features on people because the current reader is interested in people, their problems and how they solve them, as well as their successes. Throughout, John exposes the reader to people whose lives are changed because of their encounter with Jesus. What is known about Andrew? Only what John wrote. John identifies a disciple named Nathanael, not mentioned in the other gospels, and it is only on the basis of John that we know about "doubting Thomas." While the other gospels speak of a disciple who smote a servant at the betrayal of Jesus, it is John alone who identifies the servant as Malchus and records that it was Peter who held the sword.

E. A Precise Style. One cannot read this gospel written some sixty years after the events occurred without being impressed with the amazing number of details. John remembers the very hour (4:00 P.M.) he met Jesus (1:39), that there were six waterpots at the marriage in Cana (2:6), the fact that a woman left her waterpot at the well (4:28), the number of years a man had been sick (5:5), the estimated cost of feeding the five thousand (6:7), and the one who discovered the five barley loaves and two small fishes (6:8,9). Such details tend to verify his claim to have witnessed these things (see section III, G, earlier in this chapter).

F. The Jerusalem Setting. Finally, the Gospel of John is unique in its description of Jerusalem. The other gospels almost ignore the capital city of the Jews, recording only one visit to Jerusalem in Christ's public ministry, though many others are implied (see Matthew 23:37). John, however, puts Jesus in Jerusalem on at least five different occasions, these being the feast days. In so doing, John pictures Jesus as an obedient Jew who goes to Jerusalem as commanded (Deuteronomy 16:16). While the ministry of Jesus in the synoptic gospels is almost exclusively in Galilee, the ministry of Jesus in John is almost exclusively in Jerusalem. In Galilee, Jesus ministers to the multitudes who generally receive Him, but in Jerusalem, Jesus is confronted with "the Jews" who dispute His claim of deity and crucify Him.

V. THE CHRONOLOGY OF THE GOSPEL

The authors of some commentaries say the events in the life of Christ could be compressed into six months, while others, taking into account the unrecorded events in the life of Christ, feel that He could have been seventy years old to have accomplished what He did.

There is no better authority to establish the chronology of Jesus' ministry than the Word of God. Jesus began His ministry at His baptism, where we see that "Jesus was about thirty years of age" (Luke 3:23). In telling how old Jesus was at the beginning of his ministry and baptism, Luke might have been drawing a connection to the initiation of the Old Testament priest who was dipped in water at age thirty. According to Jewish law and custom, the priest was inducted into the priesthood at age thirty by being cleansed with clean water. Jesus, being initiated into His anointed offices (prophet, priest, and king), followed this practice with His baptism, declaring the beginning of His ministry.

Based on this fact, only John reveals that Christ ministered for three and a half years, hence showing Christ was approximately thirty-three and a half years old when he died. After Jesus was baptized, He immediately began His ministry by calling Andrew, Peter, and one other unnamed person, probably the Apostle John (1:35–42). On the next day, Christ found Philip, who in turn brought Nathanael, and they both followed Him (1:43–51). Notice the words in these verses: each day is connected by the phrase, "the next day," or "the day following," pointing out a day-by-day progression. In John 2:1 notice the "third day," indicating that this is the third day following Christ's baptism. On this day, we see Christ and His disciples at the wedding feast in Cana of Galilee. Here Jesus performs His first miracle, by changing water into wine. Although not mentioned in the Gospel of John, it is following this miracle that Jesus is thought to have been led into the wilderness to be tempted.

At this point in chronology, the Passover feasts are used to date the life and ministry of Christ. The Passover is a feast of the Jews which every Jewish male is legally required to attend in Jerusalem. There are four Passovers mentioned in the Gospel of John, implying that Christ ministered three years (2:13; 5:1; 6:4; 11:55). Approximately five months elapse between the temptation of Christ and the first Passover feast, the phrase "not many days" (2:12) being an indefinite length of time.

In the first Passover recorded in John (2:13), Christ cleansed the temple of money changers and merchants. The second Passover is in John 5:1, and the third occurs in John 6:4. Between the fifth and sixth chapters of John, the second year of Christ's ministry, there is no record of any activities of Jesus. We might ask, "Is not this time of Jesus' life noteworthy? Why did John not record anything in the entire second year of Christ's ministry?" These questions cause us to review the purposes of John once more. His goal is not to write a complete, sequential, chronological history of the life and ministry of Christ, but to prove that Christ is deity and that if the readers will believe in Him, they will have eternal life. John writes selectively under the influence of inspiration.

The third year of Christ's ministry begins with the Passover in John 6:4. The fourth Passover, the one at which Christ was crucified, begins in John 11:55. Noting the chronology carefully, we can conclude that Christ ministered three and a half years after His baptism and died when He was approximately thirty-three and a half years old.

A second fact that proves John writes selectively is that he spends the first eleven chapters on the thirty-three and a half years of the life of Christ. Then he devotes the last ten chapters to what amounts to only one week. That last week covers the final instructions to His disciples, the crucifixion, and the postresurrection events. So the most important emphasis in John is the death of Christ. He undoubtedly sees the life that Christ lived as being valuable and foundational, but he emphasizes the death and resurrection of Christ as the ultimate purpose of his book.

VI. THE AUTHENTICITY OF THE GOSPEL

A. Apologetics of John. During the last century, certain scholars have chosen to question and challenge the authenticity of most books of the Bible. As a result, they argue that certain books are really the result of several authors and claim chapters and verses either do not belong or are misplaced in the book. The Gospel of John has not escaped these attacks. Still, it has not only survived, it may well be that in challenging the authenticity of this gospel, liberal scholars have threatened the credibility of their other works.

The fact that John's gospel was written long after the other gospels makes it surprising that it was even received by the church. Not every book or letter written by the apostles made it into the New Testament. Apparently two Pauline epistles and one Johannine epistle were written to churches and did not make it into the canon (see 1 Corinthians 5:9; Colossians 4:16; 3 John 9). It was not beyond the dignity of the early church to question the theological accuracy of even apostolic statements (see Acts 17:11). Despite this, the Gospel of John was accepted quickly by the early church as authentic and enjoyed widespread circulation within fifty years of its writing.

The earliest apparent allusion to John is found in the Epistle of Barnabas. Ignatius, Papias, Justin Martyr, Theophilus of Antioch, and many other early church leaders make reference to this gospel in their writings. Not only is John identified in the Muratorian Canon (A.D. 170), it was also cited by heretics, including Basilides and Valentinus. Only a small sect known as "Alogoi" appears to have had any opposition to the gospel in the early years of Christianity. This sect followed the teachings of a Gnostic named Cerinthus, a contemporary of the apostle's later years and one whose teaching was bitterly opposed by John. One tradition of the early church tells of a time when the aged apostle was at a public bath when he learned that Cerinthus was in another part of the same building. Convinced the roof would cave in upon everyone present as a judgment of God on this false teacher, John urged his companions to leave with him immediately. It is therefore only natural to expect the followers of Cerinthus to challenge anything even remotely associated with the Apostle John. Apart from the Alogoi, there was no challenge to the authenticity of John until the nineteenth century.

During the nineteenth century and into the early part of the twentieth century, form critics delighted to give this gospel a late date. Traditionally it was accepted that the Gospel of John had been written about A.D. 90. But these critics began with the assumption that it could not have been written prior to the second, third, or even fourth century. As these conclusions were being suggested by higher critics, a remarkable discovery was made in England. In 1920, Grenfell acquired some Egyptian papyri for the John Rylands Library of Manchester. Upon later examination, C. H. Roberts discovered one fragment contained five verses from the Gospel of John (18:31–33,37,38). The latest possible date of this fragment is A.D. 150, making it the oldest of all New Testament documents. Obviously, by the middle of the second century the Gospel of John not only had been written but had even reached a provincial town in Egypt.

B. *Secondary Purposes.* There may be several other reasons why John wrote this gospel. Although they are not as clearly stated as his primary purpose (20:31), they are implied by what John has chosen to emphasize. These secondary reasons relate primarily to the historical context of the gospel.

As a former disciple of John the Baptist, the author of this gospel may have been disturbed by the existence of a sect that elevated the Baptist. This group flourished within orthodox Judaism into the third century. The Apostle Paul encountered a dozen men in Ephesus who may have been affiliated with this sect and on the fringe of the church (Acts 19:1–7). As one reads this gospel, it becomes apparent that the author continually portrays John the Baptist in a respectable but lesser light than Jesus. This distinction is not as clearly emphasized in the synoptic gospels.

A second sect that created theological problems for early Christians was gnosticism. Gnostics believed that all matter was essentially evil. In an effort to deny the possibility of God in any way being related to matter, these heretics essentially denied both the deity and the humanity of Christ. Some held He was a kind of semi-god, while others claimed Jesus was really a spirit who only seemed to be a man. Still others tried to define Him as a man with unusual divine power from His baptism to the cross. While there are many subtle attacks on the errors of the Gnostic teachers in John's writings, perhaps his boldest challenge is the statement of the incarnation, "the Word was made flesh" (1:14). God, who is spirit, touched earth by becoming flesh. In this statement, John attacked the Gnostics, who believed flesh was sinful.

Still a third minor or secondary purpose for John's writing was to correct the mistaken belief some had that John would not die but would live until Christ returned. Many conservative scholars agree the last chapter was added by John after completing his gospel to clarify any misunderstanding about his death. John, perhaps aware he would soon die, wanted to make it plain that Jesus had never promised him immortality (*see* chapter 21).

TWO

CHRIST—
THE WORD OF GOD
JOHN 1:1–18

Christ is called "the Word" (*ho logos*) six times in Scripture, and all occurrences appear only in the writings of John (1:1,14; 1 John 1:1; Revelation 19:13). Historically, *logos* meant a collection of ideas or words. It can mean both inner thought and the outward expression of that thought. The Septuagint translators used *logos* with reference to both the law and wisdom of God (Exodus 34:28; Proverbs 8:1–33).

Scholars debate where John got the term *word*, hence they disagree on its meaning. First, some believe John borrowed the term from the Greeks and is answering the Gnostics by implying Jesus is God's answer to philosophic questions. Second, some think the term is Hebrew, and John may be making reference to Christ as the wisdom of God as presented in Proverbs (*see* Proverbs 3:18–20; 4:5–13; 8:1—9:2). Third, some believe Jesus is called "the Word of God" because this phrase is used over twelve hundred times in the Old Testament to refer to the revelation of God or His message to men. Jesus is the final revelation and is the personification of the written and spoken word in the Old Testament. Referring to Christ as the "word" is more easily understood when we reflect on our purpose for using words. Words are used to communicate, express, and convey mean-

Chart 6

TITLES OF CHRIST IN JOHN 1			
Verse	Title	Verse	Title
1	Word	23	Lord
1	God	29	Jesus
3	Him	29	Lamb of God
4	Life	30	A Man
4	Light of Men	34	Son of God
9	True Light	38	Rabbi
11	He	38	Master
14	Flesh	41	Messiah (RSV)
14	Only Begotten of the Father	45	Jesus of Nazareth
17	Jesus Christ	45	Son of Joseph
18	Only Begotten Son	49	Son of God
20	Christ	49	King of Israel
		51	Son of Man

ing. Therefore, Jesus is the expression, revelation, and communication of the Lord. Christ is the incarnate Word of God.

Twenty-five titles are used for Jesus Christ in this first chapter of the Gospel of John, more than in any other chapter of the Bible. Through these titles Jesus is defined as being totally man and totally God, the God-man. This is illustrated in Chart 6.

I. THE REVELATION OF THE WORD OF GOD (1:1–18)

John begins this section with eternity prior to creation and concludes with a point in time, the incarnation. John is emphasizing the deity of Christ, stressing both His preexistence and eternalness. Most of the things he says about Jesus in this introduction are highlights of what he will cover in greater detail later in the gospel. Because John's purpose is different from that of the synoptic gospel writers, he includes material in his introduction that is ignored by the other biographers of Jesus. John stresses the preincarnate Word becoming flesh and the witness of John the Baptist to His divine nature and purpose. The synoptic writers stress the conception, physical birth, reaction by family and strangers, flight to Egypt, and human growth of the boy Jesus. Each book's purpose is reflected in its introduction.

> In the beginning was the Word, and the Word was with God, and the Word was God.
> 2 The same was in the beginning with God.

A. His Deity (1:1,2). John introduces Christ as the Word by emphasizing His deity. The first five verses of this gospel have an obvious parallel in structure and thought with the first chapter of Genesis. While similar, there is also an important difference between these two passages. Genesis begins with the creation of the world, at a point that began time, while John reaches back beyond time into eternity. Creation is not specifically mentioned until verse three, so the first two verses must refer to an earlier period. This thought is particularly evident in the description "In the beginning was the Word." The verb *was* is imperfect *en*, conveying the idea of continuous existence rather than the more usual term *egeneto*, which is also translated "was" but has the idea of coming into being. The concept of the eternal preexistence of the Word is conveyed by the New English Bible translation, "When all things began, the Word already was."

Not only does John emphasize the eternal preexistence of the Word, he also notes the intimacy of fellowship that existed between the Word and God. In the phrase "the Word was with God," the use of the preposition *pros* (with) with the accusative case denotes motion toward a particular direction. This grammatical structure is used to represent intimacy and communion and implies the Word and God were in face-to-face relationship. The Word was not only with God, He was communing with God.

John very carefully concludes the first verse of this gospel with a statement declaring the deity of the Word—"the Word was God." In this expression, *theos en ho logos*, the definite article belongs to the Word, not God. The New World Translation has erroneously translated this phrase "the Word was a god," a translation which violates both the context of the phrase and the rules of Greek grammar but fits in well with their Jehovah's Witness denial of the deity of Christ. *Theos* without the article emphasizes quality rather than individuality. Had John included the article, this phrase would tend to support the error of Sabellianism, which taught one God, manifested in three different modes. John, however, used this form because he wished to identify who the Word is, not who God is. The idea conveyed is that the Word is of the very same character, quality, essence, and being as God. While the Word does not by Himself complete the Godhead, all the divinity belonging to the rest of the Godhead also belongs to Him.

> 15 John bare witness of him, and cried, saying. This was he of whom I spake. He that cometh after me is preferred before me: for he was before me.
> 16 And of his fulness have all we received, and grace for grace.
> 17 For the law was given by Moses, but grace and truth came by Jesus Christ.
> 18 No man hath seen God at any time; the only begotten Son, which is in the bosom of the Father, he hath declared him

B. His Creation (1:3). In the third verse, John specifically emphasizes the creative work of the Word. Again, the absence of the definite article is significant. Greek philosophers uses the expression *ta panta* (the whole of creation). When John here used *panta* (all things) without the article, he refers to all creation with its infinite parts. He speaks not only of the vastness of creation as seen through the telescope but also of the wonders of creation observed with the microscope. Also, John means more than the creation that we see; he implies the creation of the heavens (plural) including the inhabitants thereof (angels), as seen in Genesis 1:1, and the creation of the earth.

Concerning this creation John writes, "All things came into being at a point in time by him" (1:3, literal translation). The use of an aorist (*egeneto*) with reference to the creative activity of the Word contrasts the event of creation with the continuous existence of the Word. *Egeneto* is one of three words in the New Testament that expresses the creation of substance from nothing. The other two, *ktizein* and *poiein,* tend to emphasize the place of the Creator, whereas this verb refers to substance that was created.

According to John, not even one thing came into being apart from the Word. The Word is here portrayed as the intermediate agent in the work of creation. This thought is also conveyed by Paul in 1 Corinthians 8:6. This does not limit the Word as a mere instrument of God but rather recognizes the relationship between the Father and Son. This statement concerning the creative work of the Word is a clear expression of John's personal faith in the creative power of God (*see* Hebrews 11:3).

> 4 In him was life; and the life was the light of men.
> 5 And the light shineth in darkness; and the darkness comprehended it not.

C. His Illumination (1:4,5). One of the significant metaphors Christ uses to describe Himself is light. One of the seven "I am's" is "I am the light of the world" (8:12; 9:5). Light is also the theme of chapters eight and nine in the gospel. John mentions three things in introducing the concept of light.

First, the light "shineth" (1:5). The verb *phainei* is a linear present active indicative, which indicates not merely a point in time but that the light has continued to shine from the beginning until now and is still shining. Even today Christ is the Light "which lighteth every man that cometh into the world" (1:9).

Second, light stands in contrast to the darkness that is everywhere present. The Greeks had two words for darkness. *Zophos* was a poetic term signifying the ideas of gloom, nebulousness, or a kind of half darkness. John uses the stronger term, *skotia*, nine times in his gospel. John calls darkness the natural sphere of those who hate good (3:19,20), and he contrasts it with Jesus, the Light of the World (8:12; 12:35,46). On three occasions John uses the term to describe physical darkness, yet also implies spiritual darkness (3:19; 6:17; 20:1). In using *skotia* here, John reminds the reader that the moral darkness associated with sin is deep, like midnight, not a mere dusk.

The third thing John emphasizes concerning the light is the state of hostility that exists between it and the darkness.

The verb translated "comprehended" is *katelaben*. This word is used in a variety of ways in the New Testament including a runner obtaining a prize in a race (1 Corinthians 9:24), the Gentiles attaining righteousness (Romans 9:30), a demon taking possession of a man (Mark 9:18), and the day of the Lord overtaking as a thief (1 Thessalonians 5:4). The verb in Greek literature can refer to a grasping by the mind ("comprehend," "understand"), a grasping by force ("overtake," "seize"), or overwhelming. Since John did not use the middle voice, he did not mean passive understanding or comprehension. John here uses an aorist active indicative, meaning that the darkness has not overtaken or extinguished the light. The aorist emphasizes there has never been one instance of such a defeat.

> 6 There was a man sent from God, whose name was John.
> 7 The same came for a witness, to bear witness of the Light, that all men through him might believe.
> 8 He was not that Light, but was sent to bear witness of that Light.
> 9 That was the true Light, which lighteth every man that cometh into the world.

D. His Forerunner (1:6–9). Before following Jesus, the author of this gospel was a follower of John the Baptist. It is therefore natural to expect John the Apostle to emphasize the place of the Baptist in his introduction. Yet in every reference to the Baptist, John demonstrates the superiority of Christ. Earlier, John observed the Word was (*en*), implying Christ's self-existence or eternalness. Here, John the Baptist merely comes into being (*egeneto*). The Christ was the true light, John merely the witness of that light.

This does not, however, minimize the importance of the Baptist. He was a man uniquely sent from God. The verb translated "sent" is *apestalmenos*, from which the word *apostle* is derived. This verb carries the sense of sending out an envoy with a special commission. Elsewhere in the New Testament it is used of both Christ and His apostles. It is distinguished from the usual word *pempo*, which simply refers to the relation of the sender to the sent. In the case of John the Baptist, he was sent "from God." The preposition *para* means "from beside" and invests the messenger with greater authority and significance than had he simply been sent "by God." This expression is used elsewhere in this gospel of the Holy Spirit, who is sent "from the Father" (15:26).

> 10 He was in the world, and the world was made by him, and the world knew him not.
> 11 He came unto his own, and his own received him not.

E. His Rejection (1:10,11). John summarizes the life of Jesus in just two short verses. The story of Jesus Christ is a story of rejection. Although He was in the world and was the Creator of it all, yet the world failed to recognize Him for who He was. The verb *egno* (knew) refers to the idea of recognition. Throughout this gospel, various individuals and groups speculate as to who Jesus is, but most of them fall short of recognizing Him as the Christ, the Son of God and One through whom life is received (20:31).

In recognizing the Word as the rejected one, John suggests the Word has personality. The pronoun *auton* (him, 1:10) is a masculine form. Every other previous reference to the Word, life, or light is a form that could be interpreted as a thing or a person. The word *auton* here establishes that John was speaking of a person all along.

The severity of Christ's rejection is emphasized by John's use of the term *parelabon* (received). This verb is used to mean "taking one's side" or "welcoming a person to a place" (Matthew 4:5; 17:1; Acts 16:33). It is the same verb used by Jesus of the welcome that awaits His disciples in His Father's house (14:3). It is also used to mean "accepting one to be what he claims to be," or "accepting something transmitted" (1 Corinthians 11:23; Galatians 1:12). Not only was Christ rejected and His gift refused, His own people were unprepared to even acknowledge His identity.

> 12 But as many as received him, to them gave he power to become the sons of God, even to them that believe on his name:
> 13 Which were born, not of blood, nor of the will of the flesh, nor of the will of man, but of God.

F. His Offer (1:12,13). Such treatment would leave most people bitter against those who rejected them. But such was not the case with Jesus. His rejection by His own people resulted in a wider offer of salvation to others (*see* Romans 11:11). Christ's offer of salvation is no longer limited to the lost sheep of the house of Israel, but salvation is offered to as many as receive Him. The verb *elabon* (received) refers to the actual gaining of a possession. While the expression "receive Christ" is commonly used by evangelists, this is the only place in the New Testament where the verb is used in this sense.

The word for "power," *exousian* (1:12), is one of six words used in the New Testament that are translated "power." Each word has a different shade of meaning. *Bia* is the violent exhibition of a repressive force (Acts 5:26; 27:41). *Dunamis* refers to a natural ability (2 Peter 2:11). *Energeia* is energy in exercise and is used exclusively by Paul and only of supernatural power, both good and evil (Ephesians 1:19; 3:7; Colossians 2:12). The word *iselus* refers to strength (2 Peter 2:11), and *kratos* refers to the dominion and might of God (Ephesians 1:19; 6:10; 1 Timothy 6:16; 1 Peter 4:11). The idea behind *exousian* is that of liberty of action or authority. The one who receives Christ by faith not only has the ability but also the right to be a child of God.

When John refers to a believer as a child of God, he uses the word *teknon* rather than *huios*, which is used by Paul. The use of these two words reflects the soteriological emphasis of each writer. *Teknon* shares a common root with *tikto* (to beget) and is probably preferred by John because of his emphasis on the doctrine of regeneration (3:3) and the community of the family of God (11:52). Paul, emphasizing the doctrine of adoption in his soteriology, prefers the legal term *huios* when discussing sonship. It is interesting that John often speaks of the children of God in his writings but never of a child of God.

One becomes and has the right to be known as a child of God as a result of believing on the name of Christ. This is more than an intellectual acceptance of the revealed truths concerning Jesus Christ. His name expresses the sum of all the qualities that mark the character and nature of Christ. To believe on, or believe in that name involves the absolute transfer of trust from self to the Saviour. Anything short of this falls short of saving faith.

14 And the Word was made flesh, and dwelt among us, (and we beheld his glory, the glory as of the only begotten of the Father,) full of grace and truth.

G. *His Incarnation (1:14).* One of the great mysteries of Christology is the doctrine of the incarnation, summarized here by John in a single verse. Briefly stated, the incarnation means Christ became the God-man. The word *sarx,* here translated "flesh," signifies human nature in and according to its corporeal manifestation. It means more than merely acquiring a physical body, although that is undoubtedly part of the incarnation. Christ also assumed human nature, thus identifying completely with mankind, having a human body, a human soul, and a human spirit. Of course Jesus did not acquire a sin nature, as that was not originally part of human nature.

Not only did the Word become flesh, He also condescended to dwell among men. John uses the verb *eskenosen,* which literally means "to pitch a tent or tabernacle." This verb is used exclusively by John in the New Testament (*see* Revelation 7:15; 12:12; 13:6; 21:3). Some have suggested this verb is used to emphasize the transitory nature of the Lord's stay on earth, but the same verb is used of the Lord's stay in the eternal city (Revelation 21:3). The figure in John's mind was probably the Old Testament tabernacle (Exodus 26:1–37; Leviticus 26:11; 2 Samuel 7:6; Psalms 78:67). The tabernacle was the dwelling place of God and the meeting place of God and Israel, making it the most perfect type of Christ, the Word incarnate, in the Old Testament. Chart 7 shows the parallels between the tabernacle and Christ.

Chart 7

TWENTY-FOUR TYPES OF CHRIST IN THE TABERNACLE	
Items in the Tabernacle	**Applied to Christ**
1. Gate (Exodus 27:16)	"I am the way" (John 14:6)
2. Brass altar (Exodus 27:1–8)	"We have an altar" (Hebrews 13:10)
3. Laver (Exodus 30:18–20; 38:8)	"Ye are clean through the word which I have spoken unto you" (John 15:3)

4. Five pillars (Exodus 26:37)	Five names of Christ (Isaiah 9:6)
5. Boards and bars overlaid with gold (Exodus 26:15–30)	Humanity and deity of Christ (John 1:14)
6. Blue, purple, and scarlet linens (Exodus 26:1–6)	His heavenly origin (John 7:28,29), royal title (Matthew 1:1), and shed blood (Hebrews 9:14)
7. Door (Exodus 26:36,37)	"I am the door" (John 10:7, 9)
8. Table of shewbread (Exodus 25:23–30)	Bread of God (John 6:33–35)
9. Altar for incense (Exodus 30:1–10)	High priestly prayer (John 17)
10. Golden candlestick (Exodus 25:31–40)	True Light (John 1:9; 8:12; 9:5)
11. Inner veil (Exodus 26:31–33)	Body of Christ (Hebrews 10:20)
12. Materials of the ark of the covenant (Exodus 25:10–22)	Humanity and divinity of Christ (John 1:14)
13. Mercy seat (Exodus 37:6–9)	Propitiation for the whole world (1 John 2:2)
14. The Law (1 Kings 8:9)	Christ, the fulfillment of the Law (Matthew 5:17–20)
15. Aaron's rod which budded (Hebrews 9:4)	Resurrection of Christ (Matthew 28:6)
16. Jar of manna (Hebrews 9:4)	Bread from heaven (John 6:33–35)
17. Priest (Exodus 28:1–2)	Our high priest (Hebrews 8:1)
18. Priest's robe (Exodus 28:31–35)	Righteousness of Christ (1 Corinthians 1:30)
19. Ephod (Exodus 28:6–14)	Bore our sins (1 Peter 2:24)
20. Urim and Thummim (Exodus 28:30)	Perfection of Christ (Hebrews 4:15)
21. Holy crown (Exodus 28:36–38)	Crowns of Christ (Revelation 19:12)
22. Breastplate (Exodus 28:15–29)	Righteousness of Christ (Ephesians 6:14)

| 23. Shekinah glory (Exodus 40:34–38) | Glory of Christ (James 2:1) |
| 24. Sacrifice (Leviticus 1—7) | Lamb of God (John 1:29,36) |

Just as the Shekinah glory of God rested over the holy place in the tabernacle, so John observes "we beheld his glory." The verb *etheasametha* (we beheld) is an aorist middle indicative of *theaomai* which is related to the noun *thea*, meaning "spectacle." This is the same verb used to describe John the Baptist's beholding the descending Spirit of God coming down as a dove (1:32) and his looking at Jesus when he pointed two of his disciples to Him (1:36). The verb denotes a calm, continuous contemplation of an object which remains before the spectator. Under that kind of observation, the veiled glory of God was apparent to those who had eyes to see.

The glory that was seen was "the only begotten of the Father"; the Greek word for this, *monogenous*, is used by John exclusively of Christ and can be understood in contrast with Paul's use of the term "firstborn" (*prototokos*, Romans 8:29; Colossians 1:15,18). *Monogenous* marks the unique relation of the Father to the Son and applies to no one else besides them, whereas *prototokos* places the eternal Son in relation to the universe. *Prototokos* emphasizes His existence before created things, whereas *monogenous* distinguishes the eternal relationship between Father and Son. Further, John here emphasizes that the Word was not born (*genesthai*) through receiving power, adoption, or regeneration, but rather He was (*en*), eternal before the beginning.

Also, John notes the balance of grace and truth that characterized the incarnate Word. This is a difficult balance to maintain. Often Christians who emphasize grace tend to minimize truth. Sometimes the reverse is also true. This was not the case with Jesus. Concerning this balance in the life of Christ, church historian Phillip Schaff once observed,

His zeal never degenerated into passion, nor his constancy into obstinacy, nor his benevolence into weakness, nor his tenderness into sentimentality. His unworldliness was free from indifference and unsociability, His dignity from pride and presumption, His affability from undue familiarity, His self-denial from moroseness, His temperance from austerity. He combined child-like in-

nocence with manly strength, absorbing devotion to God with untiring interest in the welfare of man, tender love to the sinner with uncompromising severity against sin, commanding dignity with humility, fearless courage with wise caution, unyielding firmness with sweet gentleness!

15 John bare witness of him, and cried, saying, This was he of whom I spake, He that cometh after me is preferred before me: for he was before me.

16 And of his fullness have all we received, and grace for grace.

17 For the law was given by Moses, but grace and truth came by Jesus Christ.

18 No man hath seen God at any time; the only begotten Son, which is in the bosom of the Father, he hath declared him.

H. His Witness (1:15–18). The final section of this prologue deals with the witness of John the Baptist. These verses reveal clearly what he thought about Jesus and how he viewed himself in relation to the Lord. As John was a highly respected popular teacher, his endorsement of Christ was significant. While John was opposed by both religious and civil leadership, the masses came to hear him preach. He was the last of the prophets, and he identified with the prophecy of Isaiah as the voice crying in the wilderness. Also, John was able to draw crowds without the use of miracles (10:41).

John uses the verb *kekragen* (cried) to describe the nature of the preaching of the Baptist. This verb denotes an inarticulate utterance and is joined with one of two words translated "saying" when used in connection with speech. It served as a technical rabbinic term for the loud voice of a prophet who intends to be heard. This voice of the Baptist crying in the wilderness had been silenced sixty years before John penned these words, yet the echo was still ringing clear in the ears of the writer.

The witness of John the Baptist was a paradox clearly understood in the context of these words. Although Jesus came after John (was born later), he was "preferred before" him (more popular than John) because "he was before" him (a reference to the eternal preexistence of the Word). This was the heart of the Baptist's appraisal of Christ. Apparently he had preached this message before, and he would preach it again the next day (1:30).

Commentators are divided as to whether John 1:16–18 are the words of the Baptist or the words of the author. If they are the words of the Baptist, the verb translated "have all we received" probably refers to all the prophets, John the Baptist being the last. If they are the words of the writer, they refer either to all the apostles, the Baptist being included (see 1:6), or more likely, to all who believe, including John the Baptist, the apostles, the reader, and perhaps even the prophets. Theologically, each interpretation is sound; however, keeping in mind the stated purpose of this gospel (20:31), the last interpretation is preferred.

As believers, we have received "of his fullness." The word *pleromatos*, while used five times by Paul of Christ (Ephesians 1:23; 3:19; 4:13; Colossians 1:19; 2:9), occurs only this one time in John's writings. It carries the idea of that which is complete in itself and can refer to either quality or quantity. John's use of this word in light of verse fourteen where the Word was "full of grace and truth" emphasizes that the believer receives from Christ all that is necessary for personal fulfillment. Whatever we need to perfect our character and complete our task for God is already provided in the fullness of Christ.

The means by which one benefits from this fullness is suggested in the phrase "grace for grace." The preposition *anti* is used to mean "to exchange in sale." The idea here, however, is not an exchange of Old Testament grace for New Testament grace, but rather the receiving of new grace upon the old grace. Here John pictures a superabounding grace continually being superimposed upon the grace already received. Like the manna in the wilderness and the faithful mercies of God, so grace is new and fresh every morning. "For the law was given by Moses, but grace and truth came by Jesus Christ" (1:17).

No one has ever seen God. The word John uses to state this fact in verse eighteen is one of three verbs he uses meaning "to see." The first, *theaomai* (1:14), implies a deliberate gazing similar to the way a spectator might gaze at a parade. Later John uses the verb *theoreo* (12:45), which implies a more critical view to acquire knowledge of what is seen. In Greek literature *theoreo* is used for a general officially reviewing or inspecting an army. The verb used in verse eighteen is *heoraken*, which denotes the physical act of seeing but also emphasizes some mental discernment of what is seen. The absence of an article accompanying *God* in this verse emphasizes that no one saw and understood the essence of God; rather they saw the forms that represent God. Jesus, of course, was God and seen by men, but only after He had emptied himself of the glory which was rightfully His (Philippians 2:7).

Though no one has seen God, God has revealed Himself to mankind. One of the means of revelation used by God was the declaration of His Son. The verb *exegesato* is a compound word based on *ek* (out of) and *hegeomai* (to lead the way). Originally, the word meant to lead or govern but later acquired the idea of leading with words, to interpret. It was a technical term used of the rabbinic interpretation of the law and the making known of divine secrets. Jesus revealed the mysteries of God to His disciples (Matthew 13) and interpreted the law in the spirit in which it was intended (Matthew 5:17–48). Of all religious teachers, He alone possessed the authority to declare truths concerning God without having to appeal to a greater authority. While the prophets taught much concerning the attributes of God, it was Jesus who declared Him as the Father.

THREE

CHRIST—
THE WILL OF GOD
JOHN 1:19–51

This section is the human introduction of Jesus Christ, just as the last section was His divine introduction. This human introduction is carried out in one week, during the seven days identified in the text. What Jesus did in these seven days is indicative of what He does for the rest of His ministry. On the first day, John summarizes the message of the Baptist concerning Christ. On the second day, Jesus was baptized. In the next two days Jesus attracts His first disciples. On the seventh day, He performs His first miracle.

I. AN INTRODUCTION TO JOHN THE BAPTIST (1:19–34)

John the Baptist was probably the most significant religious teacher of his time, apart from Christ. At the time the evangelist wrote these words, the Baptist had been dead sixty years. A century and a half later, followers of John the Baptist were still a significant sect both in Christianity and Judaism. Even today some Baptist groups attempt to trace their origins back to this mighty prophet.

It is difficult to imagine the nature of the popularity he enjoyed while preaching in the wilderness and baptizing in the Jordan River. It was unusual for the religious leaders in

Jerusalem to leave that city to investigate a rural preacher, but that is what the Pharisees did. What was even more unusual was their apparent readiness to recognize him as the Messiah. As a result of their investigation, they came to better understand both his motive and his message.

19 And this is the record of John, when the Jews sent priests and Levites from Jerusalem to ask him, Who art thou?

20 And he confessed, and denied not; but confessed, I am not the Christ.

21 And they asked him, What then? Art thou Elias? And he saith, I am not. Art thou that prophet? And he answered, No.

22 Then said they unto him, Who art thou? that we may give an answer to them that sent us. What sayest thou of thyself?

23 He said, I am the voice of one crying in the wilderness, Make straight the way of the Lord, as said the prophet Esaias.

24 And they which were sent were of the Pharisees.

25 And they asked him, and said unto him, Why baptizest thou then, if thou be not that Christ, nor Elias, neither that prophet?

26 John answered them, saying, I baptize with water: but there standeth one among you, whom ye know not;

27 He it is, who coming after me is preferred before me, whose shoe's latchet I am not worthy to unloose.

28 These things were done in Bethabara beyond Jordan, where John was baptizing.

A. The First Day (1:19–28). Had John the Baptist wanted to gather his own following and declare himself the Messiah, he certainly had opportunity to do so. For the first time in this gospel, a group identified as "the Jews" (*hoi Ioudaioi*) is seen as they investigate John as to his possible messianic claims. In this gospel, the title "the Jews" refers to the religious bureaucracy, particularly those Pharisees hostile to the Gospel. They were the leadership who lived in Jerusalem, not the common Jew who lived outside the capital city. According to verse nineteen, both priests and Levites were sent to John. The priests were descendants of Aaron, the first

high priest of Israel. Levites included others from the tribe of
Levi who were not in the priestly function. According to the
synoptic gospels, this group probably included Sadducees
(*see* Matthew 3:7; Luke 3:7), but that group is never mentioned in this gospel. After the destruction of Jerusalem in
A.D. 70, the Sadducees disbanded as a religious sect of Judaism. Since John is writing this gospel after they were dis-
solved, he does not mention the Sadducees. There also is no
mention of the scribes.

Apparently the Jewish leaders came to John the Baptist
after he had been preaching for a while. They wanted to
question him, and they probably remained for a few days to
examine his ministry. In the sovereignty of God, it was the
next day that Jesus appeared and was baptized. Notice the
seven questions listed in Chart 8 that "the Jews" asked John
the Baptist that first day. These questions reflect the intensity
of their desire to know about him.

When the Baptist denied being the Christ, he was given
two other choices. First, he was asked if he was Elijah. Malachi had prophesied the appearance of Elijah before the coming of the Messiah (Malachi 4:5). Second, he was asked if he
was "that prophet," probably a reference to the prophet like
Moses who was to appear (Deuteronomy 18:15). While
Christians and some Jews identify that prophet as the Messiah, apparently other Jews, including these questioning
John, saw the prophet as another forerunner of the Messiah.
John chose to deny both these identities.

John's denial of being Elijah creates a problem in light of
Christ's later identification of John with Elijah (Matthew
17:10–13). Three possible solutions to this problem have been

Chart 8

THE JEWS' QUESTIONS
1. Who art thou? (1:19)
2. What then? (1:21)
3. Are you Elijah? (1:21 RSV)
4. Art thou that prophet? (1:21)
5. Who art thou? (1:22)
6. What sayest thou of thyself? (1:22)
7. Why baptizest thou then? (1:25)

suggested. First, the Jews were looking for a literal incarnation of Elijah, whereas John was merely the spirit of Elijah and not the physical Elijah they were asking about. A second possibility is that John was ignorant as to his complete significance in history and had not yet realized he was Elijah. Some give as a third option that this is the law of double fulfillment, that John the Baptist was the first fulfillment, and there will be a second, literal fulfillment before Christ comes in His glorious appearing (Revelation 11:6). Jesus indicated to His disciples that the literal fulfillment of the Elijah prophecy was still for a future time (Matthew 17:11).

John the Baptist identified himself closely with the prophecy of Isaiah (Isaiah 40:3). His purpose was summarized in the statement, "Make straight the way of the Lord" (1:23). John's purpose in life was to prepare, straighten, and smooth out a road that would make the entrance of the Messiah easier. This was accomplished in part by (1) leading people to repentance, (2) creating messianic expectation, (3) baptizing Jesus, and (4) introducing some of his own disciples to Jesus.

The Baptist's high respect for Christ is emphasized in the particular words and expressions he used to describe both himself and Jesus. Most Old Testament prophets claimed they were speaking the word of God, but in this chapter, only Jesus is the Word. John merely identifies himself as a "voice" (1:23). The Greek word *phone* literally means a "sound" or "tone." As important as the ministry of John was in the fulfilling of Scripture and preparation for Jesus' ministry, in contrast with the Word, John saw himself only as a noise in the wilderness.

A second word that emphasized John's attitude toward Jesus is the verb "standeth" (1:26). *Stekei* means "stands" in the sense of a firm or persistent standing. John recognizes Jesus as the Messiah standing in their midst and here bears witness of Him, emphasizing the dignified attitude of Christ.

Third, the Baptist declares himself unworthy to loose the latchet of Jesus' shoes. In ancient times, the loosing of shoe latchets was the duty of the lowest slave in the household. John the Baptist's reference to this practice in this context emphasizes his humility. It is no wonder the later popularity of Jesus at his expense was welcomed by the Baptist (3:30).

John the Baptist was an itinerant prophet preaching and

baptizing converts in the Jordan River. The New Testament refers to his ministry in various places, including Bethabara beyond Jordan (1:28) and Aenon near Salim (3:23). The events in John 1:19–51 cover a period of four days at the site of John's ministry at Bethabara in Perea.

29 The next day John seeth Jesus coming unto him, and saith, Behold the Lamb of God, which taketh away the sin of the world.

30 This is he of whom I said, After me cometh a man which is preferred before me: for he was before me.

31 And I knew him not: but that he should be made manifest to Israel, therefore am I come baptizing with water.

32 And John bare record, saying, I saw the Spirit descending from heaven like a dove, and it abode upon him.

33 And I knew him not: but he that sent me to baptize with water, the same said unto me. Upon whom thou shalt see the Spirit descending, and remaining on him, the same is he which baptizeth with the Holy Ghost.

34 And I saw, and bare record that this is the Son of God.

B. *The Second Day (1:29–34)*. The following day John the Baptist saw Jesus coming to him (1:29). The verb *blepo* is one of two Greek words for seeing. *Horao* designates the idea of seeing in general, *blepo* the idea of a single look. The spiritual perception of John the Baptist was such that a single glance was all that was necessary to identify the Lamb of God.

One of the twenty-five titles of Christ in this chapter is "the Lamb of God" (1:29,36). When most Jews of Jesus' day thought of their coming Messiah, they thought in terms of a political liberator, not a suffering Saviour. Two notable exceptions to this general rule were Simeon (Luke 2:25, 35) and John the Baptist. Being the son of a priest, John the Baptist was well aware of the importance of the lamb offered every morning and evening as a whole burnt offering, as well as the Passover and other sacrifices. This title of Christ probably was based on John's understanding of Isaiah 53 and the sacrificial system of Israel. Just as a lamb was offered on the altar for sin, so the Lamb of God would be offered on a cross for the sin of the world.

Chart 9

WHEN THE LAMB OF GOD TAKES AWAY SIN
1. Before the foundation of the world (Revelation 13:8)
2. At the Fall (Genesis 3:15)
3. With the offering of a sacrifice (Genesis 4:4)
4. On the Day of Atonement (Leviticus 16:34)
5. At a time of national repentance (2 Chronicles 7:14)
6. During His public ministry (John 1:29)
7. On the cross (1 Peter 2:24)
8. At conversion (Romans 6:6)
9. At the Second Coming (Romans 8:18–23)
10. At the end of the millennium (Revelation 20:15; 21:8)

The verb *airon* (taketh away) has the idea of taking something up and carrying it away to destroy it. The means whereby Jesus took away sin was to bear it in His own body (1 Peter 2:24) and so remove our transgressions from us as far as the east is from the west (Psalms 103:12). This verb is a present participle, meaning the Baptist saw Jesus as the One already taking away sin even before the cross. Throughout the Scriptures we see at least ten instances where sin is taken away.

Another interesting aspect to this message of John concerning Jesus is seen in his choice of *hamartian* rather than *hamartius*. The word used by John for "sin" is singular, not plural. While the atonement of Christ is sufficient for all sins, He died for the sin principle that has separated man from God. Under the law a lamb was sacrificed first for a man, then his family, next the nation; now the Lamb of God removes the sin of the world (*see* 1 John 2:1,2).

At the appearance of Jesus, John the Baptist calls Him a "man" (1:30). The Greeks had three words for "man," each with a different shade of meaning. *Arsen* emphasized sexual distinction, man as opposed to woman. A more generic term for man was *anthropos* from which we get the word *anthropology*, "the study of mankind." The word in John 1:30 is *aner*, most often used in this gospel to distinguish a husband but also used to mean a male. Paul used this term to describe the man endowed with attributes such as courage, intelligence, and strength (1 Corinthians 13:11; Ephesians 4:13). Of the various words for man, this is by far the most honorable. It was used by John the Baptist with a sense of dignity.

Again John the Baptist compares himself negatively with Christ as he contrasts their respective ministries (1:33). John's baptism of water was in some sense typical of Jesus' baptism of the Holy Spirit. John baptized his disciples as they prepared for the One who would later baptize them with the Holy Spirit (*see* Acts 19:1–7). Today, Christians are baptized with water because it symbolically represents the baptism of the Holy Spirit into the body of Christ whereby they are identified with His death, burial, and resurrection (Romans 6:4,5).

The conclusion of John the Baptist's message about Jesus is that he is "the Son of God" (1:34). John had earlier heard the voice of the Father identifying Jesus as His beloved Son (Matthew 3:17; Mark 1:11; Luke 3:22). In this gospel, the Baptist is the first of several who recognize Jesus as the Son of God (*see* 1:49; 11:27). While it was a messianic title, it meant more than that. The Hebraism *son of* meant "of the same nature and character." To call someone "the Son of God" was to recognize the nature and character of God in that person.

Chart 10

SEVEN THINGS JOHN THE BAPTIST KNEW ABOUT JESUS
1. He knew Jesus was the son of Mary (Luke 1:39–45).
2. He knew he was to prepare the way for Jesus (1:23).
3. He knew Jesus takes away the sin of the world (1:29).
4. He knew he was to manifest Jesus to Israel (1:31).
5. He knew he was to baptize Jesus (1:33).
6. He knew Jesus would baptize with the Holy Spirit (1:33).
7. He knew Jesus was the Son of God (1:34).

II. THE ATTRACTION OF JESUS THE MESSIAH (1:35–51)

People always gathered around Christ regardless of where He was. He never had to advertise His meetings or sermons because people always followed Him. They knew He had the solution to their problems. He met people at their point of need. And it is true today that Jesus has the solution to our individual problems and needs.

Yet Christ, knowing the most effective way to reach the world with His message, turned away from the masses and invested His energies in the men whom He had chosen to follow Him. To these men Christ concentrated His time, left His message, and delegated the responsibility of its deliverance to the world, pouring His life into them while on this earth. In the remainder of this chapter, John explains how Jesus gathered half of His disciples (six) in just two days.

35 Again the next day after John stood, and two of his disciples;

36 And looking upon Jesus as he walked, he saith, Behold the Lamb of God!

37 And the two disciples heard him speak, and they followed Jesus.

38 Then Jesus turned, and saw them following, and saith unto them, What seek ye? They said unto him, Rabbi, (which is to say, being interpreted, Master,) where dwellest thou?

39 He saith unto them, Come and see. They came and saw where he dwelt, and abode with him that day: for it was about the tenth hour.

40 One of the two which heard John speak, and followed him, was Andrew, Simon Peter's brother.

41 He first findeth his own brother Simon, and saith unto him, We have found the Messias, which is, being interpreted, the Christ.

42 And he brought him to Jesus. And when Jesus beheld him, he said, Thou art Simon the son of Jona: thou shalt be called Cephas, which is by interpretation, A stone.

A. The Third Day (1:35-42). The first two disciples to follow Jesus, Andrew and John, were originally disciples of John the Baptist and began following Jesus when John pointed them to the Lamb of God. They began following Jesus first as a religious teacher. The title "Rabbi" was a Jewish title of honor literally meaning "my great one" or "my honorable sir." It was used by Jews to address their teachers and is based on a Hebrew root meaning "great." Though a title of respect, as the apostles came to understand

who Jesus was, it became less popular to ascribe this title to
Christ. It never occurs in Luke. Matthew uses it only twice as
Judas betrayed Christ (Matthew 26:25,49). In John's Gospel,
the use of this title usually introduces an inadequate question or action (1:49; 3:2; 4:19; 6:25; 9:2; 11:8; 20:16). The title
"Rabbi," which was normally an honor to receive, was an
indication that the disciples did not fully realize who Christ
really was and how great He was.

Andrew and John were sincerely seeking the appearance
of the Messiah. They had enough spiritual insight to abandon the religious hypocrisy of the status quo and become
followers of John the Baptist. When John introduced Jesus as
the Lamb of God, they were prepared to follow Jesus immediately. Jesus' invitation, "Come and see" (1:39), was a common rabbinical way of inviting someone to come and learn
from him. By the end of that visit, Andrew was convinced he
had found the Messiah (1:41). John himself was so impressed
that over sixty years later he could still remember the very
hour he met Jesus—the tenth hour (1:39), which according to
Jewish time was 4:00 P.M. They probably spent a great deal of
the early evening learning about Jesus.

One of the first things these new disciples did was to introduce others to Christ. Andrew was the first to find his
brother. The verb *heuriskei* implies Andrew may have had to
engage in a search before finding his brother.

John was the second to find his brother; Andrew was the
first to find his brother. *The Companion Bible Commentary* interprets this event: "Andrew is the first to find his brother,
and afterwards John finds his."[1] The *proton* (nominative adjective) means Andrew was first to do it, not that Andrew
did it first before anything else. When Andrew found his
brother, he announced, "We have found the Messiah" (1:41
NIV). It is interesting to note John the Baptist never used this
title of Christ. Andrew's statement, therefore, is an indication of his personal faith in Christ. Had he merely adopted
the opinion of his former teacher, he would have said they
had found "the Lamb of God." Both of these titles of Christ
are true, but their use reflects something of the experience
the user had with Christ. Andrew spent a day with Jesus and
immediately accepted Him as his Saviour. There are over six
hundred titles of Christ in Scripture. As we grow in our

Christian life, we come to understand these names in our experience and to understand more fully who Jesus is.

When Jesus first saw Peter coming to Him, He responded, "Thou shalt be called Cephas," which is by interpretation "a stone" (1:42). Jesus here exercises the right of giving names which is an expression of sovereignty. Only Christ gives names with a divine knowledge of that person. He knew Peter, what he was, and more importantly, what he could become. Peter's undisciplined and impetuous nature did not prevent Jesus from seeing his potential as a strong and unwavering pillar of the church. While Jesus is the Rock upon which the Church is being built (Matthew 16:18), Peter was an important stone placed close to the foundation in the early construction of the building.

43 The day following Jesus would go forth into Galilee, and findeth Philip, and saith unto him, Follow me.

44 Now Philip was of Bethsaida, the city of Andrew and Peter.

45 Philip findeth Nathanael, and saith unto him, We have found him, of whom Moses in the law, and the prophets, did write, Jesus of Nazareth, the son of Joseph.

46 And Nathanael said unto him, Can there any good thing come out of Nazareth? Philip saith unto him, Come and see.

47 Jesus saw Nathanael coming to him, and saith of him, Behold an Israelite indeed, in whom is no guile!

48 Nathanael saith unto him, Whence knowest thou me? Jesus answered and said unto him, Before that Philip called thee, when thou wast under the fig tree, I saw thee.

49 Nathanael answered and saith unto him, Rabbi, thou art the Son of God; thou art the King of Israel.

50 Jesus answered and said unto him, Because I said unto thee, I saw thee under the fig tree, believest thou? thou shalt see greater things than these.

51 And he saith unto him, Verily, verily, I say unto you, Hereafter ye shall see heaven open, and the angels of God ascending and descending upon the Son of man.

B. The Fourth Day (1:43–51). Having been introduced to the nation by John the Baptist and having acquired four disciples, Jesus determined to begin the three-day journey from

Bethabara to Cana of Galilee. Perhaps He may have just received details of the marriage He had to attend (2:1–11). Before arriving in Cana, however, Jesus acquired two more disciples.

The first of these two disciples was Philip. Like Andrew, Philip had a purely Greek name. In the synoptic gospels, he is only mentioned in the lists of disciples. In each of the four lists, his name always appears fifth, leading some to conclude he was appointed by Jesus as a leader over certain disciples. (The second group of four disciples included Bartholomew, Thomas, Matthew, and himself). In John's gospel, Philip is mentioned as an important character on several occasions (6:5–7; 12:21,22; 14:8,9).

When Jesus found Philip, perhaps with the assistance of Andrew, He simply spoke two words, "Follow me" (1:43). The verb *akolouthei* is an imperative and was often used by Jesus to call disciples to Himself. It means "to follow with a sense of cleaving steadfastly to someone and conforming to that person's example." Outside of the Gospels, this verb occurs only once (1 Corinthians 10:4).

Apparently, later that day Philip found Nathanael and told him about Jesus. Nathanael was skeptical, especially when he learned Jesus was from Nazareth. The city of Nazareth had a negative reputation. The residents of this town would customarily express their animosity toward the Romans by throwing their garbage into the streets. While this forced the Roman troops to march through garbage, it also earned the town the reputation of being "the city of garbage." Also, Nazareth had a reputation of being a very immoral town. Thus, being called a Nazarene was to be suspected of moral impurity. Also, Jesus appeared at a time when several Galilean messiahs had appeared and failed to accomplish their objectives (Acts 5:36,37). When confronted with Nathanael's skepticism, Philip invited him to "come and see," to investigate Christ for himself (1:46).

There is a bit of a mystery surrounding Nathanael. He is mentioned only here and in the last chapter of this gospel. While it is generally agreed he was one of the twelve, not everyone agrees which one he was. Some have suggested he may be Matthew, as both names mean "a gift of God." But the character of Nathanael described here makes it highly unlikely he was the same as the one who describes himself as "the publican" (Matthew 10:3). A more likely suggestion is that Nathanael should be identified as Bartholomew, which is really a surname meaning "Son of Ptolemy." If this was so, Nathanael's full name was Nathanael Bartholomew (or Son of Ptolemy).

When Jesus saw Nathanael coming, He commented, "Behold an Israelite indeed, in whom is no guile" (1:47). He recognized Nathanael as a true Israelite living up to the covenant name (Romans 2:29). The word *dolos* (guile) was originally a fishing term meaning fish bait. Here it is used in the sense of catching something with bait or beguiling. Jacob, the father of the twelve sons of Israel, became the true Israelite after he ceased to be a supplanter (meaning "deceiver"). While most Christians tend to think negatively of Jacob, it is interesting to note he is called a plain man (Genesis 25:27). The Hebrew word translated "plain" has been variously interpreted as a perfect or upright man, or a man of quiet and simple habits. The Septuagint translators used the word *aplastos* here, meaning "unfeigned, simple, without disguise, or guileless." To be recognized as a true Israelite without guile was among the highest compliments a Jew could receive.

Naturally, Nathanael wondered how a total stranger could know him well enough to make such a compliment. Responding to Nathanael's question, Jesus referred to seeing him under the fig tree before Philip found him. The significance of the fig tree is threefold. First, it was a place of security. When Israel was at peace, men could rest under the fig tree (1 Kings 4:25; Micah 4:4). Second, the fig tree was the place of meditation in Jewish religious practice. Because it is a leafy tree, rabbis would sit under its branches to meditate upon the things of God. Therefore, in the third place, the fig tree was the place of most intimate fellowship with God. Philip had found Nathanael under the fig tree and told him of Jesus. When Christ told Nathanael He had seen this (1:48), Nathanael recognized the divinity of Christ.

After confessing, "Thou art the Son of God," Nathanael added, "Thou art the King of Israel" (1:49). At first this title of Christ seems anticlimactic after confessing Jesus as the Son of God. Both of these titles, however, were ascribed to the Messiah in the second Psalm (Psalms 2:6,7). Nathanael recognized Jesus both in His personal dignity as the Son of

God and in His official capacity as the King of Israel. In calling Jesus the King of Israel, Nathanael was acknowledging the authority of Christ in his life.

The last verse in this chapter contains the first of the twenty-five double verilies ("verily, verily") in the Gospel of John. This expression is literally *amen amen* and is based on the Hebrew word *aman* meaning "truth" or "worthy of faith." One of the Old Testament names of God is *Elohe Amen*, the God of Truth (Isaiah 65:16). The expression was used in the Old Testament whenever one was affirming something that may have been doubted in the hearer's mind (Numbers 5:22; Nehemiah 8:6). When Jesus says, "Verily, verily," He reveals truths worthy of being believed even though they may at first sound incredible.

Of the twenty-five names of Christ in this first chapter, only one is claimed by Jesus Himself—"Son of Man." Jesus uses this title for Himself more than any other. The fact that in the Gospels only Jesus used this name for Himself indicates something of the significance of it. Outside of the Gospels, only Stephen once referred to Jesus as the Son of Man (Acts 7:56). This title does not deny the deity of Christ but rather emphasizes His humanity. Christ, who had no doubt about His deity, used this title as an expression of His awareness of being related to humanity. Christ knew He was God, but He also knew He had a human nature, and so He designated Himself as the representative man (*see* 1 Corinthians 15:47). In this context (1:51), it is clear that the Son of Man is the ladder to heaven. The angels did not descend onto Him as if to come down on top of an object. Rather they used Christ as one might use a ladder, because Christ is the only way from heaven to earth. Herein is the reason for the incarnation. God became a man that man might be able to come to God. Christ is the ladder for all to go to heaven.

While the human element is emphasized in His title "Son of Man," it does not exclude His divine nature or claims. The One who called Himself the Son of Man also called God His Father and said, "I and my Father are one" (10:30), and, "He that hath seen me hath seen the Father" (14:9).

FOUR

CHRIST—
THE CREATOR
JOHN 2:1–25

The second chapter of the Gospel of John describes two major events in the life of Jesus—first, the miracle of changing water into wine, and second, the cleansing of the temple. These two events are tied to the previous chapter and continue the introductions of Jesus. In chapter one Jesus is introduced to the world through the baptism of John and described as "the Lamb of God" (1:29,36). Seven days later (2:1), He is again revealed to the world by His first miracle. After this, Jesus is manifested to Israel by His public cleansing of the temple. With His first miracle at the marriage festival in Cana of Galilee, Jesus demonstrates His creative power, and at the first of four Passovers mentioned in this gospel, He demonstrates His religious authority by cleansing the temple.

I. A DEMONSTRATION OF THE POWER
OF CHRIST (2:1–12)

The marriage in Cana of Galilee was attended by Jesus and His disciples. Probably six disciples were with Christ at this time, those who were mentioned in the previous two days (Andrew, Peter, Philip, Nathanael—the friend of Andrew—John the writer of this book, and his brother James). It was at

this wedding celebration that Jesus performed His first of
many miracles (2:11). Little is known about the wedding
itself, the name of the bride and groom, or the identity of the
other guests. Whereas the bride is usually the central attraction at her wedding, attention is focused on Christ, perhaps
symbolizing that Christ is love and is the fountainhead of
love that is usually manifested at weddings. Also, this miracle symbolizes our (the bride's) relationship to Christ (the
bridegroom). He is preeminent and must increase in glory:
we are inconsequential in comparison.

Some have asked why Christ chose such an inconspicuous
miracle to begin His ministry. Of course no miracle is inconspicuous in that the Son of God is superseding the laws of
nature. Most of the guests did not know that Jesus had demonstrated divine power, and from a human perspective,
changing water to wine would not be considered as great as
raising the dead or calming a terrifying storm on the sea.
Christ begins His ministry and demonstrates His first miracle
in a private, family setting.

> And the third day there was a marriage in Cana of Galilee;
> and the mother of Jesus was there:
> 2 And both Jesus was called, and his disciples, to the
> marriage.

A. The Marriage in Cana (2:1,2). According to John, Jesus
arrived at this wedding on the third day, probably the day
He returned to Galilee. The sequence of events began when
Jesus was in Bethabara beyond Jordan (1:28), which is normally a three-day journey from Cana. The third day probably
refers to the third and final day of the journey. The wedding
festival had probably been in process for some time when
Jesus and His disciples arrived. This accounts for the wine
running out. Since it was customary that the marriage of a
virgin should begin on a Wednesday afternoon, the miracle
probably took place toward the end of the week. This helps
to more accurately date the events of the first recorded week
in this gospel.

The Greek word *gamos*, here translated "marriage," refers
not to the ceremony but to the marriage festival which normally consisted of a series of celebrations often lasting a week
or more. Because of this, the word was normally used as a

plural (see Matthew 22:2). Here, however, *gamos* is singular, perhaps reflecting the poverty of the family. Also note that the wine ran out, again suggesting inability of the family to purchase all they needed.

Jesus' mother was already present when He arrived. John never gives the name of the mother of Jesus in his gospel. Since John later takes her as his own mother (19:25–27), he would not call her by her name but would use the title "Mother." The absence of Joseph at this family celebration or any later point in the gospel suggests Joseph may have died as Jesus was growing up. When Jesus and His disciples arrived, they were invited to join in the celebration. Some commentators conclude the disciples might have been acquainted with the family, to be welcomed, but this is not necessary. It may have been that they were welcomed only because they were with Jesus, who was invited to the marriage.

> 3 And when they wanted wine, the mother of Jesus saith unto him, They have no wine.
> 4 Jesus saith unto her, Woman, what have I to do with thee? mine hour is not yet come.

B. The Problem with Wine (2:3,4). At a certain point in the festivities, there was a lack of wine. The word translated "wanted" (*husteresantos*) in verse three is an aorist active participle of the verb *hustereo,* meaning "late" or "lacking." It may have been that the groom had ordered wine, some of which was late in arriving at the feast. More likely, however, is the suggestion that the wine ran out due to poor planning or lack of finances. The most natural translation of this phrase is "when the wine gave out" (NEB). Possibly, if the disciples of Jesus were not originally expected at the wedding, that may have been part of the reason the wine ran out.

It seems Mary was aware of this need before it became evident to the ruler of the feast. A wedding in Galilee was a family affair, and female relatives of the bride were usually helpers or in charge of the kitchen. Since Mary took the initiative to do something about the problem of no wine, many commentators have concluded that she was related to the bride, hence Jesus was also related to her. If Mary was in charge of the kitchen and had the responsibility of the food, she would naturally turn to Jesus for help.

What did Mary mean when she told Jesus that the wine was all gone? Various Bible teachers have suggested possibilities: first, she may have hinted to Jesus to leave and thus minimize the embarrassment to the groom. After all, if Jesus brought uninvited guests, there was no wine for them. Second, Calvin and others suggest she wanted Jesus "to offer some religious exhortation, for fear the company might be wearied, and also courteously to cover the shame of the bridegroom."[2] Third, others think Mary in desperation was turning to her son to do something, possibly even going out to buy more wine. Fourth, Mary may have been calling on Jesus to perform a miracle. Knowing Jesus was from God, she probably remembered the supernatural events that accompanied His birth. She may have thought He would begin to reveal His messianic power. However, it is more conceivable that Mary was simply informing Jesus of the need, not ordering or commanding Him. Her statement is in fact much like a prayer made to Jesus. She knew He could so something.

At first glance, Jesus' response to His mother in verse four presents a problem. How could One who claimed to fulfill the law (Matthew 5:17), which required children to honor their parents (Exodus 20:12), apparently speak to His mother in a disrespectful way. Actually, the word *woman* was one of respect and affection rather than a term of abuse. It was frequently used when any adult addressed a woman. Jesus also used this expression addressing His mother from the cross (19:26), which obviously implied love because He was shielding her from criticism. Some have suggested Jesus' choice of the word *gunai* (woman) over the more natural selection *meter* (mother) showed Mary she could not exercise maternal authority in His messianic work.

The phrase, "What have I to do with thee?" (*Ti emoi kai soi*, 2:4) literally translates, "What is it to me and to thee?" H. A. Ironside interprets it in keeping with the nature of Christ, "What is it that you would have of me?"[3] William Barclay interprets it as meaning, "Don't worry; you don't quite understand what is going on; leave things to me, and I will settle them in my own way."[4] Christ here maintains

His authority with both courtesy and respect for His mother.

Jesus responded to Mary's statement with the words, "Mine hour is not yet come" (2:4). What did He mean by this? First, some have interpreted the statement to mean the guests had not yet exhausted the supply of wine. This is an unlikely interpretation in light of verse three. The second suggestion is that Jesus wanted the governor of the feast to suggest the need. Again, the context of the passage makes this an unlikely conclusion. A third possible explanation is it was not time for Jesus to start His miracles. It is interesting to note that Jesus did not turn the stones into bread as the devil tried to tempt Him (Luke 4:2–4). He performs His miracles at His appointed time and for the purpose that men might believe that He is the Son of God and that men might have life through His name. Christ does not perform a miracle for Satan, for the tempter cannot believe, nor does Christ have any ministry to him.

Most Bible commentators believe that "mine hour" refers to the fulfillment of His messianic expectation, which was His upcoming death on the cross. Eight times in the Gospel of John there is a reference to this "hour" (2:4; 7:30; 8:20; 12:23,27; 13:1; 16:32; 17:1). His "hour" (*hora*) was the total revelation of all that was to be accomplished by the Messiah.

5 His mother saith unto the servants, Whatsoever he saith unto you, do *it*.

6 And there were set there six waterpots of stone, after the manner of the purifying of the Jews, containing two or three firkins apiece.

7 Jesus saith unto them, Fill the waterpots with water. And they filled them up to the brim.

8 And he saith unto them, Draw out now, and bear unto the governor of the feast. And they bare *it*.

9 When the ruler of the feast had tasted the water that was made wine, and knew not whence it was: (but the servants which drew the water knew;) the governor of the feast called the bridegroom,

10 And saith unto him, Every man at the beginning doth set forth good wine; and when men have well drunk, then that which is worse: but thou hast kept the good wine until now.

C. The Miracle Accomplished (2:5–10). The actual accomplishment of the miracle began when Mary instructed the servants to do whatever Jesus asked them to do. The verb *do it (poiesate)* is the aorist active imperative of *poieo* for instant execution. There was to be no question on the part of the servants; they were to act immediately upon Jesus' command. This illustrates the law of the division of labor in the Scriptures. Jesus could have created wine without the assistance of the servants, but He chose to use them. God expects us to do what we can, then God will do what only He can do. Many people are prepared to do something for Christ, but He wants us to do whatever He asks.

Why did Jesus start His miracles with one that might be seen as insignificant? Here are some possibilities worth considering:

1. Jesus, knowing that wine is a symbol of joy, wanted the world to know there was joy with His coming (grace) where the Old Testament law only brought judgment.
2. Jesus was putting His stamp of approval on marriage as a divine institution by His presence in Cana.
3. Jesus was setting the stage for His ministry. The God-man demonstrated His desire to be with the multitudes and to eat and drink with the common man.
4. The Old Testament began with an act of creation; therefore, it is significant that Jesus began His ministry with an act of creation.
5. The first miracle communicates typical truths in our relation to Christ in the area of the bride and bridegroom.
6. Jesus had to begin His miracles at the level of His disciples' understanding.
7. Jesus had to begin His ministry at home with His family and friends.
8. The remnant theory suggests Jesus would begin with a small group.
9. Symbolically, He was showing the insufficiency of the old Judaic system and the abundance of Christianity.

John carefully notes the presence of six stone waterpots, "after the manner of the purifying of the Jews" (2:6). Some commentators see the number and nature of these waterpots as important in understanding the spiritual significance of the miracle. The pots themselves were required for the various cleansings prescribed by the law and traditions of Israel and are specifically identified with the group, "the Jews." This is not just a common word to identify people who were Jewish: "the Jews" were Jewish leaders, usually from Jerusalem. Just as today Americans use the term *Washington* to express the corporate power of the United States , so John identifies the corporate authority of Israel, with all its bureaucracy and hatred of Christ. It is "the Jews" who oppose and eventually crucify Jesus. There were six waterpots, the number of imperfection and man. Symbolically, John may here point out the imperfection of Judaism especially when contrasted with the perfection of Christ.

Each of these large waterpots could contain two or three firkins. A firkin was a goatskin used for storing wine. It was also a measure of volume. Although the actual size of a firkin would vary depending upon the original size of the goat and elasticity of the skin, a firkin was generally six to eight gallons. When Jesus commanded the servants to fill the waterpots, He was requiring the servants to draw eighteen to twenty-four gallons of water in each pot.

From the servants' point of view, this action may have appeared foolish. The need of the hour was for wine, but Jesus told the servants to fill the pots with water and then to draw some out to take to the governor of the feast. In simple terms, that was foolishness. This may have caused fear, but the servants obeyed, and the miraculous resulted.

The verb translated "draw out" (*antlesate*, 2:8) is an aorist active imperative derived from the noun *antlos* meaning "bilge water" or "the place where the water settles." While the English translation appears to permit the idea of the servants drawing water from the waterpots, the Greek verb implies to draw out water from the well. This is the same verb used when Jesus spoke to the Samaritan woman (4:7,15) where the meaning is even clearer in the English translation. The filling up of the six waterpots pictures Christ completely keeping or fulfilling the ceremonial law, but even then something was lacking.

"The governor of the feast" (*architriklinoi*, 2:8) literally means "the chief of the banquet hall with three couches" and was the title of the person whose duties included arranging the table and the courses of the meal and tasting the food before it could be served to the guests. When this man tasted the wine, he was surprised that it was of such quality yet reserved until the end of the feast. It was customary to serve the finest foods and wines first, then after the senses of the guests had been dulled through overindulgence, to serve inferior foods and wines.

This miracle of changing water into wine has been the center of controversy and debate among Christians for years. Did Christ create intoxicating wine? The Bible speaks of two kinds of wines: first, alcoholic, usually referred to as the adder's sting, and second, sweet wines—nonalcoholic fruit juices. Some claim Jesus here created the alcoholic variety of wine, noting the phrase "have well drunk" (*methusthosin*, 2:10) is often used in Greek literature to identify intoxication. But the verse does not refer to the sobriety or lack of the same among the guests. There are reasons to suspect all the wine at this marriage was of the sweet wine variety. A marriage festival was a family affair and not the kind of place where alcoholic beverages would be served. Also, the Passover was near (2:12,13), and Jews avoided the use of leaven, the source of fermentation, around the Passover season.

> 11 This beginning of miracles did Jesus in Cana of Galilee, and manifested forth his glory; and his disciples believed on him.
>
> 12 After this he went down to Capernaum, he, and his mother, and his brethren, and his disciples: and they continued there not many days.

D. *The Development of Faith* (2:11,12). John identifies the turning of water into wine as the first miracle of Jesus. This statement in itself denies the apocryphal accounts of the hidden years of the life of Christ. These nondocumented accounts abound with tales of the boy Jesus performing miracles like magic tricks. According to John, Jesus did not begin performing miracles until as a man He had begun to gather His disciples.

Miracles were performed by Jesus in this gospel for a variety of reasons. First, the ultimate objectives of the signs was to bring glory to God (2:11) and develop the faith of those who witnessed or heard about these miracles (20:31). Second, miracles were performed by Christ to demonstrate how He fulfilled prophecy (6:14), and third, perhaps as an expression of His compassion upon people (11:5,35).

After accomplishing this miracle, Jesus went to Capernaum. Capernaum was a fenced town (as opposed to an unfenced village) on the north shore of the Sea of Galilee. It was located on the major trade route from Damascus and the interior of Asia to the Mediterranean Sea. Godet suggests it was "the Jewish capital of Galilee" in the sense that Tiberias might be considered the Gentile or Roman capital of that region.[5] From this point on, Capernaum becomes the prominent center of Jesus' Galilean ministry. While John does not specifically state how long Jesus remained in Capernaum, the nearness of the Passover is emphasized to suggest that He went to Jerusalem from Capernaum for the Passover.

II. A DEMONSTRATION OF THE AUTHORITY OF CHRIST (2:13–22)

When Jesus arrived in Jerusalem for the Passover and Feast of Unleavened Bread, He found conditions in the temple less than desirable. His subsequent actions resulted first, in the fulfillment of a messianic prophecy and second, in His prophesying as to how He, the Messiah, would rise from the dead. The events in this chapter at the beginning of His ministry should not be confused with His cleansing of the temple right before His death (Matthew 21:22,13; Mark 11:15–17; Luke 19:45,46).

13 And the Jews' passover was at hand, and Jesus went up to Jerusalem,

14 And found in the temple those that sold oxen and sheep and doves, and the changers of money sitting:

15 And when he had made a scourge of small cords, he drove them all out of the temple, and the sheep, and the oxen; and poured out the changers' money, and overthrew the tables;

16 And said unto them that sold doves, Take these things hence; make not my Father's house an house of merchandise.

17 And his disciples remembered that it was written, The zeal of thine house hath eaten me up.

A. The Purification of the Temple (2:13–17). Entering the temple, Jesus first encountered a group of businessmen engaged in the sale of sacrificial animals and currency exchange. The use of the definite article identifying those selling animals (*tous polountas*) suggests an identifiable group of sellers who were well-known in Jerusalem. The word *kermatistas*, translated "changers of money" (2:14), is derived from the verb *kermatizo*, meaning "to cut into small pieces." This, the only occurrence of the word in the New Testament, was used in later Greek writings to identify those in the business of currency exchange.

The sale of sacrifice animals and exchange of currency was an extremely profitable and very necessary service industry in the temple, especially during the feasts such as Passover. Since pilgrims came to Jerusalem from around the world, they would need animals to sacrifice. Also, although their foreign currency might be accepted by the city businessmen, it could not be used in the temple itself. What was going on was not in itself wrong, but the place and manner in which it was done may have been wrong. The temple was divided into four courts, the outer court being the Court of the Gentiles. This was the only part of the temple a Gentile convert to Judaism could enter. This was also the place where these businessmen had set up shop. Because their commercial activities made it practically impossible for a Gentile to come and meditate upon the things of God in the temple, this service had actually become a hindrance to worship.

Jesus responded to this scene by first making "a scourge of small cords" (*phragellion ek schoinion*). The noun *schoinion* is a diminutive of a word for rope which literally meant "a rush." This is the only mention of a scourge (*phragellion*) in the New Testament. Here it represents a symbol of both authority and judgment. Jesus apparently did not use a scourge when He cleansed the temple at the end of His ministry (Matthew 21:12,13; Mark 11:15–17; Luke 19:45,46). Jesus may have used this as a goad in driving the sheep and goats out of the temple.

The verb translated "drove . . . out" is *exebalen*, literally, "cast out" (2:15). It is the same verb used by the other gospel writers to describe the casting out of demons. Here John uses the verb to refer only to "all . . . the sheep, and the oxen." Some have suggested Jesus was symbolically announcing the end of animal sacrifices was at hand. While expelling the animals from the temple site, Jesus did not apparently expel any people, with the possible exception of the dove sellers, who were told to remove the birds (2:16).

The removal of the animals, upsetting of the tables, and pouring out of the exchangers' coins naturally created a commotion in the temple. This action caused His disciples to remember the messianic prophecy, "The zeal of [literally for] thine house hath eaten me up" (2;17; see Psalms 69:9). Jesus' actions may have caused the Jews to think of another messianic prophecy. Malachi wrote of the Lord coming to His temple and purifying the sons of Levi (Malachi 3:1–3). If the Jews recognized the similarities between this temple cleansing and that of Malachi, it would be natural to expect them to verify Jesus' authority and then follow Him.

> 18 Then answered the Jews and said unto him, What sign shewest thou unto us, seeing that thou doest these things?
> 19 Jesus answered and said unto them, Destroy this temple, and in three days I will raise it up.
> 20 Then said the Jews, Forty and six years was this temple in building, and wilt thou rear it up in three days?
> 21 But he spake of the temple of his body.
> 22 When therefore he was risen from the dead, his disciples remembered that he had said this unto them; and they believed the scripture, and the word which Jesus had said.

B. The Prophecy Concerning the Temple (2:18–22). When the Jews asked for a sign, Jesus spoke prophetically of the resurrection as a sign. While His hearers did not immediately understand, the disciples remembered it later as a sign that pointed to His divinity. The verb *lusate* (destroy) is an aorist active imperative. It is the permissive imperative, not necessarily a command to do it. He was not telling them to kill Him. Jesus knew these religious leaders would later plot to have Him crucified. Although it would appear they had destroyed Him, three days later He would rise up again, as He said.

John uses two words in this passage that are both translated "temple," and his use of them is significant. Whenever he describes Jesus entering the temple structure, he uses the word *hieron* (2:14). When speaking of the temple as the body of Jesus (2:19,21), John uses the word *naos*, meaning "holy place" or "sanctuary." In doing this, he emphasizes that the real temple of God was never a structure erected by human hands, but rather the temple is where the presence of God dwelt (1:14), which was Jesus Christ.

The Jews apparently thought Jesus was referring to the temple structure itself. Later, they would misquote this saying, claiming Jesus predicted He would destroy the temple. This charge appears in both the trial of Jesus and the trial of Stephen (Matthew 26:61; Acts 6:14). They could only reason that the temple had already been forty-six years in the building and that it was impossible for anyone to rebuild it in a mere three days.

While John did not write this gospel primarily as a historian, this reference to forty-six years is another evidence to the amazing historical accuracy of his account. This temple, known as Herod's temple, was really a massive renovation of Zerubbabel's temple. The reconstruction of this temple began in 20 B.C. and was not completed until A.D. 63. If, as the Jews here suggest, the construction project had already lasted forty-six years, that would date the events of this chapter to A.D. 26. If Jesus was born in 4 B.C., the generally accepted date of His birth based upon conditions in Luke 2, then Jesus was "about thirty years of age" (Luke 3:23) as He began His ministry.

It was not until after the resurrection that the disciples completely understood what Jesus was saying. Later, they would remember this prophecy concerning the temple and believe not only the word of Jesus, but also the Old Testament Scripture which spoke of the resurrection of Christ (Psalms 16:10).

III. A DEMONSTRATION OF THE KNOWLEDGE OF CHRIST (2:23–25)

23 Now when he was in Jerusalem at the passover, in the feast day, many believed in his name, when they saw the miracles which he did.

24 But Jesus did not commit himself unto them, because he knew all men,

25 And needed not that any should testify of man: for he knew what was in man.

The events of these verses and the meeting with Nicodemus in chapter three took place in the days immediately following the Passover. Strictly speaking, the Passover was a one-day feast followed by the seven-day Feast of Unleavened Bread. But in common usage, the term *Passover* came to refer to all eight days. Most commentators agree the word *heortei* refers not to the feast day (the Passover proper) but to the feast (the Feast of Unleavened Bread). A reference to the Passover proper would have probably used the word *pascha* (*see* 2:13).

John notes that many believed when they saw Jesus' miracles. This is in contrast with the nation that should have believed when their Messiah came to the temple (1:11). But even those who did believe did not have the right kind of faith. Like Simon Magus (Acts 8:13), these believers were apparently impressed with the evident power to do miracles but did not have faith that results in a commitment to follow Christ. Their faith was incomplete. It may have affected their attitude but appeared to have little impact on their actions.

The nature of one's faith may be indiscernible to others, but Jesus knew (*ginoskein*) these believers were not genuine and so would not commit Himself to them. The verb *ginoskein* implies experiential knowledge. Because of their empty life-styles, Jesus knew it was head belief but not a divine, implanted faith from God. In the Greek text of John 2:25, the word for "man" is preceded by a definite article. Jesus knew the heart of all men in general (2:24) and of specific men (2:25). This introduces the next chapter and refers to Nicodemus. Because Jesus knew the man— Nicodemus—He could bluntly tell him to be born again. Perhaps this teaching on Jesus' omniscient knowledge of men's hearts is indicative of the rest of the gospel. Jesus responds as He does because "he knew what was in man" (2:25).

FIVE

CHRIST—
THE SAVIOUR
JOHN 3:1–36

The previous chapter ends with a statement concerning Jesus' omniscience. Jesus would not commit Himself to the multitudes, "for he knew what was in man" (2:25). That statement not only applies to the Jerusalem pilgrims but is also the introductory statement to chapters three and four. Jesus appears to be blunt in His interview with Nicodemus because "he knew what was in man." Jesus understood the woman at the well and told her to call her husband because "he knew what was in man." Jesus knew the nobleman had faith because "he knew what was in man." His supernatural knowledge of people helped Him quickly understand the specific needs of these individuals and speak directly to the issues confronting them.

The third chapter of John is the one thousandth chapter in the Bible. It is one of the best-known chapters because it records Jesus' explanation of the new birth to Nicodemus. Many Christians have committed this entire chapter to memory. Verse sixteen, often the first verse memorized by new Christians, has been called "the Gospel in a nutshell" and "the greatest verse in all Scripture." John Wesley is said to have preached on the text "Ye must be born again" (3:7) over three hundred times. When asked why he so often chose that text, he responded, "Because, ye must be born again." The message of this chapter is foundational to our Christian experience.

The teaching of this chapter is arranged around two individuals who were among the followers of Jesus. First Nicodemus, a seeker of truth, comes to Jesus by night to learn about the new birth. Then John the Baptist, a servant of truth, explains to his disciples why he rejoices over the success of Jesus' ministry. When we have learned the lesson Nicodemus learned that night, we will find ourselves constantly needing the lesson John the Baptist tried to teach his disciples.

I. A SEEKER OF TRUTH (3:1–21)

The name *Nicodemus*, though a Greek name, was common among Jews. It is derived from two Greek words: *nike*, meaning "victory," and *demos*, meaning "people." John identifies this Nicodemus as both a Pharisee and ruler of the Jews. The word *archon* (ruler) suggests he was a lay member of the Sanhedrin and not one of the chief priests (*archiereus*). He is mentioned in the Talmud as one of the four richest men in Jerusalem and one considered a disciple of Jesus. According to Hoskyns, he was a member of the same aristocratic family that had furnished the Hasmonaean King Aristobulus II with his ambassador to Pompey in 63 B.C. His son apparently was the man who negotiated the terms of surrender to the Roman garrison in Jerusalem prior to the final destruction of that city in A.D. 70.

The meeting between Jesus and Nicodemus occurred at night. Some have suggested the night meeting was due to fear on the part of Nicodemus. However, it was common for teachers to gather in conversation during the cool of the early evening. Also, Nicodemus may have come to Jesus by night because the crowds that surrounded Jesus by day made a private conversation impossible at that time. Also, the use of plural verbs connected with Nicodemus suggests he may have come representing a party within the Sanhedrin that was sympathetic to or at least interested in knowing more about Jesus' teachings (3:2,7,10,11,12). This interview became the occasion where Jesus presented the concept of the

new birth, without which man cannot see or enter the kingdom (3:3,4).

> There was a man of the Pharisees, named Nicodemus, a
> ruler of the Jews:
> 2 The same came to Jesus by night, and said unto him,
> Rabbi, we know that thou art a teacher come from God: for
> no man can do these miracles that thou doest, except God
> be with him.
> 3 Jesus answered and said unto him, Verily, verily, I say
> unto thee, Except a man be born again, he cannot see the
> kingdom of God.
> 4 Nicodemus saith unto him, How can a man be born
> when he is old? can he enter the second time into his
> mother's womb, and be born?

A. The Nature of the New Birth (3:1–4). Nicodemus was
prepared to accept Jesus as a religious teacher, even though
He had not had formal training or been otherwise accredited
by the religious leadership of the city. That Nicodemus
should use the title *Rabbi* for Jesus demonstrates something
of the respect he had for Jesus. But Nicodemus goes beyond
this. He also expresses his conviction that Jesus had come
from God as a teacher. In the expression "a teacher come
from God" (3:2), *apo theou* (from God) is first in order and
holds the place of emphasis. Nicodemus was convinced of
this by the miracles (*semeia*, literally "signs") which Jesus
performed. In this gospel, John records the miracles of Christ
only to bring people to faith in Christ (*see* 20:30,31).

Nicodemus had much going for him by the standards of
his world. He was a member of the Pharisees, a disciplined
and highly respected sect in Judaism. He was a man of extreme wealth and a member of a distinguished family with
an illustrious history. He himself was a respected ruler of the
Jews and teacher of Israel. Still, Jesus immediately turned
this conversation to Nicodemus's need—the need to be born
again.

The expression *gennethei anothen* (3:3) can be translated
various ways depending upon the implied meaning of *anothen*. This word is used in the New Testament thirteen times
with at least four different meanings. It can be translated
"from the top" (19:23; Matthew 27:51; Mark 15:38) "from

above" (3:31; 19:11; James 1:17; 3:15,17), "from the first/from the beginning" (Luke 1:3; Acts 26:5), or "again" (Galatians 4:9). In this context Nicodemus seems to think of the new birth in terms of a second birth, "born again." But Nicodemus may have been incorrect in his conclusion. Throughout this gospel *anothen* refers to "from above" (3:31; 19:11). This also seems more consistent with the idea of being "born of God" in John's writings (1:13; 1 John 3:9; 5:18). The new birth is a second birth in the sense that it occurs after a physical birth. But it is also a birth from above as it is "of God."

The necessity of the new birth is emphasized for the first time in this chapter. Jesus explains that without it one cannot see the kingdom. The verb *idein* implies more than mere physical sight. It includes the idea of actively participating in that which is seen (*see* 8:51; Revelation 18:7). In Jewish eschatology, part of the suffering in hell was that men could see heaven (*see* Luke 16:23) but not participate in it. Jesus here explains that men cannot participate in the bliss of heaven without first being born again from above.

The new birth is mandatory for one to see the kingdom. Its nature is exclusive. Because it is an imperative, this statement divides mankind. All men will fall into one of two classifications—those who have been born again or those who have not been born again. Understanding the importance of the new birth, Nicodemus twice asks questions concerning it (3:4,9). Although the questions are similar, there is an important difference. The first question concerns the possibility of the new birth. The second question concerns the process of the new birth.

Nicodemus's question to Jesus is puzzling. Apparently he not only missed what Jesus was saying but failed to think of a more plausible physical explanation than that of an old man being physically born again from his mother's womb. Nicodemus does not use *anothen*, the word Jesus used concerning the new birth, but *deuteron* (3:4) to refer to the second birth. His use of this term demonstrates his failure to grasp the spiritual or heavenly nature of this new birth. If Nicodemus was going to interpret Jesus' statements in a purely physical context, there was a better explanation than the one he proposed. Greeks sometimes used the expression "born again" to describe the birth of a son. The idea was that

Chart 11

BORN OF WATER AND OF SPIRIT (John 3:5)			
View	Water	Spirit	Key to Interpretation
Baptismal regeneration	Water baptism	Fullness of the Holy Spirit	Sacramental view of baptism
Pardon and sanctification (Godet)	Baptism as a symbol of pardon	Holy Spirit as a symbol of sanctification	Sacramental view of baptism and typical interpretation of the expression
Born of the Holy Spirit (Calvin)	Water as a symbol of the Holy Spirit (7:38, 39)	Spirit is the Holy Spirit	Translation of *kai* as "even" rather than "and"
Repentance and faith	Baptism of John unto repentance	Saving faith as a gift of the Holy Spirit	Identification of water with baptism of John and hyper-Calvinistic view that saving faith is the gift of God in Ephesians 2:8
Word of God (Scofield)	Water as a symbol of the Word of God which is the instrument of regeneration (Ephesians 4:22–25)	The Holy Spirit as agent of regeneration	Application of biblical doctrine of regeneration to this verse

| Natural birth | Breaking of the water sack at birth | Spiritual re-birth = the new birth | The parallel thought in the argument of verses four and six |
| Judeo-Christian har-mony | Water as a symbol of the law | Spirit as a symbol of re-generation | Rabbinic teaching re-garding water as a symbol of the law |

in the birth of a son, the father started life again because he was reproduced in his son. That Nicodemus did not refer to this use of the phrase "born again" suggests he may have understood to some degree that the new birth was different from a normal physical birth.

5 Jesus answered, Verily, verily, I say unto thee, Except a man be born of water and of the Spirit, he cannot enter into the kingdom of God.

6 That which is born of the flesh is flesh; and that which is born of the Spirit is spirit.

7 Marvel not that I said unto thee, Ye must be born again.

8 The wind bloweth where it listeth, and thou hear-est the sound thereof, but canst not tell whence it cometh, and whither it goeth: so is every one that is born of the Spirit.

9 Nicodemus answered and said unto him, How can these things be?

10 Jesus answered and said unto him, Art thou a master of Israel, and knowest not these things?

11 Verily, verily, I say unto thee, We speak that we do know, and testify that we have seen; and ye receive not our witness.

12 If I have told you earthly things, and ye believe not, how shall ye believe, if I tell you of heavenly things?

13 And no man hath ascended up to heaven, but he that came down from heaven, even the Son of man which is in heaven.

B. The Method of the New Birth (3:5–13). Jesus explained
the new birth in terms of being "born of water and of the
Spirit" (3:5). What did Jesus mean by this expression? Several interpretations have been offered throughout the years.
Often these interpretations have been based on preconceived
theological concepts rather than a sound exegesis of the
Word of God. Chart 11 summarizes the major interpretations
of this phrase.

Interpreting this verse in context and in light of the overall
teaching of Scripture, any suggestion that it means baptismal
regeneration or a sacramental view of baptism must be ruled
out. The three viewpoints in which "water" means (1) the
Holy Spirit, (2) the Word of God, or (3) natural birth, are in
keeping with sound biblical interpretation. The Hebrew parallelism of verses four, five, and six tends to favor the natural
birth interpretation. The method by which the new birth
takes place is spiritual regeneration. (See Chart 12.)

Jesus went on to explain that that which is born is of the
same nature as that which gives it birth. This principle is
fundamental to all of life and is emphasized in Genesis where
everything that reproduces does so "after his/their kind"
(Genesis 1:11,12,21). Therefore, "that which is born of the
flesh is flesh" (3:6). The word sarx (flesh) is used by John to
express humanity (1:14; 1 John 4:2,3; 2 John 7) and sometimes implies a hint of the sinful and corrupt nature of man
(8:15; 1 John 2:16). In this context, he probably means humanity as opposed to that which is born of the Spirit.

As He instructs Nicodemus further concerning the new
birth, Jesus emphasizes the sovereignty of the Holy Spirit in
the new birth. It is difficult to be conclusive concerning
whether Jesus speaks directly or indirectly concerning the
Holy Spirit in verse eight. The word pneuma can be translated
"spirit" or "wind" and is translated "spirit" in Wycliff's original English translation. Of the 370 times this word occurs in
the New Testament, it means "spirit" everywhere except in
one quote from the Old Testament (Psalms 104:4; Hebrews
1:7). In contrast, the verb pneo (bloweth) occurs six times in
the New Testament and in every other case clearly refers to
the wind (see 6:18). Likewise, phone could refer to the sound
of the wind or the voice of the Spirit. Both are perfectly
acceptable translations. If Jesus was speaking directly of the
Holy Spirit, He was emphasizing that no one can tell where

the Spirit has been or is going. If He is talking about the wind, the same truth is applied to the Holy Spirit by the last line of the verse, "So is every one that is born of the Spirit" (3:8).

When Nicodemus again questions concerning the new birth, Jesus addresses him as "the teacher of Israel" (3:10, literal translation). The use of a definite article accompanying both *teacher* and *Israel* serves to emphasize the position that Nicodemus held. He was not just another rabbi but rather the well-known, illustrious teacher of the nation. Still he was unable to grasp what Jesus was teaching. The assumption that Nicodemus should have known is probably based on several Old Testament passages that teach the doctrine of regeneration (Psalms 143:10,11; Jeremiah 31:33; Ezekiel 36:26–28).

In addressing this teacher, Jesus also resorts to the use of the plural verb four times (3:11). Hoskyns suggests Jesus was here speaking of the testimonies of both Himself and John the Baptist. Another possibility could be that Jesus is identifying with the testimony of the prophets with which He assumed Nicodemus was familiar. Supporting this second view is the use of the verb *eipon* in the next verse, which is more correctly translated, "they told." The prophets had spoken of earthly things, and Jesus intended to build on their message to teach heavenly things.

Jesus identified the content of His instruction as *ta epourania* (the heavenly things). This expression does not mean holy or spiritual things in contrast with sinful or temporal things but rather the things that are in heaven and take place in heaven. The teaching of Christ was concerned with the great mysteries and secrets of God concerning God's purpose in the cross and the salvation of man. This heavenly teaching was not revealed in the past but rather by Jesus and

Chart 12

INTERPRETATION BY HEBREW PARALLELISM

	First Birth	Second Birth
Verse 4	Enter the second time into his mother's womb	Be born again
Verse 5	Born of water	Born of the Spirit
Verse 6	Born of flesh	Born of the Spirit

His apostles (*see* Romans 16:25,26; Ephesians 3:4–11). While there was no conflict between the teaching of Christ and that of the apostles, the teaching of Christ went far beyond that of the Old Testament.

14 And as Moses lifted up the serpent in the wilderness, even so must the Son of man be lifted up:

15 That whosoever believeth in him should not perish, but have eternal life.

16 For God so loved the world, that he gave his only begotten Son, that whosoever believeth in him should not perish, but have everlasting life.

17 For God sent not his Son into the world to condemn the world; but that the world through him might be saved.

C. The Basis of the New Birth (3:14–17). The basis of the new birth is found in the cross. Jesus used an illustration from the Old Testament to explain this truth to Nicodemus. When Israel was plagued by serpents, Moses erected a brass serpent as directed by God. Those who in faith looked to the serpent were physically healed (Numbers 21:9). By drawing this parallel, Jesus signified His death and the spiritual healing that will come when anyone looks to Him and believes on Him. The expression "lifted up" in this gospel always refers to the cross.

The parallelism of Christ to the serpent is an intriguing one. The serpent was a symbol of the sin of Israel. Because the Israelites sinned in unbelief, God sent the serpents in judgment. Those who looked on the brazen serpent were acknowledging that their sin was the cause of judgment and death. For them to "look and live" was an act of repentance

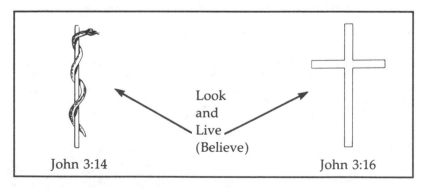

John 3:14   John 3:16

and belief. Just as the serpent was a sign of sin, so Christ was made sin (2 Corinthians 5:21) in the act of imputation. When a sinner acknowledges that Christ became sin for him, it is an act of repentance and belief.

The result of faith in Christ is eternal life. John speaks of eternal life sixteen times in this gospel. In doing so, he associates the adjective *aionios* with the noun *zoe*. The phrase means a life that is endless, beginning at the moment of faith (5:24) but never ending. But John makes the phrase refer to more than endless existence. It also involves a sharing of the divine life (5:26; 17:3). There is no difference between *eternal life* and *everlasting life*, as both translate from the same Greek expression.

Verses sixteen through twenty-one represent John's summary of the teaching of Christ concerning the new birth. There are several reasons for not attributing these words to Jesus. First, the verbs in verse sixteen, *loved* and *gave* are past tense and are better understood from a postcrucifixion context. This type of explanatory comment is typical in the gospel (*see* 1:16–18; 12:37–41). The tone of verse nineteen is similar to that of 1:9–11 and suggests the rejection of Christ as already past. Also, the phrases "believed in the name," "only begotten," and "doeth truth" (3:16,18,21), while used elsewhere by John, are never elsewhere used by Jesus. While these reasons support the conclusion that the next six verses of the chapter are not part of the interview with Nicodemus, it should be noted that several conservative commentators disagree and do include them as part of the discourse of Jesus.

Although one of the purposes and ministries of Jesus is to judge (5:27), that was not His primary purpose in coming to earth. The verb *krinei* originally referred to the act of separating or distinguishing and later came to refer to the act of pronouncing judgment upon that which was separated. Jesus' primary purpose in coming was to save the world. As some believed and others rejected His offer, the net result has been to separate the world into two distinct groups, the saved and the lost. The lost are already under judgment because of their failure to accept the deliverance offered them. When Christ returns and judges, He will be merely identifying the state of those who chose, for whatever rea-

Chart 13

JOHN 3:16—THE GREATEST VERSE IN THE BIBLE	
For God	The greatest being
so	The greatest degree
loved	The greatest affection
the world,	The greatest object of love
that he gave	The greatest act
his only	The greatest treasure
begotten	The greatest relationship
Son,	The greatest gift
that whosoever	The greatest company
believeth	The greatest trust
in him	The greatest object of faith
should not perish,	The greatest deliverance
but have	The greatest assurance
everlasting	The greatest promise
life.	The greatest blessing

sons, to remain under judgment rather than accepting deliverance.

Four times John refers to the *kosmos* (world, 3:16,17). The world is the object of the love of God, and Jesus was sent into the world. Christ's object during His earthly ministry was not to judge the world but rather to save the world. As the world rejects Christ later in this gospel, it is described as under judgment (9:39), under the control of its prince—Satan (12:31), and overcome by Christ Himself (16:33).

In this author's opinion, John 3:16 is the greatest verse in the Bible. This is illustrated in Chart 13.

18 He that believeth on him is not condemned: but he that believeth not is condemned already, because he hath not believed in the name of the only begotten Son of God.

19 And this is the condemnation, that light is come into the world, and men loved darkness rather than light, because their deeds were evil.

20 For every one that doeth evil hateth the light, neither cometh to the light, lest his deeds should be reproved.

21 But he that doeth truth cometh to the light, that his

deeds may be made manifest, that they are wrought in God.

D. *The Opposition to the New Birth* (3:18–21). The only opposition to the new birth comes when men who are in darkness refuse to turn to the light, Jesus Christ. Men, in fact, love darkness and desire to remain in that darkness because of their sin. The light makes visible the sin of man and makes a way for repentance and belief on the person of Christ. So the only opposition to the light that has come into the world is the desire of men to remain blind. They do not and will not allow themselves to see.

For John, the faith that produces life is not only believing the truth, it also involves doing the truth (3:21). The phrase *poion ten aletheian* (doeth the truth) occurs only twice in the Scriptures and is used only by John (3:21; 1 John 1:6). In contrast with the plural in the previous verse (evil, 3:20), truth here is singular. It includes all right deeds in a supreme unity. There is also a contrast in the two words translated "doeth" in these two verses. The first verb, *prasson*, emphasizes the means or practice of doing, with the idea of continuity or repetition. The verb *poion*, however, emphasizes the object and end of doing—doing once and for all. While men in darkness are continually doing evil, those who are in the light have once and for all done the truth by receiving Christ by faith.

The case is clear. The options are presented bluntly and truthfully to all. Everyone must be born again if he desires to enter the kingdom. Those who oppose this doctrine do so because they prefer remaining in darkness rather than coming to the light.

II. A SERVANT OF TRUTH (3:22–36)

22 After these things came Jesus and his disciples into the land of Judaea; and there he tarried with them, and baptized.

23 And John also was baptizing in Aenon near to Salim, because there was much water there: and they came, and were baptized.

24 For John was not yet cast into prison.

John introduces the second part of this chapter with the often repeated phrase "after these things" (3:22; see 2:12; 5:1; 6:1; 7:1). The expression identifies a period later chronologically but does not specify how much later. John does not try to write a comprehensive biography of Christ but only records select incidents that are in keeping with his purpose (20:30,31). Some days are recorded in great detail, whereas many months are virtually ignored. The events that begin in verse twenty-two take place some time after that first Passover season in Jerusalem.

Only this gospel records the parallel ministries of Jesus and John the Baptist. While Jesus' disciples baptized in Judea (see 4:2), John was baptizing in Samaria. As the forerunner of Christ, he preached to the Jews, preparing the way for Jesus. Now the Baptist is portrayed as preparing the way for Jesus' later ministry in Samaria. Some commentators have seen a significance in the meaning of the names of the places where John was baptizing. Aenon means "spring" or "fountain," and Salim, a nearby village, means "peace." It has been suggested that the ministry of John only brought his converts near the peace of reconciliation that Jesus offered to all. John adds, concerning the time of these events, that the Baptist had not yet been imprisoned (3:24). The synoptic gospels do not record the public ministry of Christ until John is imprisoned (see Mark 1:14).

25 Then there arose a question between some of John's disciples and the Jews about purifying.

26 And they came unto John, and said unto him, Rabbi, he that was with thee beyond Jordan, to whom thou barest witness, behold, the same baptizeth, and all men come to him.

27 John answered and said, A man can receive nothing, except it be given him from heaven.

28 Ye yourselves bear me witness that I said, I am not the Christ, but that I am sent before him.

29 He that hath the bride is the bridegroom: but the friend of the bridegroom, which standeth and heareth him, rejoiceth greatly because of the bridegroom's voice: this my joy therefore is fulfilled.

30 He must increase, but I must decrease.

A. A Humble Servant (3:25–30). John the Baptist was the forerunner and witness of Christ. He was the one who baptized and saw the Spirit of God descend on Jesus. He had heard the voice of the Father saying, "Thou art my beloved Son, in whom I am well pleased" (Mark 1:11). Therefore, John knew Christ and realized his primary purpose in life was complete—to announce Christ to the world. He could genuinely say to his followers, "He must increase, but I must decrease" (3:30). Unfortunately, some of John's disciples did not share his humble spirit or devotion to Christ.

The evangelist records a dispute between some of the disciples of the Baptist and a Jew or group of Jews over some matter of purification. The word *zetesis* (3:25) refers to a process of inquiry usually resulting in a meticulous dispute (*see* 1 Timothy 6:4). Perhaps there was some concern over John's willingness to baptize in Samaria, probably baptizing Samaritans as well as Jews. The Jews would have considered these people unclean and unworthy of baptism. As a result of the dispute, his disciples came to John complaining of the success of Jesus' ministry.

The statement of these disgruntled disciples suggests a degree of bitterness in their spirits. They carefully avoid naming Jesus, referring to Him only as "he that was with thee . . . to whom thou barest witness" (3:26). The word *ide* (behold), used rarely in the writings of John, suggests in this context a sense of shock at the audacity of Jesus to baptize disciples. The real problem, however, was not that Jesus or, more correctly, the disciples of Jesus were baptizing but that they were apparently baptizing more disciples than John the Baptist. As they heard of Jesus' increasing crowds and saw their own crowds decrease, they could only conclude "all men come to him" (3:26). When one sees the expressions of pride and jealousy which too often characterize those involved in the ministry of Christ today, one begins to realize not much has changed in the last two thousand years.

John the Baptist reminded his disciples that the source of their former success was not their charismatic personalities or exciting programs but rather God. He had faithfully told his disciples he was not the Messiah and even pointed to Jesus as "the Lamb of God" (1:29,36). John the Baptist was not only content to allow Jesus to enjoy success without his personal opposition, he "rejoiced greatly" in that success. The expression *charai chairei* (3:29) literally translates "rejoicing with joy." It occurs only here and in Isaiah 61:10 (Septuagint). It was a Hebrew idiom meaning "rejoicing to the full." John the Baptist was rejoicing with such great joy over the success of his friend, the bridegroom, that even his own dwindling ministry or the bitter negative attitude of his disciples could not discourage him in his rejoicing.

The great humility of this man of God is evidenced by his sincere statement, "He must increase, but I must decrease" (3:30). The word *dei* (must) occurs only once in this verse although the translators have supplied it a second time. The first *must* is clearly stated; the second only implied. The secret of great humility is often only a matter of emphasis. Humility is not so much the result of vigorous self-abasement as it is the result of raising Christ to His proper place. He *must* increase even if it means I may decrease.

> 31 He that cometh from above is above all: he that is of the earth is earthly, and speaketh of the earth: he that cometh from heaven is above all.
> 32 And what he hath seen and heard, that he testifieth; and no man receiveth his testimony.
> 33 He that hath received his testimony hath set to his seal that God is true.
> 34 For he whom God hath sent speaketh the words of God: for God giveth not the Spirit by measure unto him.
> 35 The Father loveth the Son, and hath given all things into his hand.
> 36 He that believeth on the Son hath everlasting life: and he that believeth not the Son shall not see life; but the wrath of God abideth on him.

B. An Honored Son (3:31–36). Once again John interrupts a discourse to include his own explanatory note. The change in style in the final verses of this chapter from those just examined suggests a different speaker. The last words of the Baptist in this gospel are those of verse thirty where he affirms the preeminence of Jesus in his life and ministry. It is John the Apostle who makes what amounts to a major Christological statement of the faith.

1. His divine origin (3:31). All men must decrease as they see Jesus Christ and recognize who He is. When they acknowledge Jesus' deity, they accept that He is God. In these closing verses, John identifies three reasons why Christians recognize the deity of Christ. The first relates to His divine origin. Jesus, though born in a Bethlehem barn at a point in history, really came from above. His origin is in heaven rather than on earth; therefore he "is above all."

2. His divine testimony (3:32,33). John's second argument for the deity of Christ is that the testimony of Christ is also from heaven. He has authority given by God, and the things that Jesus says are from God, because Jesus is God in the flesh.

Emphasizing this point, John uses the verb *esphragisen*. The practice of sealing was used for various reasons including that of security (Matthew 27:66; 2 Corinthians 1:22; Ephesians 1:13; 4:30; Revelation 7:3–8; 20:3), concealment (Revelation 10:4; 22:10), and authentication (6:27; Esther 8:8). Here it is used for attestation or authentication. The one who accepts the witness of Jesus attests that Jesus speaks the message of God.

3. His divine authority (3:34–36). Finally, John argues that Christ is God because all authority has been given to Christ by God the Father. Jesus Christ has the total support of God. He has the Spirit completely filling Him and speaks the words of God. God has put everything into the hands of His Son.

John uses the phrase "into his hand" not only here but also in John 13:3. Also, Jesus Himself made similar claims during His ministry (5:19–30; Matthew 11:27; 28:18). This expression signifies not only possession but also the power of free disposal. The Father has given the Son "all things into his hand" (3:35), meaning Jesus is free to administer these things according to His own will.

This chapter concludes with another reminder of the decision all must make to have eternal life. Unbelief for John is not passive but active. The verb *apeithon* (believeth not, 3:36) could be understood in terms of willful disobedience. It is formed by the application of a Greek negative *a* to the verb *peitho*, which means "to persuade," "to cause belief," or "to induce one to do something by persuading."

Those who believe receive eternal life. Those who do not

become the objects of the wrath of God. There are two words in the New Testament for "wrath," *orge* and *thumos*. John here uses the more severe term—*orge*—describing a deeper, more settled and permanent attitude toward the unbeliever. When confronted with the option to believe, can there be any question what our response should be? A person can believe on the Son and have everlasting life, or he can refuse to believe and suffer the wrath of God.

SIX

CHRIST—
THE WATER OF LIFE
JOHN 4:1–54

Jesus practiced the same strategy for world evangelization that He later gave His disciples to follow (Acts 1:8). This strategy is illustrated in chapters three and four of John as different individuals and groups come to faith in Christ. He began in Jerusalem, explaining the Gospel to a prominent leader of the Jews and followed this by preaching to the Jewish multitudes (3:22). The major part of chapter four deals with Jesus' successful ministry in Samaria, reaching an outcast woman from an outcast people, followed by ministry to many in that region. Finally, Jesus reached out to lead a Gentile to faith in the Word of God. (*See* Chart 14.)

The public ministry of Christ was conducted primarily in three geographic regions: Judea, Samaria, and Galilee. Mat-

Chart 14

ACTS 1:8 IN JOHN CHAPTERS THREE AND FOUR	
Jerusalem	Nicodemus (3:1–15)
Judea	Judean ministry (4:1–3)
Samaria	Samaritan ministry (4:4–42)
The uttermost part of the earth	Healing of the nobleman's son (4:46–54)

thew and Mark tend to emphasize the Galilean ministry, neglecting any mention of Samaria. Luke, more than any other Gospel writer, emphasizes the ministry of Christ among the Samaritans. John tends to emphasize the Judean ministry of Christ though not completely ignoring His ministry in Samaria and Galilee. In this chapter, the evangelist makes specific mention of the ministry of Christ in each of these three regions.

I. MINISTRY IN JUDEA (4:1–4)

When therefore the Lord knew how the Pharisees had heard that Jesus made and baptized more disciples than John.
2 (Though Jesus himself baptized not, but his disciples.)
3 He left Judaea, and departed again into Galilee.
4 And he must needs go through Samaria.

John does not record specifically how long Jesus remained in Judea after the Passover, but it seems He is on the way home from the Passover in Jerusalem discussed in chapter three (April). The reference to "four months until harvest" (4:35), if understood literally, suggests it was April or May, because those were planting months, and it took four months for the crops to ripen for harvest. Apart from Jesus' interview with Nicodemus at Jerusalem, we do not know the success of His first Judean tour, but the disciples of the Baptist claimed "all men come to him" (3:26). According to the evangelist, "Jesus made and baptized more disciples than John" (4:1). In light of the great crowds that attended John the Baptist's ministry, Jesus must have experienced extreme popularity during these months (*see* Matthew 3:5; Mark 1:5).

There is some question as to what is meant by Jesus' baptizing. John explains it was His disciples who did most of the actual immersing. The word *ebaptizen* is in the imperfect tense, meaning Jesus was not "in the habit of baptizing." This does not mean Jesus never practiced baptism, only that He was not the one who normally immersed His converts. Some Baptists argue Jesus baptized the twelve, who then baptized others, thus establishing a succession from John the Baptist. While that may or may not be an accurate conclusion, it should be remembered that the New Testament makes a distinction between the nature of Christian baptism and that of John the Baptist (*see* Acts 19:3–5). Those who submitted to John's baptism were looking for the coming Messiah and repenting to get ready for the Messiah. Those who receive Christian baptism fulfill a different symbolism. They are identifying with the death, burial, and resurrection of Christ (Romans 6:4,5).

John uses an unusual verb to describe the departure of Jesus from Judea. The word *aphiemi* literally means "to send away" or "to dismiss"; it is used of forgiving offenses (James 5:15), yielding up (Matthew 27:50), and letting alone (Matthew 19:14). The word is used here of Jesus leaving Judea (4:3) and later of His leaving the world (16:28). After His ministry in Jerusalem, Jesus suddenly dismissed Himself from Judea. A comparison of the Gospels, as shown in Chart 15, suggests several reasons why He left Judea so abruptly.

As this Judean ministry concludes, John mentions the necessity of going through Samaria. The normal route for a Jew travelling from Judea to Galilee involved walking up the Jordan River valley to avoid any contact with the Samaritans. So great was the hostility between the Jews and Samaritans that a Jew would only take the route through Samaria if he was in a great hurry. In light of Jesus' later decision to remain in a Samaritan city for two days (4:40), it is unlikely Jesus chose this route because He was in a hurry to get to Galilee.

A more probable interpretation of this statement is that He went through Samaria because it was necessary for Him to do the will of His Father in preaching to the Samaritans (*see* 4:34). Normally, the verb commonly translated "it is necessary" (4:4) denotes a divine requirement in this gospel (*see*

Chart 15

WHY JESUS LEFT JUDEA FOR GALILEE	
1. To avoid a confrontation with the Pharisees	(John 4:1)
2. To accomplish His ministry in Samaria	(John 4:4)
3. To avoid an imprisonment similar to that of John the Baptist	(Matthew 4:12)
4. Because He was led to do so by the Holy Spirit	(Luke 4:14)

3:7,14,30; 4:20,24; 9:4; 10:16; 12:34; 20:9). Though it may have been a faster route to Galilee, the delay of Christ for two days in Sychar suggests He must have gone through Samaria for the purpose of meeting the spiritual needs of the people living there.

II. MINISTRY IN SAMARIA (4:5–42)

5 Then cometh he to a city of Samaria, which is called Sychar, near to the parcel of ground that Jacob gave to his son Joseph.
6 Now Jacob's well was there. Jesus therefore, being wearied with his journey, sat thus on the well: and it was about the sixth hour.

Jesus' Samaritan ministry in this chapter centers around a city called Sychar (4:5). There is some disagreement among Bible commentators concerning the exact identity of this city. Many identify the city as the site of El-Ascar, a city in the plain of Soukar, near the spring of Sonkar and close to Shechem. It has been known as Sychar or Soukar in the past and is close to Jacob's well at the foot of Mount Ebal. Some believe this may have been an important city during the Roman occupation of Palestine. Other writers choose to identify Sychar with Shechem, which is also in the same geographic area. The name *Shechem* means "portion" and was generally held to be the portion of land Jacob had given Joseph, who was later buried there (Genesis 33:19; 48:22; Joshua 24:32; Acts 7:16). Also, John here identifies the city noting it was "called Sychar." The name *Sychar* may have been a popular or intentional corruption of the name *Shechem*, based on the term *scheker*, meaning "falsehood" (city of liars or heathens, see Luke 9:51–56), or *schekar*, meaning "liquor" (city of drunkards, see Isaiah 28:1). Such an identification of a major Samaritan city like Shechem was the natural result of the deep animosity which existed between the Jews and the Samaritans. Both of the above-named cities are close to Jacob's well where Jesus met the Samaritan woman. Also, both could be identified by the term *polis* (city) since throughout the Gospels of Mark and John this term is used to identify communities of various sizes. Also, John's use of the term *choriou*, a diminutive identifying the "parcel of ground" (4:5) probably refers to the area around Jacob's well and Joseph's grave and may have no bearing at all on the size of the city. One could argue that the city was small because the area of the well was small, or that the area of the well seemed small next to such a large city. John spends more time in this chapter describing the meeting at the well, rather than the ministry of Jesus to the city.

About the sixth hour, noon according to Jewish time, Jesus sat to rest at Jacob's well. The participle *kekopiaos* describes a state of weariness and is closely related to the verb meaning "excessive toil" (*see* Luke 5:5). Although this gospel emphasizes the deity of Christ, it does not neglect His humanity. Actually, John tends also to emphasize the emotions of Christ throughout (2:14–16; 11:3,33,35,38; 12:27; 13:21; 19:28). Jesus in this gospel is described as "the Word became flesh" (1:14 RSV). After a day of travelling, the flesh became weary. Tired, hungry, and thirsty, He sat at the edge of the well. The picture implied by the Greek words is that of a man collapsing by a cool well because He was too tired to go on. His disciples went into the city to buy food, leaving Jesus alone at the well (4:8).

7 There cometh a woman of Samaria to draw water: Jesus saith unto her, Give me to drink.

8 (For his disciples were gone away unto the city to buy meat.)

9 Then saith the woman of Samaria unto him, How is it that thou, being a Jew, askest drink of me, which am a woman of Samaria? for the Jews have no dealings with the Samaritans.

10 Jesus answered and said unto her, If thou knewest the gift of God, and who it is that saith to thee, Give me to drink; thou wouldest have asked of him, and he would have given thee living water.

11 The woman saith unto him, Sir, thou hast nothing to draw with, and the well is deep: from whence then hast thou that living water?

12 Art thou greater than our father Jacob, which gave us the well, and drank thereof himself, and his children, and his cattle?

13 Jesus answered and said unto her, Whosoever drinketh of this water shall thirst again:

14 But whosoever drinketh of the water that I shall give him shall never thirst; but the water that I shall give him shall be in him a well of water springing up into everlasting life.

15 The woman saith unto him, Sir, give me this water, that I thirst not, neither come hither to draw.

16 Jesus saith unto her, Go, call thy husband, and come hither.

17 The woman answered and said, I have no husband. Jesus said unto her, Thou hast well said, I have no husband:

18 For thou hast had five husbands; and he whom thou now hast is not thy husband: in that saidst thou truly.

19 The woman saith unto him, Sir, I perceive that thou art a prophet.

20 Our fathers worshipped in this mountain; and ye say, that in Jerusalem is the place where men ought to worship.

21 Jesus saith unto her, Woman, believe me, the hour cometh, when ye shall neither in this mountain, nor yet at Jerusalem, worship the Father.

22 Ye worship ye know not what: we know what we worship: for salvation is of the Jews.

23 But the hour cometh, and now is, when the true worshippers shall worship the Father in spirit and in truth: for the Father seeketh such to worship him.

24 God is a Spirit: and they that worship him must worship him in spirit and in truth.

25 The woman saith unto him, I know that Messias cometh, which is called Christ: when he is come, he will tell us all things.

26 Jesus saith unto her, I that speak unto thee am he.

A. Building the Faith of a Sinful Woman (4:4–26). Jesus was interested in meeting the needs of people regardless of who those people were. Sometimes that involved ministry among the rich and famous like Nicodemus. At other times He found Himself with the outcasts of society like this Samaritan woman. While the message of Christ never changed, nor was it in any way ever compromised, His strategy of ministry changed with each person as He determined the best way to meet his or her needs. This is evidenced when

Chart 16

HE KNEW WHAT WAS IN MAN (John 2:25)	
Jesus and Nicodemus (3:1–15)	**Jesus and the Samaritan Woman (4:7–26)**
A man with a name	A woman unnamed
Good reputation	Bad reputation
A wealthy man	A poor woman
He came to Jesus	Jesus came to her
Outstanding in society	Outcast of society
A Jew	A Samaritan
Religious (morally upright)	Worldly (immoral)
No immediate response recorded	Immediately told a city
Jesus was blunt	Jesus was tactful
Began talking of spiritual things	Began talking of physical things

one compares the meetings of Jesus with Nicodemus and the Samaritan woman (*see* Chart 16).

Jesus initiated His conversation with the woman at the well by asking for a drink. This statement not only began the meeting but also identified His racial background. The woman immediately identified Christ as a Jew. While some commentators argue this identification was based upon Jesus' physical appearance, sociological studies suggest Jews tend to look like others in the society in which they live. Apart from anti-Semitic literature, there seems to be little evidence of any distinctive physical features of Jews in contrast with other people groups. There are, however, in every ethnic group linguistic characteristics—accents that often betray a person's cultural background (*see* Judges 12:6). One of these distinctive Jewish accents would have been pronounced in the request for a drink. A Jew would say *teni lischechoth*, whereas a Samaritan would have said *teni lisechoth*.

That Jesus should be talking with the woman caught her by surprise. The Samaritans claimed they were the true Israel and prided themselves on their worship. They had a temple of their own on Mount Gerizim and to this day continue to offer the blood sacrifices required in the Pentateuch. In actual fact, they are the descendants of heathen colonists from five Mesopotamian cities who had adopted the worship of Jehovah as a sort of tribal god (2 Kings 17:24–41; 2 Chronicles 30:6,10; 34:7). According to the rabbis, "To eat bread with the Samaritan was like eating swine's flesh." John uses the compound word *sunchrontai* with a strong negative to describe the relationship between Jews and Samaritans. The word *chraomai* means "to make use of" or "to treat a person well" (*see* Acts 27:3). The word *sun* implies the idea of togetherness. John here explains, "The Jews would never work together with or have great respect for the Samaritans" (4:9, literal translation).

Jesus chose not to engage in an ethnic-oriented debate with the woman but rather turned the focus to "the gift of God" (4:10). While some commentators interpret this gift as the living water, it is more probable that the gift is Himself, the Messiah, given by God (3:16). The expression *gift* should be viewed as one of the many descriptive titles of Christ. The word *kai*, here translated "and" can also be translated "even," in which case Jesus would be identifying Himself as "even the gift of God." Paul described Christ as the unspeakable gift of God (2 Corinthians 9:15).

The expression *hudor zon* (living water, 4:10) is used to contrast the quality of water Jesus would offer with that which He had requested. Jacob's well was fed largely by rainwater percolating into the cistern or well itself. Although it was good water, a well fed by springs (living or running water) was always preferred (Genesis 26:19; Leviticus 14:5; Numbers 19:17). While the woman appeared to understand Jesus' discussion of the living water only in terms of physical water, Jesus was also referring to water in its deeper sense of being a fountain of life (*see* Proverbs 13:14).

Water is a fundamental necessity of life and was used for several purposes in those days. Although He was asking for water, Jesus desired far more to give the "living water" to the woman who so desperately needed it. Water is useful for (1) producing growth, (2) cleansing, and (3) refreshing, but Jesus was using this expression to show her how to find (4) satisfaction in life.

Not understanding that Jesus was talking about spiritual water, the woman questioned Him about how He could draw the water from the well. She described the well as "deep" and noted He had nothing with which to draw water. It is estimated that the well was about thirty to fifty feet deep at that time, and although a bucket of skin was normally left at the well, Jesus did not have the rope to lower and raise the bucket.

The woman's question in verse twelve was stated in such a way as to assume a negative answer. The Samaritans believed they were descendants of Jacob through Joseph. For a Samaritan to acknowledge someone as "greater than our father Jacob" would be like an American identifying someone as a greater American than George Washington, or a Roman Catholic identifying someone as a better Catholic than the pope. The question might be expressed, "You are not greater than our father Jacob . . . are you?"

Jesus told her that the physical water of the well would not quench thirst forever, but the water that He was able to give would bring eternal satisfaction. John uses the words *ou me* (4:14, translated "never") which forms a double negative. Its appearance with a future indicative verb (*dipsesei*, "he shall thirst") constitutes the strongest possible negative expression in Greek. The emphasis of Christ is that His living water satisfies so that the drinker will never ever thirst again.

It is interesting to note how Jesus successfully avoided getting into controversial side issues that would hinder His spiritual ministry to this woman. On at least three occasions in this dialogue, the woman asked what could be described as loaded questions. On each occasion Jesus took the question and used it as an opportunity to further reveal Himself while carefully avoiding the controversy reflected in the question (*see* Chart 17). Perhaps the woman was testing the messenger before believing the message. If so, Jesus passed the test with flying colors.

When Jesus described His living water to the woman, she responded, "Sir, give me this water, that I thirst not" (4:15). Probably, she was still thinking of water in a physical sense and made the request somewhat sarcastically. Jesus responded to her request with two imperatives, "go," and "call thy husband" (4:16). Some commentators suggest the woman's request was made mockingly as she gathered her waterpot to return to the city. The verb *hupage* (go) is a present active imperative. If the woman was starting to walk

Chart 17

THE CONTROVERSIAL QUESTIONS OF THE WOMAN AT THE WELL		
The Woman's Question	Area of Controversy	Response of Jesus
"How is it that thou, being a Jew, askest drink of me, which am a woman of Samaria?" (4:9)	Social tensions between Jews and Samaritans	Began talking about living water
"Art thou greater than our father, Jacob?" (4:12)	Heritage tensions between Jews and Samaritans	Emphasized the different nature of His water
Where should you worship God: this mountain or Jerusalem? (see 4:20)	Religious distinctives of Jews and Samaritans	Emphasized the nature of genuine and spiritual worship

away, Jesus was in essence saying, "Go on your way, and call your husband." The second imperative, *phoneson* (call), is in the aorist tense and emphasizes the idea of a specific action to be accomplished.

Whatever the woman's motive in asking for the living water, Jesus knew what was in her heart (2:25) and issued the command to call her husband for a specific reason. The woman needed to confront her own sin if she was to receive the eternal life springing up from this well of water (4:14). She carefully answered, "I have no husband" (4:17). The word translated "husband" is *andra* and can mean a man or a husband. Although the woman had her "man," he was not her "husband." When Jesus further clarified the woman's marital status, He was producing conviction and motivating her to be truthful with Him and herself. For the first time in this dialogue, the woman began to discuss spiritual issues.

This woman's worship of Christ was not a sudden conclusion but rather the result of a gradual change in attitude toward Jesus. This change in attitude is reflected in the various titles of Christ used by the woman. She began by calling him "a Jew" (4:9), which was for her a term of contempt. Then she called Him "greater than . . . Jacob" (4:12), with a suspicious attitude assuming He was not. After being confronted with her sin, she called him "a prophet" (4:19), which, although it still fell short of Jesus' true identity, was probably meant as a title of respect. Her final reverence for Jesus was evidenced when she identified Him as the "Christ" (4:25,29).

The woman's question about the place of worship was of grave importance to a Samaritan. Jacob's well is at the foot of Mount Gerizim, and the woman may have pointed to the mountain as she identified the place where her fathers had worshipped (4:20). This was the mountain where Sanballat had built a temple which was eventually destroyed by John Hyrcanus in 129 B.C. Still, the Samaritans continued to worship on the mountain. To justify this action they noted both Abraham (Genesis 12:7) and Jacob (Genesis 33:20) had established altars at Shechem. Gerizim was the mountain from which the blessings of Deuteronomy 28 were proclaimed, and, according to the Samaritan Pentateuch, it was this mountain and not Ebal where an altar was built (Deuteronomy 27:4 Peshitta). Samaritans also tried to identify Gerizim as the mountain on which Isaac was offered to God.

She had the wrong approach, for she was talking about a form or a place of worship, and Christ was talking about the object of worship, which is God. True worshippers are not searching for a place or a form, for they worship in Spirit and in truth. God is seeking worshippers, not workers. He doesn't just want people to serve Him, for serving people are not always worshipping people. In contrast, if a man really worships God, he will also serve Him.

Jesus explained to the woman that the Jews knew more about this subject as they had a fuller revelation than the Samaritans (see 4:22). The Samaritans had rejected the Psalms and Prophets and therefore did not have that material in their canon of Scripture. In contrast, the Jews not only included that literature in their Scripture, it was also an integral part of their literature, especially the Psalms of David (Psalms 1—72). These Psalms are so often repeated in the Jewish expressions of worship that it is not uncommon to find a Jew who can recite all seventy-two from memory. Further, Jesus explained that this salvation of which they had been speaking came "out of" (*ek*) the Jews. This does not identify salvation with Judaism, as the Judaizing teachers later taught (Acts 15:1), but rather emphasizes the racial origin of the One who brought salvation. Lest there be any confusion as to His identity, Jesus used the expression "I am" (*ego eimi*, 4:26), identifying Himself not only as the Messiah but also with Jehovah in the Old Testament.

When this dialogue ended, the woman's new life was just beginning. She left her waterpot and ran back to the city to share her newfound faith. She was not commanded to witness but rather took it upon herself. That she left her waterpot shows she was in a hurry to tell others about Christ. A heavy waterpot would have only slowed her progress (*see* 2:6). Also, the fact she left her waterpot probably indicates her intention to return. Perhaps she remembered Jesus' earlier command to call her husband and thought of returning with her man to introduce him to the Messiah.

27 And upon this came his disciples, and marvelled that he talked with the woman: yet no man said, What seekest thou? or, Why talkest thou with her?

28 The woman then left her waterpot, and went her way into the city, and saith to the men,

29 Come, see a man, which told me all things that ever I did: is not this the Christ?

30 Then they went out of the city, and came unto him.

31 In the mean while his disciples prayed him, saying, Master, eat.

32 But he said unto them, I have meat to eat that ye know not of.

33 Therefore said the disciples one to another. Hath any man brought him ought to eat?

34 Jesus saith unto them, My meat is to do the will of him that sent me, and to finish his work.

35 Say not ye, There are yet four months, and then cometh harvest? behold, I say unto you, Lift up your eyes, and look on the fields; for they are white already to harvest.

36 And he that reapeth receiveth wages, and gathereth

fruit unto life eternal: that both he that soweth and he that reapeth may rejoice together.

37 And herein is that saying true, One soweth, and another reapeth.

38 I sent you to reap that whereon ye bestowed no labour: other men laboured, and ye are entered into their labours.

B. Building the Faith of His Skeptical Disciples (4:27–38). When the disciples returned toward the end of Jesus' dialogue with the woman, they "marvelled." The verb *ethaumazon* is an imperfect active describing the disciples' astonishment. The reason for this astonishment is here identified "that he talked with a woman" (4:27, there is no definite article in the Greek). Though suspicious, they kept their thoughts to themselves, probably out of respect for Jesus. These disciples viewed Jesus as a rabbi (1:38,49), yet He was engaged in an activity that most rabbis would have avoided. According to rabbinical teaching, "Let no one talk with a woman in the street, no, not with his own wife."[6] This principle was usually followed regardless of the context in which the conversation occurred. For instance, another maxim of the rabbis stated, "Let a man burn the words of the law rather than teach them to a woman."[7] It is, therefore, no wonder that the disciples marvelled, much as the woman herself had at the beginning of their conversation.

When the disciples returned, they insisted He eat the food brought to Him. The verb *eroton* is an imperfect active meaning "they kept beseeching" Him (4:31). Jesus told them, "I have meat to eat that ye know not of" (4:32). The disciples were puzzled with this statement, certain that no one else had brought Him food while they were gone. The question of verse thirty-three implies a negative answer. Jesus reminded His disciples that His "meat" was not only to do the will of His Father, but also to finish it. In both Judea and Samaria, Jesus and the disciples had been doing the will of the Father with tremendous success. Jesus was still doing the will of the Father and would continue until He accomplished the task (*see* 5:26; 17:4; 19:30). Sometimes, after a period of great blessing in the work of God there is a tendency to take it easy for a while. The disciples had to be reminded by Jesus of the need to complete the task.

Jesus also reminded the disciples they were four months from harvest—mid to late summer (4:35). Normally the harvest season would also include a pilgrimage to Jerusalem to keep the feast. Perhaps the disciples were thinking of their return to Judea, anticipating as great a harvest of souls in the future as they had received during the previous months. Gently rebuking that idea, Jesus told His disciples to "lift up" their eyes and "look on the fields" which were already white. Jesus could be referring to (1) the surrounding fields, which may have been prematurely ripe, (2) to their task of

Chart 18

THE CHRISTIAN AND THE HARVEST		
Look ye	John 4:35	Vision
Pray ye	Matthew 9:38	Compassion
Go ye	Matthew 28:19	Service

evangelism, or (3) the Samaritan men already making their way to hear Him teach the Word of God. These men were the white harvest field. The disciples were guilty of looking forward to harvesting while ignoring the harvest that was already ripe.

Jesus reminded the disciples of a familiar saying, "One soweth, and another reapeth" (4:37). Sometimes Christians quote this saying to justify their own lack of success in soul winning and claim to be sowers and not reapers. But we should be certain we understand the saying before applying it. "He that soweth the good seed is the Son of man" (Matthew 13:37). To His disciples Jesus said, "I sent you to reap that whereon ye bestowed no labor" (4:38). While the disciples had gone to the city to buy food, Jesus had sent them to reap a harvest. But they had no impact in Sychar. These disciples who had been involved in an abundantly successful ministry with Jesus did not see the harvest in Samaria. While the disciples failed to "finish" the will of the Father, the purpose of God would not be frustrated. Jesus had entrusted the task of winning a city to a woman who had known Him for less than an hour because she was more willing than others who no doubt were better trained but did not respond to the need. The greatest ability Christ seeks in His workers is availability.

Our mission as "disciples" (Acts 11:26) can be summarized in the three steps shown in Chart 18. First, we need vision, and we get it as we look to the ripened harvest fields (4:35). Second, we should share the compassion of Christ for the lost and pray that the Lord of the harvest will send laborers into the harvest (Matthew 9:38). Finally, we must engage in the service of Christ and go to others with the Gospel (Matthew 28:18–20).

> 39 And many of the Samaritans of that city believed on him for the saying of the woman, which testified, He told me all that ever I did.
>
> 40 So when the Samaritans were come unto him, they besought him that he would tarry with them: and he abode there two days.
>
> 41 And many more believed because of his own word;
>
> 42 And said unto the woman, Now we believe, not because of thy saying: for we have heard him ourselves, and know that this is indeed the Christ, the Saviour of the world.

C. *Building the Faith of a Samaritan City (4:39–42).* The evangelization of a Samaritan city emphasized the power of a testimony. No doubt the woman was well-known in the city, and the change in her life resulted in many people believing on Christ simply because of what she said. They invited Jesus to remain in their city, and He did so for two days, and many more believed. In his summary of this revival, John is careful to distinguish between the saying of the woman (*lalia*, 4:42) and the word of Christ (*logos*, 4:41).

The faith of the Samaritans pointed out that Christ had a much broader scope in His ministry than most people realized. This was the first time Jesus was identified as "the Saviour of the world" (4:42). Although the early church had no question but that Jesus was the only Saviour (Acts 4:12), they were not convinced initially that salvation could be received except by the Jews (*see* Acts 10:45). Even before the cross, the Samaritans understood the salvation of Christ was sufficient to meet the need of the whole world (*see* 1 John 2:2).

III. THE MINISTRY IN GALILEE (4:43–54)

43 Now after two days he departed thence, and went
into Galilee.
44 For Jesus himself testified, that a prophet hath no
honour in his own country.

Between John's accounts of the ministries in Samaria and
Galilee, he reminds the reader, "For Jesus himself testified,
that a prophet hath no honour in his own country" (4:44).
When this expression is used in the synoptic gospels, it is
always applied to Nazareth (Mark 6:1,4), but in this gospel it
applies to a broader scope, probably to the entire Jewish
nation (1:11). John records the continual rejection of Christ
(1:11; 2:13–21,24; 4:1–3; 7:1), but He is to some extent received by the Samaritans (4:39), the Galileans (4:45), and the
Gentiles (12:20–22).

45 Then when he was come into Galilee, the Galilaeans
received him, having seen all the things that he did at
Jerusalem at the feast: for they also went unto the feast.
46 So Jesus came again into Cana of Galilee, where he
made the water wine. And there was a certain nobleman,
whose son was sick at Capernaum.
47 When he heard that Jesus was come out of Judaea
into Galilee, he went unto him, and besought him that he
would come down, and heal his son: for he was at the
point of death.
48 Then said Jesus unto him, Except ye see signs and
wonders, ye will not believe.

A. The Fickleness of the Galileans (4:45–48). Although the
Galileans received Christ, they did so for the wrong reasons. The Samaritans had received Christ for who He was,
the Saviour of the world. The Galileans received Christ for
what He did, the miracles in Jerusalem (4:45). This fickle
attitude of the Galileans is particularly contrasted with the
faith of a Gentile leader, as John records His second of
eight miracles.

In verse forty-eight Jesus says, "Except ye see signs and
wonders, ye will not believe." The phrase "signs and wonders" was a popular Old Testament expression identifying

miracles (Deuteronomy 28:46; 34:11; Nehemiah 9:10; Isaiah 8:18; 20:3; Jeremiah 32:20,21). In the New Testament, the word *wonder* is never used by itself of miracles performed by Jesus or His disciples, although the expression is repeated several times (Matthew 24:24; Mark 13:22; Acts 2:22,43; Romans 15:19; 2 Corinthians 12:12; 2 Thessalonians 2:9; Hebrews 2:4). Its usage tends to denote a failure of perception on the part of those who witness these miracles. Although Jesus addressed His remarks to the nobleman, His use of the plural verbs for *see* (*idete*) and *believe* (*pisteusete*) indicates His remarks were intended not for the one who by faith came to Him, but rather for the crowd who had only received Him because of the "signs and wonders" they saw in Jerusalem.

49 The nobleman saith unto him, Sir, come down ere my child die.

50 Jesus saith unto him, Go thy way; thy son liveth. And the man believed the word that Jesus had spoken unto him, and he went his way.

51 And as he was now going down, his servants met him, and told him saying, Thy son liveth.

52 Then enquired he of them the hour when he began to amend. And they said unto him, Yesterday at the seventh hour the fever left him.

53 So the father knew that it was at the same hour, in the which Jesus said unto him, Thy son liveth: and himself believed, and his whole house.

54 This is again the second miracle that Jesus did, when he was come out of Judaea into Galilee.

B. *The Faith of a Gentile Nobleman* (*4:49–54*). There is a tendency on the part of some commentators to confuse the miracle in these verses with a similar event recorded by Matthew and Luke. Although there are several similarities in in the two healings in Capernaum, there are also several differences that make it clear this event is different from that recorded by the synoptic gospels. These differences are illustrated in Chart 19.

John here identifies the one requesting the miracle with the word *basilikos*. This term was reserved for those closely connected with the king either by blood or by office. In all

Chart 19

TWO HEALINGS IN CAPERNAUM	
Matthew 8:5–13; Luke 7:1–10	**John 4:46–54**
Jesus in Capernaum	Jesus in Cana of Galilee
Approached by elders of the Jews, sent by a centurion, Jesus offers to come to heal servant	Approached by a nobleman, Jesus tells man his son is healed
Centurion asks Jesus only to speak the word	Nobleman begs Jesus to come to his home
Jesus comments on great faith	Jesus comments on unbelief (4:48)
Later in Galilean ministry (after Sermon on the Mount)	Early in Galilean ministry

probability, this man was a courtier, a high-ranking official of Herod Antipas, tetrarch of Galilee. News of Jesus' miracles had reached Herod's court, and Herod himself had wanted to meet Jesus and witness His miracles (Luke 23:8).

The nobleman pleaded with Jesus to come with him before his child died. Like Mary and Martha later, the nobleman believed there was hope if Jesus arrived before death claimed its victim. The term *paidion*, translated "child," was a term of endearment for a small child. The nobleman's request was not that of a high-ranking official; it was the plea of a father for his dying son.

Jesus chose to heal this man's son without making the journey to Capernaum. In this gospel, signs are recorded to produce faith. Twice John mentions the faith of the nobleman. First, he "believed the word that Jesus had spoken unto him" (4:50). Later, when that word was confirmed, he "himself believed" (4:53). The first expression of faith was faith in the spoken word of God, and the second expression of faith was in the incarnate Word of God. This sign was significant in that not only the father believed but also his whole household, which would include not only his family but also his servants. This is the first example of salvation to all who believe (*see* Acts 11:14; 16:15,34; 18:8). This does not imply that the nobleman's faith brought salvation to them, for that is inconsistent with John and the rest of Scripture, which make it clear that each individual must believe. Rather this is an illustration of "oikos evangelism," reaching people through existing natural relationships. Some identify this as a "people movement" that happens when a family or larger group of people express multi-individual decisions that lead to mutually interdependent conversions.

SEVEN

CHRIST—
THE DEITY
JOHN 5:1–47

The fifth chapter of John begins simply when Jesus goes to Jerusalem for a feast and on the Sabbath heals a man who has never walked. Out of this miracle grows the key chapter to the Gospel of John. Why the key? Because it traces two major themes. First, it records the beginning of the bitter hostilities of the Jews toward Christ. A year and a half later the Jews still hated Christ for breaking their laws concerning the Sabbath (7:23). Two full years later, they will succeed in having Jesus crucified.

Second, this chapter includes the strongest arguments for the deity of Christ. He claims a unique relationship with the Father, a statement which the Jews understood as a claim to deity (5:18). Then Jesus offers four witnesses to substantiate His claim. Those who deny that Jesus ever claimed to be God either have not read or do not understand this chapter.

I. THE THIRD SIGN (5:1–16)

John begins this chapter with the familiar expression *meta tauta* (after this), connecting the events of this chapter with those of the previous chapter. If the feast mentioned here is the Passover, almost twelve months are skipped over between the second and third of the signs in this gospel. It is not John's purpose to give a complete sequential history of Jesus Christ but to prove His deity and motivate the readers to faith (20:31). Between chapters four and five, the reader is quickly transported from Galilee to Jerusalem where Jesus again gives hope to the hopeless by meeting a need in a crippled man that no one else could meet.

> After this there was a feast of the Jews; and Jesus went up to Jerusalem.
>
> 2 Now there is at Jerusalem by the sheep *market* a pool, which is called in the Hebrew tongue Bethesda, having five porches.
>
> 3 In these lay a great multitude of impotent folk, of blind, halt, withered, waiting for the moving of the water.
>
> 4 For an angel went down at a certain season into the pool, and troubled the water: whosoever then first after the troubling of the water stepped in was made whole of whatsoever disease he had.
>
> 5 And a certain man was there, which had an infirmity thirty and eight years.

A. The Setting (5:1–5). John mentions "a feast of the Jews" in connection with Jesus' journey to Jerusalem. This feast has been variously identified as Passover, the Feast of Weeks (Pentecost in Acts 2:1), the Feast of Tabernacles, the Day of Atonement, the Feast of Dedication, and the Feast of Purim. Some manuscripts include the definite article *the* in the expression "feast of the Jews," which would likely be used only of Passover. Passover was one of the three feasts every Jewish male was required to attend (Deuteronomy 16:16), and since it was the first feast to be instituted, and it marked the foundation of the nation, Passover was considered the most important for a Jew to attend. Therefore, Jesus attends this important feast. Also, John seems to be using the Passover timetable to show that Christ ministered for over three years. This is the second of four Passovers in John (2:23; 5:1; 6:4; 12:1). During the Passover, the population of Jerusalem would swell to nearly a million people. Yet, despite the multitudes, the ministry of Christ during this Passover would center around only one man. He was a man who had "no man" to help him (5:7).

The pool of Bethesda was a long rectangular pool used to clean animals about to be taken to the temple for sacrifice. The water was two to three feet deep and, according to tradition, was left filthy by the animals. From the edge of the pool down to the water was twenty to thirty feet. Archaeologists have found a pool fitting the descriptions of Bethesda. It has only one set of stairs down to the water. There was a porch on all four sides and one spanning the center that appeared to be a bridge over the pool. The name *Bethesda* means "house of mercy," and its waters were thought, under certain circumstances, to have curative powers. John describes "a great multitude" of sick gathered around the pool for this reason (5:3). Normally there would be less than three hundred by the pool; however, during the feast seasons there were two or three thousand sick sitting by the pool.

The curative powers of the waters of Bethesda were believed to be tied to the troubling of the waters by an angel (5:4). There is some question as to whether there was any historical basis for this belief. It is noteworthy that there is no recorded instance of a verified healing connected with this pool, nor is there any evidence of an angel ever being involved in a miraculous healing. Barclay argues there was a troubling of the waters, but that it was caused by a subterranean stream that passed under the pool. This verse is absent in a number of early manuscripts, but its absence is explained two ways. Some claim the words were added to explain the prevailing opinion of the people, but others suggest the words were removed from the text because they tended to be supporting pagan ideas concerning angels giving special powers to sacred rivers and streams. In the case of the man whom Jesus healed, he would not have been healed even if the waters stirred and he knew it (5:7).

While the man's age and sickness are not specifically identified, John notes he had been in his condition for thirty-eight years. Many have seen this miracle as an allegory of the experience of Israel. According to this interpretation, the man represented Israel. The five porches represented the law "which could uncover a man's weakness, but which could never cure it."[8] The thirty-eight years have been taken to refer to either the wilderness wanderings or the centuries of messianic expectation. The stirring of the waters according to this view usually represents Christian baptism. There is probably, however, no hidden meaning in this miracle apart from the one Christ later explains—an evidence of His deity.

> 6 When Jesus saw him lie, and knew that he had been now a long time in that case, he saith unto him, Wilt thou be made whole?
> 7 The impotent man answered him, Sir, I have no man, when the water is troubled, to put me into the pool: but while I am coming, another steppeth down before me.
> 8 Jesus saith unto him, Rise, take up thy bed, and walk.
> 9 And immediately the man was made whole, and took up his bed, and walked: and on the same day was the sabbath.

B. The Sign (5:6–9). Again John emphasizes the special knowledge of Christ, as he does in every chapter in this gospel (2:24). Of the great multitude, Jesus saw one man and knew (*gnous*) he had been by the pool a long time. Some commentators suggest Jesus may have overheard someone's comments about the man or even heard the man's own story, but the word *gnous* (knowledge) is often used by John to explain Jesus' supernatural knowledge about men and the will of God (*see* 2:24; 13:1). When one waits a long time for a miracle or answer to prayer, discouragement grows and with it unbelief begins to develop. Jesus, therefore, asked the man, "Wilt thou be made whole?" (5:6).

In asking the question Jesus used the verb for *will* (*theleis*), meaning in this context not only "do you wish" but "are you still earnestly desiring" to be made whole. The response of this man suggests his hope had begun to deteriorate. Rather than answering the question directly, the man explained why he had not yet been healed. Many of us might well be guilty of sitting down and waiting for an angel to come along and trouble the waters of our lives, while giving little or no thought to putting our faith in God into action. (*See* Chart 20). It is interesting to note that when the man was finally healed, all of these excuses still existed. The difference—he was willing to take Jesus at His word.

Although hope was waning, Jesus searched the heart of this man and found that he still wished to be healed. He called upon the man to do the impossible with no thought

Chart 20

EXCUSES BY THE POOL (John 4:7)	
His Excuses	**Our Excuses**
1. "I have no man"	"There is no one around to help me"—dependence upon people rather than God.
2. "When the water is troubled"	"The conditions just are not right for a miracle"—dependence on circumstances rather than God.
3. "To put me into the pool"	"This is the wrong place to expect God to do a miracle"—limiting God to work only in certain geographic areas.
4. "While I am coming, another steppeth down before me"	"Somebody always seems to be getting in my way or hindering the situation"—blaming others for past failures rather than focusing on present possibilities.
+1. "The same day was the sabbath" (5:9)	"These are not the days of great miracles"—limiting God to having only worked during a particular period in the past.

that he would do anything but obey. The verb *egeire* is a present active imperative and was used as a popular exclamation similar to the expression of a parent calling a lazy child to "get up." This word is in direct contrast with the verb *balei* in the previous verse, meaning "to throw or cast" him into the water. For perhaps as long as thirty-eight years the man had been waiting for someone else to throw him into the pool at the right moment, while what he needed to do was simply arise in obedience to the command of Christ. Some Christians are guilty of praying and then waiting for God to hand them a miracle on a silver platter. They need to put feet on their prayers by both trusting and obeying.

Why did Jesus tell this man to do what seemed so impossible? We might consider the fact that Christ wanted the man to start his new life by doing the impossible. Just as it is impossible for an unsaved man to repent, yet that is expected. When in faith he responds, God in His power saves him from his sin. Also, in choosing this man who was apparently known to the crowd as a cripple of many years, the miracle could have a significant impact on the doubters. But perhaps the biggest issue here was in the timing, for Jesus understood the Jews' legalistic observance of the Sabbath and could well have used the miracle in defiance of their unreasonable laws, thus hoping to teach a lesson concerning the meaning behind the laws of God. When this man promptly obeyed Christ, he was immediately healed, even though it was the Sabbath.

> 10 The Jews therefore said unto him that was cured, It is the sabbath day: it is not lawful for thee to carry thy bed.
> 11 He answered them, He that made me whole, the same said unto me, Take up thy bed, and walk.
> 12 Then asked they him, What man is that which said unto thee, Take up thy bed, and walk?
> 13 And he that was healed wist not who it was: for Jesus had conveyed himself away, a multitude being in that place.
> 14 Afterward Jesus findeth him in the temple, and said unto him, Behold, thou art made whole: sin no more, lest a worse thing come unto thee.
> 15 The man departed, and told the Jews that it was Jesus, which had made him whole.
> 16 And therefore did the Jews persecute Jesus, and sought to slay him, because he had done these things on the sabbath day.

C. *The Sequel (5:10–16).* Although briefly mentioned before in connection with some opposition to Jesus, John now begins to more consistently identify a group known as "the Jews" as those opposed to Christ and His work. This designation does not refer to all Jews but rather that hostile group within the Pharisees that apparently held the power in the religious bureaucracy of the day. They insisted upon a very strict observance of the law, following its letter but long since forgetting its spirit. Jesus, the lawgiver (James 4:12), knew the real meaning of the law and fulfilled it in all aspects (Matthew 5:17). The conflict between Jesus and the Jews was perhaps inevitable.

The Jews were quick to condemn when the lame man was healed. Rather than rejoicing in this great miracle, they focused on an apparent violation of the Sabbath laws (5:10). It was unlawful to carry a bed on the Sabbath, particularly so in the city of Jerusalem (Exodus 23:12; Nehemiah 13:19; Jeremiah 17:21). The punishment for this infraction was death by stoning. One can well imagine the deep sense of horror that must have come upon this man who, while rejoicing in his healing, is suddenly seized by the Jews, accused of a capital crime, and then realizes he does not even know the name of the One who healed him (5:11–13).

Even under the narrow law of the Jews, neither Jesus nor the healed man could have been found guilty of an infraction of the Sabbath. According to the Mishna, a man could not be accused of violating the Sabbath unless he had first been formally warned against such an action. There is no record of such a warning ever being given to Jesus, and it would be difficult to believe the man who had been sick for thirty-eight years would have been previously told by the Pharisees not to carry his bed on the Sabbath. The questioning of this man by the Jews reflects their true attitude. Despite the clear testimony of the man concerning his healing, when the Jews asked about the One responsible, they were not asking about the One who healed the man but rather the One who commanded the man to carry his bed (5:12). Those who have critical hearts are quick to condemn and slow to congratulate.

When Jesus later found the man, he said, "Sin no more, lest a worse thing come upon thee" (5:14). The verb *heuriskei* (found) means "to find after search for someone or something." Jesus thought it was important to give this warning to the man and went looking for him. The nature of this warning suggests the illness had been caused by a volitional act of sin. While not all sickness is the result of sin (*see* 9:3), sometimes sickness is the natural or supernatural result of violating the law of God. That had been the case in the experience of this man. It is hard to know what Jesus had in mind when He spoke of a condition worse than thirty-eight years of illness.

The man who had been healed then went to the Jews and told them that "it was Jesus, which had made him whole" (5:15). Still the miracle was the prominent thing in the mind of the man, but the Jews began actively opposing Jesus because He had, to their understanding, violated the Sabbath. The verb *ediokon* is an imperfect, meaning they "began to persecute and continued to persecute" Him (5:16). It would be two years before they would see Him hanging on the cross. The verb *epoiei* (he had done) is also an imperfect, suggesting their formal charge related not to just this miracle but that He habitually or continually broke the Sabbath (*see* Matthew 12:10–13; Luke 6:7–11). This is one of the ten reasons John suggests as to why the Jews opposed Christ (*see* Chart 21).

Chart 21

WHY DID THE JEWS OPPOSE CHRIST?	
1. Because of the cleansing of the temple	(2:18)
2. Because of His extreme popularity	(4:1)
3. Because He healed a man on the Sabbath	(5:16)
4. Because He made Himself equal with God	(5:18)
5. Because they were not of God	(8:44–47)
6. Because He identified Himself as the I Am	(8:58,59)
7. Because He was a Galilean	(9:29; *see* 7:41,52)
8. Because He claimed to be the Son of God	(10:30–33)
9. Because they were losing power over people to Him	(11:48)
10. Because they feared Rome would destroy the nation if He succeeded	(11:48–53)

II. THE THREE CLAIMS OF CHRIST (5:17-24)

The Jews also sought to kill Jesus because He claimed to be "equal with God" (5:18). He did this by revealing three areas in which He was equal with the Father. In doing so He was essentially claiming to be God, as each of these claims relates to an area unique to God.

> 17 But Jesus answered them, My Father worketh hitherto, and I work.
> 18 Therefore the Jews sought the more to kill him, because he not only had broken the sabbath, but said also that God was his Father, making himself equal with God.

A. Equal with God in Nature (5:17,18). Jesus began by referring to God as "My Father" (*ho pater mou*). By using this title of God, Jesus was claiming a unique relationship with God. The Jews understood this to be a claim to be equal with God in nature. John uses the term *idion* (his) in repeating the charge in 5:18, "God was his father." We get the English word *idiom*, meaning "a unique expression," from the Greek word *idion*. Here Jesus is described as the unique Son of God. Verse eighteen is one of the strongest statements of Christ's deity, and it comes from His enemies.

As the son of a man has the nature of man, so the Son of God has the nature of God. Jesus pointed out that He, in a unique relationship to God, had violated their Sabbath laws and had done so for some time. The verb *ergazetai* means "he keeps on working"—without a break for the Sabbath. As Westcott observes, "Man's true rest is not a rest *from* human earthly labor, but a rest *for* divine, heavenly labor."[9] Because the Father continues to work on the Sabbath, and Jesus is equal with God in nature, He too should be free to work on the Sabbath.

> 19 Then answered Jesus and said unto them, Verily, verily, I say unto you, The Son can do nothing of himself, but what he seeth the Father do: for what things soever he doeth, these also doeth the Son likewise.
> 20 For the Father loveth the Son, and sheweth him all things that himself doeth: and he will shew him greater works than these, that ye may marvel.

21 For as the Father raiseth up the dead, and quickeneth
them; even so the Son quickeneth whom he will.

B. *Equal with God in Power* (5:19–21). Jesus explained
that nothing He did was by His power, but rather He was
doing what He saw the Father do. He cited the love of the
Father for the Son as the basis for which the Son has a share
in the power of God (5:20). The word *philei* is used to emphasize the ultimate and affectionate friendship and fellowship the Father has for the Son. In other places the Scriptures
use the term *agape* to describe the love between the Father
and the Son. Both verbs are inadequate to completely express the nature of this relationship.

Jesus speaks here of the "greater works" He will do (5:20).
While the term *erga* (works) is sometimes used in Scripture
of miracles, John prefers the term *semeia* (signs), using it
seventeen times in the gospel to emphasize the spiritual significance of the eight particular miracles he describes. The
references to works in this gospel should probably be limited
to the nonmiraculous aspects of Christ's doing the will of His
Father (*see* 4:34). The use of "works" (5:20) is a reference to
His declaring the Father (1:18), fulfilling the messianic claim,
and becoming flesh (1:14).

Jesus was equal with God in power because both had the
power to give life. This theme would be emphasized in a
discourse at the next Passover season when Christ would
reveal Himself as the bread of life (6:33–35). Later, He would
also explain He was the light that gives life (8:12; 9:5), the
door to the abundant life (10:9), the shepherd who gives His
life for His sheep (10:11), the resurrection and the life (11:25),
the way, the truth, and the life (14:6), and the vine that gives
the branches life (15:5). By way of a sign to verify these
claims, Jesus would give physical life to three dead individuals (11:41–44; Matthew 9:18,23–26; Luke 7:11–17).

22 For the Father judgeth no man, but hath committed
all judgment unto the Son:
23 That all men should honour the Son, even as they
honour the Father. He that honoureth not the Son honoureth not the Father which hath sent him.
24 Verily, verily, I say unto you, He that heareth my
word, and believeth on him that sent me, hath everlasting

life, and shall not come into condemnation; but is passed
from death unto life.

C. *Equal with God in Authority* (5:22–24). The third area
in which Jesus claims equality with the Father is that of authority. Jesus explained that the Father had committed all
judgment to the Son (5:22). The verb *dedoken* (given) is a
perfect active indicative form of the verb indicating a state of
completion (*see* 3:35; 6:27,31; 10:29). The emphasis here is
that the Father has already made the commitment to leave
the execution of judgment in the hands of the Son.

The consequence of this equality is that the Son is worthy
of the same worship that is due the Father. The verb *timosi* is
a present active subjunctive meaning "may keep on honoring the Son" (5:23). Clearly, Jesus is calling on men to worship Him with the same honor they would have toward the
Father. Also, that worship should consist not only of a momentary adoration of the Son but also include constantly
putting Him first in every area of life.

Verse twenty-four was cited by J. Wilbur Chapman as the
verse upon which his assurance of salvation rested. The use
of the present tense verb *echei* (has) emphasizes that eternal
life is the present possession of everyone who hears and
believes. The believer also has the promise he "shall not
come into condemnation; but is passed from death unto life"
(5:24). The death here is not physical death but rather the
second death (Revelation 20:14).

III. THE THREE ACTS OF CHRIST (5:25–29)

When Jesus spoke here of the dead coming to life when they
hear the voice of the Son of God, He was speaking of the
spiritually dead finding new life in Christ (Ephesians 2:1,5;
5:14). He goes on to teach that He not only gives spiritual life
but also judges and raises the dead. These three acts that He
does are acts of God; therefore they are closely tied to His
claim that He is deity because He does the acts of God.

25 Verily, verily, I say unto you, The hour is coming,
and now is, when the dead shall hear the voice of the Son
of God: and they that hear shall live.
26 For as the Father hath life in himself; so hath he
given to the Son to have life in himself.

A. All Life in His Hands (5:25,26). That which makes the Creator of Life distinct from any living beings that He has created is that He has "life in himself" (5:26). As this is characteristic of the Father, it is also given to the Son. The verb *edoken* (he gave, 5:26) is an aorist, pointing back to the eternal past. The prepositions *as* and *so* indicate the fact rather than the degree of this giving of life. Jesus here claims to be engaged in the giving of life as one might expect God to give life (*see* 1:3).

27 And hath given him authority to execute judgment also, because he is the Son of man.

B. All Judgment in His Hands (5:27). As Jesus tied His work of giving life to His title "Son of God," here He ties His work of judgment to His title "Son of Man." The absence of the definite article here has led some to conclude His emphasis is "Because I am human, I can rightly judge." But John also uses this title of Christ without an article in Revelation 1:13, where there is little emphasis on the humanity of Christ. Jesus used this title most often in the context of the cross, the place where the Father judged the sin of the world. In essence, Jesus is saying, "Because I have been judged for the sin of others, I am qualified to judge others."

28 Marvel not at this: for the hour is coming, in the which all that are in the graves shall hear his voice,

29 And shall come forth; they that have done good, unto the resurrection of life; and they that have done evil, unto the resurrection of damnation.

C. All Resurrection in His Hands (5:28,29). He that has power to give spiritual life also has power to raise the dead. The dead are described as "in the graves"—the physically dead. There are two words for the grave in the New Testament. The word *taphos* emphasizes the idea of burial, whereas the word used here—*mnemeiois*—emphasizes the memorial marking the grave. During His later ministry, Jesus would demonstrate His power by raising two people from death before their bodies were buried and another after his body had begun to decompose in the grave.

Jesus divided this resurrection into two distinct parts, the resurrection to life and the resurrection to damnation. Some have mistakenly taken the word *hora* (hour, 5:28) to mean these two resurrections are really one general resurrection. The Scriptures teach this resurrection to life occurs at the beginning of the kingdom (Revelation 20:4) whereas the resurrection to damnation is a thousand years later (Revelation 20:5). It should be noted the "hour" of spiritual regeneration (5:25) has already lasted almost two thousand years; therefore, there should be no problem in this future "hour" of resurrection lasting a thousand years.

IV. THE FOUR WITNESSES TO CHRIST (5:30–47)

30 I can of mine own self do nothing: as I hear, I judge: and my judgment is just; because I seek not mine own will, but the will of the Father which hath sent me.

31 If I bear witness of myself, my witness is not true.

32 There is another that beareth witness of me; and I know that the witness which he witnesseth of me is true.

Jesus recognized His claim to be "equal with God" (5:18) would be disputed if not authenticated by two or more witnesses in accordance with Jewish law (Numbers 35:30; Deuteronomy 17:6). He noted, "If I bear witness of myself, my witness is not true" (5:31). This does not mean He is confessing to being a false witness. Later He states that His witness and that of the Father are two reliable witnesses to His deity and that two witnesses are in keeping with the requirement of Mosaic law (8:17). Here, Jesus was stating that his witness alone was not enough because the Jews would simply not accept it. Under Jewish, Roman, and Greek law, the testimony of a witness was not accepted as evidence in his own case. Though Jesus' witness was genuine, He offers the Jews twice as many witnesses as they required to verify his claims.

33 Ye sent unto John, and he bare witness unto the truth.

34 But I receive not testimony from man; but these things I say, that ye might be saved.

35 He was a burning and a shining light; and ye were willing for a season to rejoice in his light.

A. John the Baptist (5:33–35). Jesus first reminds them they had already talked to John the Baptist, and he had been a faithful witness to Christ (1:19–27). The people had trusted John, who in turn had prophesied of Christ. Each of the four Gospels mentions John the Baptist in connection with introducing Christ to the nation at the beginning of Jesus' public ministry. If the Jews had believed John, they would now be accepting Jesus.

Jesus describes John the Baptist in the past tense, suggesting the ministry of John had ended either with his imprisonment or, more probably, his death. He described John as "a burning and a shining light" (5:35). The word translated "light" here is not *phos*, which is reserved in this gospel for the true light (1:8), but rather *luchnos*, meaning "lamp" or "candle" (*see* Matthew 5:15). While Jesus is the light of the world, that light is shed abroad through many lamps such as John the Baptist and Christ's disciples. The verb *kaiomenos* (burning) is a reminder of the transitory nature of John's light.

> 36 But I have greater witness than that of John: for the works which the Father hath given me to finish, the same works that I do, bear witness of me, that the Father hath sent me.

Chart 22

THE MESSIANIC WORKS OF DANIEL 9:24
1. Finish the transgression
2. Make an end of sins
3. Make reconciliation for iniquity
4. Bring in everlasting righteousness
5. Seal up the vision and prophecy
6. Anoint the most holy

B. Jesus' Works (5:36). The second witness to which Jesus appeals is His "works." While some commentators confuse these works with the signs or miracles of Jesus, it is more probable that these works are nonmiraculous. Jesus was conscious of the need to finish the works of His Father and did so often without the aid of a miracle (4:34; 17:4; 19:30). The works to which He is specifically referring here are the distinctively messianic works prophesied by Daniel (Daniel 9:24, see Chart 22). The greatest works of Jesus involved reconciling people with God through the new birth (Nicodemus) and the offer of living water (Samaritan woman). The Jews should have recognized these works as a witness supporting His messianic claims.

> 37 And the Father himself, which hath sent me, hath borne witness of me. Ye have neither heard his voice at any time, nor seen his shape.
> 38 And ye have not his word abiding in you: for whom he hath sent, him ye believe not.

C. *The Father* (*5:37,38*). The third witness offered by Jesus is the witness of the Father. Jesus notes that "the Father . . . hath borne witness" (5:37), and "him ye believe not" (5:38). Commentators have suggested three possible expressions of the witness of the Father. First, Barclay identifies this statement with a subjective experience within man, noting, ". . . His witness is the response which rises in the human heart when a man is confronted with Christ."[10] On the other hand, Pink follows Calvin in identifying the witness of the Father with His revelation in the Scriptures. He concludes, "We think that Christ refers, rather, to the witness which the Father had borne to His Son through the prophets during Old Testament times."[11] A third possibility is that of Chrysostom, Bengel, and others that this refers to the statement of the Father at the baptism of Jesus (Mark 1:11). In any event, the Father Himself bears witness that Jesus is the Christ, the Messiah, the Son of God.

> 39 Search the scriptures; for in them ye think ye have eternal life: and they are they which testify of me.
> 40 And ye will not come to me, that ye might have life.
> 41 I receive not honour from men.
> 42 But I know you, that ye have not the love of God in you.
> 43 I am come in my Father's name, and ye receive me not: if another shall come in his own name, him ye will receive.

44 How can ye believe, which receive honour one of another, and seek not the honour that cometh from God only?

45 Do not think that I will accuse you to the Father: there is one that accuseth you, even Moses, in whom ye trust.

46 For had ye believed Moses, ye would have believed me: for he wrote of me.

47 But if ye believe not his writings, how shall ye believe my words?

D. The Scriptures (5:39–47). The fourth witness to Jesus is the Scriptures. Throughout this gospel the Scriptures are held in high esteem, often being cited authoritatively to explain an aspect of the gospel. Here John uses the plural *tas graphas,* referring to the Old Testament as a whole. When he uses the expression in the singular, he is normally referring to a particular verse of Scripture (*see* 2:22; 7:38; 10:35). Here was a common ground for both Jesus and the Jews, for both professed a high regard for the Scriptures and their authority in matters of faith and practice.

Jesus says of the Jews and their attitude toward the Scriptures, "In them ye think ye have eternal life" (5:39). John's use of the verb *dokeite* suggests they were thinking wrongly. Whenever John uses this verb in the gospel, it always indicates a mistaken opinion (5:45; 11:13,31; 13:29; 16:20; 20:15). It was not that they were mistaken in thinking eternal life could be found in the Scriptures (*see* 2 Timothy 3:15), they were wrong in thinking they had that eternal life. Had they correctly searched the Scriptures, they would have realized it testified of Christ and in believing on Him would have received eternal life. In rejecting Christ, they lost everything.

This fifth chapter of John then gives a clear picture of Christ and His deity as He reveals truth to the crowds. But, as Jesus Himself observed, He would be rejected, although other false messiahs would be accepted (5:42,43). This is the first of eight references to the name of the Father in this gospel (5:43; 10:25; 12:28; 17:5,11,21,24,25). In rejecting Christ, they had rejected the Father. While this is a Gospel of faith revealing how people came to believe that Jesus is the Christ, the Son of God (20:31), it has also been called the gospel of rejection, as that theme is also evident (*see* 1:11; 3:11,32; 12:37).

Jesus concludes this discourse by telling the Jews that
Moses not only testified of Him, he would also testify against
them (5:45). Commenting on this, Barclay notes, "Here then
is the great and threatening truth. That which had been the
greatest privilege of the Jews had become the greatest
condemnation."[12] There is an antithesis drawn between
Moses and Jesus and their respective messages. They were
hoping in Moses (5:45) rather than believing in Christ (5:46).
They failed to believe Moses' writings and could not believe
Christ's words (5:47). John uses the verb *elpikate* (5:45),
meaning "a state of resting or relaxing." Although translated
here with the English word *trust*, it is not the usual word for
faith but rather hope. Also, John uses the word *grammasin*
(5:47) to identify the writings of Moses. This term is used
elsewhere in the New Testament negatively contrasting the
letter with the spirit (Romans 2:27,29; 7:6; 2 Corinthians 3:6)
and to identify written characters such as letters (Luke 22:37;
2 Corinthians 3:7; Galatians 6:11). The scribes of the Jews
made careful copies of the letters of the law, and on that they
were resting. Their earlier response to the man who was
healed after thirty-eight years of sickness demonstrated they
had no comprehension of the spirit of the Scriptures.

The fifth chapter of this gospel gives a clear picture of
Christ and God being one and the same—deity. But it also
shows Jesus as a man—a man of strength, a man of understanding, a man capable of analyzing and dealing with men
whose life-styles are contrary to the will of His Father and
whose man-made laws are in violation of God's law—the
very law He came to fulfill.

EIGHT

CHRIST—
THE BREAD OF LIFE
JOHN 6: 1–71

This is the longest chapter in John, totaling seventy-one verses, yet it covers the events of probably less than twenty-four hours. During this time Jesus miraculously fed approximately five thousand people, spent time alone with God in prayer, walked on the water, and taught a lesson in the synagogue, on the bread of life. Within this period the multitudes determined first to crown Him as king then rejected Him as Lord. Though much is recorded in this chapter, there is approximately a year that has passed unmentioned between this and the events of the previous chapter. Chapter six records the first of the seven "I am's" in this gospel. In this chapter it is Christ—the bread of life.

I. THE FEAST OF JESUS (6:1–15)

After these things Jesus went over the sea of Galilee, which is the sea of Tiberias.

2 And a great multitude followed him, because they saw his miracles which he did on them that were diseased.

3 And Jesus went up into a mountain, and there he sat with his disciples.

4 And the passover, a feast of the Jews, was nigh.

The feeding of the five thousand with "five barley loaves, and two small fishes" (6:9) is perhaps the most popular miracle performed by Christ. It is designated as the most popular miracle because (1) it is the only miracle recorded in all four gospels and (2) it involves the largest group of people. It is difficult to imagine the volumes of food produced from that lad's meager lunch, enough to satisfy the physical hunger of five thousand men and fill twelve baskets afterward.

John begins this chapter with the familiar phrase *meta tanta* (after these things, 6:1). This expression is used by the writer when he identifies an undetermined period of time. The context of this chapter suggests that this period of time is about one year (*see* 5:1; 6:4), the feast of the Jews and the Passover being the same. According to the synoptic gospels, that year was spent largely in Galilee and was characterized by the growing popularity of Jesus. John hints at this popularity as he described the great multitude that followed Him (6:2). The verb *ekolouthei* is in the imperfect tense, suggesting the crowd followed Him not only on this occasion but were generally following Him. However, verse four suggests this was a crowd of people on their way to Jerusalem for the Passover.

Jesus went up into a mountain and sat with His disciples. John uses a definite article with the word *mountain*, suggesting he had a particular hill in mind. The verb *ekatheto* is an imperfect middle, meaning "was sitting" in the sense of someone sitting to relax. Those with Jesus at the time were His disciples, which probably included more than the twelve. Many outside of the twelve had also chosen to follow Jesus and were identified as disciples, although some of these left Him after His sermon on the bread of life (6:66). It was out of the remaining disciples that Jesus commissioned twelve as apostles (Matthew 10:2–4). The time that Jesus had alone with the disciples on the mountain is not specified, but John implies it was very brief. Very soon they saw the approaching crowds (6:5).

John makes specific mention of this Passover (6:4), probably the third one in the ministry of Christ. He may have mentioned it for several reasons. First, this is typical of John who, while not writing a chronological biography of Christ in the sense that Luke did, still gives careful attention to chronological details such as feasts, days, and even hours. A second reason for mentioning the Passover may have been to explain the crowds. Passover was one of the three feasts a Jewish man was required to travel to Jerusalem to celebrate (Deuteronomy 16:16). This would explain the presence of five thousand men with apparently few women or children. A third reason for the mention of the Passover may have been to provide the background and context of Jesus' sermon on the bread of life. The Passover season was one rich in the symbolism of unleavened bread (Exodus 12:8,15).

These obedient Jews were going to Jerusalem for a feast that was presided over by sterile priests and ungodly temple leaders. These unbelieving priests would shortly reject Jesus and crucify Him. So Jesus knew that the crowds would not have their spiritual needs met by false shepherds. Therefore, Jesus is setting up a true feast in opposition to their empty feast. As John often juxtaposes light against darkness, so here is a spiritual feast in opposition to an empty religious feast (*see* Chart 23).

> 5 When Jesus then lifted up his eyes, and saw a great company come unto him, he saith unto Philip, Whence shall we buy bread, that these may eat?
>
> 6 And this he said to prove him: for he himself knew what he would do.
>
> 7 Philip answered him, Two hundred pennyworth of bread is not sufficient for them, that every one of them may take a little.
>
> 8 One of his disciples, Andrew, Simon Peter's brother, saith unto him,
>
> 9 There is a lad here, which hath five barley loaves, and two small fishes: but what are they among so many?

Chart 23

The Feast Of Jesus	The Feast of the Jews
1. Simple—five loaves and two fishes	1. Elaborate
2. Surrounded by God's creation	2. Surrounded by magnificent temple
3. Fills body and soul	3. Fills only body

A. The Need Identified (6:5–9). As Jesus looked out from the mountain, He saw the crowds coming to Him. This crowd followed Jesus not for who He was but for what He did (6:2). Still, even before the crowds had finally arrived, He recognized a need and asked Philip where bread (*artous*, literally "loaves") could be purchased. Whereas Peter is usually the spokesman, there are three possibilities why Jesus may have asked Philip. First, Philip had been raised in this area (Cana) and might have known where such supplies were available. Second, in the four listings of the disciples (Matthew 10:2–4; Mark 3:16–19; Luke 6:14–16; Acts 1:13), Philip is always listed fifth, suggesting he is the leader of the second group of four disciples (Peter, Andrew, James, and John, making up the first group of four), and that as leader of this group it was his responsibility to care for the multitude. Third, Jesus asked Philip to test him (6:6). Philip is characterized as an analytical disciple. Whenever he is mentioned in Scripture, he usually is analyzing something (1:43–46; 12:20–22; 14:8–14). Perhaps the Lord knew his analytical nature and wanted to reveal it to him in a tangible way. The word *peirazon* means "testing" either in the sense of tempting or proving. When used in connection with deity in Scripture, it always has the latter emphasis as "God cannot be tempted with evil, neither tempteth he any man" (James 1:13).

Philip's response suggests he failed the test. Rather than realizing he was in the presence of the Son of God who turned water to wine, Philip became overwhelmed with what was needed. He estimated they needed two hundred denarii (RSV) to give everyone a taste, but it would be insufficient to completely feed them. The denarius was a Roman coin worth a day's wages for a common laborer.

Jesus knew what He would do (6:6), therefore He was expecting an expression of faith from Philip. But all He heard was a recital of facts. An expression of faith would have confessed the person of Jesus Christ as deity and recognized what He was able to do.

Apparently before Jesus could respond, Andrew, true to his character, brought someone to Jesus. Andrew brought a boy with a lunch, recognizing it was not much, but at the same time knowing it was all he had. Andrew had that rare ability to be fully aware of a great need and still be willing to consider the apparently inadequate solution. Andrew's statement, "But what are they among so many?" (6:9), reflects his little faith. The Lord uses those with small faith when it is exercised in response to Jesus Christ.

Although this miracle is mentioned in all four Gospels, John alone mentions the boy. The word *paidarion* is a double diminutive meaning literally "a very small boy." The word was sometimes used to identify slaves and hardly a term to be applied to a person one would identify as the source for feeding five thousand people. Also, the word *opsaria* (fishes) is a diminutive. It probably refers to a couple of pickled fish. Several varieties of small fish were caught in abundance in Galilee, and the pickling and selling of these fish was a major commercial enterprise of the area. There was nothing particularly significant in either the fish or the boy, except that they were not much.

Further, John identifies the bread as "barley loaves" (6:9). Bread made from barley was generally considered inferior by people of that day. It has a low protein count in comparison to wheat and corn and was called the food fit for beasts. Barley was part of the diet of soldiers being punished for losing their standard in battle. To offer barley bread to others might by some be considered an insult. What Andrew had to present to Jesus was not much, but it was all he had. What we have to offer Christ today may not seem like much in light of the great needs around us, but if it is all we have, it is enough to meet the need when placed in the hands of Jesus and blessed by Him.

There are several reasons why Jesus fed the five thousand. He could have asked them to fast, which was a religious exercise to draw the soul to God, but He did not. First, Jesus knew the people were hungry and that most of them had come a long way. He had compassion on them. Second, He may have wanted to show them the wonderful plan of God's love and His power to take care of any needs they might have. Third, considering the contrast of the feast days and the knowledge Jesus had of Jewish custom, it is certain that He could have anticipated this informal feast as an opportunity to teach them about His Father. Fourth, Jesus wanted to contrast His ministry with the emptiness of the Jews in Jerusalem.

10 And Jesus said, Make the men sit down. Now there was much grass in the place. So the men sat down, in number about five thousand.

11 And Jesus took the loaves; and when he had given thanks, he distributed to the disciples, and the disciples to them that were set down; and likewise of the fishes as much as they would.

12 When they were filled, he said unto his disciples, Gather up the fragments that remain, that nothing be lost.

13 Therefore they gathered them together, and filled twelve baskets with the fragments of the five barley loaves, which remained over and above unto them that had eaten.·

B. The Miracle Accomplished (6:10–13). The feeding of the multitude illustrates several principles of spiritual operation. First, He is a God of order and not confusion (1 Corinthians 14:33,40). Jesus first directed the crowd to be seated in an orderly arrangement (6:10). Second, Jesus gave thanks before distributing the food, emphasizing the need to honor God in all spiritual service. Third, the law of the division of labor is emphasized. God usually does not do for us what we can do for ourselves and reserves for Himself the task that only He can do. Only Jesus could multiply the fish and bread, but He used the disciples to distribute the food to the multitudes (6:11). Fourth, God is always willing to use what we willingly give Him. Although He could have produced manna as He did for Israel in the wilderness, He chose rather to multiply a small boy's lunch. That day no one left hungry (6:12,13). There was one basket left over for each disciple. Fifth, God is concerned with preservation in both the spiritual and physical realms. The abundance was collected and utilized (6:12).

Jesus instructed first that the men be seated. The word *andres* was used of men as distinct from women. This command may imply the women were not seated, they were seated separate from the men in keeping with Near Eastern custom, or, more likely, there was not a significant number of women present. The law only required that men attend the Passover in Jerusalem, and while women were not excluded, the economics of the situation usually meant the men made the trip, leaving their wives and children at home.

Before distributing the food, Jesus gave thanks. The verb *eucharistesas*, from which we get the term *eucharist*, meaning "thanksgiving," referred to the Jewish custom of saying grace at meals (*see* Deuteronomy 8:10). Jesus may have used the familiar formula, "Blessed art thou Jehovah our God, King of the world, who causes to come forth bread from the earth."

Jesus then gave the broken loaves and fishes to the disciples, who in turn gave them to the men. The only guideline given to the disciples was that they should distribute the food liberally so that everyone would get "as much as they wanted" (6:11 RSV). According to Mark's account of this miracle, the men sat in groups of fifty and groups of a hundred (Mark 6:40). The five barley loaves and two fishes were distributed equally among the disciples. Perhaps the miracle began in Jesus' hands until the twelve baskets of the disciples were filled. They in turn distributed to the multitudes, and perhaps the miracle continued in each basket, the food continually replenished as each person took his portion.

Regardless of how the disciples distributed the loaves, it was more than sufficient to satisfy the multitude. John uses two different words to emphasize this truth. The first word, *eneplesthesan* (6:12), means "to fill in," "to fill up," or "to fill completely." Later, Jesus used the verb *echortasthete* (6:26), which was normally used of feeding animals. When applied to people it meant they were glutted, fatted, or fed to repletion. The emphasis of this second word is captured in the contemporary slang expression "pig out."

When the multitude was fed, Jesus instructed them to gather the fragments "that nothing be lost" (6:12). He was attempting to teach here by example a principle he would verbalize the next day. "That of all which he [the Father] hath given me I should lose nothing" (6:39). When the gathering was accomplished, there were twelve baskets of bread (6:13).

It was customary in a Jewish feast to leave something for the servants. In allowing His disciples to assist in feeding the hungry crowd, Jesus demonstrated His confidence and trust in them. It was as if He were making them co-workers and partners in this great miracle. The significance of the twelve baskets is clear when we understand the motive of Christ as He dealt with twelve men of different backgrounds and vaious degrees of faith. He understood the nature of each and gave each an equal responsibility. Because they had taken when they had received and had given it to the multitude, Jesus provided a basket of food for each of them. The word *kophinoi* refers to the bottle-shaped basket a Jew normally carried when travelling. Each disciple was able to fill his *kophinos* with the unused fragments of the barley loaves.

14 Then those men, when they had seen the miracle that Jesus did, said, This is of a truth that prophet that should come into the world.

15 When Jesus therefore perceived that they would come and take him by force, to make him a king, he departed again into a mountain himself alone.

C. The Response of the Multitude (6:14,15). In this gospel the miracles are signs to bring people to faith in Christ and thus produce eternal life. The repeated miracles (6:2) climaxed by this spectacular miracle of the feeding of the five thousand finally began to make an impression. They began to identify Jesus as the prophet like unto Moses (6:14; Deuteronomy 18:15). However, even that understanding was tainted. The Galileans during this time were quick to identify prophets who might lead a messianic revolt against Rome and secure political independence for the Jews. They identified Jesus as a prophet not to teach them the things of God but rather to deliver them from Rome and be their king.

The language of verse fifteen paints a vivid picture of the beginning of a revolution. The verb *mellousin* is a present active indicative suggesting the leaders of the group were already starting the movement. Another active verb, *harpazein*, meaning "to seize violently," suggests the mood of the mob was such to immediately start the revolution against Pilate and declare Jesus their king. Jesus sent His disciples away immediately (Matthew 14:22; Mark 6:45) as they perhaps were sympathetic with the revolutionary mood of the crowd. Jesus went farther up the mountain to be alone and pray (Matthew 14:23; Mark 6:46).

One might well ask, "If the national acceptance of Jesus as the Messiah, the king of the Jews, was the objective of John the Baptist, why did Jesus resist efforts to make Him king?" Perhaps the answer to this question is seen in that the will of

God can only be accomplished when God's man does God's work in God's way at God's time. The end can never justify the means in any spiritual endeavor. As is evident later in this chapter, those who were ready to declare Jesus their king for political reasons were not willing to recognize Him as their Lord for spiritual reasons.

II. THE PROTECTION OF JESUS (6:16–21)

16 And when even was now come, his disciples went down unto the sea,

17 And entered into a ship, and went over the sea toward Capernaum. And it was now dark, and Jesus was not come to them.

18 And the sea arose by reason of a great wind that blew.

19 So when they had rowed about five and twenty or thirty furlongs, they see Jesus walking on the sea, and drawing nigh unto the ship: and they were afraid.

20 But he saith unto them, It is I; be not afraid.

21 Then they willingly received him into the ship: and immediately the ship was at the land whither they went.

A second miracle recorded in this chapter occurred later that same evening. Apparently the disciples waited on the shore for Jesus to arrive. When He had not come by late evening, they determined to set sail without Him. John describes the scene of their departure, noting, "It was now dark, and Jesus was not come to them" (6:17). John often uses the word *skotia* to refer not only to physical darkness but also a kind of spiritual darkness. It was the dark when Judas went out to betray Christ (13:30). Now it was dark as the disciples were about to sail into a storm without Jesus.

The trip across the Sea of Galilee is only about six or seven miles, but it can be one of the most dangerous trips one makes. The mountains around this body of water are such that a storm can rise quickly and almost instantaneously turn the calm and peaceful lake into a raging torrent. The disciples were about three and a half miles into their journey (twenty-five or thirty furlongs, 6:19) when such a storm overtook them. John uses the word *diegeireto*, an imperfect passive form of the verb meaning "to wake up thoroughly" or "to arouse" to describe the approaching storm. It was as though the sleeping lake suddenly began to wake up because of the great wind that blew. Even for experienced fishermen such a storm would have been very dangerous.

It was during this storm that the disciples saw Jesus "walking on the sea" (6:19). Those who tend to deny the miraculous like to emphasize that the word *epi* can mean "on," "by," or "along" (*see* 21:1). They argue Jesus was not walking on the sea but rather by or along the sea—on the shore. While grammatically the word may be translated with that meaning, the context rules out that possibility. Had the disciples seen Jesus on the shore, they would have been relieved that their journey was almost finished rather than being afraid. Also, it would have been difficult for the disciples to see through the stormy darkness three and a half miles and clearly identify the Lord. The record clarifies the meaning of the preposition when John speaks of Jesus coming closer to the boat.

Jesus calmed the fears of His disciples by revealing to them His true identity in the midst of the storm. He said, "It is I" (*ego eimi*, 6:20), which is the Old Testament identification of Jehovah, "I am." Jehovah was the covenant name of God in the Old Testament, the One who would not fail nor forsake (Joshua 1:5). Although the disciples were prepared to leave without Jesus, they were now learning He would not forsake them in the storm. When they were willing to receive Him (*ethelon labein*, 6:21), the storm began to end. John does not specifically say whether Jesus actually entered the boat, but the accounts of Matthew and Mark confirm He did (Matthew 14:32,33; Mark 6:51). Their immediate and miraculous arrival at the shore may have been simultaneous with either their willingness to receive Christ or, more probably, with His entering the boat. The accounts of Matthew and Mark add, "the wind ceased."

III. CHRIST—THE BREAD OF LIFE (6:22–59)

22 The day following, when the people which stood on the other side of the sea saw that there was none other boat there, save that one whereinto his disciples were entered, and that Jesus went not with his disciples into the boat, but that his disciples were gone away alone;

23 (Howbeit there came other boats from Tiberias nigh unto the place where they did eat bread, after that the Lord had given thanks:)

24 When the people therefore saw that Jesus was not there, neither his disciples, they also took shipping, and came to Capernaum, seeking for Jesus.

25 And when they had found him on the other side of the sea, they said unto him, Rabbi, when camest thou hither?

26 Jesus answered them and said, Verily, verily, I say unto you, Ye seek me, not because ye saw the miracles, but because ye did eat of the loaves, and were filled.

27 Labour not for the meat which perisheth, but for the meat which endureth unto everlasting life, which the Son of man shall give unto you: for him hath God the Father sealed.

28 Then said they unto him, What shall we do, that we might work the works of God?

29 Jesus answered and said unto them, This is the work of God, that ye believe on him whom he hath sent.

30 They said therefore unto him, What sign shewest thou then, that we may see, and believe thee? what dost thou work?

31 Our fathers did eat manna in the desert; as it is written, He gave them bread from heaven to eat.

Although John does not specifically say so, the next day was probably the Sabbath. Jesus' discourse on the bread of life occurred "in the synagogue, as he taught in Capernaum" (6:59). There was a meeting of the synagogue on Monday and Thursday as well, but there are reasons why this was probably the Sabbath meeting. First, the lesson on manna was appointed to be read at the morning service, and this appears to have been Christ's sermon text. Perhaps for this reason, or in keeping with an early tradition, several early versions and some church fathers have added the words "on the sabbath day" to verse fifty-nine. The remainder of this chapter contrasts the people's desire for physical bread and Christ's offer of the bread of life.

The passage begins by describing the people's search for Christ. They crossed the lake in boats and noted only the disciples' boat was on shore. Finally, the crowd found Jesus in Capernaum. While they made their search under the pretense of "seeking for Jesus" (6:24), Jesus noted, "Ye seek me, not because ye saw the miracles, but because ye did eat of the loaves, and were filled" (6:26). Jesus is illuminating their spiritual unbelief even though they outwardly followed Him. They were failing to grasp the nature of what it meant to be a disciple of Christ. Jesus urged them to be more concerned with eternal life than mere food to keep one alive physically.

The sermon Jesus preached on this occasion was the hardest public discourse in the life of Christ. Four times Jesus used the formula, "Verily, verily" (6:26,32,47,53), which tended to recognize a resistance by the hearers to believing the truth. This is not often an expression used in a public message, although Christ used it three additional times as He introduced the new truths recorded in the Upper Room Discourse (13:16,20,21).

Jesus appealed to men to believe Him because He had the seal of God upon Him (6:27). In the East, it was the seal rather than the signature that authenticated a document or guaranteed the contents of a package or fulfillment of a contract. The rabbis taught that the seal of God is truth.[13] This was based on a legend where a scroll was said to fall from heaven, bearing only one word, *emeth*, the Hebrew term for "truth." *Emeth* is spelled with three Hebrew letters—*aleph* (the first letter of the alphabet), *mem* (the middle letter of the alphabet), and *tav* (the final letter of the alphabet). When Jesus spoke of being sealed by God, He was emphasizing that His message was true for the beginning, the middle, and the end of life.

Twice in this meeting the people called on Christ to produce manna (6:31,34). There are several reasons why such a request might be made. First, it was widely believed that Jeremiah had hidden the jar of manna kept in the ark and that the Messiah would reveal Himself by producing the hidden manna (*see* Revelation 2:17). Also, in the identification of the prophet like unto Moses, the Messiah was thought to bring manna. The rabbis taught, "As was the first redeemer so was the final redeemer; as the first redeemer caused the manna to fall from heaven, even so shall the second redeemer cause the manna to fall."[14] A third reason for this request may have been related to their hope for a messianic revolt (*see* 6:15). Manna was thought to be characteristic of the kingdom of God.

Manna was one of several types of Christ in the Old Testament (*see* Chart 24). Given to Israel originally as their bread in the wilderness, it ended only after the nation crossed the Jordan River and began eating the grain of the land. It was widely known as "the bread from heaven."

Jesus identified Himself as the bread of life (6:35), which may mean the bread that communicates life (6:54) or the bread which is eternal life (*see* 1 John 1:2). There are several similarities and differences between the manna in the wilderness and Christ who is the bread of life.

> 32 Then Jesus said unto them, Verily, verily, I say unto you, Moses gave you not that bread from heaven; but my Father giveth you the true bread from heaven.
> 33 For the bread of God is he which cometh down from heaven, and giveth life unto the world.
> 34 Then said they unto him, Lord, evermore give us this bread.

A. The Bread of Everlasting Life (6:32–34). The crowd was asking Jesus to duplicate the miracle of Moses in providing

Chart 24

MANNA AS A TYPE OF CHRIST	
From heaven Individually received Accessible to all Sweet White (Pure)	
Manna	**Christ**
Gift of God through the mediation of Moses	Gift of God given directly by God
Given temporarily, ceased when Israel entered Canaan	Given continuously
Given only to Israel	Given to the whole world
Sustained physical life until they died	Sustains spiritual life forever

bread from heaven. Like the woman at the well, they appeared to be thinking only of their physical needs and not their spiritual needs. Jesus urged them to be concerned not with manna but rather "the true bread" (6:32). John used the word *alethinon*, meaning "true" in the sense of genuine. He was the ultimate reality of which manna was only a foreshadowing.

Jesus specifically identified the bread of God as "he which cometh down from heaven" (6:33). John uses the word *katabainon* seven times in this chapter (6:33,38,41,42,50,51,58). It serves to emphasize Christ's heavenly origin in that He "came down" from heaven. It also served as a major stumbling block, exposing the unbelief of the crowd (6:41,42).

The genuine bread of God from heaven is that which gives life. When John uses the word *zoe* for life, he is most often talking about eternal life. John Chrysostom, one of the church fathers, contrasted manna with Christ, noting that while manna brought nourishment (*trophe*), it failed to give life (*zoe*). Christ is the bread of everlasting life.

35 And Jesus said unto them, I am the bread of life: he that cometh to me shall never hunger; and he that believeth on me shall never thirst.

36 But I said unto you, That ye also have seen me, and believe not.

B. *The Bread of Satisfying Life* (6:35,36). Jesus offers a satisfying life to those who will accept it on His terms. This involves both coming and believing (6:35). The verb *erchomenos* (comes) is the first act of the soul in approaching Jesus. Godet suggests it involves approaching Christ with seriousness of heart and sense of sin. Although John does not use the word *repent* in his writings, the idea of repentance is certainly implied in the use of the term *coming*. The second verb, *pisteuon*, refers to a continuous relation of trust after coming; it is the confiding eagerness with which the heart receives Christ. Coming to Christ without faith or believing in Christ without coming to Him will fail to appropriate the satisfying life He offers. Both are necessary. This combination of verbs is repeated in John 7:37,38, where the image is that of satisfying thirst. Those who hunger and thirst after righteousness will be satisfied if they come to Christ in faith.

37 All that the Father giveth me shall come to me; and him that cometh to me I will in no wise cast out.

38 For I came down from heaven, not to do mine own will, but the will of him that sent me.

39 And this is the Father's will which hath sent me, that of all which he hath given me I should lose nothing, but should raise it up again at the last day.

40 And this is the will of him that sent me, that every one which seeth the Son, and believeth on him, may have everlasting life: and I will raise him up at the last day.

41 The Jews then murmured at him, because he said, I am the bread which came down from heaven.

42 And they said, Is not this Jesus, the son of Joseph, whose father and mother we know? how is it then that he saith, I came down from heaven?

43 Jesus therefore answered and said unto them, Murmur not among yourselves.

44 No man can come to me, except the Father which hath sent me draw him: and I will raise him up at the last day.

45 It is written in the prophets, And they shall be all taught of God. Every man therefore that hath heard, and hath learned of the Father, cometh unto me.

46 Not that any man hath seen the Father, save he which is of God, he hath seen the Father.

47 Verily, verily, I say unto you, He that believeth on me hath everlasting life.

C. *The Bread of Resurrection Life* (6:37–47). As He continues to explain the nature of the genuine bread of life, Jesus makes three references to the future resurrection of the saints (6:39,40,44). Just as none of the fragments of the barley loaves was lost, so none of those whom the Father has given Him will be lost, but all will be included in the resurrection (6:12,39). The privilege of being raised by Christ is further identified as one of the benefits of the eternal life received by faith (6:40). Jesus explains that those who will be raised are those who are drawn by the Father and come to Him (6:44).

Saving faith in Christ is closely related to our understanding of the person of Christ. John uses the word *theoron* (6:40), meaning not merely "seeing" but rather "contemplation"— seeing with the eye of faith. John often uses verbs for sight in the gospel in close association with faith (*see* 20:5,8). The Jews, however, could not or would not see beyond the obvious. They stumbled in unbelief concerning the statement of Christ's heavenly origin because they were aware of His family background. They had seen Christ (*heorakate*, 6:36), but they had not seen with the eye of faith; hence their unbelief.

Jesus explained that the Father must draw men to Christ if they are to come to Him (6:44). This statement has become a proof text to those who wrongly teach a hyper-Calvinist view of election. John, writing under the influence of divine inspiration, had two Greek words to choose from, each with a different shade of meaning. The word *suro* literally means "to drag" and is used in Scripture of dragging the body of Paul (presumed dead) out of the city of Lystra (Acts 14:19). It is interesting to note this word is never used of Christ's attraction of men. Rather John chose the word *helkusei*, meaning "to draw with a moral power" (12:32; *see* Jeremiah 31:3). This word almost always implies some form of resistance on the part of the object or person drawn. Commenting on this verse, Martin Luther observed, "The drawing is not like that of the executioner, who draws the thief up the ladder to the gallows; but it is a gracious allurement, such as that of a man whom everybody loves, and to whom everybody willingly goes."[15]

As He emphasized this truth, Jesus cited biblical authority (6:45). The statement Jesus quoted is from Isaiah 54:13, although the idea is taught throughout the Old Testament (*see* Jeremiah 31:33,34; Joel 2:28–32). The presence of the word *and* beginning the quote suggests Jesus may have at that time been holding the Isaiah scroll and paused to read the verse directly from the text.

> 48 I am that bread of life.
>
> 49 Your fathers did eat manna in the wilderness, and are dead.
>
> 50 This is the bread which cometh down from heaven, that a man may eat thereof, and not die.

Chart 25

THE LOGICAL ORDER OF SALVATION IN JOHN 6:35-65
1. The Father draws by revealing Christ as an attractive alternative to sin and its end (6:37). 2. The sinner beholds (contemplates) the gracious offer of the Father (6:40). 3. The sinner determines to trust the atoning work of Christ for his salvation (6:40). Rejection of Christ at this point ends the saving process at least temporarily. 4. The repentant sinner comes to Christ for the purpose of salvation (6:37). 5. The sinner evidences his heart of repentance by coming to Jesus (6:35,65). 6. The sinner embraces Christ as Saviour by faith (6:35). 7. The disciple is embraced by Christ, never to be cast out or lost (6:37,39). 8. The disciple enjoys a growing intimacy with Christ during his life (6:54,56). 9. Disciples shall be raised by Christ at the last day (6:39,40,44,54).

51 I am the living bread which came down from heaven: if any man eat of this bread, he shall live for ever: and the bread that I will give is my flesh, which I will give for the life of the world.

52 The Jews therefore strove among themselves, saying, How can this man give us his flesh to eat?

53 Then Jesus said unto them, Verily, verily, I say unto you, Except ye eat the flesh of the Son of man, and drink his blood, ye have no life in you.

54 Whoso eateth my flesh, and drinketh my blood, hath eternal life; and I will raise him up at the last day.

55 For my flesh is meat indeed, and my blood is drink indeed.

56 He that eateth my flesh, and drinketh my blood, dwelleth in me, and I in him.

57 As the living Father hath sent me, and I live by the Father: so he that eateth me, even he shall live by me.

58 This is that bread which came down from heaven: not as your fathers did eat manna, and are dead: he that eateth of this bread shall live for ever.

59 These things said he in the synagogue, as he taught in Capernaum.

D. *The Bread of Indwelling Life* (*6:48–59*). In this passage there is a unique relationship between two verbs for eating and two kinds of life (eternal and indwelling). Though there may be some connection between John 6:53–56 and the Lord's Supper, most interpret this passage to refer to a spiritual feeding upon Christ, first by receiving Him as Saviour and then by reading and studying the Word. The figure of speech for eating is used here to express the method by which life is transferred from Christ to the believer. The first verb for eating is *phagein* (6:50,51,52,53), used by Jesus in the aorist tense, it relates to receiving eternal life. Eating (*phagein*) His flesh is receiving Christ as Saviour and in that context is not a process but a single act. Hence Christ is describing the act of salvation. Apart from eating, "ye have no life in you" (6:53).

Beginning in verse fifty-four Jesus uses a second word for eating, *trogon*. This verb is a present active participle emphasizing a continual or habitual eating. The verb *trogo* originally referred to munching on fruit, vegetables, or cereals. The change in Greek tense emphasizes the continual satisfying of a spiritual appetite through constantly or habitually feasting on Christ. This constant communion with Christ is the result of an indwelling union with Him—the believer "dwelleth in me, and I in him" (6:56). Attempting to explain this phenomenon, Augustine observed, "We abide in Him, because we are His members; but He abides in us, because we are His temple."[16]

IV. RESPONSES TO JESUS (6:60–71)

This sermon marked a division among His followers. The consensus of His listeners was that the message was hard, not hard to understand, but hard to accept. In the remainder of the chapter John emphasizes three responses to the bread of life.

60 Many therefore of his disciples, when they had heard this, said, This is an hard saying; who can hear it?

61 When Jesus knew in himself that his disciples murmured at it, he said unto them, Doth this offend you?

62 What and if ye shall see the Son of man ascend up where he was before?

63 It is the spirit that quickeneth; the flesh profiteth nothing: the words that I speak unto you, they are spirit, and they are life.

64 But there are some of you that believe not. For Jesus knew from the beginning who they were that believed not, and who should betray him.

65 And he said, Therefore said I unto you, that no man can come unto me, except it were given unto him of my Father.

66 From that time many of his disciples went back, and walked no more with him.

A. The Unbelieving Majority (6:60–66). The primary response to this sermon was unbelief. This did not catch Jesus by surprise, "for Jesus knew from the beginning who they were that believed not" (6:64). Among those who found this sermon too hard to accept were some who had formerly chosen to be identified as His disciples. John describes the results, "From that time many of his disciples went back, and walked no more with him" (6:66).

67 Then said Jesus unto the twelve, Will ye also go away?

68 Then Simon Peter answered him, Lord, to whom shall we go? thou hast the words of eternal life.

69 And we believe and are sure that thou art that Christ, the Son of the living God.

B. The Believing Minority (6:67–69). With the desertion of many, Jesus turned to the twelve and asked, "Will ye also go away?" (6:67). Jesus does not use a future tense of the verb here but rather expresses Himself with the words— *humeisthelete*, meaning "do you wish?" and *hupagein*, meaning "to go away." As the question is asked anticipating a negative response, it could be paraphrased, "You do not wish to go away also, do you?"

Peter, apparently speaking on behalf of the others, states his faith and knowledge concerning Christ. "We believe and

are sure that thou art that Christ, the Son of the living God"
(6:69). The order of the verbs in verse sixty-nine is significant. Faith is the result of the overpowering response to
Jesus, His person, doctrine, and ministry, followed by intellectual conviction. The perfect active indicative tense of both
these verbs here suggests Peter's emphasis, "We have come
to believe and know and still believe and know." This order
was reversed in the experience of the early church. "And we
have known and believed" (1 John 4:16). There knowledge
comes before belief.

> 70 Jesus answered them, Have not I chosen you twelve,
> and one of you is a devil?
> 71 He spake of Judas Iscariot the son of Simon: for he it
> was that should betray him, being one of the twelve.

C. *The Professing Apostate (6:70,71)*. Notwithstanding the
confession of Peter on behalf of the disciples, Jesus identified
the presence of His betrayer in the midst of the disciples a
full year before the act was accomplished. Here Judas is indirectly described as "a devil" (6:70). The word *diabolos* literally means "slanderous" and almost always occurs as a
noun with the definite article to identify Satan. It is interesting that the disciples were aware of a devil in their midst for
at least a year but were unable to identify Judas as such even
as he went out to betray Christ (13:29). They thought he was
going to prepare for the feast. Although we may not always
be aware of another's true spiritual nature, the Lord is. He
alone was not deceived by Judas the betrayer. The name
Judas comes from the Hebrew *Judah*, meaning "praise." Only
John identifies Judas' father, Simon (6:71). The name *Iscariot*
literally means "man of Kerioth" and probably refers to his
family's home. Kerioth was one of the towns settled by the
tribe of Judah (Joshua 15:25). Judas is apparently the only
disciple of the twelve who was not a native of Galilee. He
comes from Judah, that country most hostile to Jesus.

NINE

CHRIST—
THE HEAVENLY ONE
JOHN 7:1–53

The previous chapter ends in the spring of the year with the events prior to the Passover. John begins chapter seven after six months of silence and describes the events surrounding the Feast of Tabernacles, which occurs in October. Once again Jesus returns to the city of Jerusalem, where "the Jews" are more determined than ever to kill Him because He broke the Sabbath law. Although there will be attempts on His life during this extended visit, it will not be until a later visit that He will be crucified as the Lamb of God.

I. CHRIST AND HIS BRETHREN (7:1–13)

After these things Jesus walked in Galilee: for he would not walk in Jewry, because the Jews sought to kill him.

2 Now the Jews' feast of tabernacles was at hand.

3 His brethren therefore said unto him, Depart hence, and go into Judaea, that thy disciples also may see the works that thou doest.

4 For there is no man that doeth any thing in secret, and he himself seeketh to be known openly. If thou do these things, shew thyself to the world.

5 For neither did his brethren believe in him.

A. Setting (7:1–5). As the Feast of Tabernacles drew near Jesus was approached by His half brothers about going to Jerusalem to the feast with them. This feast was thought of by some Jewish writers as the greatest national feast of Israel. It was established in the Jewish calendar by the law (Leviticus 23:33–43). This feast, beginning annually on 15 Tishri (early October), had a twofold emphasis. First, it was the natural time for a harvest festival, and second, during the duration of the feast the people would live in booths (small tents or temporary shelters made of palm branches) outside the city of Jerusalem as a reminder of God's care for Israel during their forty years of wandering in the wilderness. Sometimes these booths were small tents, hence the name Feast of Tabernacles. This was one of three feasts every mature Jewish male was expected to attend (Deuteronomy 16:16). Of all the feasts, the Feast of Tabernacles tended to be the one characterized by celebrations and parties.

The term *brethren* (*adelphoi*) has been variously interpreted. To safeguard their doctrine of the perpetual virginity of Mary, the Roman Catholic Church follows the tradition of Jerome in identifying the brethren as cousins of Jesus. Another popular view in the early church suggests these brethren were sons of Joseph by a former marriage. A third explanation spiritualizes the term to refer to a group of Jesus' followers; however, in this gospel John uses the term *disciples* exclusively of the followers of Jesus. The most natural and probable interpretation of this is a reference to children of Joseph and Mary born after Jesus. While Jesus was virgin born, the New Testament nowhere intimates anything of the perpetual virginity of Mary or suggests Jesus might have been an only child.

The Hebrew character of verses three and four suggests John quotes the actual words of Jesus' brothers. They urge Jesus to expand the narrow limits of His ministry. The expression *en parresiai*, translated "openly" (7:4), literally means "in boldness." Their reasoning is that no man may assert the unique position Christ was claiming for Himself while at the same time keeping His works secret. The nature of their urging is similar in many respects to the urging of the devil for Jesus to jump from the pinnacle of the temple and attract attention (Matthew 4:5,6). John uses a negative and the imperfect tense *episteuon* (were believers) to refer to the fact that the brothers of Jesus did not have a habitual or controlling faith in Jesus as Messiah. This being so, this urging of the brethren may have carried a hint of sarcasm. They may be calling on Him to perform His miracles in Jerusalem, before discerning religious authorities, thinking "the Jews" will find flaws in Him. Some have even suggested the brothers were aware of the danger awaiting Jesus in Jerusalem and are here urging Him to walk into a trap.

> 6 Then Jesus said unto them, My time is not yet come: but your time is alway ready.
> 7 The world cannot hate you; but me it hateth, because I testify of it, that the works thereof are evil.
> 8 Go ye up unto this feast: I go not up yet unto this feast; for my time is not yet full come.
> 9 When he had said these words unto them, he abode still in Galilee.

B. Timing (7:6–9). Jesus turned down His brothers' invitation with the expression, "My time is not yet come" (7:6). The word *kairos,* translated "time," is not the usual word found in this expression and occurs only here in the Gospel of John. The usual word *hora* refers to the appointed hour. The term used here is broader, suggesting the appropriate season. When Jesus spoke of His hour (2:4; 13:1), He was referring to the hour of messianic revelation on the cross. When He spoke here of His season, He may not have had the same thing in mind. He may have meant that it was not appropriate to go to Jerusalem at that moment.

One of the problems in this chapter is Christ's statement in verse eight in light of His subsequent actions. Several early texts and translations suggest the reading "I go not up to this feast, for my time is not yet fully come" (7:8). At least one writer has accused Christ of a deliberate falsehood in making the statement, while others have argued that the Father may have ordered Jesus to go to the feast after His brothers left. The key, however, to understanding and resolving this apparent conflict is in the interpretation of the word *anabaino* (I go up). The verb has the idea of ascending, and in the context of this feast, ascending to Jerusalem in celebration of a completed task—the harvest. What Jesus was therefore telling His brethren was that He had decided not to be a part of

Chart 26

JESUS AND THE THREE MAJOR FEASTS OF ISRAEL			
Feast	Time	Typical Meaning	Christ's Fulfillment
Passover	April	Redemption	Death on the cross
Pentecost	June	Church (loaves with leaven)	Coming of the Holy Spirit, sent from the Father and the Son
The Feast of Tabernacles	October	End of harvest, beginning of rest	Second advent to establish the kingdom

the celebrations which tended to characterize this feast because His work was not completed.

A second possibility which resolves this problem is seen in Christ's fulfillment of the three major feasts of Israel, the Passover, Pentecost, and Tabernacles (*see* Chart 26). The time for Jesus to celebrate Passover was during His last Passover in Jerusalem, when He as the high priest offered Himself as the Paschal Lamb of God (Hebrews 9:14). The time for Jesus to celebrate Pentecost was fifty days later, when He gave the Holy Spirit to His disciples (14:16; Acts 2:1–4). The season for Christ to celebrate the Feast of Tabernacles is yet future, when He returns to Jerusalem to establish His kingdom (Revelation 19:11—20:5).

10 But when his brethren were gone up, then went he also up unto the feast, not openly, but as it were in secret.

11 Then the Jews sought him at the feast, and said, Where is he?

12 And there was much murmuring among the people concerning him: for some said, He is a good man: others said, Nay; but he deceiveth the people.

13 Howbeit no man spake openly of him for fear of the Jews.

C. *Hostilities* (7:10–13). When His brothers left for the feast, Jesus remained behind in Galilee. Later, He went to the feast secretly. The word *kruptoi*, translated "in secret" (7:10), is placed in contrast with the public way (celebration) in which his brothers had urged Him to go. The terms *phaneros*, translated "openly" (7:10), and *parresiai* (7:4) both come from the same root and convey the idea of telling it all. Jesus used these words in His Sermon on the Mount to urge His followers to walk humbly with God (*see* Matthew 6:4,6). The arrival of Jesus secretly in Jerusalem means more than His merely being absent from the caravan of pilgrims from Galilee. It identifies the nature of His walk with God in contrast to a more natural inclination to identify with the crowds.

John uses the imperfect active form of the verb *zeteo* (I seek) to show the attitude that characterized "the Jews." The emphasis of the verb is that they kept seeking or persistently sought for Him. This reveals something of the strong animosity the Jewish leaders had toward Jesus. It had been a year and a half since Jesus healed the man by the pool of Bethesda on the Sabbath, and their animosity had not been quenched. "The Jews" were persistently seeking Christ to achieve their destructive plans.

This attitude of the leadership only served to make Jesus the talk of the people. The verb *goggusmos* (murmuring) tended to have a negative overtone. It is used repeatedly in the Septuagint for the murmuring of Israel in the wilderness. Here, the murmuring was both friendly and hostile to Christ. There seems to be a continual controversy between believers, nonbelievers, and half believers in this chapter. Some thought He was a good man (*agathos*, meaning "good" or "upright" in contrast to an impostor), but others accused Him of deceiving people. This chapter reveals Jesus as the divider of men, and although this is more apparent on the final day of the feast, it is obvious even before Jesus begins teaching (*see* Matthew 10:34,35). Although the people were discussing Christ, it was all done quietly for fear of the response of "the Jews."

II. CHRIST AND HIS HEAVENLY CLAIMS (7:14–39)

The Feast of Tabernacles was a seven-day feast followed by a special Sabbath. Jesus did not begin teaching in the temple until "the midst of the feast," the fourth day. His appearance and heavenly claims served to cause some to consider His messianic claims, but for most it served to demonstrate the degree of their bias against Him. The clarity and authority of His teaching caught the religious leaders by surprise. They marvelled at Jesus, wondering how He was familiar with the literary methods of His time, having not received formal training.

The Greek noun *grammata* (letters) originally meant the characters of the alphabet, later it meant a letter or epistle; then it identified the Scriptures, and finally the learning of literature. The verb *memathekos* (learning) is a perfect active participle. Because Jesus had not attended one of the two rabbinical colleges, the rabbis considered Jesus illiterate and uninstructed. It was not the wisdom of Jesus that upset the Jewish leaders as much as the fact that He was not an alumnus of their schools.

Chart 27

FOUR CLAIMS OF CHRIST IN THE MIDST OF THE FEAST (John 7:14–36)
1. Concerning His heavenly message (7:14–24) a. My doctrine is from God (7:16) b. I have performed a miracle (7:21)
2. Concerning His heavenly mission (7:25–36) a. I am from God (7:28) b. I will return to God (7:33)

14 Now about the midst of the feast Jesus went up into the temple, and taught.

15 And the Jews marvelled, saying, How knoweth this man letters, having never learned?

16 Jesus answered them, and said, My doctrine is not mine, but his that sent me.

17 If any man will do his will, he shall know of the doctrine, whether it be of God, or whether I speak of myself.

18 He that speaketh of himself seeketh his own glory:

but he that seeketh his glory that sent him, the same is true, and no unrighteousness is in him.

19 Did not Moses give you the law, and yet none of you keepeth the law? Why go ye about to kill me?

20 The people answered and said, Thou hast a devil: who goeth about to kill thee?

21 Jesus answered and said unto them, I have done one work, and ye all marvel.

22 Moses therefore gave unto you circumcision; (not because it is of Moses, but of the fathers;) and ye on the sabbath day circumcise a man.

23 If a man on the sabbath day receive circumcision, that the law of Moses should not be broken; are ye angry at me, because I have made a man every whit whole on the sabbath day?

24 Judge not according to the appearance, but judge righteous judgment.

A. His Message from Heaven (7:14–24). In announcing the heavenly origin of His message, Jesus first emphasized the need for His listeners to willingly listen to Him. The verbs *thelei poiein*, here translated "will do" (7:17), really communicate the idea of the will of the personality in the role of gaining knowledge. What Jesus is saying is "if one is willing to do," if his moral purpose is in harmony with God's will, then that person will come to know the true origin of Jesus' doctrine. The yielding of self-will to the will of God is the key that unlocks spiritual discernment.

Because of the attitude of "the Jews," they cannot meet this condition, so they cannot understand His doctrine. Moses gave them the law, yet they are plotting to break the law (the sixth commandment). Jesus challenges the hypocritical attitude of the Jews, asking, "Why go ye about to kill me?" (7:19).

Apparently the people were unfamiliar with the personal ambitions of their leaders. John here uses the term *ochlos* (crowd, people, 7:20) to refer to the pilgrims visiting the city, probably from Galilee. He uses this word especially in this chapter and chapter twelve to distinguish the masses from the leaders. It would be unthinkable to these people that their leaders would plot to kill a man. The natural conclusion then is that Jesus must be controlled by a demon (7:20).

(John uses the word *daimonion*, meaning "demon," rather than *diabolos*, reserved in Scripture for the devil himself.) In all probability, the people suspected Jesus of some form of paranoia.

Jesus reminded the people that circumcision regularly resulted in the breaking of Sabbath laws (7:22). The law required the circumcision of a male child on the eighth day, regardless of when he was born. If the eighth day fell on a Sabbath, anything that was necessary to accomplish the circumcision was permissible to do. The logic of Jesus' argument was that if it is permissible to treat one part of the body on the Sabbath, then what was wrong with healing the whole body on the Sabbath? (7:23). The Jews were not totally unfamiliar with this line of reasoning; it was actually their own. According to Rabbi Eliezer, "If circumcision, which concerns one of a man's 248 limbs, displaces the Sabbath, how much more must a man's whole body [*i.e.*, if his life be in danger] displace the Sabbath" (*Yoma* 85b).

Again John uses a particular term to reveal the degree of animosity "the Jews" had toward Jesus. The verb *cholate* (translated "are ye angry," 7:23) occurs only here in the New Testament. It is a derivative from the word for *gall* and literally means "to be full of bile." It was a term used to express the horror one feels at a monstrous act. What was the monstrous act of Jesus that brought rise to this intense anger on the part of the Jews? Nineteen months earlier He had healed a man who had been sick thirty-eight years, and He did it on the Sabbath (5:16).

Jesus had done more than meet the physical need of this man; He had met his spiritual need as well. The phrase *holon anthropon hugei* literally means "a whole [*holon*] man [all the man] sound [*hugei*, well]." In contrast with the rite of circumcision, Jesus' action had not merely affected one part of a man's anatomy but rather corrected his entire being. Jesus had not only said, "Take up thy bed, and walk" (5:8), He had also said, "Sin no more, lest a worse thing come unto thee" (5:14).

25 Then said some of them of Jerusalem, Is not this he, whom they seek to kill?

26 But, lo, he speaketh boldly, and they say nothing

unto him. Do the rulers know indeed that this is the very Christ?

27 Howbeit we know this man whence he is: but when Christ cometh, no man knoweth whence he is.

28 Then cried Jesus in the temple as he taught, saying, Ye both know me, and ye know whence I am: and I am not come of myself, but he that sent me is true, whom ye know not.

29 But I know him: for I am from him, and he hath sent me.

30 Then they sought to take him; but no man laid hands on him, because his hour was not yet come.

31 And many of the people believed on him, and said, When Christ cometh, will he do more miracles than these which this man hath done?

32 The Pharisees heard that the people murmured such things concerning him; and the Pharisees and the chief priests sent officers to take him.

33 Then said Jesus unto them, Yet a little while am I with you, and then I go unto him that sent me.

34 Ye shall seek me, and shall not find me: and where I am, thither ye cannot come.

35 Then said the Jews among themselves, Whither will he go, that we shall not find him? will he go unto the dispersed among the Gentiles, and teach the Gentiles?

36 What manner of saying is this that he said, Ye shall seek me, and shall not find me: and where I am, thither ye cannot come?

B. His Mission from Heaven (7:25–36). If the crowds from Galilee did not know the ambitions of "the Jews," the people of Jerusalem certainly did. The title *Ierosolumiton* occurs only here (7:25) and in Mark 1:5. It refers specifically to the residents of the city of Jerusalem as distinct from both the crowds who invaded the city during the feasts and the religious bureaucracy identified by John as "the Jews." The presence of Jesus boldly teaching in the temple causes this group to begin to think of Jesus as a possible Messiah. The interrogative *mepote,* used by John to introduce their conclusion, suggests they wondered, Can it possibly be that "the rulers know indeed that this is the very Christ?" (7:26). This possibility created another dilemma for them.

Jewish tradition had taught the coming of the Messiah would be veiled in mystery. It was thought by some that the Messiah Himself might not even know who He was until He was anointed by Elijah. But the people knew something of the background of Jesus; therefore He could not be the true Messiah. Had they been willing to consider Jesus' response to this dilemma, they might have understood Him as the Messiah. He claimed to be sent from God and to know God (7:28,29).

Jesus said, "He that sent me is true" (7:28). The word *alethinos* means "true" in the sense of genuineness rather than veracity. While both aspects of truth are attributes of God, the emphasis here identifies God as the ultimate reality. It is this reality of God that Jesus knows and by whom He is commissioned. This claim stirs some to attempt to take Him, but their attempt fails. His hour is not yet come (7:30).

Still others in the crowd now begin to believe. They are convinced the Messiah will perform the kind of miracles (literally "signs") Jesus performs. Here John focuses on the strategy of this gospel. John records these signs so that the reader comes to believe and, believing, comes to receive eternal life (20:31).

When the Pharisees began to receive reports of some of the people following Jesus as Messiah, they sent out the temple police (*huperetas*) to arrest Jesus (7:32). Apparently they were commissioned not only to arrest Him but also to gather evidence that could be used against Him in His trial. The officers were not merely to be His captors but also His accusers. They did not report back to the Sanhedrin until four days later.

Jesus continued His teaching, claiming He was not only from God but also would return to God (7:33). In their spiritual blindness, the Jews unwittingly prophesied concerning the future of His mission (7:35). "The dispersed" (*diasporan*) was a technical term identifying Jews living outside of Palestine. These Jews were identified by two names, "the captivity" (expressed by three Greek words) and "the dispersion." The first name suggests their relation to their homeland, whereas the second name refers to their relationship to the foreign land. "The Jews" suggest Jesus might take His message to these Jews outside of Palestine and then even to the Gentiles. This is exactly what the early church did as they spread the Gospel throughout the world.

> 37 In the last day, that great day of the feast, Jesus stood and cried, saying, If any man thirst, let him come unto me, and drink.
> 38 He that believeth on me, as the scripture hath said, out of his belly shall flow rivers of living water.
> 39 (But this spake he of the Spirit, which they that believe on him should receive: for the Holy Ghost was not yet given: because that Jesus was not yet glorified.)

C. His Gift from Heaven (7:37–39). It was not until the final day of the feast that Jesus made His first announcement concerning the coming of the Holy Spirit. There could not have been a better time for such a statement. For seven days the nation had lived in booths, reminding them of God's provision for the nation in the wilderness. For seven days they had rejoiced in the harvest of that year. Now the eighth day was a special Sabbath and served as a fitting climax to this week of celebration. As part of the ritual of this day, a priest would draw water from the pool of Siloam and take it to the temple. The entire procedure would be accomplished with all the pageantry worthy of a temple service. The priest would be followed by a crowd of worshippers from the pool of Siloam to the altar of the temple. Then the water was poured out upon the altar. At that moment, the religious ecstasy of the Jews knew no bounds. The people would begin singing Isaiah 12:3. Their minds would be focused not only upon the past blessing of God but also the promises of God's future blessings. Most Bible commentators believe it was at that moment Jesus made His announcement, "If any man thirst, let him come unto me, and drink. He that believeth on me, as the scripture hath said, out of his belly shall flow rivers of living water" (7:37,38).

The Greek word *koilias* can be translated with one of three different meanings. It may refer to an organ of nourishment such as the stomach. A second use described an organ of reproduction such as the womb. Probably the meaning here is a reference to the hidden innermost recesses of the human body. Sometimes this word was used as a synonym for *kardia* (heart) referring to the seat of intellect, emotion, and will, the real person.

John uses the expression, "as the scripture hath said" (7:38). Normally, when he uses this expression in the gospel, he is referring to a particular verse, but there is no place in the Old Testament that refers to rivers of living water flowing from within a man. While many explanations have been suggested to resolve this apparent problem, the answer is probably to be found in the setting itself. Among the various Scriptures read during this ceremony were several speaking of water from the rock in the wilderness. Godet sees a number of parallels between the Septuagint translation of these verses and the statement of Jesus. In Exodus 17:6, the word translated "out of it" shares a common root with the word here translated "belly." The "abundant waters" from this rock (Numbers 20:11) is very similar to the Greek expression here translated "rivers of living water." The verb "shall flow" recalls a similar Old Testament form, "shall come out" (Exodus 17:6). In all probability, Jesus' reference to the Scriptures here was a reference to the rock that supplied water in the wilderness. Although the Old Testament speaks of two occasions when Moses produced water from the rock in two different locations, Jewish tradition held that the rock was a kind of theophany that travelled with the nation in the wilderness so that, in fact, it was the same rock which produced water on both occasions.

As to the meaning of this statement there can be little doubt. John here incorporates into his text a footnote explaining that Christ was speaking of the Holy Spirit. According to this and other verses, the Holy Spirit indwells all who believe and not just some who have a particular experience. The presence of the Holy Spirit in the life of the believer results in many benefits, some of which are listed on Chart 28.

III. THE RESPONSE OF THE MULTITUDE (7:40–53)

Like a catalyst in chemistry which produces a reaction but is itself unaffected, Jesus inevitably separated every crowd of people into two groups—believers and unbelievers. In the concluding verses of this chapter, John shows how three

Chart 28

WHAT THE HOLY SPIRIT BRINGS	
1. Indwells the believer	Romans 5:5
2. Fills for service	Ephesians 5:18
3. Gives quality life	Galatians 5:22,23
4. Illuminates	John 14:26
5. Secures heaven	Ephesians 1:13,14

groups present on that day were divided in their opinions about Jesus.

40 Many of the people therefore, when they heard this saying, said, Of a truth this is the Prophet.
41 Others said, This is the Christ. But some said, Shall Christ come out of Galilee?
42 Hath not the scripture said, That Christ cometh of the seed of David, and out of the town of Bethlehem, where David was?
43 So there was a division among the people because of him.

A. Divided Multitude (7:40–43). People began to look at Jesus with new interest after He disrupted the great procession into the temple. Some were prepared to identify Him as the Prophet (*see* Deuteronomy 18:15–19). Others were prepared to recognize Him as the Messiah. But some who thought He might be the Messiah stumbled at a problem. The Scripture taught the Messiah would come from Bethlehem (Micah 5:2), but Jesus was identified as a Galilean. One wonders what the result might have been if they had investigated further to learn the true birthplace of Jesus. They did not, and as a result the crowd was divided.

The term *schisma* (7:43), here translated "a division," comes from a verb that means "to rend." In other places, the word is translated with the idea of being torn apart (*see* Matthew 9:16). Here it emphasizes a clear split in the crowd. When it comes to making a decision about Jesus, He is either accepted or rejected. There is no middle ground.

44 And some of them would have taken him; but no man laid hands on him.

45 Then came the officers to the chief priests and Pharisees; and they said unto them, Why have ye not brought him?

46 The officers answered, Never man spake like this man.

B. Divided Officers (7:44–46). What was true of the crowd was also true of the officers who were sent to collect evidence and arrest Jesus. After four days on the job, some would have arrested him (7:44). But others were deeply impressed by both His teaching manner and His message (7:46). As a result, the plan of the Sanhedrin to arrest and destroy Jesus was again frustrated.

47 Then answered them the Pharisees, Are ye also deceived?

48 Have any of the rulers or of the Pharisees believed on him?

49 But this people who knoweth not the law are cursed.

50 Nicodemus saith unto them, (he that came to Jesus by night, being one of them,)

51 Doth our law judge any man, before it hear him, and know what he doeth?

52 They answered and said unto him, Art thou also of Galilee? Search, and look: for out of Galilee ariseth no prophet.

53 And every man went unto his own house.

C. Divided Sanhedrin (7:47–53). The division here caused by Jesus reached even into the Sanhedrin itself. Most were incensed with the failure of the officers to arrest Jesus, but at least one of these seventy leaders was prepared to question their actions. The Pharisees thought the opinion of the religious leadership of the nation was unanimous in its opposition to Jesus. The force of the Greek expression in verse forty-eight is, "Is there a single one of the rulers or Pharisees who believes on Him?" It is in this context that Nicodemus ("he that came to Jesus by night, being one of them," 7:50) speaks somewhat on behalf of Jesus. He reminds his colleagues of an important principle of law they appear to be overlooking.

The response of the Pharisees (7:52) may be interpreted two ways. First, they may be urging Nicodemus to search the Scriptures and see that no prophet had ever appeared in Galilee. In response to such an argument it should be noted that God is not confined to precedent. If there had indeed never been a prophet from Galilee, God would still have been able to call a man to this office from that place. But, in fact, the Jews held that six prophets—Jonah, Hosea, Nahum, Elijah, Elisha, and Amos—had come from Galilee. While five of these might be disputed by some, Jonah definitely came from the same part of Galilee where Nazareth is located.

A second way of interpreting this expression is to assume the verb *search* does not refer to the Scriptures but the place. The statement might then be paraphrased, "From your knowledge of Galilee, is it the kind of place to produce a prophet?" This reflects the same kind of attitude held by Nathanael when he first heard of Jesus (1:46). The difference here is that the Pharisees are not interested in determining if their statements are accurate or not. Apparently they forgot about the Galilean ministry of the Messiah (Isaiah 9:1,2). Their plot frustrated and group divided, "every man went unto his own house" (7:53).

TEN

CHRIST—THE LIGHT OF THE WORLD
(IN MORAL DARKNESS) JOHN 8:1–59

This eighth chapter of John begins with the Jews trying to stone a sinful woman and ends with the same group attempting to stone the sinless Messiah. Both attempts fail. All of these events probably take place between the Monday morning following the Feast of Tabernacles (8:2) and the Sabbath ending that same week (9:14). While we are not sure the events cover just one week, this seems to be implied in the narrative.

This chapter also presents a major textual problem in the New Testament. John 7:53—8:11 is missing in some ancient manuscripts, which has led some scholars to conclude it was not originally part of this gospel but was added later. Some newer translations of the Bible have gone so far as to omit this section from the main text of the gospel (NEB) or to disclaim it in the text (NIV). When one examines the history of this textual problem more closely, however, there can be no question but that it is an authentic part of the gospel.

There are several arguments for its authenticity, hence including it in the canon. First, the internal argument claims the contents are consistent with the rest of Scripture. The actions and teachings of Jesus as well as the actions of the Jews reflect the rest of God's revelation. Second, the story of the woman caught in adultery was cited in the third-century *Apostolic Constitutions* as biblical grounds for accepting pen-

160

itents who had been disciplined by the church. Third, the narrative was considered authentic by church fathers such as Jerome, Ambrose, and Augustine. In fact, it is Augustine who has preserved the reason why some older texts omit this story. Apparently the account was rejected and removed from the gospel by some men Augustine describes as "weak in faith" because they feared their wives would use it to justify immorality. When the story is correctly understood, there is no way that such conclusions could be reached. Finally, it is never permissible to remove even part of a verse from the Scriptures simply because one does not understand it or disagrees with its conclusions. Still, despite the foolish actions of these early Christians, God has preserved His Word even to this generation, and the account of an unnamed woman caught in the act of adultery remains a part of the gospel written for our edification.

I. CHRIST, THE LORD OF AN IMMORAL WOMAN (8:1–11)

The presentation of the woman caught in the act of adultery to Jesus by a group of scribes and Pharisees was not so much to get Jesus to carry out the law against adultery as it was a trap to snare Him. They wanted Jesus to react in an embarrassing situation so they might have something with which they could accuse Him. If He condemned her and called for her execution, He would never again be known as the friend of sinners. Also, He would be placing Himself against Rome, which did not allow the Jews to practice capital punishment for infractions of Jewish law (see 18:31). If He condoned her act, He would be upholding her sin and opposing the Law of Moses. Jesus essentially found Himself in a no-win situation.

Earlier it was suggested that in every chapter of John the omniscience of Jesus was manifested. In this chapter Jesus seems to know the heart of the woman and the intention of His enemies. Whether this is a supernatural act or His human wisdom is not evident, but He does know what is in mankind.

Jesus went unto the mount of Olives.

2 And early in the morning he came again into the tem-

ple, and all the people came unto him; and he sat down, and taught them.

3 And the scribes and Pharisees brought unto him a woman taken in adultery; and when they had set her in the midst,

4 They say unto him, Master, this woman was taken in adultery, in the very act.

5 Now Moses in the law commanded us, that such should be stoned; but what sayest thou?

6 This they said, tempting him, that they might have to accuse him. . . .

A. A Snare Produced (8:1–6a). During the Feast of Tabernacles the Jewish people erected booths outside the city of Jerusalem and lived in them as a reminder of their pilgrimage and God's provision in the wilderness (Leviticus 23:42,43). The previous chapter concludes with the note that "every man went unto his own house" (7:53), implying that more than their discussion with Jesus was over, so they went home. They had lived in booths and returned to their homes for the first time in eight days.

With all Israel outside the city in a tenting or camping experience, there was probably a vacation atmosphere among the people. In this environment it would have been easy for a man to tempt a woman to adultery. Also, it would have been easier to detect a man and woman "in the very act" (8:4) in a booth as opposed to detection in a house behind closed doors.

John describes Jesus beginning His teaching "early in the morning" (8:2), using the word *orthrou*, referring to the early dawn hours just before sunrise. The delegation of scribes and Pharisees that brought the woman to Jesus was probably small, perhaps only a half dozen men. However, there is a crowd of "all the people" (8:2) who came to hear Him teach.

John makes special mention of Jesus sitting to teach in the temple area, using the participle *kathisas*. Although this is the only specific mention of Jesus sitting to teach in this gospel, it was probably Jesus' practice as it was common for a rabbi to sit as he taught. Jesus was sitting when He talked with the woman at the well (4:6), for the Sermon on the Mount (Matthew 5:1), and during the Upper Room Discourse (13:12). In mentioning His sitting, John is here emphasizing His authority as a teacher of the law.

Both scribes and Pharisees were involved in bringing this woman to Jesus (8:3). This is the only reference to scribes in the gospel, though they are often mentioned in the synoptics. The scribes were the copiers of the law and therefore became its teachers. The illegality of their actions here is significant. If they had been concerned with upholding the law, they would have taken the woman to their court to try this kind of case.

The accusers arrived with a woman who they say was caught in the very act of adultery. The adjective *autophoroi* is a compound word based on the words *autos* (self) and *phor* (thief). Originally it referred to a thief caught in the very act of stealing. Her crime is identified with the word *moicheuomene* (adultery) which always refers to sexual infidelity involving married people, hence implying she was married. Note that she was not taken to her husband, which would have been the natural reaction even before taking her to a Jewish court. Also note her husband is not present in the temple. As we feel sympathy for both the woman and Jesus because the Jews were trying to trap Him, do not forget that she broke the law and her marriage vow to her husband. With the large influx of pilgrims in the city and the campground setting of the week, immorality tended to be prevalent during the Feast of Tabernacles, so common it usually was overlooked by religious leaders. They probably had no difficulty in finding the bait for their trap, if in fact the whole situation had not been arranged by the Jews.

Their reference to the Law of Moses was little more than a pretense. Stoning was the penalty only in the case of a betrothed woman guilty of adultery (Deuteronomy 22:22–24). In other cases death was prescribed, but the means of execution not specified (Leviticus 20:10). Normally, the Jews punished adultery by strangulation. Further, since they chose to remind Christ of the Law of Moses, it seems strange that they forgot to bring the man who also should have been stoned under the same law. It takes two persons to be caught "in the very act" of adultery.

Some have suggested that there was a plot involved to set a trap for the woman caught in adultery by permitting a man to be with her that she might be caught and accused. By doing this the Jewish leaders would have been accomplices to the sin. However, on this occasion they were doubtless not only plotting to catch the woman but also wanted to plan a way to be able to accuse Jesus, not knowing that He knew what was already in their hearts.

> . . . But Jesus stooped down, and with his finger wrote on the ground, as though he heard them not.
> 7 So when they continued asking him, he lifted up himself, and said unto them, He that is without sin among you, let him first cast a stone at her.
> 8 And again he stooped down, and wrote on the ground.
> 9 And they which heard it, being convicted by their own conscience, went out one by one, beginning at the eldest, even unto the last; and Jesus was left alone, and the woman standing in the midst.
> 10 When Jesus had lifted up himself, and saw none but the woman, he said unto her, Woman, where are those thine accusers? hath no man condemned thee?
> 11 She said, No man, Lord. And Jesus said unto her, Neither do I condemn thee: go, and sin no more.

B. A Sentence Produced (8:6b–11). At first Jesus ignored the accusers and began writing on the ground. Perhaps this was a deliberate stalling technique to give the accusers time to think clearly about their actions and understand their sin. Some have wrongly thought Christ was caught in a dilemma and did not know what to say, so He wrote on the ground to get time to think. But Christ was the Son of God and knew perfectly what He was going to do. Initially Jesus just sat writing with His finger.

For the early Christians who first read this gospel, the act of Jesus writing with His finger was significant. First, many who could not write looked to this story to prove Jesus was literate. Second, some saw this event as shedding light on Christ the Lawgiver. Although the Jews claimed that Moses gave the law (8:5), one of the early titles of Christ was that of "Lawgiver" (James 4:12). Jesus not only gave the law, He also pronounced the sentence regarding the law. The finger of God was involved in writing the law (8:6; Exodus 31:18). Here the Lawgiver is symbolically using His finger to remind the audience of His right to judge a woman by the law.

John uses two different words for writing in this account. The first word, *kategraphen* (8:6) literally means "to write against" (*see* 13:26). There are many suggestions concerning what Jesus wrote on the ground. First, some interpreters hold that Jesus was listing the sins of the accusers. This view finds some support in the Armenian New Testament which states, "He Himself, bowing His head, was writing with His finger on the earth to declare their sins; and they were seeing their several sins on the stones." Second, others feel Jesus was writing the number seven or the seventh commandment, "Thou shalt not commit adultery"(Exodus 20:14). Third, some feel He wrote the name of the man who committed adultery with the woman, implying he was also guilty or that he too should be condemned. If the Jews had planned this act of adultery to trap Jesus, He reversed the situation by writing the guilty man's name on the ground, hence revealing His knowledge of their plot. Fourth, some have suggested Jesus wrote something about the mercy or forgiveness of God. The fifth suggestion comes from the other word for writing, *egraphen* (8:8). Some have suggested this writing may have been little more than Jesus doodling on the ground.

Jesus responded to the persistent questioning of the scribes and Pharisees by announcing His sentence. "He that is without sin among you, let him first cast a stone at her"(8:7). In essence He upheld the law and its authority, but He required that the law be observed in its proper spirit (*see* Matthew 5:18). The word *anamartetos* (without sin) means "one who has not sinned" or "one who cannot sin," although the latter meaning of this word was never expressed in the Septuagint or New Testament. A.T. Robertson calls this a verbal adjective which suggests, "He who has not committed this same sin."[17] When they left the presence of Jesus, beginning with the older Jewish leaders, it implies they were guilty of this same sin.

Obviously, Jesus was not claiming only the sinless could pronounce the penalty of the law. In this context, He is requiring that the men so eager to execute this woman do so only if they themselves are innocent of sin in their lives. Even if they had not entrapped this woman, those who caught her and let the man go were guilty as conspirators or of conflict of interest.

John records the departure of the accusers, noting the reason, "being convicted by their own conscience" (8:9). The verb *elegchomenoi* here used by John literally means "to bring to light and expose." John chose to include this unusual event in the life of Christ to show Christ was Light both on the law and in the consciences of men. Christ follows this event with the declaration, "I am the light of the world" (8:12). As Light, Christ was reminding these hardened scribes and Pharisees of their own history of sin, illuminating their very conscience, and exposing them. It is interesting to note the order in which the accusers left the scene that day. Perhaps those who lived longest were more aware of their own failings or may have more often engaged in this sin.

The accusers left the woman "in the midst" (8:9). This woman with a stained reputation was not left alone with Jesus. The Jewish leaders left, but not the crowd who witnessed this confrontation. Jesus asked, "Hath no man condemned thee?" (8:10). John uses a very appropriate verb here which he rarely used in the gospel, *katekrinen*, literally meaning "to give judgment against or down on." Stoning as practiced by the Jews involved taking large rocks, raising them over one's head with both hands and thrusting them down upon the victim. At the beginning of this episode, her accusers were inviting Jesus to support the Law of Moses in casting stones down upon the woman. Now, in the presence of the Light of the World, they were unable even to speak against her.

Jesus told the woman, "Neither do I condemn thee" (8:11). Was this a pardon or a promise of forbearance to give the woman time to repent? Godet argues the woman had not come to Him on the basis of repentance and faith and therefore could not be pardoned with these words. Westcott argues Jesus' words are not words of forgiveness. On the other hand, how could Jesus expect anyone to "go, and sin no more" (8:11) unless there was a transformed heart to make that possible? (*see* 5:14). Perhaps after the woman was dragged against her will into the presence of Jesus, the light that had driven away the proud scribes and Pharisees had a special attraction for her.

Jesus condemned adultery as He did all sin, but He accepted her, for He does not love the act of sin, but He accepts the sinner. We should not reverse the order of judgment and condemn sinners but accept their sin.

II. CHRIST, THE LIGHT IN MORAL DARKNESS (8:12–30)

After the encounter with the woman about to be stoned, Jesus taught His followers that He was the Light of the World. This is the second use of the formula "I am" (*ego eimi*) with an object. To make such a statement was to capitalize on several recent events. In the Court of the Women in the temple were four golden candelabras each with four golden bowls. As part of the celebration surrounding the Feast of Tabernacles, these bowls had been filled with oil and lit. Contemporary observers claimed the light was so brilliant it lit the entire city of Jerusalem. The memory of this event would have still been in the minds of His listeners.

There were also things in the Old Testament to which Jesus may have compared Himself as light. The illumination of the temple was a reminder to the people of the cloud/pillar of fire that led Israel through the wilderness. Most Jews would have considered the cloud/pillar of fire a theophany which was a manifestation of God Himself. If Jesus was thinking of this background, His statement was a clear claim to deity. Also, the name *Light* is applied to the Messiah in several Old Testament passages (Isaiah 9:2; 42:6; 49:6; 60:1–3; Malachi 4:2). It is interesting to note the previous day the Pharisees said Jesus couldn't be the Messiah or a prophet, because none came from Galilee. Perhaps the Lord reminded the people of the messianic prophecy concerning the light arising in Galilee (Isaiah 9:1,2). The Jews rejected Christ because He came from Galilee. Now He is claiming to be the Light of the World.

But there may also be a more immediate context that prompted His statement about light. Jesus began teaching just before the sun rose above the mountains. In mountainous regions like Jerusalem, the day approaches very quickly. Within a few minutes, the misty darkness of early dawn will break forth into the brilliance of day. As Jesus said "I am the light," perhaps day was finally arriving in Jerusalem. Perhaps it was the arrival of the sun "which is as a bridegroom coming out of his chamber" (Psalms 19:5) which prompted this claim at this moment. Later Jesus would remind His disciples, "If any man walk in the day, he stumbleth not, because he seeth the light of this world" (11:9). Later the apostle would urge believers to "walk in the light, as he is in the light" (1 John 1:7). Jesus is the Light of the World for every hour of our day.

More than any other Gospel, John is the Gospel of people, often identifying those who are otherwise unknown. It is only natural, therefore, that this claim be understood in the context of the people immediately involved. Jesus was that light which drove away the proud, unrepentant scribes and Pharisees and attracted the sinful woman (8:9,11). He was the light that caused the blind man to first see the light of day (9:1–7). He is "the true Light, which lighteth every man that cometh into the world" (1:9). As light illuminates, thus revealing what was formerly hidden in the darkness, so the Light of the World accomplishes His work through revelation.

12 Then spake Jesus again unto them, saying, I am the light of the world: he that followeth me shall not walk in darkness, but shall have the light of life.

13 The Pharisees therefore said unto him, Thou bearest record of thyself; thy record is not true.

14 Jesus answered and said unto them, Though I bear record of myself, yet my record is true: for I know whence I came, and whither I go; but ye cannot tell whence I come, and whither I go.

15 Ye judge after the flesh; I judge no man.

16 And yet if I judge, my judgment is true: for I am not alone, but I and the Father that sent me.

17 It is also written in your law, that the testimony of two men is true.

18 I am one that bear witness of myself, and the Father that sent me beareth witness of me.

19 Then said they unto him, Where is thy Father? Jesus answered, Ye neither know me, nor my Father: if ye had known me, ye should have known my Father also.

20 These words spake Jesus in the treasury, as he taught in the temple: and no man laid hands on him; for his hour was not yet come.

Chart 29

ARE THERE NOT TWELVE HOURS IN THE DAY? (JOHN 11:9)
1. The hour of the Son of Man's shining (2:4; 12:23)
2. The hour of the Savior's suffering (7:30; 8:20; 17:1)
3. The hour of the seeker's summons (1:39)
4. The hour of the sinner's salvation (4:6,29)
5. The hour of the supplicant's certainty (4:52,53)
6. The hour of the saint's service (19:27)
7. The hour of spiritual sanctimony (4:21,23)
8. The hour of the shepherd's sabbatical (13:1)
9. The hour of the soul's sorrow (12:27; 16:21)
10. The hour of the students' scattering (16:32)
11. The hour of the sovereign's showing (19:14)
12. The hour of the Son of God's supremacy (5:25–29)
"If any man walk in the day, he stumbleth not, because he seeth the light of this world" (11:9).

A. By Revealing the Christ (8:12–20). When Jesus made the claim to be light, the Pharisees immediately responded, "Thy record [witness] is not true" (8:13). According to the accepted rules of evidence among the rabbis, no man could give witness for himself. The law required a matter could only be verified in the presence of two or more witnesses (8:17; *see* Numbers 35:30; Deuteronomy 17:6; 19:15; Matthew 18:16; 2 Corinthians 13:1; 1 Timothy 5:19). When the Pharisees said Jesus' witness was not true, they were using the expression *ouk alethes,* meaning His witness was irrelevant or not pertinent. Jesus had earlier recognized this principle and suggested four additional witnesses that would verify His own witness (5:30–47). In the context of Jesus' claim to be light, the rules of evidence are irrelevant. One might as well argue that the sun is not shining if it is the only one declaring itself to be the sun.

The verb *gegraptai* is in the perfect tense, meaning it "has been written and stands written" (8:17). In His statement, Jesus includes the word *humeteroi* (your) in an emphatic position emphasizing their prior claim to having a monopoly on the law (*see* 7:48,49). Jesus offered the Pharisees two witnesses in keeping with the Scriptures. His two witnesses were His own witness and the witness of His Father who sent Him (8:18). The response of the Pharisees ignores Jesus' own witness and questions that of His Father. Jesus' response identifies the problem that they do not know or accept Him or His Father (8:19).

Jesus taught these things in one of the most popular areas of the temple, the area surrounding the treasury (8:20). The treasury was adjacent to the Court of the Women and was the area where all gifts were made to the temple. John mentions the area of Jesus' ministry here to emphasize the tremendous liberty Jesus had. The word *kai* is used with the emphasis "and yet no man laid hold on Him." Jesus taught publicly in the most popular area of the temple, and yet despite the obvious opposition of the Jews, "no man laid hands on him; for his hour was not yet come" (8:20).

21 Then said Jesus again unto them, I go my way, and ye shall seek me, and shall die in your sins: whither I go, ye cannot come.

22 Then said the Jews, Will he kill himself? because he saith, Whither I go, ye cannot come.

23 And he said unto them, Ye are from beneath; I am from above: ye are of this world; I am not of this world.

24 I said therefore unto you, that ye shall die in your sins: for if ye believe not that I am he, ye shall die in your sins.

25 Then said they unto him, Who art thou? And Jesus saith unto them, Even the same that I said unto you from the beginning.

26 I have many things to say and to judge of you; but he that sent me is true; and I speak to the world those things which I have heard of him.

27 They understood not that he spake to them of the Father.

B. By Revealing the Father (8:21–27). Jesus told His listeners He would go where they could not go and that they would die in their sins (8:21,24; *see* Ezekiel 3:18; 18:18). The first time Jesus made this statement He used the singular *hamartiai* (sin, 8:21) whereas the second and third times He used the plural *hamartiais* (sins, 8:24). He was emphasizing both sin in its essence which is the sin principle and sin in its many expressions. Because "the Jews" would not repent and believe Him, they would die in both their sin and their sins. The essential idea of this word for sin is that of missing the mark. To die in this state means to be eternally separated from God.

The Jews, completely ignoring this warning, capitalized upon Christ's claim they could not go where he was going and asked, "Will he kill himself?" (8:22). The use of the interrogative particle *meti* suggests a negative answer was expected, "Surely He will not kill Himself, will He?" It was widely held in Judaism that anyone who took his own life would go to Gehenna. In arrogance, no Pharisee could ever consider the idea that he might go to Gehenna. Their conclusion therefore, was that Jesus would have to kill Himself to go to the one place no Pharisee would or could go. Commenting on this statement, Vincent observes, "The mockery in these words is alike subtle and bitter. . . . The remark displays alike the scorn and the self-righteousness of the speakers."[18]

Attempting to correct the misconception of the Jews, Jesus reminds them that the conflict between them finds its source in their different origins. He uses two words in contrast, *kato*, meaning "beneath," and *ano*, meaning "above" (8:23). The difference between Jesus and the Jews was the difference between the heavenlies and the sensual (*see* James 3:15–17). Jesus states emphatically, "I am from above. . . I am not of this world. . . . if ye believe not that I am he, ye shall die in your sins" (8:23,24).

The expression *ego eimi* used here may be interpreted one of several ways. In its immediate context Jesus may be saying they must believe He is from above (8:23). Perhaps thinking back to a recent discussion with these same people, Jesus was telling them they must believe He is the One sent by the Father (7:28). In the context of this extended discourse, Jesus may have meant they must believe He is the Light of the World (8:12; *see* 7:52). A fourth possible meaning is explained later where Christ describes Himself as the deliverer from sin (8:28,31,32,36). Also, when John uses this expression in this gospel, he does so most often identifying with the Old Testament name of God—Jehovah (*see* Deuteronomy 32:39). Supporting this latter view is the interesting note that the phrase used here is identical to the

Septuagint translation of Isaiah 43:10. Also, Jesus definitely makes the claim of identifying with Jehovah before the discourse is ended (8:58).

The Jews responded by asking Jesus to identify Himself (8:25). Commentators are divided over the nature of Jesus' response. Some interpreters view the statement as a question, "How is it that I even speak to you at all?"[19] Others recognize the statement as an affirmation, "I am essentially that which I even speak to you."[20] Both views are acceptable so far as the grammar and context are concerned, and a survey of English translations of the verse reveals no general agreement as to which is preferred.

John notes that these comments referred to the Father (8:27). But those who could not comprehend the Light (1:5) also failed to perceive *egnosan*, "that he spake to them of the Father" (8:27).

> 28 Then said Jesus unto them, When ye have lifted up the Son of man, then shall ye know that I am he, and that I do nothing of myself; but as my Father hath taught me, I speak these things.
>
> 29 And he that sent me is with me: the Father hath not left me alone; for I do always those things that please him.
>
> 30 As he spake these words, many believed on him.

C. *By Revealing the Cross* *(8:28–30)*. Jesus reminded them of the cross (8:28), a constant theme in His ministry. The time would come when they would possess knowledge of who He was, but that knowledge would arrive late. Referring to Himself as "the Son of Man," the favorite title used by Christ, He made the second of three references in this gospel to His being lifted up (3:14; 8:28; 12:32,34). Darby notes Christ constantly uses the title "Son of Man" with reference to the cross. Here Christ says that it is the cross which will finally cause the world to recognize Him as the "I am" *(ego eimi)* and agree with His claim that He did the will of the Father. The word *pantote* (always, 8:29) is in the emphatic position, meaning Christ was habitually and continuously doing those things that please the Father.

John notes briefly the results of this discourse by recording that "many believed on him" (8:30). Commentators are divided on the nature of this faith, whether it was saving faith or natural faith. (These disciples, like those in John 6:66, apparently had some kind of faith in Christ but later chose to stop following Him.) Some argue it was natural faith pointing to the conflict in the remaining verses of this chapter. However, it is more likely that those who believed on Him in verse thirty are different from those in verse thirty-one. John identifies those in verse thirty with the expression *episteusan eis* (believed into), which is used to identify those who become the children of God (1:12). In the next verse, John identifies another group with the expression *pepisteukotas autoi* (believed him), meaning those who accepted His messianic claims but probably added their own political interpretation to His words. It is this second group who were guilty of only natural faith, whereas the first group seems to have experienced saving faith.

III. CHRIST, THE LIBERATOR OF MORAL SLAVERY (8:31–59)

Up to this point the message of Christ was broad, having a public appeal, whereas now His comments will become more pointedly directed at a specific group who had been following Him. These believed in the same way that those in Jerusalem at the first Passover had believed (2:23,24). Jesus' message to this group was to emphasize a greater liberation from the bondage of moral slavery. His offer was simple and direct. If they would continue in His Word, they would be His disciples. One of the fringe benefits of such a commitment was genuine liberty. While the offer of Christ was liberty, to refuse His offer resulted in bondage.

31 Then said Jesus to those Jews which believed on him, If ye continue in my word, then are ye my disciples indeed;
32 And ye shall know the truth, and the truth shall make you free.
33 They answered him, We be Abraham's seed, and were never in bondage to any man: how sayest thou, Ye shall be made free?
34 Jesus answered them, Verily, verily, I say unto you, Whosoever committeth sin is the servant of sin.
35 And the servant abideth not in the house for ever: but the Son abideth ever.

36 If the Son therefore shall make you free, ye shall be free indeed.

A. Bondage Declared (8:31–36). Jesus began this more private discourse on liberty from moral slavery by emphasizing the nature of true discipleship. Christ taught that discipleship begins with faith, involves constantly remaining in the Word of Christ, issues in the knowledge of truth, and results in genuine freedom. When the Jews heard this they immediately understood the implication and claimed they "were never in bondage to any man" (8:33). Yet at that time the Jews were in fact under Roman authority. Most patriotic Jews did only the bare minimum that was required by Rome and did what they could to irritate their Roman masters. Many had gone so far as to follow one of the many self-proclaimed messiahs in their civil rebellions against Roman authority. But although they did what they could to deny it, the fact remained that they were under the bondage of Rome.

Jesus, however, was not speaking of political bondage but rather of the bondage of sin. Jesus uses the word *doulos,* meaning "slave," to describe the one who practices sin. He further reminded them of the insecurity of a slave in contrast with the security of a son. A slave could be expelled from the house at any time, whereas a son was always free to come and go as he pleased. The Apostle Paul later used this same analogy contrasting the slave of sin and the Son of God (*see* Romans 6—8).

36 If the Son therefore shall make you free, ye shall be free indeed.

37 I know that ye are Abraham's seed; but ye seek to kill me, because my word hath no place in you.

38 I speak that which I have seen with my Father: and ye do that which ye have seen with your father.

39 They answered and said unto him, Abraham is our father. Jesus saith unto them, If ye were Abraham's children, ye would do the works of Abraham.

40 But now ye seek to kill me, a man that hath told you the truth, which I have heard of God: this did not Abraham.

41 Ye do the deeds of your father. Then said they to

We be not born of fornication; we have one Father, even God.

42 Jesus said unto them, If God were your Father, ye would love me: for I proceeded forth and came from God; neither came I of myself, but he sent me.

43 Why do ye not understand my speech? even because ye cannot hear my word.

44 Ye are of your father the devil, and the lusts of your father ye will do. He was a murderer from the beginning, and abode not in the truth, because there is no truth in him. When he speaketh a lie, he speaketh of his own: for he is a liar, and the father of it.

45 And because I tell you the truth, ye believe me not.

46 Which of you convinceth me of sin? And if I say the truth, why do ye not believe me?

47 He that is of God heareth God's words: ye therefore hear them not, because ye are not of God.

B. *Bondage Explained* (*8:36–47*). The ethnic heritage of the Jews hindered them from understanding their need to be liberated from the bondage of moral slavery. They equated their liberty with their physical relationship with Abraham. It was as though they reasoned, "Because Abraham was the friend of God, we his children are certainly acceptable to God." In the discussion which follows, the Jews kept referring back to Abraham for their authority, while rejecting Christ.

In the course of this discussion, the Jews explained, "We be not born of fornication" (8:41). Most commentators agree the emphasis of this statement was directed toward the circumstances of Jesus' birth. They were spreading the rumors about Jesus' birth, that Mary conceived before Joseph publicly married her. From Scripture we know Christ was born by the miraculous conception of the Holy Spirit. The Jews were attempting to embarrass Christ by suggesting He was conceived out of wedlock. Rejecting the doctrine of the virgin birth, or anything supernatural about His birth, the Jews thought Jesus was born as the result of an immoral union. What is significant, however, is that the emphasis of the Prophet Hosea was exactly contrary to their conclusion: the nation had become the children of a whore (Hosea 1:9—2:4).

Jesus' premise was that they were children of Satan. This satanic fatherhood should not be limited only to Jews but rather applied to all men. Outwardly they were religious, but inwardly they were followers of Satan. Their ultimate role in the crucifixion of Christ only demonstrated they were of their father, the devil. The devil is a liar and the father of lies, and they were influenced by him. They could not find sin in Christ (8:46); still they rejected Him. If they had been of God, they would have believed, but their unbelief demonstrated they were not of God (8:47).

48 Then answered the Jews, and said unto him, Say we not well that thou art a Samaritan, and hast a devil?

49 Jesus answered, I have not a devil; but I honour my Father, and ye do dishonour me.

50 And I seek not mine own glory: there is one that seeketh and judgeth.

51 Verily, verily, I say unto you, If a man keep my saying, he shall never see death.

52 Then said the Jews unto him, Now we know that thou hast a devil. Abraham is dead, and the prophets; and thou sayest, If a man keep my saying, he shall never taste of death.

53 Art thou greater than our father Abraham, which is dead? and the prophets are dead: whom makest thou thyself?

54 Jesus answered, If I honour myself, my honour is nothing: it is my Father that honoureth me; of whom ye say, that he is your God:

55 Yet ye have not known him; but I know him: and if I should say, I know him not, I shall be a liar like unto you: but I know him, and keep his saying.

56 Your father Abraham rejoiced to see my day: and he saw it, and was glad.

57 Then said the Jews unto him, Thou art not yet fifty years old, and hast thou seen Abraham?

58 Jesus said unto them, Verily, verily, I say unto you, Before Abraham was, I am.

59 Then took they up stones to cast at him: but Jesus hid himself, and went out of the temple, going through the midst of them, and so passed by.

C. Bondage Demonstrated (8:48–59). The Jews responded to Jesus' logic by calling Him a Samaritan and claiming He was demon possessed (8:48). The animosity between the Jews and the Samaritans was so strong that to call someone a Samaritan was among the worst insults. There is also a linguistic connection between the Aramaic words *Shomeroni*, meaning Samaritan, and *Shomeron*, being a title of the devil. Barclay argues that the word *Shomeroni* could also mean "a child of the devil" and that this was the probable emphasis of the Jews.[21] They later tried to use His claim, "If a man keep my saying, he shall never see death" (8:51) to prove He had a demon.

When the Jews asked Jesus if He was greater than Abraham, the form of their question anticipated a negative response, "You do not think you are greater than Abraham— do you? "(*see* 8:53). This was the same argument used by the Samaritan woman who was convinced Jesus was not greater than Jacob (4:12).

Jesus responded, "Abraham rejoiced to see my day: and he saw it, and was glad" (8:56). He did not, however, explain when Abraham saw His day. There are at least seven explanations of when this happened. First, it was held Abraham was living in paradise at that time and could see the events on earth (*see* Luke 16:22–31). Therefore, Abraham was at that time seeing the day of Jesus and rejoicing. Another similar view was later proposed in the apocryphal books the Gospel of Nicodemus and The Acts of Pilate. Both of these books include a passage describing Abraham rejoicing to see the light of the approaching Christ when He descended into hell between the cross and the resurrection. The problem with these two views is the consistent use of aorist verbs implying Abraham saw at a point of time, probably in the past.

The Jews had four interpretations of passages in the life of Abraham which could have accounted for this claim. First, Abraham knew the Messiah would come from him and so rejoiced and saw Him by faith (Genesis 12:3). Also, some rabbis held that Abraham's vision in Genesis 15:8–21 included a prophetic view of the history of Israel and the Messiah. A third interpretation claimed that Abraham's laugh at the prophecy of Isaac's birth was not a laugh of unbelief but rather a laugh of joy because he knew the Messiah would eventually come through the line of Isaac (Genesis 17:17). A final view is based on the interpretation of the phrase "well stricken in age" (Genesis 24:1) which is literally "gone into days." Some rabbis believed that Abraham had a prophetic odyssey into the future history of the nation. At that time he saw the coming Messiah, Jesus Christ. Perhaps the correct interpretation was the theophany appearance of Jehovah to Abraham (Genesis 18) where judgment against Sodom and Gomorrah was revealed to him. At that time Abraham interceded to Jehovah for the souls to be judged. Since Christ has all judgment (5:30), and this was a physical appearance of Jehovah (He ate), then it must have been Christ that Abraham saw.

The key to understanding when Abraham saw Jesus' day, however, may not be the context of the day but rather the nature of Christ. Jesus' claim, "Before Abraham was, I am" (8:58), was clearly interpreted by the Jews as blasphemy worthy of punishment by stoning—He was claiming to be God. In this context, any revelation of Jehovah (I am) to Abraham could be viewed as a time when Abraham rejoiced to see Christ.

The Jews found Jesus' statement difficult to interpret. They asked, "Thou art not yet fifty years old, and hast thou seen Abraham?" (8:57). Some commentators have mistakenly taken this statement to argue Jesus was approaching fifty years of age and therefore claim He died an older man. Others, recognizing that the Gospels clearly teach Jesus died in His mid-thirties, claim the pressure of the ministry so aged Jesus that he looked like an old man. The key to understanding this phrase, however, is in recognizing that fifty years was the age at which a Levite retired from active service (Numbers 4:3). In essence the Jews were saying, "You are still a young man, not even old enough to retire." They were guessing His age and allowing enough room to not embarrass themselves. The comment here should be understood as an idiom and has no bearing on the age of Christ.

The response of the Jews to Christ's revelation of Himself as the "I am" demonstrates just how severely they were blinded to truth. Despite the fact that they were in the temple area (8:20), it was the Sabbath (9:14), and Jesus had not been formally charged before the Sanhedrin, the Jews took steps to stone Him. The verb *balosin* (cast) suggests a picture of at least some members of the mob already beginning to throw stones. Jesus escaped by hiding Himself. Some have suggested He hid by physically vanishing or blinding His enemies, but the verb *ekrube* should probably be interpreted to mean He hid Himself in a group of people—He was lost in the crowd. Jesus did not run away, as a victim might run from a mob that is trying to kill him. Jesus knew His time had not come (13:1). The next chapter describes Him calmly leaving the temple and pausing on the stairs to answer a question about a blind man.

The chapter begins with the Jews attempting to stone a sinful woman, and in the process catch Jesus in a self-contradictory trap. In the end, they try to stone the sinless Christ because they were caught in their own trap.

ELEVEN

CHRIST—
THE LIGHT OF THE WORLD
(IN PHYSICAL DARKNESS) JOHN 9:1–41

This chapter has two major themes, light and opposition. It begins when Jesus becomes the physical light to the man born blind and ends with the healed man receiving spiritual light. The Jewish bureaucracy reject the light and persecute those who respond to it.

But this chapter also is tied to the previous one in that the revelations of Christ in chapter eight are applied in chapter nine. This is illustrated in Chart 30.

Belief is the key topic of John, and in this chapter it appears that there were more in opposition to Christ than believers in Him. However the testimony and undaunted faith of one man have proved to be stepping-stones for many. This blind beggar shares his testimony several times, but it seems no one will listen to him. The authenticity of his experience

Chart 30

Chapter 8	Chapter 9
Christ the Light	Opens blind eyes
Christ the Liberator	Delivers from darkness
Christ the Sinless One	Forgives the sinner
Christ the "I AM—I AM"	Worshipped as God

is evidenced in that he never changes his story and his enemies never deny the reality of a life-changing miracle. This particular miracle was a favorite in the early church, being referred to often in writings and art. While skeptics and their lives are forgotten, the man who was healed from darkness is a living example of the power of Christ—the Light of the World.

I. THE HEALING OF THE BLIND MAN (8:59—9:7)

59 Then took they up stones to cast at him: but Jesus hid himself, and went out of the temple, going through the midst of them, and so passed by.

9:1 And as Jesus passed by, he saw a man which was blind from his birth.

2 And his disciples asked him, saying, Master, who did sin, this man, or his parents, that he was born blind?

3 Jesus answered, Neither hath this man sinned, nor his parents: but that the works of God should be made manifest in him.

4 I must work the works of him that sent me, while it is day: the night cometh, when no man can work.

5 As long as I am in the world, I am the light of the world.

6 When he had thus spoken, he spat on the ground, and made clay of the spittle, and he anointed the eyes of the blind man with the clay,

7 And said unto him, Go wash in the pool of Siloam, (which is by interpretation, Sent.) He went his way therefore, and washed, and came seeing.

As chapter eight concludes, John paints a picture of crisis with the Jews ready to stone Jesus. The verb *balosin,* here translated "to cast," is actually an aorist active subjunctive form of *ballo,* suggesting that some had already begun to throw stones. Those who hated Christ and tried to stone Him in chapter eight continue their severe opposition to Jesus in chapter nine. Even though it was a Sabbath (9:14) and Jesus was in the temple proper (8:59), still some of these religious leaders were prepared to break their religious laws to destroy Jesus. Their attempt is unsuccessful as Jesus "hid himself" and left the temple, "going through the midst of them"(8:59).

How Jesus made His escape is a matter of conjecture. Some of the suggestions are: (1) He became invisible; (2) those who would stone Him became blind temporarily or could see everything but were blinded to Jesus; (3) Jesus hid Himself in the mob because of the confusion; or (4) the disciples came between the stone throwers and Jesus, hiding Him from them.

Most would think that if a person was fleeing an attempted assassination, he might be running or he might hide out. But not Jesus. He is pictured as leaving the temple, probably by the Gate Beautiful. Traditionally, there were a number of beggars there because their physical imperfection would keep them out of the temple. Jesus carries on a casual conversation with His disciples about the causes of blindness rather than escaping His potential pursuers. Jesus knew who He was, and He knew that His time had not yet come (13:1).

According to John, the miracle of healing occurred "as Jesus passed by" (9:1). That Jesus should even notice, let alone heal a blind beggar under such circumstances may be thought by some as the real miracle in this chapter. Actually, this action was characteristic of the One who came not to be ministered unto but to minister. The contrast of this action of Jesus and the circumstances under which the miracle took place so impressed Oswald J. Smith that it resulted in the writing of one of his best-known hymns, "Then Jesus Came."[22]

Although Jesus healed many blind people during His public ministry, this miracle is unique in that this person was the only individual afflicted from birth. This may be why the early Christian writers often referred to this miracle as an illustration of conversion. When an individual becomes a Christian, he does not recover what he had formerly lost but rather receives a completely new ability to see and understand the things of God (1 Corinthians 2:14,15). For the first time in his life this man was going to see. And one of the first things he would see would be the Son of God.

The appearance of this blind man prompted the disciples of Jesus to ask what appears to be an unusual question. If a man is blind from birth, how could that be the result of that person's sin? If sin was involved in his blindness, then it would be natural to assume that his parents were responsible for that sin. Several Old Testament passages suggest the sin of the parents brings consequences to the children (see Exodus 20:5; 34:7; Numbers 14:18; Deuteronomy 5:9; Jeremiah 31:29,30; Ezekiel 18:2). Another popular Jewish thought that could explain how a man could be responsible for the sin was that sin began not at birth but at conception. The child in the womb had committed some sin prior to his birth and as a result was born blind. The third popular Jewish view, particularly among Hellenistic Jews, was that souls existed prior to birth and were assigned to different kinds of physical bodies as a reward or punishment for their prior actions. In this case, the thought was that the man's soul had committed some evil prior to being assigned to a particular body.

Jesus answered the disciples' question by telling them that sin was not the only reason to suffer from physical afflictions. In this case, a man was born blind "that the works of God should be made manifest in him" (9:3). While it is true that personal sin can result in physical affliction (see 5:14) and the sin of parents may be visited upon the children even to the third and fourth generation, it is also sometimes in the plan of God to bring physical infirmities or suffering into the life of an individual to demonstrate the works of God. There are many great Christian leaders of the past who might fall into the category "handicapped," but their handicaps became the channels through which the works of God were manifest in an unusual way.

Jesus told His disciples, "We must work the works of Him that sent Me" (9:4, literal translation). The first personal pronoun in this statement is hemas (we) and not eme (I). To whom was He referring—God and Christ, or Christ and the disciples? While only God can do the works of God, there is a responsibility for every disciple to be engaged in that work. The last personal pronoun is me (Jesus). While Christians are sent by Christ into the world, only Christ is sent by the Father (see 20:21). That this work must be done "while it is day"(9:4) stresses the urgency with which a work of God should be undertaken.

Again Jesus reminded His disciples, "I am the light of the world" (9:5; see 1:4; 8:12). Here Jesus qualifies this claim limiting it to, "As long as I am in the world." The word hotan, here translated "as long as," has the emphasis of "whenever." When Jesus is in the world, He is its light. While Jesus never ceased to be light by nature, He is actually "the light of the world" only when He is in the world. This applies not only to His incarnation, life, and ministry as recorded in the Gospels, but also to the various Christophanies in the Old Testament. Even in the eternal city, Jesus is the light (Revelation 21:23). When Christ is not physically present in the world, He indwells the believer, making His disciples the light of the world (see Matthew 5:14).

Unlike the healings of other blind men in the Gospels, Jesus here made use of clay and spittle to heal the blind man. On other occasions Jesus healed the blind by touch or speaking. Why clay and spittle? First, spittle was believed to have special curative powers. Jesus made use of spittle in only two miracles (see Mark 7:33). Pliny observed "that ophthalmia can be cured by anointing, as it were, the eyes every morning with fasting spittle."[23] Had Jesus shared this opinion, He would probably have made wider use of spittle in His miracles. That this superstition still exists to some degree today is evidenced by the initial reaction of many people when they burn or cut a finger. The most natural reaction is to put the finger in the mouth. A second suggestion is that kneading clay with spittle is specifically forbidden by the Sabbath laws of the Jews. As this miracle occurred on a Sabbath (9:14), Jesus is again challenging the authority of the traditions of men. A third suggestion is that Jesus is reminding them that man was originally made from the dust of the ground and he owes all life to his Creator.

After anointing the eyes of this blind man, Jesus sent him to the pool of Siloam. Some have wondered why Jesus sent the man so far away when the pool of Bethesda was much closer. First, the answer is seen in the typical significance of this pool, from which water was drawn on the eighth day following the Feast of Tabernacles. In that ceremony the waters of Siloam were likened unto the "wells of salvation" (Isaiah 12:3). Also, as John here emphasizes, the name Siloam means "sent" (9:7, see 9:4). Not only is this idea closely related to the sending of the Messiah into the world by God, but also one of the titles of the Messiah, "Shiloh" (Genesis 49:10; Isaiah 8:6), is actually translated "Siloam" by the Septuagint translators of Isaiah 8:6. The sending of this man to the "wells of salvation," which also spoke of the sending of the Messiah, was the beginning of Jesus' revelation of Himself to this blind man (see 9:37). A second reason is to test the faith of the man born blind. He might not have been healed if he went to a closer well or if he washed in a nearby basin. By sending the blind man as far as possible to a natural spring, Jesus was bringing out faith in obedience to the promise of Christ (which brings spiritual light).

The healing of this man was accomplished when the man obeyed and washed. He then came seeing. In this gospel, John often uses expressions of physical sight to identify faith. While the primary meaning of *blepon* indicates the blind man was no longer blind but could see, in the context of this chapter, this man's physical sight was the first step toward his spiritual sight.

II. THE WITNESS OF THE BLIND MAN (9:8–34)

As soon as this blind man received his sight, he became a witness of the miraculous power of Jesus in the life of an individual. When he first began to testify concerning the One who had given him his sight, he did not know a great deal about Christ. But as he began to tell others about Jesus, his own faith grew. At first, he simply identified this One as "a man that is called Jesus" (9:11), then "a prophet" (9:17), next "a worshipper of God [who] doeth his will" (9:31), and ultimately he recognized Jesus as the Son of God and his Lord. He became a worshiper of Jesus (9:36,38). (See Chart 31.)

After the miracle, the bulk of this chapter deals with the healed man giving witness of his faith to different groups. The first to learn of this man's life-changing miracle were his friends (9:8–12). These friends brought him to the Pharisees,

Chart 31

PROGRESSION OF FAITH	
1. Recognized Jesus	9:11
2. Told the facts	9:15
3. Testimony (how it happened)	9:25
4. Defended his faith	9:30–33
5. Became a seeker	9:36
6. Finally was a worshiper of Christ	9:38

where he was able to share his experience with the leaders of Israel (9:13–18a). While the Bible does not specifically mention his witness to his family, John makes it clear that his family knew what had happened (9:18b–23). The man appears before the Pharisees a second time, but they are more confrontational with him and become his enemies (9:24–34).

> 8 The neighbours therefore, and they which before had seen him that he was blind, said, Is not this he that sat and begged?
> 9 Some said, This is he; others said, He is like him; but he said, I am he.
> 10 Therefore said they unto him, How were thine eyes opened?
> 11 He answered and said, A man that is called Jesus made clay, and anointed mine eyes, and said unto me, Go to the pool of Siloam, and wash: and I went and washed, and I received sight.
> 12 Then said they unto him, Where is he? He said, I know not.

A. Witness to His Friends (9:8–12). When those who previously knew the man in his blind state saw him after the miracle, their curiosity was greatly aroused. John identifies two groups who began to question him, first his neighbors and then others who had from time to time observed him begging at the temple. The verb *theorountes* is a present active participle of *theoreo* and has the emphasis "who used to observe him." As they recognized him, they recognized he was not only a blind man, but a beggar (*prosaites*) "that sat and begged." The final expression of verse eight denotes his customary practice. He had his regular place and was a familiar figure, but now his eyes were wide open.

The difference in this man after he had received his sight was so great that some refused to believe he was the same man. The statement translated, "He is like him" (9:9), begins with the Greek negative *ouchi*, denoting a vigorous denial concerning the identity of the man. If his own friends found it hard to believe this was the same man after he met Jesus, it is perhaps not so difficult to understand why some of the Pharisees later questioned if the man had ever been blind (9:18).

His friends may not have been sure of his identity, but the blind man knew who he was and what had happened to him. He emphatically told the story of what happened to him. The verb *aneblepsa*, translated "I received sight" (9:11), is an aorist active indicative of *anablepo*, meaning "to see and continue seeing." Originally, the verb meant "to look up," such as to look toward heaven in faith (*see* Matthew 14:19). As this man related his experience to others, he recognized the change in his life was the result of faith.

> 13 They brought to the Pharisees him that aforetime was blind.
> 14 And it was the sabbath day when Jesus made the clay, and opened his eyes.
> 15 Then again the Pharisees also asked him how he had received his sight. He said unto them, He put clay upon mine eyes, and I washed, and do see.
> 16 Therefore said some of the Pharisees, This man is not of God, because he keepeth not the sabbath day. Others said, How can a man that is a sinner do such miracles? And there was a division among them.
> 17 They say unto the blind man again, What sayest thou of him, that he hath opened thine eyes? He said, He is a prophet.
> 18 But the Jews did not believe concerning him, that he had been blind, and received his sight, until they called the parents of him that had received his sight.

B. *Witness to the Pharisees (9:13–18a).* When the man was unable to tell the people about the person who healed him, they brought him to the Pharisees. This miracle had raised several questions. Again Jesus had broken the Sabbath laws, but the result was the healing of a blind man. What did this mean? If Jesus was of God, were the Sabbath laws no longer binding? Perhaps questions like these prompted his friends to take him to the Pharisees. As the teachers of Israel, the Pharisees should have been able to provide spiritual answers.

But rather than providing spiritual leadership, they stumbled over their own traditions and failed to recognize Jesus was from God (*para theou*, 9:16). Jesus had now broken their concept of the Sabbath law several times. He had healed a man on the Sabbath a year and a half earlier (5:8,9), and now he had made clay with spittle, anointed the eyes of a blind man (9:6), and healed him. These actions were normally forbidden on the Sabbath. The Pharisees could not offer a clear affirmative statement about who Jesus was, but they did deny that He was from God.

The Pharisees were not unanimous in this conclusion. Some apparently were not ready to make a complete denial of Jesus in light of the growing evidence. "How can a man that is a sinner do such miracles?" (9:16). The rift among "the Jews" which began in chapter seven now becomes even more pronounced. John continues to use the expression "the Jews" to identify that part of the Pharisaic party still opposed to Jesus. The first act of "the Jews" in this chapter is to deny the man was ever blind at all. To prove this, they stop questioning the man and begin to investigate his background.

18 But the Jews did not believe concerning him, that he had been blind, and received his sight, until they called the parents of him that had received his sight.

19 And they asked them, saying, Is this your son, who ye say was born blind? how then doth he now see?

20 His parents answered them and said, We know that this is our son, and that he was born blind.

21 But by what means he now seeth, we know not; or who hath opened his eyes, we know not: he is of age; ask him: he shall speak for himself.

22 These words spake his parents, because they feared the Jews: for the Jews had agreed already, that if any man did confess that he was Christ, he should be put out of the synagogue.

23 Therefore said his parents, He is of age; ask him.

C. *Witness to His Family* (9:18b–23). While the Bible does not specifically mention this man's witness to his family, John strongly implies his family was aware of their son's healing but refused to endorse it for fear of the Jews. When called before a hostile group of religious leaders, they were asked three questions: (1) Is this your son? (2) Do you testify that he was born blind? (3) How is it that he now sees? (9:19). In the Greek, these three questions are combined into one, perhaps in an attempt to confuse the parents into making a misstatement which they could use to minimize the miracle. They were looking for some loophole to deny the testimony of the blind man concerning Jesus. If their desire was devious, they failed to see it accomplished.

The parents substantiated the essential facts of their son's condition but refused to comment on how the miracle occurred. Normally, parents of a son born blind, who was healed, would be thrilled to tell everyone how it happened, but the conditions surrounding this miracle changed that normal response. The word *ephobounto*, translated "they feared" (9:22), is an imperfect middle and refers to a continuing fear. The parents knew of the consequences of identifying too closely with Jesus, and although they were no doubt happy their son was healed, they were not prepared to follow Jesus and be excommunicated from the synagogue.

The phrase "put out of the synagogue" (9:22) is translated from the two Greek words *aposunagogos genetai*. For a Jew to be put out of the synagogue meant that he was ostracized by everyone in the community, and since they lived in Jerusalem, that meant everyone. The Jews had three kinds of excommunication. The first was called "rebuke" and lasted from seven to thirty days. The second was referred to as "casting out" and lasted at least thirty days and normally sixty days. It was usually accompanied by curses and sometimes proclaimed with the blasting of a horn. People would keep a distance of six to seven feet from one under this discipline and stones were thrown on his coffin when he died. The third and most severe form was "cutting off." The duration of this excommunication was indefinite, and the individual was treated as dead. Absolutely no communication would exist between the one under discipline and others in the Jewish community. While John does not identify the level of excommunication the parents feared, it appears their son became the subject of the second, "casting out," before the day was through (9:34).

24 Then again called they the man that was blind, and said unto him, Give God the praise: we know that this man is a sinner.

25 He answered and said, Whether he be a sinner or no,

I know not: one thing I know, that, whereas I was blind, now I see.

26 Then said they to him again, What did he to thee? how opened he thine eyes?

27 He answered them, I have told you already, and ye did not hear: wherefore would ye hear it again? will ye also be his disciples?

28 Then they reviled him, and said, Thou art his disciple; but we are Moses' disciples.

29 We know that God spake unto Moses: as for this fellow, we know not from whence he is.

30 The man answered and said unto them, Why herein is a marvellous thing, that ye know not from whence he is, and yet he hath opened mine eyes.

31 Now we know that God heareth not sinners: but if any man be a worshipper of God, and doeth his will, him he heareth.

32 Since the world began was it not heard that any man opened the eyes of one that was born blind.

33 If this man were not of God, he could do nothing.

34 They answered and said unto him, Thou wast altogether born in sins, and dost thou teach us? And they cast him out.

D. Witness to His Foes (9:24–34). Again the man is questioned by the Pharisees, but this time by that hostile group which were opposed to Jesus. They begin their cross-examination with the phrase, "Give God the praise" (9:24). This was not a call to worship but rather an insinuation the man had been lying. It was an idiom meaning, "Speak the truth in the presence and the name of God." The first recorded use of the phrase is that of Joshua speaking to Achan, calling on him to confess his sin to the nation (Joshua 7:19). From the beginning of this second interview, these Pharisees place themselves as this man's foes, who doubt the veracity of his testimony. They declare emphatically, "We know that this man is a sinner" (9:24).

The opposition of the Jews did not cause this man to change his story. He refused to engage in a theological discussion with the Pharisees over whether Jesus was or was not a sinner; he simply explained how Jesus had changed his life. Philip P. Bliss has paraphrased this man's testimony

Chart 32

THE PROGRESSION OF OPPOSITION	
1. Mockery	9:8,9
2. Skepticism	9:10,15
3. Attacked the source	9:16
4. Created peer pressure	9:18–22
5. Accused of being dishonest	9:24
6. Open rebuke	9:28
7. Rejection	9:34

with the words, "Once I was blind, but now I can see. The light of the world is Jesus." In the face of the continual questioning of the Jews, the man finally asks them, "Will ye also be his disciples?" (9:27). The construction of the question begins with the negative *me*, implying the one asking expected a negative response. Perhaps the most amazing thing about this whole discussion is that the man being questioned still did not know who Jesus was, nor had he put his trust in Jesus. He was simply giving honest answers about what had happened to him.

The healed man's final question cuts deep. "The Jews" were no longer civil in their response to the beggar. The word *eloidoresan*, here translated "reviled" (9:28), means "to reproach or scold in a loud and abusive manner." It is a word that describes harsh and bitter statements made for the purpose of offending. They claimed to be disciples of Moses who received the law, whereas this man was the disciple of someone who broke the law. The pronoun *ekeinou*, translated "his," has a contemptuous force implied.

Still this man is unmoved in his recounting of the miracle. His argument concerning the identity of Jesus is based upon three commonly held views. First, God does not answer the prayers of sinners. Second, God does and will hear the prayers of those who worship God and do His will (9:31). His third observation is that no one had ever before healed someone born blind from birth (9:32). The logical conclusion of these facts was that the One who had given sight to the blind must be from God or He could do nothing (9:33).

The Jews responded to this logical argument with insult

and excommunication. Some commentators argue that the phrase "cast him out" (9:34) means he was physically removed from that place rather than formally excommunicated. They argue that a man could not be excommunicated by a small gathering. The word *ekballo* (cast out), however, was the formal designation of the second kind of excommunication noted above, and Jewish practice did not require a formal meeting of the whole Sanhedrin. As few as ten men could meet to sentence a man in this way. In this context, there is no reason to doubt the word refers to an excommunication (*see* 9:22).

III. THE WORSHIP OF THE BLIND MAN (9:35–41)

35 Jesus heard that they had cast him out; and when he had found him, he said unto him, Dost thou believe on the Son of God?

36 He answered and said, Who is he, Lord, that I might believe on him?

37 And Jesus said unto him, Thou hast both seen him, and it is he that talketh with thee.

38 And he said, Lord, I believe. And he worshipped him.

39 And Jesus said, For judgment I am come into this world, that they which see not might see; and that they which see might be made blind.

40 And some of the Pharisees which were with him heard these words, and said unto him, Are we blind also?

41 Jesus said unto them, If ye were blind, ye should have no sin: but now ye say, We see; therefore your sin remaineth.

John records that when Jesus heard the man had been expelled, He found him. Many Christians have found that when they are rejected by others, there is a unique and intimate fellowship that one has with the Lord. When Jesus found the man, He asked, "Do you believe . . . ?" (*see* 9:35). The Greek construction *su pisteueis* suggests an affirmative answer is anticipated and could be translated, "You do believe, don't you?" This suggests the man had physical sight but had not yet come to spiritual sight.

The man had not come to faith because he did not know

what to believe. Jesus solved this problem by revealing His true identity. When questioned by those antagonistic to His message, Jesus often refused to reveal who He was. But in every case where people were seeking truth, Jesus revealed Himself (*see* 3:27;4:26).

When the man knew who Jesus was, he worshipped Him (9:38). While the title "Lord" was used in the New Testament many times as an expression of respect, here it is clearly a title of reverence (*see* 9:36). The word *prosekunesen*, translated "worship," literally means "to fall down in reverence." John uses this verb exclusively to refer to the worship of God. Unlike the apostles, Jesus makes no protest over being worshipped (*see* Acts 10:25,26;14:18). As God, He is worthy to receive our worship (Revelation 4:11).

This meeting between Jesus and the blind man was not private in nature. They met in a public place, and others were observing this conversation, including some of the Pharisees. In the remaining verses of this chapter, Jesus turned His attention to them. He told them that one of His purposes in the world was that of judgment (9:39). This judgment refers not so much to the act as the result. The word *krima* (judgment) is closely related to *krisis* (sifting) and the verb *krino* (to separate). One of the purposes of Jesus was to sift the hearts of men and separate believers from those who reject Him.

This judgment results in the blind receiving sight and those professing to have sight being made to realize that they are blind. When the Pharisees heard this, they recognized the insinuation and asked, "Are we blind also?" (9:40). The emphasis of their question anticipated a negative response— "We are not also blind, are we?" But they did not get the answer they were looking for. Because they were unprepared to recognize their spiritual blindness, their sin remained. If, like the blind man, they had been willing to recognize Jesus as God, they could have resolved the sin problem once and for all.

TWELVE

CHRIST—
THE GOOD SHEPHERD
JOHN 10:1–42

Shepherding the flocks was very much a part of the culture during biblical times. Often a man's wealth was determined by the size of the flock he owned. Much of the economy throughout the biblical history of Israel was dependent largely upon this industry. In addition to the prominent role of the lamb in Old Testament worship, the Jews also identified the Lord as "the Shepherd of Israel" (Psalms 80:1; see 23:1) and spoke of themselves as "the sheep of [His] pasture" (Psalms 74:1; 79:13; 100:3).

Shepherds were the first group to worship Christ at His birth, being told of it by the angels (Luke 2:15–18). No doubt Christ had often encountered shepherds leading their flocks through the fields as He grew up. As a good teacher will try to relate new truth to known truth, one would come to expect the Master Teacher to use the familiar images of shepherding to teach spiritual truth. Much of this chapter of John records the spiritual applications Jesus drew from shepherding as He taught in the city of Jerusalem.

I. THE PROVERB OF A SHEPHERD (10:1–6)

Verily, verily, I say unto you, He that entereth not by the door into the sheepfold, but climbeth up some other way, the same is a thief and a robber.

194

2 But he that entereth in by the door is the shepherd of the sheep.

3 To him the porter openeth; and the sheep hear his voice: and he calleth his own sheep by name, and leadeth them out.

4 And when he putteth forth his own sheep, he goeth before them, and the sheep follow him; for they know his voice.

5 And a stranger will they not follow, but will flee from him; for they know not the voice of strangers.

6 This parable spake Jesus unto them; but they understood not what things they were which he spake unto them.

Unlike the synoptics, there are no parables in this gospel. The Gospel of Luke includes twenty-seven parables, more than any other Gospel. Sometimes people point to the parable of the Good Shepherd in this chapter as an exception by John. But the word translated "parable" (10:6), is not *parabole*, but *paroimian*, meaning "a wayside saying or proverb." Even though this word was sometimes used of an allegory, it was not used of a parable. The language of this proverb or allegory is deliberately indefinite, while a parable usually has definite characters, narration, and development of action. This proverb in John does not have narrative by the persons in the proverb, nor is there any unfolding action.

Jesus draws a distinction between thieves and robbers and the shepherd. Rustling is always a problem in livestock farming, and there are two kinds of rustlers. The word *kleptes* (thief) always refers to those who steal by means of a plan, usually carefully thought out. The thief is constantly attempting to plan and execute the perfect crime. The word *leistes* (robber) on the other hand relates to those who use violence to accomplish their end. This word is closely related to the verb *to plunder* and would identify the common mugger. The New Testament carefully preserves the distinction between the thief and robber.

These two types of rustlers attempt to enter the sheepfold some other way than by the carefully guarded gate. It was customary for shepherds to gather their flocks into an enclosed area at night for their protection. Then the shepherd would sleep across the gate to protect his sheep. Hence,

Jesus called Himself the door (gate) to the sheepfold. In the morning the shepherds led their sheep out through the gate to pasture. Rustlers would sometimes attempt to steal sheep at night by climbing the fence or otherwise entering the fold. Jesus' use of the rare word *allachothen* (from some other way) is significant (10:1). The shepherd always came *from* a well-known direction, unlike the rustler. In the previous chapters, (3:13; 8:42) and at other times, Jesus had used the word *from* to identify His divine origin.

Sometimes the shepherds left their sheep in the fold in the care of an undershepherd, known as a "porter" (10:3). The word *thuroros* comes from two other Greek words, *thura*, meaning "door," and *ora*, meaning "care." The porter was the gatekeeper of the fold and opened the gate only to the shepherd. While it is uncertain how definitely Jesus intended this proverb to be applied, commentators have suggested at least two possible identities of the porter. Some suggest he is the Holy Spirit, who opens the heart of men to allow Christ to enter (1:12). A more probable interpretation in light of the context identifies the porter as John the Baptist, the forerunner of Christ (*see* 10:40–42).

The description of a shepherd leading the flock from the sheepfold illustrates several distinctive traits of the Near Eastern shepherd. Some commentators believe Jesus was speaking here of David, the shepherd-king of Israel and one of the fullest personal types of Christ in the Old Testament. But the absence of a definite article with *shepherd* suggests Jesus was not thinking of any particular shepherd. The emphasis clearly rests on the character of shepherds in general rather than any particular person.

The close relationship between a shepherd and his sheep is emphasized when Jesus observes, "The sheep hear his voice: and he calleth his own sheep by name" (10:3). The verb *phonei* (calleth) emphasizes the personal aspect of his call. The sheep might be mixed with other flocks in the fold but were gathered with their own flock when they responded to the voice of the shepherd. Even today it is not uncommon to find the eastern shepherd calls his sheep by name. If someone other than the shepherd were to call them, even by their own names, the sheep would not respond.

In every flock there were some reluctant sheep who needed an extra incentive to get them out of the fold. Often a shepherd would have to get into the fold and find the reluctant sheep and drive them out of the fold to join the rest of the flock. The verb *ekbalei* (putteth forth, 10:4) literally means "thrust out" and is used in other Gospels of Jesus casting out demons. Once out of the fold, his flock follows the shepherd to the selected pasture.

When Jesus told this proverb, His listeners (the Pharisees, 9:40) failed to understand its meaning. Earlier that day He had proved Himself the Good Shepherd to the woman caught in the act of adultery and to the man born blind. In both cases the Pharisees had demonstrated themselves first thieves in their plot concerning the woman, then robbers in the way they treated the blind man whom Jesus healed. Their failure to comprehend this proverb resulted in Jesus explaining more fully its spiritual truths.

II. THE LESSON OF THE PROVERB (10:7–21)

Jesus used two particular aspects of this story to teach truths concerning Himself. Using the familiar "I am" (*ego eimi*) formula twice, He declared Himself both the door (10:9) and the shepherd (10:11). As was becoming increasingly the case, the response of the crowd who heard this lesson was divided. While some were cautiously supportive of Christ, others were certain He was mad and/or demon possessed.

> 7 Then said Jesus unto them again, Verily, verily, I say unto you, I am the door of the sheep.
> 8 All that ever came before me are thieves and robbers; but the sheep did not hear them.
> 9 I am the door: by me if any man enter in, he shall be saved, and shall go in and out, and find pasture.
> 10 The thief cometh not, but for to steal, and to kill, and to destroy: I am come that they might have life, and that they might have it more abundantly.

A. The Door (10:7–10). When Jesus identified Himself as the door, He was emphasizing the purpose or function of a door. This was the means whereby the sheep entered into the fold. By way of application, Jesus is the door to the fold of salvation. Jesus emphasizes the exclusiveness of Himself as Saviour by using the definite article (*the* door); He was not just another door or offering another way of salvation. By identifying salvation exclusively with entering the fold through that door (10:9), He denied syncretism. The expression *di'emou* (by me) is in an emphatic position so as to clearly identify the door by which men find salvation. As Robertson notes, "One can call this narrow intolerance, if he will, but it is the narrowness of truth. If Jesus is the Son of God sent to earth for our salvation, he is the only way."[24] Notice in Chart 33 the benefits to the sheep provided by the door.

Jesus uses the verb *sothesetai* (saved, 10:9), which is the key word in the biblical doctrine of salvation. This word includes the ideas of being both safe and sound. The security of the sheep is a theme developed later in this discourse. The order of the verbs describing the thief is significant. Although stealing is his primary purpose, he will kill or destroy to accomplish his goal. The Pharisees were prepared to kill the woman caught in the act of adultery and destroy the man born blind, but their ultimate purpose was to steal from Christ the glory that was rightfully His as the Light of the World. The similarity between the purpose of the thief (10:10) and the action of the wolf (10:12) will again identify the Jews with Satan (8:44).

11 I am the good shepherd: the good shepherd giveth his life for the sheep.

12 But he that is an hireling, and not the shepherd, whose own the sheep are not, seeth the wolf coming and leaveth the sheep, and fleeth: and the wolf catcheth them, and scattereth the sheep.

13 The hireling fleeth, because he is an hireling, and careth not for the sheep.

14 I am the good shepherd, and know my sheep, and am known of mine.

Chart 33

I AM THE DOOR (10:9)	
"By me, if any man enter in . . .	
1. He shall be saved	Salvation
2. He shall go in and out	Liberty
3. He shall find food	Spiritual food

15 As the Father knoweth me, even so know I the Father: and I lay down my life for the sheep.

16 And other sheep I have, which are not of this fold: them also I must bring, and they shall hear my voice: and there shall be one fold, and one shepherd.

17 Therefore doth my Father love me, because I lay down my life, that I might take it again.

18 No man taketh it from me, but I lay it down of myself. I have power to lay it down, and I have power to take it again. This commandment have I received of my Father.

B. The Shepherd (10:11–18). The Pharisees were not part of God's ordained plan for the leadership of Israel. The anointed office of the priests had been appointed by God as the spiritual leaders and teachers of the nation. Like the hireling (10:12), the priests were the legitimate guardians of the sheep in the absence of the shepherd. Unfortunately, like the hireling (10:13), the priests had abdicated their responsibility. The approach of the wolf is identified with the thief and robber mentioned earlier. Note the identities of the principal persons or groups as shown in Chart 34.

Jesus twice identifies Himself as the Good Shepherd

Chart 34

	Description	Relation to Sheep	Aim	Symbolizes
1.	Porter	Care	Open door to Christ	John the Baptist
2.	Shepherd	Owner	Lead (10:3), feed (10:9), give life for sheep (10:11,15,17)	Christ
3.	Thief and robber	Rustlers	Steal, kill (10:10)	Pharisees
4.	Wolf	Enemy	Destroy	Satan
5.	Hireling	Legal guardian	Self-interest, indifference toward sheep (10:13)	Priests and/or Levites

(10:11,14). The word *kalos* (good) used here is a term with moral overtones. In classical Greek this word was used to describe that which was beautiful, useful, auspicious, noble, wholesome, competent, and morally good. It would be correct to use any or all of these adjectives to describe "the good shepherd." Commenting on this word, Vincent notes, "The epithet *kalos*, applied here to the shepherd, points to the essential goodness as nobly realized and appealing to admiring respect and affection."[25]

Four times Jesus speaks of laying down His life for His sheep (10:11,15,17,18). When the wolf or rustler comes to the flock, his object is to steal the sheep. Normally, if he accomplishes this object unhindered, he will leave everything else alone. The shepherd, of course, is not prepared to allow the enemy to accomplish his purpose unhindered. In defending the flock, a shepherd necessarily defends his sheep with his life. He suffers the wrath of the wolf in order to save a lamb or sheep (*see* 1 Samuel 17:34,35). In the case of this Good Shepherd, Christ took the consequences of sin upon Himself, laying down His life for the sheep. Notice that Christ twice uses the preposition *huper* (on behalf of) describing the substitutional nature of His sacrificial death (10:11,15). The sacrificial death of the Good Shepherd springs from two facts. First, as the Son of God He was free from sin and He could therefore become sin (2 Corinthians 5:21) and a sacrifice (10:15,17,18). Second, as the Shepherd of the sheep, His love for them made it a voluntary sacrifice. Jesus maintained control over His life, even in allowing it to be destroyed by the enemy (10:18).

Much of the ministry of Christ on earth was limited to the lost sheep of Israel (*see* Matthew 10:6). Jesus also speaks of "other sheep . . . which are not of this fold" (10:16). By "other sheep" Christ could mean the members of future generations, while those who were listening to Him were "the sheep." However, it is more likely that He was recognizing the biblical distinction between Israel and the Gentiles. The flock of this Shepherd includes sheep from two folds—Israel and the Gentiles.

19 There was a division therefore again among the Jews for these sayings.

20 And many of them said, He hath a devil, and is mad; why hear ye him?

21 Others said, These are not the words of him that hath a devil. Can a devil open the eyes of the blind?

C. The Response (10:19–21). Once again the teaching of Jesus resulted in a schism or division in the crowd (*see* 6:52, 60,66; 7:12,43; 9:16). One group sought to write Jesus off as a madman or one who was demon possessed (10:20). This was not a new or unusual response by those who opposed Christ (*see* 8:48,52). The other group was reluctant to accept this appraisal of Christ. The logic of His teaching was inconsistent with the alleged theory of madness. The nature of His miracles hardly seemed the result of a demon. There is, however, no indication that those who rejected the erroneous explanations were at this point ready to believe in Jesus Christ for salvation.

III. THE DISCOURSE AT THE FEAST OF DEDICATION (10:22–39)

22 And it was at Jerusalem the feast of the dedication, and it was winter.

23 And Jesus walked in the temple in Solomon's porch.

24 Then came the Jews round about him, and said unto him, How long dost thou make us to doubt? If thou be the Christ, tell us plainly.

25 Jesus answered them, I told you, and ye believed not; the works that I do in my Father's name, they bear witness of me.

26 But ye believe not, because ye are not of my sheep, as I said unto you.

27 My sheep hear my voice, and I know them, and they follow me:

28 And I give unto them eternal life; and they shall never perish, neither shall any man pluck them out of my hand.

29 My Father, which gave them me, is greater than all; and no man is able to pluck them out of my Father's hand.

30 I and my Father are one.

31 Then the Jews took up stones again to stone him.

32 Jesus answered them, Many good works have I
shewed you from my Father; for which of those works do
ye stone me?

33 The Jews answered him, saying, For a good work we
stone thee not; but for blasphemy; and because that thou,
being a man, makest thyself God.

34 Jesus answered them, Is it not written in your law, I
said, Ye are gods?

35 If he called them gods, unto whom the word of God
came, and the scripture cannot be broken;

36 Say ye of him, whom the Father hath sanctified, and
sent into the world, Thou blasphemest; because I said, I
am the Son of God?

37 If I do not the works of my Father, believe me not.

38 But if I do, though ye believe not me, believe the
works: that ye may know, and believe, that the Father is in
me, and I in him.

39 Therefore they sought again to take him: but he escaped out of their hand.

Approximately three months passed between Jesus' last
discourse at the time of the Feast of Tabernacles (October)
and His return to Jerusalem for the Feast of Dedication (De-
cember). In the interim, Jesus had returned to Galilee for the
last time before His death. The Gospel of John, unlike the
synoptics, almost totally ignores Jesus' Galilean ministry, fo-
cusing rather on His miracles, discourses, and works in Jerusalem. In this discourse at the Feast of Dedication, Jesus
continued to refer to the shepherding illustration to draw out
spiritual truths.

This is the only mention of the mid-December Feast of
Dedication in Scripture. The feast was instituted by Judas
Maccabaeus in 165 B.C. to commemorate the dedication of the
temple after it had been cleansed following its desecration by
Antiochus Epiphanes. One of the principal features of this
eight-day celebration was the lighting of lights in the temple
and in homes. This feast is today celebrated by Jews and is
known by its Hebrew name, Hanukkah.

When the Jews saw Jesus in that part of the temple known
as Solomon's Porch, they immediately surrounded Him and
began questioning Him (10:23). They asked Christ for a clear
statement concerning His identity, particularly as it related
to "the Christ" (10:24). The question was probably asked by

some in an effort to trap Christ into making a statement that could be construed as blasphemy, but for some of the questioners there may have been an element of sincerity. The current festival was closely connected with that part of Israel's heritage known as the Maccabean revolt. The Jews had political dreams for the coming Messiah (6:15), and the celebration of this feast, especially under the yoke of Rome, again revived their messianic hopes. It is interesting that Jesus carefully avoids applying the title of Christ to Himself at this feast. Perhaps the Jews were ready to accept a political Messiah, so Christ did not foster this dream. They were still not prepared to receive the Son of God (10:36).

Jesus was not at all intimidated by the presence of those who three months earlier had attempted to stone Him (8:59). In His omniscience He knew that they would moments later attempt to do the same again (10:31). Still He began to again explain the consequence of their real problem, unbelief. Because they would not believe, they were not His sheep and could not partake in any of the privileges of the Shepherd (10:26).

One of the key texts in Scripture emphasizing the security of the believer is John 10:28,29. Jesus emphasizes the safety of the sheep in two ways. First, He promised they would never perish. John here uses a double negative (*ou me*) which although poor English grammar is an emphatic way of stat-

Chart 35

THE SHEPHERD AND HIS SHEEP (10:27,28)		
The Problem of the Sheep	The Work of the Shepherd	The Privilege of the Sheep
Lost	He seeks and calls the sheep	Hears His voice
No sense of direction	He leads the flock	Follows the Shepherd
Unable to find food	He feeds the flock	Receives eternal life
Unable to defend itself	He protects the flock	Never perish—safe in the hand of the Shepherd

ing the case in Greek. The Lord's emphasis is "They will certainly never ever perish." Second, Jesus taught that the believer is secure in His hand and the hand of His Father. The believer could not be removed. Jesus uses the verb *harpazo* twice in verses twenty-eight and twenty-nine, first stating the fact that none would be snatched away from His hand, and second, noting the impossibility of a believer being snatched away from His Father's hand. This verb conveys the idea of being removed by force.

As before, Jesus' use of the title "My Father" (10:29) together with His identification as one with the Father (10:30) resulted in yet another attempt to stone Him. Jesus defended His right to identify with God by citing Psalms 82:6 in His defense (10:34). His argument was that God inspired the psalmist to call Israel's leaders "gods." This phrase, "ye are gods," recognized the leaders' authority to require obedience and execute justice. Jesus was therefore not guilty of blasphemy by simply calling Himself the "Son of God." He was using Scripture the way they used Scripture, looking for the smallest detail to prove their point. As a Jew and messenger from God, Jesus was claiming what God Himself had declared true. In this context Jesus noted, "the scripture cannot be broken" (10:35), meaning the Scriptures cannot be treated as though they do not exist. This word *broken* is the same word used to annul a marriage. A marriage is a sacred union of man and woman by God, and no one can annul or break what God has done. So no one can break or annul the Scriptures. This demonstrates Jesus' attitude toward inerrancy. In essence, Jesus was stating that the Scriptures are authoritative in what they state and no one can take any of it away. The Jews attempted again to take Him (arrest Him), but once again they failed (10:39).

IV. SUMMARY OF THE PEREAN MINISTRY (10:40–42)

40 And went away again beyond Jordan into the place where John at first baptized; and there he abode.

41 And many resorted unto him, and said, John did no miracle: but all things that John spake of this man were true.

42 And many believed on him there.

Jesus left Jerusalem to spend much of the remaining months of His life in the region of Perea (10:40), particularly in the area of Bethabara (*see* 1:28). It was in this area about three years earlier that Jesus had begun to gather His disciples. It had also been one of John the Baptist's principal centers of ministry. Though the Baptist had been killed about two years earlier, he was still alive in the memory of those who had heard him preach. They could not help but draw comparisons between Jesus and the former prophet of this region. And the comparisons were for the most part favorable. Many came to Jesus and believed on Him during this ministry (10:42). They came largely because of the testimony of John the Baptist. Although he had no miracles authenticating his ministry, the people recognized the fulfillment of John's prophecy in the life of the One he had identified as "the Lamb of God" (1:29,36).

THIRTEEN

CHRIST—
THE RESURRECTION
JOHN 11:1–57

This chapter records one of the most touching accounts in the life of Christ, the raising of Lazarus from the dead. During the ministry of Christ, Lazarus and his two sisters had become His special friends, and this is the first mention of His relationship with this family in the gospel. Still, John knew his readers were well aware of Jesus' relationship with them, either because they had read of it in other Gospels, or because they had heard preachers tell of it in their explanation of the Gospel message (12:3; see Mark 14:9). Here John tells of the event of raising Lazarus, a miracle recorded in no other Gospel.

Some commentators have attempted to identify this Lazarus with the beggar who died and went to paradise (Luke 16:19–31). This Lazarus, however, does not appear to have lived in the abject poverty that described the beggar. The name *Lazarus* was an abbreviated form of *Eleazer*, meaning "God has helped." Although there are only two men so named in the New Testament, the name appears also in Josephus and the rabbinical writings. This sort of name would not be uncommon among the Jews. After the miracle, the multitude flocked to see the man who came back from the dead (12:9), but Jesus, the One who knew all concerning the afterlife, is the focus of attention.

Because the death and resurrection of Lazarus is the focal point of this chapter, it is interesting to note the various attitudes toward death by the people mentioned. The attitude of the disciples was doubt, and they expressed fear. Martha responded to the death of her brother with disappointment and reflected that Christ could have helped if He had arrived before it was too late. The more emotional Mary responded to Lazarus' death with discouragement; she cut herself off from others and approached a state of depression. Jesus' attitude toward death was deliverance, and He raised Lazarus from the dead as He will some day raise all men. The concluding verses of this chapter reflect the attitude of the Jews toward Christ—now they are deliberately trying to destroy Him.

I. ATTITUDE OF DISCIPLES TOWARD DEATH— DOUBT (11:1–16)

John begins this chapter by describing the growing circumstances of a crisis. In describing Lazarus's condition, he used the word *asthenon* (sick, 11:1), literally meaning "without strength." The seriousness of this disease is noted later in the announcement of his death. While we are not told what the sickness was, it was evidently severe. Lazarus was probably dead by the time the messenger got to Jesus.

A second aspect of this crisis is alluded to in John's mention of Lazarus's home. Bethany was only two miles east of Jerusalem, separated from it only by the Mount of Olives. Earlier in His ministry, Jesus had spent a great deal of time with this family (*see* Luke 10:38–42), but the memory of the recent attempts to stone Jesus in Jerusalem would have been fresh in the mind of Jesus as they were in the minds of His disciples (11:8). The disciples realized that Jesus faced danger if He went to minister to Lazarus. Jesus could have helped from a distance, as He did before (*see* 4:49–53), but He had other plans.

Then John adds the note further identifying Mary as the one who had anointed the feet of Jesus (11:2). This was perhaps one of the best-known events in the life of Christ during the early centuries of Christianity (Mark 14:9). Although John does not describe this anointing here, his reference to it in this context would remind his readers of the real danger to Jesus in Jerusalem. In the last year Jesus had several times escaped the attempts of the Jews to arrest Him or stone Him. The reader of this gospel might have begun to believe the Jews would never be successful in capturing Jesus. By being reminded of the anointing of Jesus for His burial, the reader would understand this was a real crisis.

> Now a certain man was sick, named Lazarus, of Bethany, the town of Mary and her sister Martha.
>
> 2 (It was that Mary which anointed the Lord with ointment, and wiped his feet with her hair, whose brother Lazarus was sick.)
>
> 3 Therefore his sisters sent unto him, saying, Lord, behold, he whom thou lovest is sick.
>
> 4 When Jesus heard that, he said, This sickness is not unto death, but for the glory of God, that the Son of God might be glorified thereby.
>
> 5 Now Jesus loved Martha, and her sister, and Lazarus.
>
> 6 When he had heard therefore that he was sick, he abode two days still in the same place where he was.

A. Fearful of Dying (11:1–6). The sisters of Lazarus sent a simple message to Jesus. "He whom thou lovest is sick" (11:3). The word for love here is *phileis,* which means "to love as a friend." The fact that the message does not include a specific request for help suggests something of the depth of Jesus' friendship with Lazarus. The sisters were confident Jesus would help when informed of the need (*see* 11:21,32).

When Jesus received the message of Lazarus's sickness, He noted the sickness was not unto death but rather for the glory of God (11:4). This statement was probably intended not only for the messenger to pass on to the sisters but also for the disciples. They would have known something of the relationship between Jesus and Lazarus, and perhaps they had eaten many times at his table. The disciples, like the sisters, were fearful that Lazarus would die (*see* 11:12). As Bethany is only a one-day journey from Bethabara, Lazarus was probably dead before Jesus received the message. His statement concerning the sickness not being unto death obviously did not mean Lazarus would not die, only that death would not be the final result of the sickness. Though he died, in being raised again, God would be glorified; therefore the sickness ended in the glorification of the Son of God.

Rather than returning immediately to Bethany, Jesus remained where He was for two days. This delay was not due to a lack of concern. John notes in this context that Jesus loved the family, using the verb *agape* (11:5), the stronger word for self-sacrificial love. This word was stronger than the one used by the sisters. Some have suggested He delayed because He feared stoning or wanted to wait until Lazarus was dead so as to raise the dead and promote faith, but the raising of Lazarus established conditions that would seal His death (11:53). Going immediately was not necessary because Lazarus was probably dead by the time Jesus received the message, and in His omniscience, He knew it. Perhaps the real reason why Jesus waited related to the mourning customs of the Jews.

According to Edersheim, the burial of the deceased invariably took place on the day of the death.[26] The mourning began immediately and lasted a month but was divided into three periods. The first three days were the most intense in mourning and often involved the practice of hiring professional mourners. During the rest of that first week, mourning was less intense and friends were expected to visit expressing their condolences and sympathy. The fourth day after the death was, therefore, the first day Jesus could have arrived if He wished to come as a friend and visit with Lazarus's sisters. When He arrived at the home of Lazarus, it was generally believed that He had arrived too late (11:21,32, 37). In reality Jesus was right on time.

> 7 Then after that saith he to his disciples, Let us go into Judaea again.
>
> 8 His disciples say unto him, Master, the Jews of late sought to stone thee; and goest thou thither again?
>
> 9 Jesus answered, Are there not twelve hours in the day? If any man walk in the day, he stumbleth not, because he seeth the light of this world.
>
> 10 But if a man walk in the night, he stumbleth, because there is no light in him.
>
> 11 These things said he: and after that he saith unto them, Our friend Lazarus sleepeth; but I go, that I may awake him out of sleep.

12 Then said his disciples, Lord, if he sleep, he shall do well.

B. *Fearful of Stoning (11:7–12)*. After the delay, Jesus announced His desire to return to Judea (11:7). The disciples recalled the recent attempts to stone Jesus in Jerusalem and could think of no valid reason for taking such a risk in entering that dangerous territory. When the disciples asked, "Goest thou thither again?" (11:8), they used the verb *hupago* (goest thou), meaning "to withdraw." In essence they reminded Jesus of the danger in Judea and asked, "Doest thou withdraw from this safe retreat?"[27] With the Passover approaching (11:55), the disciples no doubt had concluded that Jesus' desire to return to Judea would mean He wanted to visit the temple in Jerusalem for the Passover.

Jesus reminded His disciples there were twelve hours of light in a day (11:9). Dawn was probably breaking when Jesus said these words and, realizing a full day's journey would take them to Bethany, He was suggesting they travel during the safer daylight hours. Also, this proverb has a spiritual application to Christians who are to "walk in the light, as [Christ] is in the light" (1 John 1:7). As the sun is the light of the world during the twelve hours of daylight, Jesus is the Light of the World for every hour of our lives (*see* Chart 29 in chapter ten).

Jesus then further clarified His motives for returning to Judea by noting Lazarus was sleeping. Sleep is a common biblical figure for death in both Old and New Testaments (2 Samuel 7:12; Psalms 13:3; 1 Corinthians 15:20,51; 1 Thessalonians 4:13,14). The idea has no relation to the state of the soul, which some cults say happens at death (soul sleep). The soul is eternally conscious. Sleep refers to the physical body which is "laid to rest" awaiting the resurrection of the dead. In speaking of Lazarus's "sleep," Jesus used the verb *kekoimetai*, a perfect passive indicative meaning "he has fallen asleep and continues to sleep." The disciples completely misunderstood the meaning of Jesus' expression thinking He was referring to physical rest. Natural rest is in itself part of the healing process and is usually a sign that the crisis of an illness is passed (*see* 11:12). They could not understand, therefore, why Jesus had remained where He was when His friend was on his deathbed. The disciples probably assumed that if Lazarus were sleeping, he was improving and the crisis was past. So the disciples could not understand why Jesus was eager to go to Judea.

13 Howbeit Jesus spake of his death: but they thought that he had spoken of taking of rest in sleep.
14 Then said Jesus unto them plainly, Lazarus is dead.
15 And I am glad for your sakes that I was not there, to the intent ye may believe; nevertheless let us go unto him.
16 Then said Thomas, which is called Didymus, unto his fellow disciples, Let us also go, that we may die with him.

C. *Fearful of Death (11:13–16).* Jesus, recognizing the confusion of His disciples, told them plainly that Lazarus was dead (11:13,14). The adverb *parresiai* (plainly) means "without metaphor." Jesus often used parables, proverbs, and metaphors to teach truth, but at times He spoke plainly to His disciples.

In discussing the death of Lazarus, Jesus speaks of being glad He was not there when Lazarus died (11:15). Obviously Jesus was not glad Lazarus had died, nor did He rejoice in the sorrow of the family surrounding that death. He was glad because of the opportunity He now had to build His disciples' faith. The implication is that if Jesus had been there, He would have healed Lazarus (*see* 11:21,32). Some commentators have suggested it was physically impossible for anyone to die in the presence of Jesus who is the Prince of Life. Therefore, Jesus was glad because Lazarus could not have died if He had been there.

The closeness of the relationship between Jesus and Lazarus is emphasized by the Lord's statement, "Nevertheless let us go unto him" (11:15). Even though Lazarus was dead, Jesus spoke of going "unto him" as though he were still alive. Not even physical death could hinder the personal relationship between Jesus and the one whom He loved. Paul later explained that nothing can separate us from the love of God (Romans 8:38,39).

It was Thomas who was the first to declare his willingness to follow Jesus to the death (11:16) and the last to accept the testimony concerning the resurrection of Jesus from the grave (20:24–28). The doubt of Thomas is embryonically reflected in his statement of death. He does not believe Jesus could protect him from death, so doubt leads to discouragement and then to despair, "that we may die with him." John identifies both the Aramaic name, *Thomas*, and his Greek name, *Didymus*. Both of these names mean "twin" in their respective languages and suggest Thomas had a twin brother or sister. Probably he used these names interchangeably depending on the cultural context in which he found himself. Thomas the pessimist is ready to think the worst and later refuses to believe the good news concerning the resurrection. As Westcott observes, "He will die for the love which he has, but he will not affect the faith which he has not."[28]

II. ATTITUDE OF MARTHA TOWARD DEATH—DISAPPOINTMENT (11:17–27)

17 Then when Jesus came, he found that he had lain in the grave four days already.

18 Now Bethany was nigh unto Jerusalem, about fifteen furlongs off:

19 And many of the Jews came to Martha and Mary, to comfort them concerning their brother.

20 Then Martha, as soon as she heard that Jesus was coming, went and met him: but Mary sat still in the house.

21 Then said Martha unto Jesus, Lord, if thou hadst been here, my brother had not died.

22 But I know, that even now, whatsoever thou wilt ask of God, God will give it thee.

23 Jesus saith unto her, Thy brother shall rise again.

24 Martha saith unto him, I know that he shall rise again in the resurrection at the last day.

25 Jesus said unto her, I am the resurrection, and the life: he that believeth in me, though he were dead, yet shall he live:

26 And whosoever liveth and believeth in me shall never die. Believest thou this?

27 She saith unto him, Yea, Lord: I believe that thou art the Christ, the Son of God, which should come into the world.

Because everyone is different, each person will respond differently to a given situation. This is certainly evident in the contrasting reactions of the two sisters of Lazarus to the loss of their brother. Martha, who seems to be characteristically the more pragmatic of the two, responded by carrying on as best she could. She was the active sister, probably the manager of the house (see Luke 10:38–42). When the messenger came to the house to tell them Jesus was near, Martha was probably fulfilling her social duties. Mary, on the other hand, sat in seclusion still mourning. This did not mean Martha loved her brother less than Mary, only that they responded to his death differently.

Jesus arrived on the fourth day following Lazarus's death and apparently chose to remain outside the city limits, perhaps near the local cemetery (see 11:30). Bethany was only two miles from Jerusalem, and Lazarus was apparently well-known among the Jews. Perhaps Jesus realized that many of the Jews would arrive on the fourth day to comfort the women. He probably thought it best to simply send for the sisters, perhaps intending to raise Lazarus in the presence of His disciples and the sisters.

Often in times of mourning, a recurring thought crystallizes itself in one's mind and becomes an often repeated expression during that period. How many times had Mary and Martha looked at each other over the previous four days and said, "If only Jesus had been here . . ."? Perhaps the one word that best describes the feeling of Martha is *disappointment*. The first thing she said to Jesus upon meeting Him was, "Lord, if thou hadst been here, my brother had not died" (11:21). Then, as if she regretted her words, she added, "But I know, that even now, whatsoever thou wilt ask of God, God will give it thee" (11:22). She probably did not intend a rebuke or complaint in her words; she was only expressing her disappointment that her brother had not been healed but had died.

The theology one learns at funerals is often contrary to that taught in the Scriptures. When people are emotionally disturbed, often they are unable to think clearly and may grasp only one aspect of truth. In their failure to understand other balancing truths, they end up believing something that falls short of what the Bible teaches. Martha evidenced this characteristic in expressing three erroneous views during their brief conversation.

The first of these is found in her statement concerning

Jesus asking of God (11:22). Martha uses the verb *aiteo*, the usual word for men praying to God which implies the inferior asking the superior for favors. Jesus, however, was an equal with God and never used this verb but rather *erotao*, which referred to one making a request of an equal. Concerning the use of *aitesei* here, Trench observes, "Martha plainly reveals her poor unworthy notions of his person, and in fact declares that she sees in Him no more than a prophet."[29]

The second area of doctrinal error expressed here regards her view of the resurrection. Jesus promised, "Thy brother shall rise again" (11:23). While this could be taken as a Jewish expression of comfort, in light of Jesus' message (11:25) and His subsequent actions, it was probably intended by Christ as a personal promise or statement that He would raise Lazarus immediately. Martha responded with a general statement of the resurrection, one consistent with Jewish theology. The doctrine of the general resurrection at "the last day," however, cannot be adopted as the biblical view in light of the New Testament revelation of two distinct resurrections (Revelation 20:4–15), the first of which contains several stages (1 Corinthians 15:22–24).

Jesus again uses the "I am" (*ego eimi*) formula to reveal Himself. This is the fifth "I am" in John. Jesus tells Martha, "I am the resurrection, and the life" (11:25). Martha had expressed her faith in the resurrection as a *principle*, but Jesus now reveals the resurrection as a *person*. He is the embodiment of all life, including the resurrection. As Godet explains, "If He is the principle of the physical resurrection, it is because He is. . .life in the most exalted sense of that word."[30] Jesus as the resurrection, therefore, is only one manifestation of life, as Jesus the light was also that manifestation (1:4,5).

Jesus then asked Martha if she believed that He is the resurrection (11:26). Martha responded using the perfect tense, literally "I have believed" (11:27). Her expression of faith is in keeping with John's stated purpose (20:31) but in this context falls short because it fails to evidence faith as an internalization of the truth concerning Christ as the resurrection and the life. She was prepared to express her faith in Christ as the Son of God (11:27) but was not prepared to say she believed her brother could be raised before the resurrection at "the last day."

Christ did not rebuke Martha for her erroneous beliefs but rather sought to help her grow in faith. This emphasizes an important truth concerning the Christian life. Because we are incapable of grasping all truth at one time, we must constantly grow "from faith to faith" (Romans 1:17). The Lord will sometimes overlook our weak faith (Romans 14:1). When He knows our heart is right, He will receive us (Romans 15:7).

III. ATTITUDE OF MARY TOWARD DEATH—DISCOURAGEMENT (11:28–39)

28 And when she had so said, she went her way, and called Mary her sister secretly, saying, The Master is come, and calleth for thee.

29 As soon as she heard *that*, she arose quickly, and came unto him.

30 Now Jesus was not yet come into the town, but was in that place where Martha met him.

31 The Jews then which were with her in the house, and comforted her, when they saw Mary, that she rose up hastily and went out, followed her, saying, She goeth unto the grave to weep there.

32 Then when Mary was come where Jesus was, and saw him, she fell down at his feet, saying unto him, Lord, if thou hadst been here, my brother had not died.

33 When Jesus therefore saw her weeping, and the Jews also weeping which came with her, he groaned in the spirit, and was troubled.

34 And said, Where have ye laid him? They said unto him, Lord, come and see.

35 Jesus wept.

36 Then said the Jews, Behold how he loved him!

37 And some of them said, Could not this man, which opened the eyes of the blind, have caused that even this man should not have died?

38 Jesus therefore again groaning in himself cometh to the grave. It was a cave, and a stone lay upon it.

39 Jesus said, Take ye away the stone. Martha, the sister of him that was dead, saith unto him, Lord, by this time he stinketh: for he hath been *dead* four days.

If Martha was the pragmatic sister, Mary was the idealist. Her response to her brother's death reveals she was by nature more expressive and emotional. When Martha went to meet Jesus, Mary remained in the house alone. When she did get up to go to Jesus, those who saw her thought she was going to the tomb to mourn. Perhaps she had turned her grief inward and cut herself off from others during her period of mourning. If that were the case, it would be a reasonable conclusion of the Jews to suspect she was about to break emotionally. The verb *klausei,* translated "to weep" (11:31; *see* 11:33), means "to weep loudly" or "to wail" and referred to the normal response of a Jew in mourning.

Mary met Jesus in the same place Martha had met Him (11:30). When she arrived at the place where Jesus was, she fell at Jesus' feet, repeated Martha's initial statement, and began to weep (11:32,33). It is interesting to note that every time Mary is described in the Gospels, she is at the feet of Jesus (*see* 12:3; Luke 10:39). Also, in comparing the two statements of the sisters, Mary put the pronoun *autou* (my) in an emphatic position and used a more vivid tense of the verb *apethanen* (died, 11:32). Unlike her sister, when Mary made that statement, she began to cry uncontrollably (11:33).

Both Mary and Martha had expressed their devotion and faith in Christ earlier, but their faith and hope fell short of Jesus' expectation. When Lazarus was sick, they had contacted Jesus believing as long as there is life, there is hope. Jesus knew Lazarus was dead when He got the news of his sickness, but He believed as long as there is hope, there is life. In Mary's emotional state, it was impossible to encourage her with words, so Jesus makes no attempt here.

Jesus was not unaffected emotionally by these events and the circumstances of Lazarus' death. Although the weeping of Mary was genuine, the weeping of the Jews (11:33) was probably at least in part a performance that stirred groanings in Jesus. John uses the verb *enebrimesato* (11:33), which is translated "groaned" but literally means "to snort with anger like a horse." This verb is used in the Septuagint for an expression of violent displeasure (Daniel 11:30). John also uses the verb *etaraxen* (troubled), meaning He was disturbed or agitated. While Jesus was in sympathy with Mary, He was disturbed by the loud wailing of the Jews.

The shortest verse in the English Bible simply records, "Jesus wept" (11:35). The verb used here is *edakrusen*, meaning "to shed a tear" or "to weep silently." This verse has been variously paraphrased, "Jesus burst into tears" (MOF-FATT) or, "Tears came to Jesus' eyes" (TLB). Concerning this verse, A. T. Robertson notes, "Often all that we can do is to shed tears in grief too deep for words. Jesus understood and understands. This is the shortest verse in the Bible, but no verse carries more meaning in it."[31] Godet correctly observes, "The very Gospel in which the deity of Jesus is most clearly asserted is also that which makes us best acquainted with the profoundly human side of His life."[32]

When the Jews witnessed the tears in the eyes of Jesus, they had various responses. Some concluded, "Behold, how he loved him!" (11:36). The verb *ephilei* (he loved) speaks of a close friendship or brotherly love (*see* 11:3). Others remembered the healing of the man born blind (9:6,7) and wondered if Jesus could not also have prevented the death of Lazarus (11:37). Commentators are divided on the intent of these words. Some believe the statement was made in derision, whereas others interpret it as a natural conclusion of Jewish theology similar to that of the sisters earlier. They may have wondered, if Jesus really loved Lazarus that much, why did He not do something earlier? In this chapter it appears everyone thought Jesus arrived too late, but the Lord is never late.

Even in recognition of the relationship between Jesus and Lazarus, the Jews failed to understand the meaning of the tears in Jesus' eyes. If His tears had been caused by His sense of loss, He would no doubt have smiled knowing what He was about to do. Jesus wept not for Himself but for others (*see* Chart 36). Jesus knew what was in the heart of each one gathered there by the tomb (2:25). He expressed His compassion for Mary who was hurting. He recognized the callousness of the Jews who should have been comforting but were condemning. He could identify in His disciples their

Chart 36

WHAT BROUGHT TEARS TO THE EYES OF JESUS?
1. The deep hurting and sorrow of Mary—compassion (11:32,33)
2. The callousness of the Jews (11:33,37)
3. The ignorance of His followers concerning His power (11:16,40)
4. The unbelief of a few of the Jews present (11:42)
5. The indecision of some who professed faith in Christ (11:46)
6. His love for Lazarus

ignorance of His power over death. He saw the unbelief of those who that day would not "be persuaded, though one rose from the dead" (Luke 16:31) and in unbelief seal their eternal fate. And He knew the indecision of those who would believe but continue to be loyal to the Pharisees, those who would declare Him king but within a week of that action call for His crucifixion.

When Jesus came to the tomb, He made an unusual request. Lazarus had been buried in a tomb carved into the rock and covered with a large stone. Jesus commanded that the stone be removed (11:39). Immediately Martha objected, referring to the òdor that one expects after a body is dead four days. Although several famous paintings of this scene suggest the observers were repelled by odor, it is more likely that Martha only assumed there would be an odor if the stone were removed. Some Jews believed the soul of the deceased hovered around a body for three days after death but departed finally on the fourth day as the body began to decompose. From that perspective, Lazarus was beyond even a miraculous resurrection, and the opening of the tomb would only serve to release an offensive odor. There is nothing unreasonable about Martha's objection. She probably assumed Jesus' request was related to His groaning at the tomb (11:38) and may have seen it as a sort of unreasonable request sometimes made by emotionally upset people. Obviously she did not expect Jesus to raise her brother from the dead.

IV. ATTITUDE OF CHRIST TOWARD DEATH—DELIVERANCE (11:40-46)

40 Jesus saith unto her, Said I not unto thee, that, if thou wouldest believe, thou shouldest see the glory of God?

41 Then they took away the stone from the place where the dead was laid. And Jesus lifted up his eyes, and said, Father, I thank thee that thou hast heard me.

42 And I knew that thou hearest me always: but because of the people which stand by I said it, that they may believe that thou hast sent me.

43 And when he thus had spoken, he cried with a loud voice, Lazarus, come forth.

44 And he that was dead came forth, bound hand and foot with graveclothes: and his face was bound about with a napkin. Jesus saith unto them, Loose him, and let him go.

45 Then many of the Jews which came to Mary, and had seen the things which Jesus did, believed on him.

46 But some of them went their ways to the Pharisees, and told them what things Jesus had done.

Sometimes Christ will ask us to obey Him in an area we do not understand or might view as abnormal. He does this in order that He might demonstrate the greater glory of God. Jesus reminded Martha of the response He had sent back with their messenger (11:4,40). By the time Martha had received that message, Lazarus was dead, perhaps even buried. She had failed to understand the meaning of this message that if she would believe, she would see God's glory. Now Jesus would demonstrate the glory of God for all those present to see. But first He required that the stone be removed. Often God waits for us to do what only we can do, so that He can do what only He can do. Until we obey Him, He cannot work. D. L. Moody began his great Chicago campaign preaching on the phrase, "Take . . . away the stone" (11:39), and suggested the cause of revival would be hindered if the stone of unbelief, prejudice, and sectarianism were not set aside.

Jesus prayed a prayer of thanksgiving to the Father before the raising of Lazarus. In the presence of others Jesus acknowledged His belief that God would answer His prayer concerning Lazarus. Robertson suggests an earlier unrecorded prayer of Jesus concerning the raising of Lazarus. Jesus thanks the Father "that thou hast heard me" (11:41), implying He had previously asked for this miracle. Here Jesus prays as a testimony that the crowd around the tomb might come to believe (11:42). In so doing, Jesus was illustrating a principle of "say-it faith" which He had earlier taught His disciples (Mark 11:23).

Someone has suggested Jesus called Lazarus by name (11:43) because if He had not, every dead person would have been revived. Regardless of the accuracy of that statement, Lazarus was revived at the call of Christ. The word of Christ gave life to Lazarus, just as the Word of God gives spiritual life today (Hebrews 4:12; 1 Peter 1:23). Jesus "cried with a loud voice" (11:43) not so much to wake the dead as to insure the crowd could hear Him. Some of them may still have been engaged in their mourning wail (11:33). There is no verb recorded in Christ's command to Lazarus, although it is obviously implied. Literally, Jesus said, "Lazarus, out here!" When he appeared, he was still in the grave clothes in which he was buried, and a cloth was covering his face. Jesus instructed either His disciples or some of the Jews nearby to release Lazarus from these hindrances.

Lazarus's miraculous appearance at the call of Christ was proof that a man can have a new life. Lazarus did not experience a resurrection life of the Spirit. Lazarus was resuscitated or returned to the physical life he previously had. Christ solved the problem of death, which is the greatest enigma facing man. Many evangelical writers have drawn parallels between the raising of Lazarus and the new life in Christ found by those who are dead in their trespasses and sin. Even after we are saved, the grave clothes—habits and attitudes of the world which bind our hands and feet thereby hindering our activity for Christ or cover our face and hinder our vision of the things of God—must be removed. After this is accomplished, many will come to believe because of the difference Jesus has made in our lives.

The result of this miracle was that "many of the Jews . . . believed on him" (11:45). This is the normal expression for saving faith in this gospel. By this time in the ministry of Christ, the rift between Jesus and the Jews was so great that following Christ involved cutting oneself off or being cut off from the Jews. Some of those who believed, however, were not prepared to make a clean break and reported this miracle to the Pharisees (11:46). Perhaps they thought the news of this resurrection, an evidence of the credibility of Jesus, might have released some of the tension or calmed some of the animosity the Pharisees had developed toward Him. More likely, however, these believers may have desired the best of both worlds, and were prepared to follow Jesus but not prepared to leave the world.

V. THE ATTITUDE OF THE JEWS TOWARD JESUS—DESTRUCTION (11:47–57)

Since many were convinced by this miracle, those of the religious hierarchy of Israel were all the more intense in their enmity toward Jesus (11:47–53). They insisted upon decisive action. In a meeting of the council, the high priest unknowingly spoke prophetically when he recommended that Jesus be put to death (11:50). Now it became their established purpose to apprehend Him in such a way as to not incite a rebellion. They failed to realize that their goal was subject to a higher purpose. However Jesus, recognizing this higher purpose, retired from the scene until the divinely appointed hour (13:1). Notice in Chart 37 how many times "the Jews" attempt to arrest and/or destroy Jesus in this gospel.

47 Then gathered the chief priests and the Pharisees a council, and said, What do we? for this man doeth many miracles.

48 If we let him thus alone, all men will believe on him: and the Romans shall come and take away both our place and nation.

A. The Problem (11:47,48). The popularity of Jesus created a problem for the leaders of the Jews. The Sanhedrin had a degree of liberty in their rule over the people but were held responsible to Rome for any perceived rebellion against the Roman authorities. The absence of an article accompanying *sunedrion* (council, 11:47) suggests this was an informal meeting and may not have included all of its members. While the raising of Lazarus resulting in the defection of many Jews gave rise to this meeting, the real concern of council members was how to hold on to their power and privileges. Robertson, commenting on the significance in the word order of that which concerns the council members, interprets the word *place* to mean "position." If his interpretation is correct, then the problem is when *place* (job) is put before *nation* (patriotism). However, the word *topon* (place) is probably a reference to the temple and reveals their preference for a building over their desire to glorify God who inhabited the building.

> 49 And one of them, named Caiaphas, being the high priest that same year, said unto them, Ye know nothing at all.
>
> 50 Nor consider that it is expedient for us, that one man should die for the people, and that the whole nation perish not.
>
> 51 And this spake he not of himself: but being high priest that year, he prophesied that Jesus should die for that nation;
>
> 52 And not for that nation only but that also he should gather together in one the children of God that were scattered abroad.

B. The Prophecy (11:49–52). Caiaphas responded to this problem with a politically expedient plan. His proposal was that Jesus be killed and the nation thereby saved from destruction at the hands of the Romans (11:49,50). The verb *sumpherei* (expedient, 11:50) literally means "to bear together" in the sense of being profitable. Caiaphas also used the preposition *huper* (in behalf of) in comparing the death of one man versus a whole nation. This preposition is used throughout the New Testament in reference to the substitutionary death of Christ.

John identifies Caiaphas's statement as prophetic in nature (11:51). It is doubtful Caiaphas realized he was speaking prophetically as his intended meaning was for Jesus to be martyred instead of thousands of Jews being killed by Roman soldiers. The high priest was in this context counselling the murder of an innocent man for reasons of political expedience. Prophetically, however, Caiaphas was speaking of the substitutionary death of Christ for the nation. While this was true, John correctly notes Jesus did not die only for Israel, "but that he should gather together in one the chil-

Chart 37

THE JEWS' ATTEMPTS AGAINST JESUS
1. They challenge His authority at the cleansing of the temple (2:18–20).
2. They persecute Him for healing a man on the Sabbath (5:10,16).
3. They sought to kill Him for claiming equality with God (5:18).
4. They sought Him as the Feast of Tabernacles began (7:11).
5. They sent officers to arrest Him during the latter part of the Feast of Tabernacles (7:32,44,45).
6. Some of them were involved in the plot concerning the woman caught in adultery (8:6).
7. They attempted to stone Him when He identified with the Old Testament "I am" (8:58,59).
8. They attempted to stone Him at the Feast of Dedication for the statement, "I and my Father are one" (10:30,31).
9. They attempted to arrest Him at the Feast of Dedication when they could not refute Him (10:39).
10. They determined in council to put Him to death (11:53).
11. They sought Him among the pilgrims who arrived early for Passover (11:56).
12. They issued requests for information leading to His arrest (11:57).
13. They privately acknowledged their failure after His triumphant entry into Jerusalem (12:19).
14. They arranged with Judas Iscariot to arrest Jesus in secret (13:2,21–30)
15. They attempted to arrest Jesus in the garden but fell back in the presence of His self-revelation (18:6).
16. Jesus surrendered to the arresting party and was bound (18:8,12).
17. They formally condemned Him in a series of illegal trials (18:13,14,19–24).
18. They delivered Him to Pilate for execution (18:28–32).
19. They refused Pilate's attempts to release Him (18:38–40; 19:12).

| 20. They called for His crucifixion (19:6,7,15). |
| 21. They led Him away to be crucified (19:16). |
| 22. They crucified Him (19:18). |
| 23. They witnessed His dying (19:20). |
| 24. They sought to alter the title of the cross (19:21). |
| 25. They sought to have His legs broken (19:31). |

dren of God that were scattered abroad" (11:52)—a prediction of the coming Church.

> 53 Then from that day forth they took counsel together for to put him to death.
>
> 54 Jesus therefore walked no more openly among the Jews; but went thence unto a country near to the wilderness, into a city called Ephraim, and there continued with his disciples.
>
> 55 And the Jews' passover was nigh at hand: and many went out of the country up to Jerusalem before the passover, to purify themselves.
>
> 56 Then sought they for Jesus, and spake among themselves, as they stood in the temple. What think ye, that he will not come to the feast?
>
> 57 Now both the chief priests and the Pharisees had given a commandment, that, if any man knew where he were, he should shew it, that they might take him.

C. The Plot (11:53–57). The opposition of the Jews and their hatred toward Jesus had apparently been sporadic to this time. As they listened to Jesus, their anger would be incited and in a fit of rage they would try to arrest or stone Him. When Jesus was not in Jerusalem, He was ignored. Now it became their official policy "to put him to death" (11:53). Because of this action of the Sanhedrin, Jesus left the area, travelling to Ephraim, a village near the wilderness about twenty miles north of Jerusalem and five miles east of Bethel (11:54). He remained there with the disciples until He returned to Jerusalem for His final Passover.

As the Passover season approached, the Jews suspected Jesus might try to enter the city unnoticed to celebrate the feast. As the first pilgrims arrived, they began searching for

Him and issued requests for information leading to His arrest. Privately they may have believed Jesus would not attend this Passover. The question "What think ye, that he will not come to the feast?" (11:56) is asked anticipating a negative response. John uses the double negative *ou me*, emphasizing a degree of certainty on the part of those searching that Jesus would not come.

FOURTEEN

CHRIST—
THE CENTER
OF ATTRACTION
JOHN 12:1–50

This chapter in the Gospel of John marks the beginning of Christ's final week before the cross. According to Sir Robert Anderson's calculations in *The Coming Prince*, the sixty-ninth week of Daniel ended on the day Jesus rode into Jerusalem on a young ass (12:14). This gives the chapter a special significance in light of Jesus' claim that day that the "hour" had finally arrived (12:23). Within a week Jesus would complete His messianic work on a cross outside the city walls.

Among conservative Bible teachers, there is some dispute over the exact chronology of this last week. The traditional view is that Christ was crucified on Friday. Others hold the reconstructed view that Christ was crucified on Wednesday. The traditional is based first on the chronology of Mark (Mark 11:1–12,20; 14:1,30; 15:1,25,33; 16:1,2). Second, it is based on the Jewish custom of identifying any part of a day as the whole day, the three days Christ was in the grave were identified as late Friday afternoon through early Sunday morning. The third argument states Christ arose on "the third day," which would exclude the actual third night (Matthew 16:21; Mark 8:31; 9:31; 10:34; 1 Corinthians 15:4). Fourth, the fact that the Feast of the First Fruits (resurrection) followed the day after Passover (Leviticus 23:6–11). The fifth argument is from history—the early church celebrated Friday as the day Christ was crucified.

The reconstructed view argues the express "three days and three nights" (Matthew 12:40) must be interpreted more literally—six twelve-hour periods. To allow for this amount of time, they teach Christ was crucified on Wednesday. Next, they assume the Jews followed a revolving calendar and that the Passover came on a different day each year, not on the Sabbath before the Feast of First Fruits. Therefore, they say the Passover came on a Thursday the year Christ was crucified. Also, they assume Jesus would not have violated the Sabbath law in making a journey from Jericho to Bethany.

Even though some modern scholars teach Jesus was crucified on Wednesday, the overwhelming argument is for Friday. The reconstructed view has difficulties in that references in both John (12:1,12) and Mark (Mark 14:1; 15:1; 16:1) would assume the triumphant entry occurred on Sunday. They teach otherwise. Also the reconstructed view suggests Jesus spent three days and four nights in the tomb. Since Jesus was buried late Wednesday afternoon, he must have been raised, according to them, at 6:00 P.M. on Saturday. But the biblical record suggests the resurrection occurred early Sunday morning. Matthew 12:40 suggests that there must be three twenty-four hour days, including three days *and* three nights. This means Jesus was raised at the same hour which He was buried, which is not the case. In the Jewish mind, a part represents the whole, and part of the day represents day *and* night. Therefore, this chapter begins on Saturday, six days before the Passover (12:1).

In this chapter Christ is the center of attraction at the banquet (12:1–11), the triumphant entry (12:12–22), and at the cross (12:23–36). The rest of the chapter records the response of the people to Jesus (12:37–43) and the Lord's final public message in John (12:44–50). Throughout this gospel, John has emphasized the various reactions of groups and individuals to Christ. In studying this chapter, note the contrasting attitudes toward Christ represented in the various groups and individuals mentioned as shown in Chart 38.

Chart 38

THE CONTRASTING ATTITUDES TOWARD CHRIST	
1. Martha (12:2)	Tireless service
2. Lazarus (12:2)	Speechless adoration
3. Mary (12:3)	Sacrificial worship
4. Judas Iscariot (12:4–6)	Inbred selfishness
5. Chief priests (12:10,11)	Calculated craft
6. Pharisees (12:19)	Confounded frustration
7. Greeks (12:20)	Spiritual curiosity
8. Crowd (12:34)	Blinded questions
9. Some rulers (12:42)	Secret belief

I. THE BANQUET IN BETHANY (12:1–11)

Then Jesus six days before the passover came to Bethany, where Lazarus was which had been dead, whom he raised from the dead.

2 There they made him a supper; and Martha served: but Lazarus was one of them that sat at the table with him.

3 Then took Mary a pound of ointment of spikenard, very costly, and anointed the feet of Jesus, and wiped his feet with her hair; and the house was filled with the odour of the ointment.

4 Then saith one of his disciples, Judas Iscariot, Simon's son, which should betray him,

5 Why was not this ointment sold for three hundred pence, and given to the poor?

6 This he said, not that he cared for the poor; but because he was a thief, and had the bag, and bare what was put therein.

7 Then said Jesus, Let her alone; against the day of my burying hath she kept this.

8 For the poor always ye have with you; but me ye have not always.

9 Much people of the Jews therefore knew that he was there: and they came not for Jesus' sake only, but that they might see Lazarus also, whom he had raised from the dead.

10 But the chief priests consulted that they might put Lazarus also to death;

11 Because that by reason of him many of the Jews went away, and believed on Jesus.

According to John, Jesus arrived in Bethany "six days before the passover" (12:1), on the Sabbath before His death. Some commentators argue Jesus would never have made such a long journey from Jericho to Bethany on the Sabbath day as it was a violation of the Sabbath laws. It should be noted that the Lord was not as concerned with keeping these laws as were the Pharisees, so this objection is not a major issue. Also, if part of the journey had been made Friday so that He arrived late Friday (after sundown, therefore on the Sabbath), He could still have made the journey, arrived on the Sabbath, and violated neither the spirit nor letter of the Jewish law. Others seek to resolve this problem by suggesting Jesus made the journey the day before and stopped somewhere just outside of Bethany.

A more serious chronological problem in this passage relates to the time of this supper and the anointing. Most commentators argue this is the same banquet as was held in the home of Simon the leper (see Matthew 26:6–13; Mark 14:3–9). While there are many remarkable similarities between these accounts, John appears to date his account on the Sabbath six days prior to Passover (12:1), whereas in both Matthew and Mark the anointing appears to have occurred on the following Tuesday. Also, in John it is the feet of Jesus that are anointed (12:3), whereas in the synoptic gospels the anointing of His head is emphasized (Matthew 26:7; Mark 14:3). Commentators are divided on the resolution of the first problem. Hindson, Cheney, and Brown suggest the banquet and anointing were on the Sabbath, following John's chronology; however, Robertson, Taylor, and Templeton argue for the Tuesday anointing. Concerning the solution to the second problem, Godet suggests Mary broke the neck of the flask of ointment over the head of Jesus thus spilling some and anointing His head and then proceeding to anoint His feet.

Perhaps a more plausible harmony of these accounts is to view them as two very similar but different events—one on Saturday and the other occurring the following Tuesday. There were usually a number of banquets surrounding the Passover because of the festival season and because friends were present from all over (Deuteronomy 16:16). Two banquets and two anointings would be a natural interpretation in the light of the significance of both the anointing and the One anointed. When burying the dead, the Jews typically would wash and anoint the body of the dead, wrap it in grave clothes, and then anoint the grave clothes a second time. This certainly appears to be the intent in the burial of Christ. The first anointing is recorded by John as done by Nicodemus and Joseph of Arimathea (19:38–40), yet according to the synoptic gospels the women who witnessed this burial returned home to prepare spices and return to the tomb Sunday to finish what these men only began (Matthew 27:61; 28:1; Mark 15:47—16:3; Luke 23:55—24:1). It is interesting to note that in both type and fulfillment, the Gospel of John records only the first anointing, whereas the synoptic gospels record only the second. Also, as Jesus was the fulfillment of the type of the Passover lamb, it is interesting that the four days according to Jewish reckoning between the first and second anointing correspond with the four days between the initial selection and final approval of the lamb for slaughter (Exodus 12:3–6). It was following the second anointing that Judas Iscariot contacted the Sanhedrin and made arrangements to betray Jesus (Matthew 26:14–16; Mark 14:10,11).

The giving of a banquet was a common means of honoring a guest in the Near East. While this dinner was in Bethany, the exact location is not specifically identified. If, as Hindson suggests, Simon the leper was the father of Mary, Martha, and Lazarus, both anointings may have occurred in the same place. The context of John's gospel would seem to suggest the anointing occurred in the home of the latter three. Martha is portrayed as serving and again Mary is found at the feet of Jesus, the customary descriptions for both these women. Lazarus, presumably hosting this meal, sat at the table with Jesus.

At some point during the festivities Mary expressed her overflowing love for Jesus by anointing His feet. John describes this ointment with several particular words (12:3). The word *murou* (ointment) is a generic term for liquid perfume. A second word, *nardou* (spikenard) is probably derived from the Sanskrit term *nalada*, referring to a particular very fragrant plant grown primarily in India. Some lesser varieties of this plant also grew in and around Syria, but the third word, *pistikes*, meaning "faithful," "reliable," or "genuine," suggests this ointment was the real thing, probably imported from India. This ointment was used as a perfume for both bodies and wine. John identifies the measure of ointment used as a literal "pound" (12:3), about twelve ounces, and Judas Iscariot estimated its market value at three hundred denarii (12:5 RSV), a denarius being a day's wage for a common laborer. If his estimate was accurate, that would place the value of the ointment at twenty-five denarii per ounce, or (accounting for 1990 wage and price scale) about $800 per ounce. No wonder John uses the adjective *polutimou* (very costly), a compound word from *polus*, meaning "much," and *time*, meaning "value" (of great value or very valuable), to describe this ointment.

After anointing them, Mary began to wipe the feet of Jesus with her hair. Such an act would usually have been extremely humiliating for a woman of Mary's status and character. In the custom of the day, it was generally considered a disgrace for a woman to appear in public with her hair unbound. So ingrained was this into the thinking of the Jews that when Kamith, a mother who had seven sons who had served as high priests of the nation, was asked to what she owed such an honor, she responded, "To the fact that the beams of my chamber have never seen the hairs of my head." Perhaps hearing of a woman in Galilee who had similarly wiped Jesus' feet with her hair had prompted such a response from Mary (*see* Luke 7:36–50).

Writing of this event some sixty years later, it seemed as if John could still smell the fragrance of that very expensive perfume. He remembers the scent filling the room and notes, "The house was filled with the odour of the ointment" (12:3). Because the story of Mary's sacrificial expression of worship was so often repeated in the early preaching of the Gospel, some church fathers interpreted this statement allegorically meaning that the whole church was filled with the memory of Mary's act. Perhaps there is some truth in both the literal and mystical interpretations of this statement.

At the later anointing of Jesus, the disciples questioned the wisdom of spending so much money on such an act when the money could have been used for the relief of poverty, but here it was Judas Iscariot alone who voiced the concern (12:4,5; *see* Matthew 26:8; Mark 14:4). John is careful to point out that the only person Judas Iscariot was concerned about was himself. He identifies Judas as a thief, using the word *kleptes* which referred to those who steal according to a carefully devised plan. Probably the disciples first learned of his thievery after his death when an audit of their resources was conducted. John further hints at Judas's activities noting he bore what was put into the bag (12:6). The verb *ebastazen* means "to carry, bear, or lift" in the sense of taking away from. This idea would be best expressed with the English idiom "carried off" or the slang use of "lifting" in the sense of shoplifting. Judas was not only in control of the disciples' finances, he was stealing from them on the side.

Mary's actions were defended by Jesus when He said, "Against the day of my burying hath she kept this" (12:7). This expression is interpreted in two different ways by conservative commentators. First, He may have been pointing out that Mary had kept this ointment aside for His burial when she had prepared Lazarus's body for the grave. It appears only Mary had taken Christ's statements about the cross seriously. Perhaps she first learned of this truth as she sat at the feet of Jesus (Luke 10:39–42). A second interpretation of this expression assumes a paradox. Jesus taught that in losing one's life, one keeps it. Perhaps He meant Mary had "kept" this ointment by giving it in worship of Himself.

Jesus' statement, "For the poor always ye have with you" (12: 8), should not be used as a justification for ignoring the needs of the poor. What the Lord is here emphasizing is the need to establish correct priorities. It is not possible for one individual to do everything there is to do for God, yet everyone can do something. When someone attempts to do God's will, he may at the same time neglect other things that are also important. The faithful missionary in Africa might in this sense be accused of neglecting the spiritual needs of the lost in Asia. A missionary to the highlands could be accused of neglecting the·boat people. That is why it is so important for the Christian to walk in and be led by the Spirit. One aspect of discovering God's will is discerning between the permissive and the perfect will of God (*see* Romans 12:1,2; 1 Corinthians 6:12).

When the crowds in Jerusalem learned Jesus was in Bethany, they came to that place (12:9). Throughout this gospel

John uses the word *ochlos* (people) to identify the common people of the land, as distinguished from both the natives of Jerusalem and the leaders of the Jews. These were the worshipers who came to Jerusalem for Passover. John records that these came to Bethany not only to see Jesus but also to see the one He had raised from the dead. Lazarus's presence was such a credible evidence of Christ's power that large numbers began following Jesus because of him. This created a major problem for the chief priests in particular. Not only were they in danger of losing their place in the nation, the presence of Lazarus alive after he had been dead challenged one of their fundamental beliefs—that the dead are not raised. Both of these concerns probably had some part in influencing the decision that Lazarus also had to be put to death. If Lazarus was still alive when the synoptic gospels were written, this commitment of the Sadducees to kill him may have been the reason why they neglected to include the account of his resurrection. John, writing later, after the fall of Jerusalem and demise of the Sadducees as a religious sect, recorded many details that may not have been wise to include earlier.

II. THE RECEPTION IN JERUSALEM (12:12–22)

The next day, the Sunday before the Passover, Jesus entered the city of Jerusalem as a triumphant king accompanied by two groups of people. While one group accompanied Jesus as He rode into the city, the second came out of the city to meet Him with palm branches chanting part of the Great Hallel, a series of Hebrew hymns. Although this had been prophesied by the prophet Zechariah (Zechariah 9:9), the disciples failed to understand the significance of this until after Christ was glorified. As He arrived in the city that day, He was (1) received by the crowds, (2) rejected by the Pharisees, and (3) requested by the Gentiles.

> 12 On the next day much people that were come to the feast, when they heard that Jesus was coming to Jerusalem,
> 13 Took branches of palm trees, and went forth to meet him, and cried, Hosanna: Blessed is the King of Israel that cometh in the name of the Lord.

14 And Jesus, when he had found a young ass, sat thereon; as it is written,

15 Fear not, daughter of Sion: behold, thy King cometh, sitting on an ass's colt.

16 These things understood not his disciples at the first; but when Jesus was glorified, then remembered they that these things were written of him, and that they had done these things unto him.

17 The people therefore that was with him when he called Lazarus out of his grave, and raised him from the dead, bare record.

18 For this cause the people also met him, for that they heard that he had done this miracle.

A. Received by the Crowds (12:12–18). John describes the crowds coming out of the city with the expression *ho ochlos polus* (much people), meaning literally "the people much or in large numbers." This expression was also used idiomatically to refer to the common people, but while it may mean that here, the context of this passage suggests it also referred to large numbers (*see* 12:19). According to one census, there were 256,500 lambs slain in Jerusalem during one Passover season. If a minimum of ten people per lamb are assumed to be present celebrating the feast, that would put the estimated size of the crowd above 2.6 million people in the city during the feast season. While some of these may not have arrived in the city before Jesus arrived, the numbers involved would no doubt have given an observer an impression similar to that of the Pharisees, "Behold, the world is gone after him" (12:19).

The arrival of Jesus into Jerusalem is the picture of a triumphant king coming to the city in peace. Palms were a symbol of strength, beauty, joy, and salvation. Palms were cut for the triumphant entry of Simon and Judas Maccabaeus during an earlier era of Jewish history (*see* 1 Maccabees 13:51; 2 Maccabees 10:7). To carry palms was the mark of triumphant homage to a victor or king (*see* Revelation 7:9). Also, while today an ass's colt is not a sign of honor, these animals were highly regarded as noble beasts. If a king were coming to a city to make war, he rode his horse. If he was coming in peace, however, he would ride into the city on a donkey. It is interesting to note John in his writings twice records seeing Jesus riding. First, he enters Jerusalem on an ass offering peace and, second, on a white horse coming with His armies to make war (Revelation 19:11–16).

As the crowds met Jesus, they recited Psalms 118:25,26 (12:13) which was regarded by the rabbis as messianic in nature. The word *Hosanna* is transliterated from the Hebrew meaning "save now, I pray thee." This psalm was part of the Great Hallel composed of Psalms 115—118 used in the observance of the Passover meal and also part of the Egyptian Hallel composed of Psalms 113—118 sung at the feasts of Passover, Weeks (or Pentecost), Tabernacles, and Dedication. It was a psalm well known by the people. Ironically, this psalm was probably the last song Jesus and His disciples sang together at the Last Supper (*see* Matthew 26:30).

John makes no mention of the two disciples sent out to find the colt Jesus rode into Jerusalem but implies the search using the verb *heuron* (found) which suggests finding after searching (12:14). John, one of the two unnamed disciples involved in the search, neglects to mention it because of humility. Also, that event may not have fit in with John's purpose. He does note, however, the Scripture fulfilled in this action (Zechariah 9:9). As noted above, the idea of a king riding an ass was not as incompatible with his dignity as it might seem today (*see* Judges 10:4; 2 Samuel 17:23). As was typical in the experience of the disciples, they apparently did not realize they were seeing the fulfillment of messianic prophecy until some time later (12:16).

Of the four Passovers in this gospel, this one is unique in that it is the only one in which Jesus was so readily received. John attributes this to the witness of those who had seen Lazarus raised from the dead. The day before, news of Lazarus's resurrection attracted the people to Bethany. Now it was attracting masses to Christ. In light of the earlier accounts of the people's willingness to recognize Jesus as Messiah (*see* 6:15), it is likely most of the mob were still thinking of Him primarily as a political saviour from the bondage of Rome.

19 The Pharisees therefore said among themselves, Perceive ye how ye prevail nothing? behold, the world is gone after him.

B. Rejected by the Pharisees (12:19). An event such as the triumphant entry of Jesus into Jerusalem would hardly have gone unnoticed by the Jews. Earlier they had joined efforts with the Sadducees in an attempt to find Jesus among the pilgrims coming to the feast. But now that they found Him, there was another problem—"the world is gone after him" (12:19). This comment circulating among the Pharisees was a confession to themselves that they had failed to achieve their ends. Their use of hyperbole was not all that inaccurate. While they had only witnessed masses of Jews following Jesus, John uses their statement to introduce an incident indicating the interest of Gentiles.

20 And there were certain Greeks among them, that came up to worship at the feast:

21 The same came therefore to Philip, which was of Bethsaida of Galilee, and desired him, saying, Sir, we would see Jesus.

22 Philip cometh and telleth Andrew: and again Andrew and Philip tell Jesus.

C. Requested by the Greeks (12:20–22). The identity of the Greeks at the feast is difficult to ascertain. Some believe they were Hellenistic Jews; others believe they were Gentile proselytes to Judaism who wanted to meet Jesus; others believe they were Gentiles who lived in Galilee. As Jesus taught publicly in the temple area known as the Court of the Women, the first two groups could have contacted Him directly as He taught. The fact that they could not get to Jesus (if He were in the temple) suggests they were Gentile Greek tourists or philosophers who were curious to see the latest Jewish Messiah. A fourth view identifies them as monotheistic Greeks who had come to worship the God of Israel without accepting the yoke of the law and were known as God fearers. If this were the case, they may have wanted to thank Jesus personally for the cleansing of the temple, thus restoring their place of worship. A fifth view holds these Greeks represented an embassy from a Gentile nation. According to the early church father Eusebius, when the King of Edessa in Syria saw the obstinacy of the Jews in rejecting Jesus, he sent an embassy to Jesus to invite Him to come to his home promising Him a royal welcome. However, this view is questioned in light of the Jewish exclusiveness and Gentile hostility toward Jews in general.

The Greeks first approached Philip with their request, who then consulted with Andrew. Philip, the analytical disciple, might also have been the most open to outsiders, hence the Greeks came to him. He went to Andrew because Andrew is often characterized as bringing people to Jesus. To bring people to Jesus, he would know where Jesus was and how to get there. Andrew and Philip together told Jesus. Did Jesus meet the Greeks? His response was to give His disciples further insight concerning the results of the cross. The essence of His statement was that the cross must come before Gentiles can have access to Christ. Christ was the Lamb of God who would die for the world (1:29). Although the Scriptures are silent in this area, Jesus probably did meet with these Greeks as He passed through the Court of the Gentiles on His way out of the temple. Although most of Christ's ministry was limited to Israel, it is interesting to note the willingness of the Gentiles to recognize Him as king at both His birth and His death.

III. THE SHADOW OF THE CROSS (12:23–36)

23 And Jesus answered them, saying, The hour is come, that the Son of man should be glorified.

24 Verily, verily, I say unto you, Except a corn of wheat fall into the ground and die, it abideth alone: but if it die, it bringeth forth much fruit.

25 He that loveth his life shall lose it; and he that hateth his life in this world shall keep it unto life eternal.

26 If any man serve me, let him follow me; and where I am, there shall also my servant be: if any man serve me, him will my Father honour.

27 Now is my soul troubled; and what shall I say? Father, save me from this hour: but for this cause came I unto this hour.

28 Father, glorify thy name. Then came there a voice from heaven, saying, I have both glorified it, and will glorify it again.

29 The people therefore, that stood by, and heard it, said that it thundered; others said, An angel spake to him.

30 Jesus answered and said, This voice came not because of me, but for your sakes.

31 Now is the judgment of this world: now shall the
prince of this world be cast out.

32 And I, if I be lifted up from the earth, will draw all
men unto me.

33 This he said, signifying what death he should die.

34 The people answered him, We have heard out of the
law that Christ abideth for ever: and how sayest thou, The
Son of man must be lifted up? who is this Son of man?

35 Then Jesus said unto them, Yet a little while is the
light with you. Walk while ye have the light, lest darkness
come upon you: for he that walketh in darkness knoweth
not whither he goeth.

36 While ye have light, believe in the light, that ye may
be the children of light. These things spake Jesus, and
departed, and did hide himself from them.

Jesus began His final public discourse of this gospel noting, "The hour is come, that the Son of man should be glorified" (12:23). This was the hour of messianic expectation to
which John often referred—when Jesus would be glorified
on the cross. The "suffering glorification" was contradictory
to Jewish ideas. In the Book of Enoch, the Son of Man is
viewed as a powerful conqueror (see Daniel 7:13). The idea of
His glorification by means of crucifixion would have been
difficult for them to understand.

Those who say Jesus gave this sermon to the Greeks view
His statement concerning the cross as a particular judgment
on Hellenism. The essence of Greek society was the pursuit
of happiness in an effort to live the good life—pleasure without sacrifice. Jesus likened His death to the planting of a seed
from which there comes forth "much faith" in resurrection
(12:24). The same principle is also applied to discipleship
(12:25). Nature teaches us that the higher form of existence
can be obtained only by the extinction of the lower. This law
holds true in the spiritual world as well as in the natural
world. To those Greeks who sought to meet Him, He spoke
of the need to follow Him if they desired to serve Him.

As Jesus taught these principles, it was as though the
shadow of the cross passed over Him. John uses the verb
tetaraktai (troubled, 12:27), meaning "to be agitated or dis-

turbed," in describing Jesus' emotional response to the cross. The tense of this verb suggests Jesus' emphasis, "I have been troubled and continue to be troubled" (see 11:33; 13:21). If there was ever a moment of decision in the life of Christ, this was it. He asks, "What shall I say?" knowing the only two possibilities. First, He could request salvation from that hour. From the human perspective, the death of Christ was the greatest tragedy of human history. But, second, the cross was the purpose of His coming. From God's point of view, the death of Christ was the greatest victory of all history. Such was the contradiction of His death. There was both the bruising of the heel of Christ and the crushing of the head of Satan (see Genesis 3:15). If He had been saved from that hour, we should have been lost.

At that crisis moment, the voice of God was heard. This was the third time God broke the silence of heaven and spoke audibly to the people during the life of Christ. Each of these instances marked the beginning of a new phase of Jesus' ministry. Previously the Father stated He was well pleased with Jesus' life; now He is to be glorified in His death, and Jesus Himself will be glorified as well.

Some commentators attempt to minimize the significance of the voice of the Father, claiming it was nothing more than a clap of thunder which occurred at an opportune moment. The responses of those who heard the voice, however, deny this possibility. Just as there may be different interpretations of a statement made by a human voice, so there were different explanations of the divine voice. If a man makes a statement, a wild animal may hear a noise but the man's pet will understand his meaning. Only another man, however, may discern the thought. When the voice was heard from heaven,

Chart 39

THE VOICE OF THE FATHER IN THE GOSPELS	
1. At the baptism (Mark 1:11)	The beginning of Jesus' ministry
2. At the transfiguration (Mark 9:7)	The beginning of the last trip to Jerusalem
3. At the temple (John 12:28)	The beginning of the passion of Christ

the three responses represent three classes of people in the world. Some said it thundered—representing those who explain God's supernatural works in terms of natural phenomena. Others claimed it was the voice of an angel—representing those who explain God's supernatural working in terms of an impersonal mighty One. Jesus recognized the voice of His Father—representing those who are in proper relationship and fellowship with God.

Jesus interpreted the cross both in terms of the beginning of the end of Satan's dominion (12:31) and the beginning of His triumph over the hearts of men (12:32). The verb *ekblethesetai*, meaning "shall be cast out," is always used in the writings of John to describe being cast out of a holy place or society (*see* 2:15; 9:34,35; 10:4; 3 John 10; Revelation 11:2). With this verb John also uses the word *exo*, meaning "clean out." The casting of Satan out of heaven is equated here with the purging of heaven. Also, the cross is viewed as a magnet drawing men to Christ. The verb *helkuso* (draw, 12:32) means "to attract" and is preferred to another common verb for drawing meaning "to drag." (*See* the notes on 6:44 in chapter eight.) Jesus made the cross, which was considered horrid and scandalous, attractive to those who seek it. It is His atoning death, not His exemplary life, that attracts men to Himself.

Jesus, the actual Messiah, was radically different from what the Jewish mind expected. The Jews misunderstood the Scriptures and were perplexed, resulting in their doubting the claims of Jesus. It did not occur to them to doubt their interpretation of messianic prophecy. Therefore, when He spoke of the death of the Son of Man, they questioned how that could be harmonized with their law that taught that Christ will abide forever (*see* Psalms 89:4; 110:4; Isaiah 9:7; Ezekiel 37:25; Daniel 7:14). What they failed to realize was the nature of their limited revelation. There are many mysteries in the Old Testament which were revealed in the New Testament. Christ died and Christ will abide forever, the mystery of God. With the fuller revelation of Scripture, we realize both these statements are true and harmonious.

Jesus, knowing that His hearers could not understand His doctrine and realizing that most of the mystery doctrines were not yet to be revealed, returned to His revelation of Himself as light, to urge His listeners to walk in the light and believe the light. Sometimes there is a tendency not to believe what is not completely understood, but that is where faith is important. Our understanding of Christ will continue to grow when we are willing to simply obey what we know.

Following these remarks, Jesus hid Himself (12:36). Jesus had done this earlier when the Jews sought to stone Him (8:59). Perhaps the presence of the Pharisees (12:19) together with the growing evidence of the unbelief of the crowds signalled a new danger for Christ and the disciples. Because His ministry for that day was over, Jesus left. John ignores the public ministry of Christ during the remainder of that week and begins to summarize the results, not only of that sermon but of over three years of public ministry.

IV. THE RESPONSE OF THE PEOPLE (12:37–43)

37 But though he had done so many miracles before them, yet they believed not on him:

38 That the saying of Esaias the prophet might be fulfilled, which he spake, Lord, who hath believed our report? and to whom hath the arm of the Lord been revealed?

39 Therefore they could not believe, because that Esaias said again,

40 He hath blinded their eyes, and hardened their heart; that they should not see with their eyes, nor understand with their heart, and be converted, and I should heal them.

41 These things said Esaias, when he saw his glory, and spake of him.

42 Nevertheless among the chief rulers also many believed on him; but because of the Pharisees they did not confess him, lest they should be put out of the synagogue:

43 For they loved the praise of men more than the praise of God.

John characterizes the general response to our Lord's public ministry as unbelief. This unbelief existed despite the many miracles which should have been signs to them. Willfully rejecting the adequate testimony to the messiahship of Jesus, the Jews were punished by judicial blindness. Willing not to believe, they made themselves incapable of believing. Judicial blindness is a two-layer blindness. They themselves first hardened their hearts, and then God hardened them in response. This did not come as a surprise to Jesus. Isaiah had prophesied this blindness many years earlier (Isaiah 6:10; 53:1). The first citation from Isaiah about Jewish or judicial blindness is quoted five times in the New Testament (12:40; Matthew 13:13; Mark 4:12; Luke 8:10; Acts 28:26).

This general state of unbelief was not universal. John notes that some did believe, even some "among the chief rulers" (12:42), but they kept their discipleship secret for fear of the Pharisees. Nicodemus and Joseph of Arimathea were probably among this group of secret disciples. To publicly identify with Christ involved being expelled from the synagogue (*see* 9:22; 16:2), and these believers were apparently not yet ready to make that kind of an open commitment. The problem with secret discipleship is that it amounts to a contradiction in terms. Sooner or later, either their secrecy will destroy their discipleship or their discipleship will destroy their secrecy.

When Christ called people to salvation in the Gospels, He called them publicly so that they made a public profession of their faith. He stated that the Son of Man would be ashamed of those who were ashamed of Him (Mark 8:38). These rulers did not make a public confession of their decision for Christ because they were more concerned with what men would think than what God thought (12:43). In doing so, they fell into a common snare set for those who begin their new life in Christ (Proverbs 29:25).

V. THE JUDGMENT OF CHRIST (12:44–50)

44 Jesus cried, and said, He that believeth on me, believeth not on me, but on him that sent me.

45 And he that seeth me seeth him that sent me.

46 I am come a light into the world, that whosoever believeth on me should not abide in darkness.

47 And if any man hear my words, and believe not, I judge him not: for I came not to judge the world, but to save the world.

48 He that rejecteth me, and receiveth not my words, hath one that judgeth him: the word that I have spoken, the same shall judge him in the last day.

49 For I have not spoken of myself; but the Father which sent me, he gave me a commandment, what I should say, and what I should speak.

50 And I know that his commandment is life everlasting: whatsoever I speak therefore, even as the Father said unto me, so I speak.

As our Lord's public ministry seems to have ended earlier (12:36), this passage may have been a private statement of Christ, a part of His earlier teachings, or an epitome of His teachings. In any case it expressed the judgment of Christ regarding the attitude of men toward Him: for those who believe, life everlasting; for those who believe not, condemnation.

Some people mistakenly limit rejection of Christ only to those who in defiance blatantly refuse His gracious offer. John here uses the word *atheton* (rejecteth, 12:48) composed of an *alpha*, which negates the verb, and the verb *tithemi*, meaning "to lay down" or "to pay a price." In essence, all who do not pay the price of being a disciple of Christ, even those with good intentions but who put off their decision, are included in those who reject Christ. Those who reject Christ belong to a dangerous group, one which is already judged.

FIFTEEN

CHRIST—
THE SERVANT
JOHN 13:1–38

John 13—16 is generally referred to as "the Upper Room Discourse." Christ is with His disciples for the last time before the crucifixion. Here He expresses His love for them and explains something of what they will face in the future. As in no other place in Scripture, the reader sees into the heart of the Saviour. This discourse served as a preparation for Jesus' sacrificial death. He was not so much concerned about Himself as about His disciples, preparing them for their future ministry. In the upper room they were completely removed from the world, and before long the last foreign element in their midst, Judas Iscariot, would leave. According to Lewis Sperry Chafer, this sermon constitutes "the seed plot of all grace teaching."[33] Everything that is uniquely Christian, the doctrinal truth of the epistles, is taught here by Jesus in its embryonic form. In these chapters we find ourselves alone in intimate fellowship with Jesus as He shares His heart with those in whom He has invested His life.

I. THE WASHING OF THE DISCIPLES' FEET AND ITS MEANING (13:1–20)

Now before the feast of the passover, when Jesus knew that his hour was come that he should depart out of this world unto the Father, having loved his own which were in the world, he loved them unto the end.

2 And supper being ended, the devil having now put into the heart of Judas Iscariot, Simon's son, to betray him;

3 Jesus knowing that the Father had given all things into his hands, and that he was come from God, and went to God;

A. The Setting (13:1–3). The first verse serves as an introduction to the entire discourse, not just the washing of the disciples' feet. John begins with a reference to time—"before the feast of the passover" (13:1). Although Passover was technically on the fourteenth day of Nisan, John uses the term *pascha* nine times in the gospel, and on every occasion refers not only to the feast of the fourteenth but also the Feast of Unleavened Bread which followed. As Jesus was crucified on the preparation day prior to the Sabbath (Mark 15:42), this discourse must have occurred on the previous Thursday evening.

John again reminds the reader of Christ's knowledge approaching this final meeting. As Jesus prepared to wash His disciples' feet, there were seven significant facts of which He was fully aware. These are listed in Chart 40.

In spite of what He knew about Himself and about His disciples, He chose to continue loving them. John uses the verb *egapesen* (loved), indicating the discriminating love of choice and selection. It is a self-sacrificial love. John adds to this the expression *eis telos* (to the end), meaning "to the uttermost" (*see* 1 Thessalonians 2:16). Jesus' own approach-

Chart 40

WHAT DID JESUS KNOW?
1. He knew His hour had come.
2. He knew His glory was near.
3. He knew all things were in His hand.
4. He knew He had come from God.
5. He knew it was time to depart and go to God.
6. He knew He was both Master and Lord.
7. He knew He was about to be betrayed and denied.

ing crisis on the cross did not in any way hinder the nature or expression of His love for His own. The idea expressed in these words is, "He loved them with a perfect love."

The events of these chapters began sometime into the evening meal. Most commentators argue the correct text of verse two uses the present participle *ginomenou* (during supper) rather than the aorist participle *genomenou*. If this is correct, the second verse should read "during supper" rather than "supper being ended." This reading seems to be supported by the context. Jesus later "riseth from supper" (13:4) and later returns to the table with the meal still in progress (13:12,26). By the time this meal began, Judas had already committed himself to betray Christ.

> 4 He riseth from supper, and laid aside his garments; and took a towel, and girded himself.
> 5 After that he poureth water into a bason, and began to wash the disciples' feet, and to wipe them with the towel wherewith he was girded.

B. The Example (13:4,5). No Gospel writer gives a complete picture of what occurred that evening, but by comparing accounts we have a fairly full picture. Luke records a dispute among the disciples that evening over which of them deserved first place (Luke 22:24–27). This only served to emphasize the need on the part of the disciples to learn the important lesson Jesus was about to demonstrate with a towel and basin. The footwashing described here probably followed the institution of the Lord's Supper.

During the Passover supper, the head of the group would take the first of four cups, the cup of thanksgiving, and pass it around the room. This was probably the cup Jesus used in instituting the Lord's Supper (1 Corinthians 10:16). After this, it was customary for the host to rise and engage in a ceremonial washing of hands. Edersheim believes it was at this point Jesus rose to wash not His hands but the disciples' feet.[34]

When Jesus rose from supper, He removed His garment. John uses the word *himatia* here referring to His outer garment. Jesus was still wearing a tunic (*chiton*), which was the normal costume for a servant (Luke 22:27). He wrapped a linen towel about His waist not so much for modesty, but because He would have needed both hands to carry the basin of water. He then began systematically washing His disciples' feet.

Footwashing in the Near East was an important but undesirable task. Because of the sandal-type footwear worn and the dusty roads, most hosts would have a servant wash the feet of their guests. Although rabbis were highly regarded and their followers would do almost anything for them, they would not normally wash their feet. That was the duty of a slave, and even then, a slave of Jewish birth could not be forced to wash feet. Whether or not the disciples had washed their feet when they arrived is not stated. Some scholars claim they had, and that this washing was merely an object lesson. It is more likely, however, that they had not.

6 Then cometh he to Simon Peter: and Peter saith unto him, Lord, dost thou wash my feet?

7 Jesus answered and said unto him, What I do thou knowest not now; but thou shalt know hereafter.

8 Peter saith unto him, Thou shalt never wash my feet. Jesus answered him, If I wash thee not, thou hast no part with me.

9 Simon Peter saith unto him, Lord, not my feet only, but also my hands and my head.

10 Jesus saith to him, He that is washed needeth not save to wash his feet, but is clean every whit: and ye are clean, but not all.

11 For he knew who should betray him; therefore said he, Ye are not all clean.

C. The Resistance (13:6–11). The Scriptures do not identify the order in which the disciples' feet were washed, and several views have been suggested. Chrysostom argued Judas Iscariot was first. This tradition has been maintained by the Eastern church, and is reflected in passion plays where Judas is portrayed pushing his way through the disciples to be first. Origen argued Peter was the last to have his feet washed, but Augustine, on the basis that Peter was the chief of the apostles, and Edersheim, on the basis of the seating arrangement at the table, both argue that Peter was first. Augustine and Edersheim may be correct, because if Peter had not been first, he could never have kept quiet until Jesus got to him.

When Jesus came to wash Peter's feet, He immediately met with resistance. Jesus explained that Peter would not understand what He was doing until later (13:7). Normally, the use of this expression refers to a time after the cross (*see* 12:16; 16:12). Some commentators have suggested Jesus was symbolically portraying the humiliation of His death in the act of washing His disciples' feet. The verbs *tithesin* (laid aside, 13:4) and *elaben* (had taken, 13:12) are normally used by John in speaking of the cross—Jesus laying down His life and taking it up again (10:11,15,17,18; 13:37,38; 15:13; 1 John 3:16). Also, an appeal is sometimes made to Paul's explanation of the *kenosis* where Christ took "the form of a servant" and "humbled himself" (Philippians 2:7,8). The suggestion here is that Christ illustrated His setting aside of His divine glory to serve during the period of His incarnation and afterward took up His glory and sat in heavenly places.

Jesus further explained, "If I wash thee not, thou hast no part with me" (13:8). The expression "to have a part with" normally referred to the involvement of a subordinate in the riches and glory of the leader (*see* Joshua 22:24; 2 Samuel 20:1; 1 Kings 12:16). The verb *echeis* (thou hast) refers not only to the present but also to the future. Peter was quick to understand this meant more than not merely enjoying the fellowship of this meal with Christ. Jesus was referring to the union and communion of the believer with Himself, a common theme in this discourse. Peter's natural response in that context was to request Jesus also to wash his hands and head (13:9).

The practical application of Jesus' example of footwashing is implied in Jesus' response to Peter's request. The key is found in the use of two Greek synonyms, both of which are translated "wash." The first verb, *leloumenos*, refers to the practice of bathing the entire body (*see* Acts 9:37; 2 Peter 2:22). The second verb, *nipsasthai*, refers to the practice of cleaning a particular soiled area of the body, such as washing one's hands before eating (*see* Matthew 6:17). Although the word *katharos* normally refers to external cleanliness (*see* Matthew 23:26; 27:59), the context of John's usage of the term *wash* here and later in this discourse (15:3) seems to refer to spiritual purity rather than physical cleanliness. The person is pictured returning from the public bath to his home. His feet get dusty in the trip and need washing, but not his whole body again. The underlying principle is that those who have received the first bath of regeneration (Titus 3:5) do not need to be bathed again (saved again), although they may need to "wash" (be cleansed of sin) from time to time (see 1 John 1:9). The first washing deals with relationship, the second with fellowship. The first washing is once and for all (Hebrews 10:1–12), but daily sins need confession and cleansing (1 John 1:9). The blood cleanses eternally from guilt before the law, but the believer needs constant cleansing from the daily defilement of sins.

There was one in the apostolic group who had never been cleansed at all (13:11). The time was coming when his identity would be revealed. Lest his defection should prove too serious a blow to the faith of others, Jesus identified him before he committed the traitorous act, thereby proving His own foreknowledge and, at the same time, sustaining the faith of the true disciples (13:19).

> 12 So after he had washed their feet, and had taken his garments and was set down again, he said unto them, Know ye what I have done to you?
> 13 Ye call me Master and Lord: and ye say well; for so I am.
> 14 If I then, your Lord and Master, have washed your feet; ye also ought to wash one another's feet.
> 15 For I have given you an example, that ye should do as I have done to you.
> 16 Verily, verily, I say unto you, The servant is not greater than his lord; neither he that is sent greater than he that sent him.
> 17 If ye know these things, happy are ye if ye do them.
> 18 I speak not of you all; I know whom I have chosen: but that the scripture may be fulfilled, He that eateth bread with me hath lifted up his heel against me.
> 19 Now I tell you before it come, that, when it is come to pass, ye may believe that I am he.
> 20 Verily, verily, I say unto you, He that receiveth whomsoever I send receiveth me; and he that receiveth me receiveth him that sent me.

D. The Explanation (13:12–20). After washing the disciples' feet, He returned to the dinner table to explain the meaning of His actions. He began first by reminding them who He was, by referring to two specific titles by which disciples commonly referred to their rabbis, "Master" and "Lord." Here Christ acknowledged, "for so I am" (13:13). The title *didaskalos* (master) referred to the authoritative teaching of Christ. In calling Jesus *kurios* (Lord) the disciples were recognizing His authority over their entire lives. If this were true of Jesus, and He was willing to wash the disciples' feet, the conclusion is that the disciples "also ought to wash one another's feet" (13:14).

Some denominations take this commandment to refer to the institution of a third ordinance or sacrament of the church, like baptism and the Lord's Supper. Among those who practice footwashing are the Roman Catholics (the Pope annually washes the feet of selected poor persons on the Thursday prior to Good Friday), Dunkards, Freewill Baptists, and Moravians. Often, the way in which the rite of footwashing is practiced contradicts the very spirit of humility which Jesus here emphasizes. Also, those groups that practice footwashing err theologically in that they tend to explain its significance with reference to a defective view of sin or in association with a second work of grace.

There are several reasons for rejecting footwashing as an ordinance of the church. First, Jesus' use of the word *kathos* (as, 13:15) emphasizes His act as an example, not an ordinance. If He were instituting an ordinance, He would probably have used the term *ho* (that which), but this use does not occur in any manuscript. Second, there is no record in the epistles that God ever commanded footwashing as an ordinance. Third, there is no example in Scripture that the early church ever practiced footwashing as an ordinance of the church. It is difficult to demonstrate footwashing was ever practiced as an ordinance before the fourth century. Fourth, the custom of wearing sandals should be remembered. It was customary for a man's feet to be washed when he entered a home. This is the probable context to the reference to footwashing in 1 Timothy 5:10. Jesus was referring to humility and a custom, not to a church ordinance. Finally, the primary symbolic meaning behind the act of footwashing is humility (*see* Chart 41). The primary symbolism of baptism

Chart 41

WHY DID JESUS WASH THE DISCIPLES' FEET?
1. As an example of humility (13:14).
2. As a rebuke to pride (Luke 22:24–27).
3. As a picture of our daily cleansing (13:10).
4. As a warning to Judas Iscariot (13:18).
5. As a picture of His humiliation (Philippians 2:5–11).
6. As a reminder of His union and communion with the believer (13:8).

and the Lord's Supper is death, burial and resurrection—the heart of Christianity. The symbolism of the two ordinances have ultimate priority, while the symbolism of footwashing only has relative importance in comparison.

Of the seven double verilies spoken in this Upper Room Discourse, the two spoken in the context of this footwashing form something of a paradox (13:16,20). First, Jesus reminds the disciples the servant is not above his master. In the second, He likens receiving the servant to receiving the master. While the servant is not greater than the master, there is another sense in that he is not less than the master. To be effective in the service of his master, the Christian must have the attitude of the Master.

In preparing to reveal His betrayer, Jesus made reference to the fulfillment of Scripture, quoting Psalms 41:9 (13:18). In its original context, David was lamenting his betrayal by Ahithophel. The difference between David and Ahithophel and Jesus and Judas is reflected in the omission of the phrase, "in whom I trusted" (Psalms 41:9). Because of His omniscience, Jesus had never trusted Judas and had warned the disciples of his action a year earlier (6:70,71). The expression "lifted up his heel" is based on the metaphor of a sudden kick of a mule or a horse. In revealing His betrayal to His disciples, Jesus helped them understand He was the "I am" (*ego eimi*, 13:19).

II. THE SENDING OUT OF JUDAS ISCARIOT
(13:21-30)

21 When Jesus had thus said, he was troubled in spirit, and testified, and said, Verily, verily, I say unto you, that one of you shall betray me.

22 Then the disciples looked one on another, doubting of whom he spake.

23 Now there was leaning on Jesus' bosom one of his disciples, whom Jesus loved.

24 Simon Peter therefore beckoned to him, that he should ask who it should be of whom he spake.

25 He then lying on Jesus' breast saith unto him, Lord, who is it?

26 Jesus answered, He it is, to whom I shall give a sop, when I have dipped it. And when he had dipped the sop, he gave it to Judas Iscariot, the son of Simon.

27 And after the sop Satan entered into him. Then said Jesus unto him, That thou doest, do quickly.

28 Now no man at the table knew for what intent he spake this unto him.

29 For some of them thought, because Judas had the bag, that Jesus had said unto him, Buy those things that we have need of against the feast; or, that he should give something to the poor.

30 He then having received the sop went immediately out; and it was night.

After finishing the lesson on humility, John described Jesus as "troubled in spirit" (13:21). The verb here used to describe Jesus' emotional state is *etarachthe*, which is used in Scripture with the idea of stirring up, disturbing, troubling, or throwing into confusion. This phrase has been variously translated or paraphrased as "disquieted in spirit" (MOFFATT), "greatly moved" (GOODSPEED), "clearly in anguish of soul" (PHILLIPS), "inwardly disturbed" (BERKELEY), "in great anguish of spirit" (LB), "deeply troubled" (TEV), and "troubled in spirit" (NIV). Although Jesus was God, He was also man. This is one of the many evidences of His humanity in this gospel.

He made a statement that may have been one of the most difficult pronouncements for His disciples to accept. "Verily,

Chart 42

CHRIST'S APPEALS (WARNINGS) TO JUDAS
1. Announcement of His betrayer a year earlier (6:70,71).
2. Seating arrangement at the table—Judas in the place of honor.
3. Jesus washed his feet (13:5,12).
4. Announcement that one of the disciples was unclean (13:10,11).
5. Appeal to the Scriptures (13:18; Psalms 41:9).
6. Double verily concerning the betrayer (13:21).
7. Identification of Judas in the presence of Matthew (Matthew 26:25).
8. Handing of the sop to Judas—an act of honor (13:26).
9. Sending Judas out to accomplish his task—forcing his hand (13:27).
10. Addressing him as a friend in the garden (Matthew 26:50).

verily, I say unto you, that one of you shall betray me" (13:21). The difficulty the disciples had in accepting this statement is later underscored in that although both Matthew (*see* Matthew 26:25) and John (*see* 13:26) were present and saw that Jesus clearly identified Judas as the betrayer, John claims no one knew the intent of Judas as he left (13:28). The word *egno* refers to knowledge with perception. Some disciples had already figured out why Judas was sent out, but their conclusions were wrong (13:29).

Jesus made at least ten appeals to Judas Iscariot as shown in Chart 42. The Lord did this not as an attempt to preserve His own life but rather to save Judas from the end of his own plans. The fact that Judas rejected these appeals indicates the exercise of his free will to reject Christ. In light of the rejected appeals, it is little wonder Jesus said, "It had been good for that man if he had not been born" (Matthew 26:24).

A careful study of the conversation and action around the table gives some clue as to the seating arrangement at the table. The table was not thirty inches high with chairs, as is customary today in the West. Rather, the table was low, perhaps twelve inches from the floor. The guests sat on mats, or reclined on pillows. Their feet were stretched behind them. Because His feet were stretched away from the table and behind Him, it was easy for Mary to wash Jesus' feet in the previous feast. John, who was "leaning on Jesus' bosom" (13:23) must have been reclining to the right of Jesus, which was the place of affection. Five times in this gospel, John describes himself as the disciple whom Jesus loved (13:23; 19:26; 20:2; 21:7,20). For John to lean on Jesus' bosom would have been difficult or awkward if they were seated in chairs. But sitting on the floor and reclining on pillows, it was natural for John to lean over to Jesus, especially when he had something to say or ask, as when John questioned Jesus, "Lord, who is it?" (13:25). When Jesus told John it was the one to whom He gave the sop, the rest of the disciples probably did not have access to this private conversation.

Judas was probably sitting to the left of Jesus, which would have been reserved for the honored guest. As it was customary to recline at the table, this means that Jesus could have rested His head on Judas' bosom, as John had done with Jesus. Peter appears to have been sitting across the table where he could easily get John's attention (13:24). When Peter speaks to John, the word *neuei* (beckoned) literally means "to nod to someone as a signal," such as to motion or gesture. Luther used the word *winkte* (winked) in his German translation.[35]

John notes concerning the departure of Judas, "and it was night" (13:30). While referring to the physical darkness of that time, John seems also to be implying the spiritual state into which Judas had entered. As Hoskyns observes, "Having surrendered himself to the Prince of this world, Judas is banished from the light, and passes out into darkness under the judgment of God."[36] It is always night when a man turns from Christ to follow his own will.

III. THE BEGINNING OF THE UPPER ROOM DISCOURSE (13:31–38)

31 Therefore, when he was gone out, Jesus said, Now is the Son of man glorified, and God is glorified in him.
32 If God be glorified in him, God shall also glorify him in himself, and shall straightway glorify him.

> 33 Little children, yet a little while I am with you. Ye
> shall seek me: and as I said unto the Jews, Whither I go, ye
> cannot come; so now I say to you.

With the departure of Judas, the whole atmosphere of the
upper room changed. Jesus said, "Now is the Son of man
glorified" (13:31). Commenting on verses thirty-one and
thirty-two, Godet suggests, "These two verses are as if a cry
of relief which escapes from the heart of the withdrawing
traitor."[37] The departure of the faithless disciple initiated the
series of events that resulted in God being glorified in
Christ's redemptive work (13:31) and in Christ being glorified in His heavenly exaltation (17:4,5; see Philippians 2:9).
The verb *edoxasthe* (glorified) is an aorist passive verb pointing to the departure of Judas as the moment of the beginning
of the glory. Although Jesus was glorified in His death, hu-
manly speaking His fate was sealed with the departure of
Judas. He speaks in this context of His death as already past.
Unlike the other Gospels, John continually emphasizes the
word *glory*. Christ was glorified by being tabernacled in flesh
(1:14). The ultimate glory is when the flesh is delivered up.
   The new spirit of intimacy between Christ and His disciples is now reflected in Jesus' use of the term *teknia* (little
children, 13:33). This is the only occurrence of the term in the
Gospel of John, although it was commonly used by John in
his first epistle, the only other place the word occurs in Scripture. It is a diminutive of *tekna* (children under twelve years
of age), but when used by Christ or John it is regarded as a
word of tender affection. A survey of 1 John reveals the deep
impression this word made on the apostle. In one sense, the
Upper Room Discourse begins with this word, everything
else being introductory to the message Jesus would now
share with His disciples.

> 34 A new commandment I give unto you, That ye love
> one another; as I have loved you, that ye also love one
> another.
> 35 By this shall all men know that ye are my disciples, if
> ye have love one to another.

A. *The New Commandment* (13:34,35). Jesus left His disciples with what he called "a new commandment" (13:34).

Some have objected to calling this a new commandment on the basis that the command to love one's neighbor as oneself was well established long before this time (Leviticus 19:18). A closer look at Jesus' new commandment, however, reveals several significant differences between this commandment and that which was known as the royal law (James 2:8). These differences are outlined in Chart 43.

This new love for others in the family of God is one of the tests of being a Christian. Love is a mark by which a believer can be identified. The observations of both the enemies and leaders of the early church suggest the Christians of the first few centuries obeyed this commandment. Lucian mocked the Christians of his day observing, "Their Master has made them believe that they are all brethren."[38] Tertullian correctly observed, "The working of such love puts a brand upon us; for see, say the heathen, how they love one another."[39] The divine commentary on this new commandment is 1 John. According to Jerome, in his old age the apostle John often repeated "love one another," justifying his statement with the words, "Because it is the Lord's commandment; and if it be fulfilled it is enough."[40]

36 Simon Peter said unto him, Lord, whither goest thou? Jesus answered him, Whither I go, thou canst not follow me now; but thou shalt follow me afterwards.

37 Peter said unto him, Lord, why cannot I follow thee now? I will lay down my life for thy sake.

Chart 43

ROYAL LAW (JAMES 2:8)	NEW COMMANDMENT (JOHN 13:34)
Love neighbor.	Love one another (fellow believers).
Love as you love self.	Love as Christ loved you.
Love because of the covenant relationship of Israel and God.	Love because of the family relationship within the family of God.
Love is an expression of human effort in keeping the law.	Love as an expression of Christ loving others through us.

Chart 44

THE CHARACTERISTICS OF A DISCIPLE
1. He continues in Christ's words (8:31). 2. He expresses love toward other believers (13:34,35). 3. He produces spiritual fruit (15:7,8).

38 Jesus answered him, Wilt thou lay down thy life for my sake? Verily, verily, I say unto thee, The cock shall not crow, till thou hast denied me thrice.

B. Peter's Denial Predicted (13:36–38). The closing verses of this chapter record Christ's words in predicting Peter's denial. Having been just moments earlier rebuked for an impetuous statement (13:8,9), perhaps Peter should have known better than to make another dogmatic statement concerning what he would or would not do. Still Peter vowed he would lay down his life for Christ (13:37). According to Mark, Peter later argued, "Although all shall be offended, yet will not I" (Mark 14:29). Jesus responded to Peter's statement here by repeating it in the form of a question, "Wilt thou lay down thy life for my sake?" Then Jesus added, "The cock shall not crow, till thou hast denied me thrice" (13:38). Before the evening ended, this prophecy had been more than fulfilled (*see* notes on 18:15–27 in chapter twenty). Barclay distinguishes between the betrayal of Judas and the denials of Peter noting, ". . . The sin of Peter was the sin of a moment's weakness and a lifetime's regret."[41]

SIXTEEN

CHRIST—
THE COMING ONE
JOHN 14:1–31

Jesus used various methods to effectively teach His disciples the things of God. In this part of the Upper Room Discourse, He used the question-and-answer method, known today as the Socratic method of teaching. This method emphasizes learning readiness because it focuses on the need in the student. This chapter can best be outlined using four questions raised by His disciples as Christ sought to explain His new relationship with them after the cross.

The first of these questions is actually asked in the preceding chapter (13:36) but is not answered until here. As we study the Scriptures, we should remember that the chapters and verses were divided long after the text was written, and occasionally the last few verses of a previous chapter will aid in understanding a chapter's contents. At the end of chapter thirteen, Christ tells the disciples, "Whither I go, ye cannot come" (13:33). When Christ told them they would not be able to go with Him, they asked where He was going. It was Peter, the spokesman for the group who asked, "Whither goest thou?" (13:36).

I. WHERE ARE YOU GOING? (14:1–4)

Let not your heart be troubled: ye believe in God, believe also in me.

2 In my Father's house are many mansions: if it were not so, I would have told you. I go to prepare a place for you.

3 And if I go and prepare a place for you, I will come again, and receive you unto myself; that where I am, there ye may be also.

4 And whither I go ye know, and the way ye know.

The departure of Jesus from this world by means of a cross was bound to have a traumatic effect on His disciples. Despite His constant references to both the cross and the resurrection, the disciples had a sense of disillusionment even after the initial reports came in concerning the resurrection (*see* Luke 24:21). In the upper room the disciples were told that one of them would betray Him, their Master and Lord. Now the hour had come when Christ would be glorified on the cross, and even Peter would deny Christ at least three times in the remaining hours of the night. It was the most natural thing in the world for the disciples to be in a state of emotional turmoil. Jesus urged, "Let not your heart be troubled" (14:1).

The word *kardia* (heart) is not a reference to the physical organ of the circulatory system but rather to the seat of man's conscious life in its moral, intellectual, volitional, and emotional aspects. It was the Jewish way of expressing the idea of a man's personality, the real person inside. In this gospel emotions are ascribed to the soul, spirit, and heart (12:27; 13:21; 14:27). Jesus understood experientially what it meant to be troubled (13:21) and here provided a faith basis for His disciples to overcome their problems.

John uses the verb *pisteuete* (believe), which could be an indicative or imperative and could be translated as a fact (ye believe) or as a command (believe). Based on the nature of this discourse, most commentators agree that both occurrences of this verb should be understood as an imperative command. The disciples had previously expressed faith in God and the deity of Christ (6:68,69). Jesus knew a troubled heart would eat away at that faith, but faith would calm a troubled heart. His command then was "Keep on believing in God and keep on believing in Me also" (*see* 14:1). After years of practicing this principle, John came to understand that this approach to faith was key to overcoming, for the Christian life (*see* 1 John 5:4).

Jesus went on to explain that there are many "mansions" in His Father's house (14:2). The word *monai* (mansions) occurs only twice in the New Testament (14:2,23) and literally refers to a place to stay—a dwelling or abode. Although expositors over the years have vividly described the ivory palaces and luxurious mansions of the believer in heaven, that idea is not implied in this word. The English word *mansion* and its Latin counterpart *mansio* both originally referred to common dwelling places, only later being used as they are at present.

The great promise of this chapter is not so much the place Christ is preparing for us, but that He will return for us (14:3). This promise relates not to (1) His return to establish the kingdom; (2) His return for us at death; (3) His return to us with peace when we are troubled; but rather, (4) His bodily return for His own—the rapture. Four times in this chapter Jesus promises to "come again" (*see* Chart 46). Each of these promises reveals a different aspect of His new relationship with the disciples.

Jesus answers the first question, "Where are you going?" by telling His disciples He is going home to the Father. Out of this answer grows the second question, "We know not whither thou goest; and how can we know the way?" (14:5).

II. HOW CAN WE KNOW THE WAY? (14:5–7)

5 Thomas saith unto him, Lord, we know not whither thou goest; and how can we know the way?

6 Jesus saith unto him, I am the way, the truth, and the life: no man cometh unto the Father, but by me.

Chart 45

FOUR GREAT FACTS JESUS GAVE ABOUT HIS HOME (JOHN 14:2,3)
1. Many mansions
2. I am preparing a place
3. I will come again for you
4. You will be where I am

Chart 46

CHRIST—THE COMING ONE
1. At the rapture (14:3)
2. By His spiritual presence (14:18)
3. Through indwelling the believer (14:23)
4. During His postresurrection ministry (14:28)

7 If ye had known me, ye should have known my Father also: and from henceforth ye know him, and have seen him.

The second question, relating to the way to the Father's house, was asked by Thomas, who was the first disciple to confess willingness to die with Jesus (11:16) but the last to believe in the resurrection (20:24–28). Thomas has been dubbed "the doubter" for his questions. This is another question that gives insight into his character. This question occasioned one of the most memorable and significant revelations of Christ. Using the "I am" (*ego eimi*) formula again, Jesus responded, "I am the way, the truth, and the life" (14:6). Any one of these three claims would have been staggering.

The word *hodos* (way) literally means "road" or "highway." In the context of the language used here, Jesus is the highway to heaven. As He Himself explained, "No man cometh unto the Father, but by me" (14:6). The New Testament teaches the exclusiveness of Christ as the only Saviour. This was not only claimed by Christ but also acknowledged by His disciples (Acts 4:12). This description of Christ was so essential to the nature of New Testament Christianity that followers of Jesus were described as being "of the way" (Acts 9:2; 19:9,23; 22:4; 24:14,22).

Jesus had earlier identified Himself with both truth and life, which are divine attributes. Since Christ is the source of life and truth, He must also be the way to God Himself. He is so closely identified with the Father that we need not look away from Jesus to see the Father. His divine words and works are a token of this fact (14:7–11).

Jesus tells His disciples that He is the way to the Father and to mansions in heaven. The third question is raised by analytical Philip, not about the house, but about God the

Father. Actually it is not a question, but it implies that Jesus should respond to the inquiry, "Shew us the Father" (14:8).

III. SHOW US THE FATHER (14:8–21)

8 Philip saith unto him, Lord, shew us the Father, and it sufficeth us.

The third question in this discourse is really a request. Jesus' constant emphasis on the Father during His ministry and the deep intimacy that existed between the Father and the Son must have often aroused the curiosity of the disciples. In the unusually free atmosphere of the upper room, perhaps Philip now felt free to request something he had wanted for a long time—he wanted to see the Father.

Philip may have had a vision or theophany in mind when he requested that Jesus show them the Father. Jesus, however, explained that the disciples were witnesses to the revelation of the Father every day they were with Christ. He indicated there was a oneness between Himself and the Father, so much so that they could be identified as the same being. "He that hath seen me hath seen the Father" (14:9). Since Christ was so conscious of His identity with His Father, He expressed surprise when the disciples failed to recognize it by now. Philip demonstrated his lack of understanding when he asked for an experience inferior to those he had experienced daily in his contacts with God incarnate (1:18). Actually, Jesus gave three answers to his question, as there are at least three ways to see the Father.

9 Jesus saith unto him, Have I been so long time with you, and yet hast thou not known me, Philip? he that hath seen me hath seen the Father; and how sayest thou then, Shew us the Father?

10 Believest thou not that I am in the Father, and the Father in me? the words that I speak unto you I speak not of myself: but the Father that dwelleth in me, he doeth the works.

11 Believe me that I am in the Father, and the Father in me: or else believe me for the very works' sake.

A. The Father Revealed Through Jesus' Words and Works (14:9–11). Jesus' initial response to Philip serves as a reminder to every believer of the need to continue growing in his Christian experience. Philip was one of the earliest of the disciples and began with perhaps the fullest understanding of Christ (1:45). Still, after three and a half years of close association with Him, he failed to understand the nature of Jesus. John uses the verb *egnokas* (know, 14:9), meaning "come to know" or "perceive." Many older Christians will agree there are always new things to learn about Christ (Philippians 3:10–14). Therefore, there is also always a need to continue growing.

The mystery of the Trinity is one of the most difficult of all doctrines to understand, and over the years there have been many erroneous views taught. One of these known as modalism taught that the Father, Son, and Holy Spirit were merely different descriptions, or different modes, of the same person. Sometimes followers of this view are characterized as "Jesus only" Christians. Their position is based in part on their interpretation of verses ten and eleven. However, when Jesus spoke of the Father and Himself as one, He was referring to their spiritual union and not claiming they were the same person. The basic error of modalism is that it denies the eternity and distinctiveness of the three Persons of the Trinity. Earlier in this gospel, John has demonstrated that both the Father and the Son have existed from eternity past (1:1,2).

Jesus again appealed to His disciples to believe Him (14:11). The use of the plural verb *pisteuete* suggests the request made by Philip was also the desire of the other disciples. Jesus calls them to faith in His person and works (14:11). These men had seen Jesus and understood who He was better than any others. They should have believed because of who He was, but if not, they should have believed because they saw Jesus accomplish His messianic works (*see* Daniel 9:24).

> 12 Verily, verily, I say unto you, He that believeth on me, the works that I do shall he do also; and greater works than these shall he do; because I go unto my Father.
> 13 And whatsoever ye shall ask in my name, that will I do, that the Father may be glorified in the Son.

14 If ye shall ask any thing in my name, I will do it.
15 If ye love me, keep my commandments.

B. *The Father Revealed Through Believers (14:12–15)*.
Jesus promised that His disciples would accomplish greater
works than even Jesus had accomplished because He was
going to His Father. Some Christians erroneously apply this
verse to contemporary miracle workers, claiming Jesus promised Christians would do greater miracles than Christ. The
word *erga* (works) when used in this gospel, however, never
refers to miracles unless those miracles were related to
Christ's completing His messianic work. Those who tend to
apply this verse to signs and wonders demonstrate an inconsistency in practicing healings but not resurrections.

These *meizona* (greater) works are not thought of here as
necessarily greater in quality but rather greater in quantity.
Christ ultimately completed His messianic works on the
cross. While Christ provided salvation not only for the nation but also the whole world, comparatively few individuals
were personally brought to faith by Christ during His earthly
ministry. These greater works refer to the conversion of great
numbers of sinners, the greatest work in all the world.

The Father is revealed through believers not only in these
greater works, but also through a new privilege in prayer.
Jesus urged His disciples to "ask in my name" (14:13). Praying in the name of Jesus means more than concluding with
the benediction, "in Jesus' name, Amen." The name of an
individual identifies his person and credibility. When we
pray in Jesus' name, we are asking on the basis of His credibility, much as a woman making a credit card purchase with
her husband's bank card. The sale is made on the basis of her
husband's credibility as expressed in his credit rating. While
most credit cards have fixed spending limits, when we pray
in Jesus' name, there is no limit for what we may ask. Twice
Christ promises concerning such prayer, "I will do it"
(14:13,14).

The true disciple will not only trust God for great answers
to prayer, he will also demonstrate his love for Christ by
keeping His commandments (14:15). The verb *teresete* (keep)
is a future active verb. The meaning here is that as long as we
love Jesus, we will be keeping His commandments. The em-

phasis is on a love that expresses itself in obedience, rather than obedience motivated by love.

16 And I will pray the Father, and he shall give you another Comforter, that he may abide with you for ever;

17 Even the Spirit of truth; whom the world cannot receive, because it seeth him not, neither knoweth him: but ye know him; for he dwelleth with you, and shall be in you.

18 I will not leave you comfortless: I will come to you.

19 Yet a little while, and the world seeth me no more; but ye see me: because I live, ye shall live also.

20 At that day ye shall know that I am in my Father, and ye in me, and I in you.

21 He that hath my commandments, and keepeth them, he it is that loveth me: and he that loveth me shall be loved of my Father, and I will love him, and will manifest myself to him.

C. *The Father Revealed Through the Indwelling Spirit (14:16–21).* In the context of Jesus promising us answers to prayer, He reveals the greatest thing for which we may ask— the presence and power of the Holy Spirit in our lives. Jesus now promises the disciples He will ask the Father to send them a Comforter (14:16). Though the Holy Spirit was already dwelling with the disciples by His omnipresence, He was to come to them in a special sense (14:17) and would fulfill a special ministry as "another Comforter" (14:16). The word *parakleton* (comforter) literally means "one summoned to the side of another to help." It was used of the advocate or lawyer who pleaded his client's case, the tutor who instructed his pupils, the doctor who comes to the bedside of a sick patient to treat the disease, a friend pleading the cause of another, or one who comes to encourage and comfort. John uses this term four times as a title of the Holy Spirit (14:16,26; 15:26; 16:7) and once as a title of Christ (1 John 2:1). His use of the word *allon* (another, 14:16) rather than the more usual *heteron* (another of a different kind) is significant in that *allon* refers to another of the same kind. The Comforter who is the Holy Spirit (14:26), like the Son is one with the Father in nature, though all are different personalities.

Another title of the Holy Spirit used by Jesus is "Spirit of truth" (14:17). The Spirit who is and has the truth of God is portrayed in Scripture as revealing truth, testifying to the truth, and defending the truth. John later contrasts Him (the Spirit of Truth) with the spirit of error (1 John 4:6). When Ananias and Sapphira attempted to lie to the Spirit of Truth, they paid with their lives (Acts 5:1–11). This title of the Holy Spirit is foundational to the teaching or illuminating ministry of the Holy Spirit.

Jesus described the Holy Spirit in two relationships with His disciples. First, He noted the Holy Spirit was "with you," and then added, "and shall be in you" (14:17). The expression *par humin* (with you) means "by your side" or "at home with you." In the Old Testament, the Holy Spirit is generally (but not exclusively) described as *with* God's people. In the New Testament the Holy Spirit is *in* believers.

Jesus promised, "I will not leave you comfortless" (14:18). John here uses the word *orphanous* (comfortless), a word used only one other time in the New Testament (James 1:27). Literally, He is promising not to leave us fatherless orphans. The Everlasting Father (Isaiah 9:6) promises to come again.

When Christ speaks in this discourse of a future coming, sometimes He means His spiritual coming at Pentecost (14:18), and sometimes His second advent (14:3). Though physically and visibly He would leave His disciples and go to the Father, yet spiritually and invisibly He would come to them and remain with them (14:23). He leaves and yet remains; He is with us always, yet comes again. Divine paradox!

Jesus began to explain the mystery of the union of Christ and the believer. He spoke of "ye in me, and I in you" (14:20). This is the phenomenon Jesus later attempted to explain with the metaphor of the vine and the branches (15:1–7). He told His disciples He would manifest Himself to

Chart 47

HOW CAN THE HOLY SPIRIT REVEAL THE FATHER TO US?
1. By indwelling us (14:16)   2. Through the Word of God (14:21)

them and not to the world. This manifestation was more than a mental exercise, remembering what Christ looked like, which would have involved the more common verb *deloo*. John here uses *emphaniso* (manifest), meaning "a manifestation of sight." Concerning this word Westcott notes, "It conveys more than the disclosing of an undiscovered presence, or the manifesting of a hidden one."[42] With the eye of faith the disciples would see Christ manifested to them but not to the world.

The disciples were told Christ would manifest Himself to them (14:20), yet He told them "the world cannot receive" (14:17). This knowledge raises a question, "How is it that thou wilt manifest thyself to us, and not unto the world?" (14:22).

IV. HOW CAN YOU MANIFEST YOURSELF TO US AND NOT TO THE WORLD? (14:22–31)

22 Judas saith unto him, not Iscariot, Lord, how is it that thou wilt manifest thyself unto us, and not unto the world?

The fourth question in this discourse was asked by Judas also called Thaddaeus and Lebbaeus. It was the final question asked of Jesus by any disciple prior to the cross. This Judas was not Judas Iscariot, who had already left to make final preparations for the betrayal of Christ. Apart from the listing of the apostles, this is the only mention of this Judas in the New Testament. What a contrast in these two Judases. At that moment Judas Iscariot was receiving thirty pieces of silver, the price of blood, for the betrayal of his Master. The other Judas was at the same time in intimate fellowship with Jesus, asking about the nature of intimate Christianity.

Jesus' statement concerning a manifestation to the disci-

Chart 48

DOUBLE TRANSFERENCE (JOHN 14:20; 15:4; 1 JOHN 3:24)	
I am in Christ!	Ephesians 2:6
Christ is in me!	Galatians 2:20

ples but not to the world must have caught Judas, and perhaps the other disciples, off guard. The expression *ti gegonen hoti* (how is it that, 14:22) suggests an expression of surprise. In essence he was asking, "What has happened to cause this change in plans?" Even forty days later, some disciples were hoping for an immediate setting up of the Davidic kingdom (Acts 1:6). Jesus' use of the verb *emphaniso* may have caused Judas to think the manifestation of the Son to the world in judgment may have been cancelled (*see* 5:27–30). Jesus answered Judas's question noting the three ways Christ is manifested to the believer and not to the world.

> 23 Jesus answered and said unto him, If a man love me, he will keep my words: and my Father will love him, and we will come unto him, and make our abode with him.

A. By Fellowship (14:23). Jesus explained that if the disciples would continue loving Him and keeping His words, both He and the Father would indwell them (14:23). Thus the believer is not only the temple of the Holy Spirit, but also the dwelling place of the Father and Son. It is interesting to note Jesus used the same word *monen* (mansion, 14:2) describing both the dwelling place He is preparing in heaven and the dwelling place the believer prepares for the Father and Son on earth.

> 24 He that loveth me not keepeth not my sayings: and the word which ye hear is not mine, but the Father's which sent me.
> 25 These things have I spoken unto you, being *yet* present with you.
> 26 But the Comforter, which is the Holy Ghost, whom the Father will send in my name, he shall teach you all things, and bring all things to your remembrance, whatsoever I have said unto you.

B. By the Indwelling Spirit (14:24–26). Again Jesus speaks of the ministry of the Holy Spirit in the lives of the disciples, this time emphasizing His role as their teacher, reminding them of all that Christ had taught. In the promise of the Holy Spirit's teaching ministry to the apostles, we have what Scofield calls "Christ's pre-authentication of the New Testament."[43] According to Alford, "It is the fulfillment of this promise to the apostles, that their sufficiency as witnesses of all that the Lord did and taught, and consequently the authenticity of the Gospel narrative, is grounded."[44]

> 27 Peace I leave with you, my peace I give unto you: not as the world giveth, give I unto you. Let not your heart be troubled, neither let it be afraid.
>
> 28 Ye have heard how I said unto you, I go away, and come again unto you. If ye loved me, ye would rejoice, because I said, I go unto the Father: for my Father is greater than I.
>
> 29 And now I have told you before it come to pass, that, when it is come to pass, ye might believe.
>
> 30 Hereafter I will not talk much with you: for the prince of this world cometh, and hath nothing in me.
>
> 31 But that the world may know that I love the Father, and as the Father gave me commandment, even so I do. Arise, let us go hence.

C. *By Inner Peace* (14:27–31). The third way Christ manifests Himself to the believer is through the unique peace He gives. The word used here is not the usual *shalom* (peace) but rather *eirenen*—the spiritual peace only Christ can give (14:27; 16:33) and which can be offered as a result of the incarnation (*see* Luke 2:14). This peace includes both peace with God (Romans 5:1) and the peace of God (Philippians 4:7).

Our Lord's going away would be a gain to Himself as well as to His disciples. It was a gain to Christ because it would involve a restoration of the divine glory which He surrendered temporarily when He became a man (Philippians 2:9–11). It was a gain to His disciples because it would mean the completion of His work on their behalf. In this way we understand the statement, "My Father is greater than I" (14:28)—not greater in nature or dignity, but greater in task. He is the Father, and Christ is the Son; He sends, and Christ is sent; and, especially at the time the words were spoken, He was God in heaven, while Christ was God-man on earth. Remember, the Trinity is the Father, Son, and Holy Spirit; equal in nature, separate in person, and subservient in duties.

This chapter concludes with the words of Jesus, "Arise, let us go hence" (14:31). Some commentators view these words as an indication that the disciples now left the upper room and began making their way through the streets of Jerusalem toward Gethsemane. Other commentators note the word *ag-omen* was used of armies going into battle to meet death (*see* 11:7,16). They argue Jesus used this word in a motivational way much as a missionary speaker might share the account of a martyrdom to motivate others to missionary service. Still a third view is that Jesus meant to leave the upper room at this time, but the disciples lingered at the table so the discourse continued. Chapters thirteen through sixteen should be viewed as a single discourse, even if it might have been taught in different places. After the conclusion of Christ's high priestly prayer, it is certain the disciples crossed into the garden (18:1).

SEVENTEEN

CHRIST—THE VINE
JOHN 15:1—16:4

The foundation of the Christian life is the believer's union and communion with Christ, which is the central truth of the metaphor of the vine and the branches. One cannot read the New Testament without realizing the tremendous importance that early Christians placed on the fact that they were in Christ and Christ was in them. The close identification of the believer with Christ is variously described in the epistles, but never so vividly as when Christ illustrated His relationship to believers by the relationship of the vine and its branches. When one examines a natural vine that is never trimmed, it is difficult to determine where the vine ends and the branches begin. So it should be difficult to tell when a believer is inspired by Christ or by self. Just as the total bush is the vine, so the total life of the believer should be inspired by Christ. The relationship between the believer and his Lord is so intertwined it is almost impossible to speak of one without the other.

The message of the vine in this chapter sets forth the vital and intimate union of the believer with Christ. Spiritual life and fruitfulness have their source in Him and are a token of the reality of that union. One might well ask what prompted Christ to use the analogy of the vine at this point. Several possibilities have been suggested. First, the fruit of the vine was in the cup used at the Passover meal, and Christ referred to it in the communion cup (Matthew 26:27). If this discussion began in the upper room, Jesus may have been drawing attention to the cup. Second, if Jesus were walking through the city, He may have seen the vines growing upon the walls. Third, it may have been possible to look out from the city and see the fires burning in the vineyards. The dead vines that were trimmed in the winter were burned during the cold spring nights to keep the frost from killing new growth. The sight of these fires could have prompted verse six. Fourth, some believe these words were spoken in or near the temple area in sight of the golden vine on the temple's bronze gate. Still others suggest the imagery of Israel as a vine in the Old Testament (Isaiah 5:1–7) was the idea that inspired these words and nothing physical in particular was involved.

The account of the vine and its branches is an analogy of the disciples' relationship with Christ (15:1–11). Jesus then instructed them concerning their relationship with one another (15:12–17). Finally, this chapter includes Jesus' words concerning the believer's relationship with the world (15:18—16:4).

I. THEIR RELATIONSHIP WITH CHRIST—A LIFE OF UNION AND COMMUNION (15:1–11)

I am the true vine, and my Father is the husbandman.

2 Every branch in me that beareth not fruit he taketh away: and every branch that beareth fruit, he purgeth it, that it may bring forth more fruit.

3 Now ye are clean through the word which I have spoken unto you.

4 Abide in me, and I in you. As the branch cannot bear fruit of itself, except it abide in the vine; no more can ye, except ye abide in me.

5 I am the vine, ye are the branches: He that abideth in me, and I in him, the same bringeth forth much fruit: for without me ye can do nothing.

6 If a man abide not in me, he is cast forth as a branch, and is withered; and men gather them, and cast them into the fire, and they are burned.

7 If ye abide in me, and my words abide in you, ye shall ask what ye will, and it shall be done unto you.

8 Herein is my Father glorified, that ye bear much fruit; so shall ye be my disciples.

9 As the Father hath loved me, so have I loved you: continue ye in my love.

10 If ye keep my commandments, ye shall abide in my love; even as I have kept my Father's commandments, and abide in his love.

11 These things have I spoken unto you, that my joy might remain in you, and that your joy might be full.

This chapter begins with the seventh "I am" spoken by Christ in this gospel, "I am the true vine." The grapevine was a common sight in Israel and vineyards so plenteous that the vine became the national symbol of Israel. A golden vine had been engraved on the temple gate and had been used as a symbol on Maccabean coins. Throughout the Old Testament, God had used the image of a vine or vineyard to describe the nation of Israel (Psalms 80:8; Isaiah 5:1–7; Jeremiah 2:21; Ezekiel 15; 19:10; Hosea 10:1). When Jesus called Himself "the true vine" (15:1), He was drawing on an obvious parallel. The word *alethine* (true) is repeatedly used by Jesus in this gospel to distinguish His reality and genuineness from that which is false and unreal. His use of *true* implies there is a false vine. Although God often talked of Israel as a vine in the Old Testament, in contrast Jesus is the real or genuine vine. A vine that is cared for and carefully pruned by the husbandman will consistently bear fruit. Israel was never a vine like this.

Jesus noted, "Every branch in me that beareth not fruit he taketh away" (15:2). Theologians debate the unfruitful branch which is apparently cast away. First, some say it represents the true believer apostasizing. Arminians make reference to this passage to claim that the Christian who does not abide in Christ is taken from Him and his salvation is lost. Second, those who believe in eternal security interpret this as a mere professor of Christianity who was never truly united to Christ. Third, others interpret this passage with a primary emphasis on fruit bearing, not salvation. The fourth and probable solution is seen in the word *airei* (taketh away).

This word is the root for *resurrection* (to take up). The focus here is fruitbearing; the vinedresser does not cut away a vine because it has no fruit but gently lifts it up to the sun so it has an opportunity to bear fruit. The first step of Christ is not judgment but encouragement.

A generally accepted view is that the branches in this illustration represent all Christians. Simply, fruitfulness is the result of being a Christian. Note in Chart 49 the four levels of fruit bearing evident in the vine.

It is interesting to note that the Husbandman (the Father) cuts both the branches that produce and do not produce fruit, but with a different purpose for each (*see* 15:2,6). The barren branches are removed so as to not affect the health of the rest of the vine (15:6), but the fruit-bearing branches are also pruned. The word *karpon* (fruit) is singular, implying one's character as in the fruit (singular) of the Spirit (Galatians 5:22). However, the abiding life will attract, convict, and lead to conversion of others. Hence, He also is implying soul winning.

John uses the verb *kathairei* (purgeth) literally meaning "he cleans." The present active indicative means He is continually at work. Vinedressers often prune severely the branches that produce fruit, resulting in a more abundant harvest in the next season. The purpose clause with *hina* and the present active subjunctive of *phero* means "that it may keep on bearing more and more fruit." Again, Jesus reminds His disciples "ye are clean through the word which I have spoken unto you" (15:3). This cleansing is the first condition of a fruitful life; here it is potentially cleansed as in 13:10 (Westcott).

The first condition of the abiding life is cleansing; the second condition of a fruitful life is abiding in Christ. By continually abiding in Christ, the one who has been pruned to

Chart 49

THE PROGRESSION OF FRUIT BEARING
1. No fruit (15:2)
2. Fruit (15:2)
3. More fruit (15:2)
4. Much fruit (15:5)

bring forth more fruit will bring forth much fruit (15:5). Apart from its attachment to the vine, the branch is totally useless. Not only is it incapable of producing fruit, the wood of the vine is of such an inferior quality, it was not even permitted to be burned on the temple altar.

The verb *meinate* (abide) essentially means "remain" or "stay." The secret of fruitfulness is found in abiding (or remaining) in the True Vine, and not by the effort of the branches trying to produce grapes. John captured the secret of abiding in his later epistle, "And he that keepeth his commandments dwelleth [abideth] in him, and he in him. And hereby we know that he abideth in us, by the Spirit which he hath given us" (1 John 3:24). Abiding cannot come without obedience. Notice again the double transference of the believer in Christ and Christ in the believer (*see* 14:20).

The challenge of verse six is interpreted at least four ways. First, the one who does not bear fruit is to lose his salvation because he is "cast forth" into the judgment of hell. Second, some see the third class condition of *if* and view it as a warning against presuming to be saved. This is the professing Christian who does not possess eternal life; he is "cast forth" into judgment. A third interpretation is that this is a believer who loses his reward. The verse begins with "a man" (singular) but ends with "they are burned" (plural), which is a reference to his rewards being lost (1 Corinthians 3:12–15). The fire is not a reference to hell, where the unsaved are punished, but to the fire of the bema judgment where Christians are judged (Romans 14:10; 2 Corinthians 5:10). The fourth interpretation implies the premature death of the believer who does not abide in Christ. "Men gather them" is a reference to the angels who take the souls of believers at death to God; the fire is a reference to the bema judgment as presented in the third interpretation. This truth is illustrated by Ananias and Sapphira (Acts 5:1–11), those who sleep because of sin at the Lord's table (1 Corinthians 11:28–30), and the sin unto death (1 John 5:16).

Jesus gives an astounding promise and command. The words *thelethe aitesasthe* (ask what ye will, 15:7) are aorist middle imperative and have the force of a direct order—"ask," not "if you ask." However, there is a condition to getting answers to prayer. The believer must be in harmony and intimate communion with Christ by abiding in His words.

The word *herein* (15:8) points backward to union with Christ and forward to fruit bearing. Abiding in Christ and producing fruit is not an end in itself but rather to the end of bringing glory to the Father. Jesus said the Father is glorified when we abide and produce fruit. Further, in producing much fruit, we are becoming Christ's disciples. The verb *genesesthe* (so shall ye be, 15:8) is in the future tense, emphasizing that true discipleship is a growing experience. Some older Christians enter a kind of semiretirement in their service for God. The result of such inaction is twofold. First, they stop glorifying the Father because they no longer produce fruit. Also, they will fall short of a level of discipleship they could have attained had they been more fruitful. In contrast, others continue to abide in Christ and "they shall still bring forth fruit in old age" (Psalms 92:14).

The third condition of a fruitful life is obedience (15:10). As emphasized previously in this discourse (14:15), there is an indissoluble bond linking our love for Christ and our subsequent willingness to obey and keep His commandments. The result of this obedience and meeting the conditions of the fruitful life is a sense of personal fulfillment. The verb *plerothei* (fulfilled) is used by John here to describe the progressive fulfillment of the disciples' joy (15:11). Their joy comes from inner fulfillment of fruit bearing and is different from and in addition to the joy of Christ which He gives His disciples (16:22).

The metaphor of the vine and the branches does not adequately express the full relationship between Christians and their Lord. The vine and branches are not human—so there can be no affection between them. Believers, on the other hand, are objects of Christ's love. Notice in Chart 50 the gifts of Christ to those who abide in Him.

II. THEIR RELATIONSHIP WITH ONE ANOTHER—A LIFE OF LOVE AND SERVICE (15:12–17)

12 This is my commandment, That ye love one another, as I have loved you.

Chart 50

CHRIST'S GIFTS TO HIS DISCIPLES
1. My love (15:9) 2. My commandments (15:10) 3. My joy (15:11)

13 Greater love hath no man than this, that a man lay down his life for his friends.

14 Ye are my friends, if ye do whatsoever I command you.

15 Henceforth I call you not servants; for the servant knoweth not what his lord doeth; but I have called you friends; for all things that I have heard of my Father I have made known unto you.

16 Ye have not chosen me, but I have chosen you, and ordained you, that ye should go and bring forth fruit, and that your fruit should remain: that whatsoever ye shall ask of the Father in my name, he may give it you.

17 These things I command you, that ye love one another.

If believers are in fellowship with one another as they are with Christ, then love surely ought to characterize all their mutual relationships (15:12,17). They constitute a company of friends, Jesus being the greatest Friend of all and proving His friendship by dying for them. Such a friendship with Jesus includes great privileges in service and in prayer. The example of Christ as our Friend serves to demonstrate the ideal nature of our relationship with other believers.

The expression of Christ's friendship was the cross, a display of sacrificial love (15:13). "If God so loved us, we ought also to love one another" (1 John 4:11). Further, the effect of Christ's friendship was a change in our relationship. Jesus no longer calls us servants but friends (15:15). The word *doulous* (servants) referred literally to slaves and was a title applied to the servants of God in both testaments (Deuteronomy 34:5; Joshua 24:29; Psalms 89:20; Titus 1:1; James 1:1). In the Old Testament, only Abraham was identified as a friend of God (2 Chronicles 20:7; Isaiah 41:8; James 2:23). But now every believer can enter this unique relationship and experience intimate communion with God.

Jesus reminded His disciples that He had chosen them and ordained them. The word *etheka* (ordained) does not refer to an ecclesiastical service, but rather means "to set," "to put," or "to place," and therefore has the idea of appointing someone to service rather than giving a religious position. While we are friends and not servants, there is still a service to which we are appointed with the end of producing fruit. Note the various kinds of fruit listed in Chart 51 that ought to be produced in the life and ministry of the believer.

III. THEIR RELATIONSHIP WITH THE WORLD—A LIFE OF ENMITY AND PERSECUTION (15:18—16:4)

The disciples of Jesus were warned not to expect any better treatment from the world than the treatment which was af-

Chart 51

"THAT BRINGETH FORTH HIS FRUIT IN HIS SEASON" (PSALMS 1:3)	
Fruit	**Evidenced In**
1. The fruit of the Holy Spirit (Galatians 5:22,23; Ephesians 5:9)	Character
2. The fruit unto holiness (Romans 6:22)	Conduct
3. The fruit of righteousness (Hebrews 12:11)	Contentment
4. The fruit of the lips (Hebrews 13:15)	Conversation
5. The fruit of our hands (Proverbs 31:16,31; 1 Corinthians 3:10,14)	Concrete service for God
6. The fruit of the righteous (Proverbs 11:30; Romans 1:13)	Converts
7. The fruit of the womb (implied in Romans 7:4)	Children (spiritual)

forded their Master. In light of the context of this statement, just hours before His arrest and crucifixion, this is indeed a solemn warning. Most Christians will never experience conditions as bad as their Master did. In light of the cross, the things that we otherwise find so irritating and bothersome somehow fade away. When we know how bad our situation could be, we can rejoice in present circumstances.

18 If the world hate you, ye know that it hated me before it hated you.

19 If ye were of the world, the world would love his own: but because ye are not of the world, but I have chosen you out of the world, therefore the world hateth you.

20 Remember the word that I said unto you, The servant is not greater than his lord. If they have persecuted me, they will also persecute you; if they have kept my saying, they will keep yours also.

21 But all these things will they do unto you for my name's sake, because they know not him that sent me.

22 If I had not come and spoken unto them, they had not had sin: but now they have no cloke for their sin.

23 He that hateth me hateth my Father also.

24 If I had not done among them the works which none other man did, they had not had sin; but now have they both seen and hated both me and my Father.

25 But this cometh to pass, that the word might be fulfilled that is written in their law, They hated me without a cause.

A. Hatred for Christ (15:18–25). Jesus began this warning by reminding His disciples the world hated Him and would also hate them. The construction *ei. . .misei* forms a first-class conditional sentence which assumes the condition to be true and existing. Translating the indicative mood of this verb in this context, Jesus' warning begins, "Since the world hates you, and it does, you know that it hated me before you" (15:18). The verb *miseo* (hate) is a strong word translated in English New Testaments as "hate," "detest," and "abhor." Jesus chose that term to describe the attitude of the world toward Him and His disciples. The world would be friendly (*ephilei*) with the disciple if the disciple were of the world, but friendship with the world results in enmity with

God (James 4:4). When given the alternatives, the disciple has no choice but to anticipate opposition from the world, knowing that when it comes it vindicates his discipleship.

Jesus reminds His disciples that a servant is not greater than his Master (15:20; *see* 13:16). Earlier He used this proverb to explain their need to serve one another. Now He reminds them of a second implication of this same proverb. If the master had been persecuted, and He had, the servants should not think they would escape the same treatment. The verb *dioko* (persecuted, 15:20) originally meant to run off as one might try to chase a dog out of his garden. Later this word was used of running quickly in order to overtake as an athlete might do in competition (*see* Philippians 3:12). Finally, it came to mean pursuing with hostile intent and was used generally of molesting or harassing an individual. These disciples had seen the Jews becoming increasingly hostile toward their Master over the last two years and were about to see those hostile attitudes achieve their desired end. Now it was to become the disciples' turn to face this opposition. (*See* Chart 52.)

One might wonder why anyone could so strongly oppose the Lord. Jesus explained that this opposition sprang from two sources. First, they were acting in ignorance (15:21). If they had known God who had sent Christ, their reaction would have been different. But they persecuted Christ because they did not know God. Second, they hated Him because He convicted them of their sin, in particular exposing their sin of unbelief (15:22). If they had listened carefully to the message of Jesus and heeded His instructions, both prob-

Chart 52

FOUR THINGS THE DISCIPLES SHOULD REMEMBER IN PERSECUTION
1. That the world hated Jesus first (15:18). 2. That hatred proves they (the disciples) are not of the world (15:19). 3. That they are sharing their Master's lot (15:20). 4. That they are not only suffering with Him but for His sake (15:21).

lems would have been resolved. They would have believed and come to know God. Therefore, Jesus was also correct when He cited the Scripture, "They hated me without a cause" (15:25; *see* Psalms 35:19; 69:4).

> 26 But when the Comforter is come, whom I will send unto you from the Father, even the Spirit of truth, which proceedeth from the Father, he shall testify of me:
> 27 And ye also shall bear witness, because ye have been with me from the beginning.

B. Testimony of the Holy Spirit (15:26,27). In the midst of hatred and persecution, God promises His presence. The Holy Spirit, God Himself, will be with us to testify of the indwelling Christ. Under the law of God, two witnesses are required to establish a matter (Numbers 35:30; Deuteronomy 17:6). Jesus here speaks of the Holy Spirit testifying and the apostles bearing witness (15:27). The New Testament was written by human authors (the apostles) who were inspired by the divine author (the Holy Spirit); it is the product of two divinely selected witnesses (15:27).

Jesus here speaks of the Holy Spirit "which proceedeth from [beside] the Father" (15:26). The phrase *para tou patros ekporeuetai* (proceedeth) should be translated "from beside the Father," because the Holy Spirit is equal with the Father in nature. If Jesus said, "from within the Father," it would have made the Holy Spirit less than equal with the Father. The Spirit would have been from within the Father, as perhaps an attribute. Christ states: (1) The Father, Son, and Holy Spirit are three separate persons. "He shall testify" has an emphatic masculine pronoun, not neuter. (2) The Holy Spirit is sent by Christ and the Father to testify of Christ. (3) The Holy Spirit sent from beside the Father implies He has always been in that position before being sent, hence the deity of the Holy Spirit. (4) The Holy Spirit is God, and the Holy Spirit is a separate person from the Father and the Son but is submissive to the duties of the Father and Son. (5) Therefore, the Father, Son, and Holy Spirit are equal in nature, separate in person, and submissive in duties. This is the key verse in the doctrine of the eternal procession of the Spirit. The eternal procession of the Spirit is similar in nature to the eternal generation of the Son (Psalms 2:7). One notable difference is that eternal generation links the Father to the Son, whereas eternal procession links both the Father and the Son to the Holy Spirit. The word *procession* is used by theologians to describe the official duty, not the essential nature, of the Holy Spirit to the other two persons of the Trinity.

> These things have I spoken unto you, that ye should not be offended.
> 2 They shall put you out of the synagogues: yea, the time cometh, that whosoever killeth you will think that he doeth God service.
> 3 And these things will they do unto you, because they have not known the Father, nor me.
> 4 But these things have I told you, that when the time shall come, ye may remember that I told you of them. And these things I said not unto you at the beginning, because I was with you.

C. Hatred for God's People (16:1–4). Jesus had a purpose for giving His disciples the bad news now and not when they began to follow Him. During His ministry, Jesus knew He would be attracting most of the opposition to Himself, but He was there to help sustain His disciples if they should stumble (16:4). Now, however, He was going to heaven and wanted to warn the disciples so they would not be offended when the persecution came. The word *skandalisthete* (offended, 16:1) means "caused to stumble." The opposition and hatred that they would receive from the world would be so severe and offensive that it could cause many to stumble in their faith. Perhaps the most difficult aspect of this opposition is that much of it comes apparently in the name of God and as an expression of blind zeal for God.

The Lord mentioned two specific expressions of this hatred that the disciples would have found extremely hard to bear (16:2). First, they would be expelled from the synagogue. While such an action may have little impact on Christians today, it could devastate the Jewish Christians of the early church. To be expelled from the synagogue was to be cut off socially from a society of family and friends. Some rabbis taught God would not hear prayers unless they were voiced within the walls of a synagogue. So for some, being expelled would seem like being cut off from God Himself. Second, men would kill Christians as a service for God. The verb *latreian* (service) was the very word used to describe the service of the priest at the altar.

Living for and serving Christ after the cross was not going to be easy. Jesus did not attempt in any way to minimize the danger ahead. In doing so, He was not trying to discourage His disciples but rather challenge them to meet the difficulties ahead with a spirit of readiness. During a particularly difficult period in the Second World War, Sir Winston Churchill motivated the British people to continue the fight with his famous "blood, sweat, and tears" speech promising the nation a long period of problems with only the remotest chance of success. The difference here is that Jesus, unlike Churchill, could unconditionally guarantee the ultimate victory (16:33).

EIGHTEEN

CHRIST—
THE PREEMINENT ONE
JOHN 16:5–33

> 5 But now I go my way to him that sent me; and none of you asketh me, Whither goest thou?
> 6 But because I have said these things unto you, sorrow hath filled your heart.

In this chapter Jesus finishes the Upper Room Discourse by pointing His disciples to the work of the Holy Spirit. Since the Holy Spirit is sent to meet a need, Jesus reminds His followers that "sorrow hath filled your heart" (16:6) because of unjust persecution. But in the center of hatred, Jesus reminds them that they will be sustained by the presence of the Holy Spirit.

The mood of the disciples had changed. They were saddened by what Jesus was telling them and had begun to realize the end was near. Four times in this chapter John uses a form of the verb *lupe*, meaning "inward grief" or "sorrow" to describe the emotional state of the disciples (16:6, 20–22). This is the only time he uses this verb in the gospel. This word was used to describe every kind of pain, physical or emotional, though the pain may not be outwardly expressed. It describes an inner pain that cuts so deep, it hurts too much to cry. In describing "have sorrow" (16:22), John was emphasizing the overwhelming nature of the grief that was gripping the disciples. One way that Jesus encourages His disciples is to liken the sorrow of the disciples to the labor pains a mother experiences immediately prior to giving birth (16:21). There is joy after the sorrows pass.

In their sorrow, the disciples had considered only themselves. Jesus noted they had been filled with sorrow (16:6). The disciples, they were thinking of their grief and pain without the Lord to sustain them. Yet in all this there was no consideration that it was Jesus who would suffer the agony of the cross. Jesus, perhaps noticing the mood change among the disciples, says, "And none of you asketh me, Whither goest thou?" (16:5). A. T. Robertson observes, "Now that they realize that Jesus is going, the thoughts of the disciples turn on themselves and they cease asking the query of Peter (13:36)."[45] It was in this context of their pressing need that the disciples would learn that the Holy Spirit would sustain them and that they could enjoy the victorious peace of Christ.

I. THE WORK OF THE HOLY SPIRIT (16:7–15)

In their sorrow the disciples first needed to learn of the One Jesus called "the Comforter" (16:7). In His explanation of the Holy Spirit's ministry, the Lord first explained that ministry in the world (16:7–11) and then spoke of His ministry to the believer (16:12–15).

> 7 Nevertheless I tell you the truth; It is expedient for you that I go away: for if I go not away, the Comforter will not come unto you; but if I depart, I will send him unto you.
> 8 And when he is come, he will reprove the world of sin, and of righteousness, and of judgment:
> 9 Of sin, because they believe not on me;
> 10 Of righteousness, because I go to my Father, and ye see me no more;
> 11 Of judgment, because the prince of this world is judged.

A. *His Ministry to the World (16:7–11)*. The disciples had difficulty conceiving of life without Jesus, but as He explained, His departure was to their benefit. The word *sumpherei* (expedient, 16:7) is a compound word from *sun* (together) and *phero* (to bear or bring). *Expedient* conveyed the idea of bringing one together with good things— profitable. This expression is used twice in the gospel, here by Jesus and earlier by Caiaphas (11:50). Both times this word recognizes a certain value in the death of Christ.

In these verses, John uses three different words to describe the departure of Christ. The first word, *apeltho* (16:7), means "go away," expressing a departure or leaving. Later in the same verse, the word *poreutho* (go) is used, meaning "to depart for a specific purpose"—so He could send the Comforter. The third word, *hupago* (I am going, 16:10), emphasizes a departure that affects a personal relationship—He is separating Himself. In this way, Jesus reveals progressively the nature of His departing from His disciples.

Because of Jesus' departure, the disciples gain the Comforter (16:7). Again, John uses *ou me*, a strong double negative, in the phrase "the Comforter will not come," to emphasize the certainty that the Holy Spirit would definitely not come if Jesus did not depart. On the other hand, when Jesus departs He sends the Holy Spirit because of His love and compassion.

Notice the use of masculine pronouns to describe the Holy Spirit in verse eight. In Greek there are three genders—masculine, feminine, and neuter. Normally a pronoun is chosen to agree with the gender of the noun it is replacing. Although the word *spirit* is neuter, John here uses masculine pronouns to emphasize the personhood of the Holy Spirit. In other places in Scripture a neuter pronoun is used for the Holy Spirit in keeping with correct grammar.

The word *elegxei* (reprove, 16:8) literally means "convict." The word *convict* means "to refute an adversary completely," "to demonstrate guilt so the truth of the charge will be acknowledged." It implies demonstrating the opponent's guilt to him. The Latin derivative of *convict* is "to cause one to see." Hence when one is convicted of sin, he sees his sin. This can result in guilt, remorse, sorrow, and fear. Although conviction is often expressed with tears, the emotional expression is not the act of conviction, just its result.

Three times John uses the preposition *peri* in verse eight. Although consistently translated "of" not only here and in the verse following, a better translation might be "in respect to" or "concerning." It is not only that the Holy Spirit will convict or cause an unbeliever to see the nature of sin, righteousness, and judgment, but the unbeliever will experience personal guilt associated with this action. These verses are quite often misinterpreted. *Sin* is taken to mean actual sins, so that the Holy Spirit would make a person feel sorrow for an actual sin. *Righteousness* is usually interpreted to mean "good works," so that the Holy Spirit convicts a person of the good works that he has not done, such as attending church or tithing. *Judgment* is usually interpreted to mean the coming Great White Throne Judgment, so that the Holy Spirit makes a person fear the coming wrath of God. Chart 53 shows the typical interpretation of these verses and the correct interpretation.

The areas in which the Holy Spirit convicts are identified as sin, righteousness, and judgment. The word *harmartias* (sin, 16:9) is a general word for sin describing it as missing the mark. Jesus identifies the one area in which all men miss the mark as unbelief (16:9). Therefore the Holy Spirit causes people to see their unbelief. The righteousness referred to is Christ Himself (16:10). The Apostle Paul identified Christ as the righteousness of the believer (1 Corinthians 1:30). Jesus Christ is the righteous standard, and when unbelievers are convicted, they see themselves in light of Christ. This is much greater than being compared to good works. Men will also be convicted to judgment because Satan has been judged (16:11). The verb *kekritai* (judged) is a perfect passive indicative form of the verb meaning "to judge." It is completed action and refers to the cross judgment of Jesus Christ (12:31–33). The Holy Spirit convicts unbelievers today, based on the past cross judgment where Satan was judged.

12 I have yet many things to say unto you, but ye cannot bear them now.

Chart 53

THE HOLY SPIRIT'S CONVICTION OF THE UNSAVED		
Conviction Concerning	Typical Application	True Interpretation
1. Sin (16:9)	Specific	Unbelief
2. Righteousness (16:10)	Doing good (such as church attendance, Bible reading, prayer)	Christ our righteousness is the standard (*see* Romans 4:5; 1 Corinthians 1:30)
3. Judgment (16:11)	Burning in hell	Sin judgment of Satan (16:11) on the cross (12:31–33)

13 Howbeit when he, the Spirit of truth, is come, he will guide you into all truth: for he shall not speak of himself; but whatsoever he shall hear, that shall he speak: and he will shew you things to come.

14 He shall glorify me: for he shall receive of mine, and shall shew it unto you.

15 All things that the Father hath are mine: therefore said I, that he shall take of mine, and shall shew it unto you.

B. His Ministry to the Believer (16:12–15). Now Jesus turns the focus of the disciples from the Holy Spirit's ministry to the world, to His ministry to the believer. "I have yet many things to say unto you, but ye cannot bear them now" (16:12). The verb *bastazein* (bear) literally means "to carry off." This word is used in this literal sense of Judas holding or bearing the purse for the disciples and of Jesus bearing the sin of the world on the cross. Here the word is used in a more figurative sense of bearing, that of internalizing (*see* Acts 15:10). He was telling the disciples they were unable to understand the rest of what He wished to teach them. This could have been because of their emotional state at the time or their spiritual blindness that made them unable to comprehend spiritual truth. Understanding the principle of learning readiness, Jesus explained that the Holy Spirit would complete their education at a later time.

One of the ministries of the Holy Spirit to believers is guiding them into truth, which is spiritual illumination. The verb *hodegesei* (guide) is a compound word from *hodos* (way) and *hegeomai* (to lead). Earlier in this discourse, Jesus had identified Himself as "the way, the truth, and the life" (14:6). Now He explained the Spirit of truth would guide them concerning that way. The word *pasan* (all) should probably be read as an adverb modifying this verb and be translated "completely": "He will completely lead you into truth." The guidance of the Holy Spirit in revealing New Testament truth to the apostles was complete, not partial. Therefore, the adverb *complete* implies the inspiration, inerrancy, and authority of the New Testament. The Holy Spirit completely led the disciples when they were writing revelation. By way of application, the means whereby the Holy Spirit guides the believer into truth today is the Word of God (*see* Psalms 25:5).

A second ministry of the Holy Spirit to these disciples was that of showing them things to come (16:13). The verb *anaggelei* (show) literally means He will "declare" or "announce." This was the verb used of formal preaching of the Gospel (Acts 20:20; 1 Peter 1:12; 1 John 1:5). The content which the Holy Spirit will declare is described as "things to come." This is the only occurrence of this phrase in the New Testament. Some interpret this to mean only eschatology or the events surrounding the second coming of Christ. Probably this is a reference to the coming doctrines that they will write in the New Testament, most of which were revealed after these words were spoken. In addition to eschatological truths, these also included the doctrines of ecclesiology, pneumatology, and the union of the believer with Christ and his transformation into the image of Christ. These areas are the underlying themes of the epistles.

A third area of the Holy Spirit's ministry to the believer is that of glorifying Christ. The duty of the Holy Spirit is to glorify Jesus Christ. Certain charismatic or pentecostal movements claim a particular relationship with the Holy Spirit. They tend to glorify the Holy Spirit. However, notice the priorities. The Holy Spirit does not glorify Himself (16:13). Also, the Holy Spirit does not glorify personalities, preachers, the virgin Mary, a church, or church ordinances. The Holy Spirit glorifies Jesus Christ. If a person or group is glorifying someone or something other than Christ, it is not biblical. When one surveys the New Testament, he sees the prominent place of Christ not only in the epistles but also in the recorded sermons in Acts.

Here we have the ministry of the Holy Spirit in the church and, in particular, in the guidance of the apostles in receiving and communicating the revelation of spiritual truth. Just as the Son revealed the Father and glorified Him, so the Holy Spirit will reveal and glorify the Son.

II. THE WORRY OF THE DISCIPLES (16:16–22)

Apparently, Jesus purposely expressed Himself in a riddle stating, "A little while, and ye shall not see me: and again, a little while, and ye shall see me, because I go to the Father" (16:16). Just as He asked questions to get His listeners to think through what He was saying, here He permitted His

Chart 54

WHAT THE HOLY SPIRIT WILL DO FOR THE BELIEVERS
1. He will guide them into all truth (16:13).
2. He will declare to them the things to come (16:13).
3. He will glorify Christ (16:14).

disciples to be puzzled over His statement, both individually and with one another.

16 A little while, and ye shall not see me: and again, a little while, and ye shall see me, because I go to the Father.

17 Then said some of his disciples among themselves, What is this that he saith unto us, A little while, and ye shall not see me: and again, a little while, and ye shall see me: and, Because I go to the Father?

18 They said therefore, What is this that he saith, A little while? we cannot tell what he saith.

19 Now Jesus knew that they were desirous to ask him, and said unto them, Do ye enquire among yourselves of that I said, A little while, and ye shall not see me: and again, a little while, and ye shall see me?

A. The Perplexity (16:16–19). Now that this statement about not seeing Him has been fulfilled, it is easy for us to recognize the meaning of this apparently contradictory statement. When Jesus said, "A little while, and ye shall not see me," He was predicting His death. As He continued, "And again, a little while, and ye shall see me, because I go to the Father," He prophesied of His resurrection and ministry among the disciples for forty days before the ascension. Many commentators interpret verse eighteen as the "I give up" attitude of the apostles. They did not understand because neither the death nor resurrection had occurred. Jesus uses two different verbs for see to describe what will eventually happen to them (16:16). The first verb, theoreite (to see) means "to behold" or "to gaze upon." It implies some degree of intensity in the physical act of seeing. The second verb, opsesthe, is used by John of insight or understanding spiritual realities (see 1:51; 16:22). This verb emphasizes the discernment that is the result of either physical or spiritual sight. Within a few hours these disciples would lose sight of Jesus as He would be physically removed from their presence. They would not see Him. But within a few days they would come to a greater realization of spiritual truth and forever after have a different vision of Christ.

Again John reminds us of the omniscient knowledge of Christ. The disciples did not understand Jesus' statement, and some were asking one another about it, but no one thought of asking Jesus Himself. Still, Jesus perceived (*egno,* 16:19) their desire. So He asked and answered the unasked question. It has been suggested the disciples may have been too embarrassed to ask another question after having already asked several. Jesus' willingness to answer even an unasked question reminds us we need never be embarrassed about coming to Him with any problem or need, even if it seems as if we have already done so recently.

20 Verily, verily, I say unto you, That ye shall weep and lament, but the world shall rejoice: and ye shall be sorrowful, but your sorrow shall be turned into joy.

21 A woman when she is in travail hath sorrow, because her hour is come: but as soon as she is delivered of the child, she remembereth no more the anguish, for joy that a man is born into the world.

22 And ye now therefore have sorrow: but I will see you again, and your heart shall rejoice, and your joy no man taketh from you.

23 And in that day ye shall ask me nothing. Verily, verily, I say unto you, Whatsoever ye shall ask the Father in my name, he will give it you.

24 Hitherto have ye asked nothing in my name: ask, and ye shall receive, that your joy may be full.

25 These things have I spoken unto you in proverbs: but the time cometh, when I shall no more speak unto you in proverbs, but I shall shew you plainly of the Father.

26 At that day ye shall ask in my name: and I say not unto you, that I will pray the Father for you:

27 For the Father himself loveth you, because ye have loved me, and have believed that I came out from God.

28 I came forth from the Father, and am come into the world: again, I leave the world, and go to the Father.

29 His disciples said unto him, Lo, now speakest thou plainly, and speakest no proverb.

30 Now are we sure that thou knowest all things, and needest not that any man should ask thee: by this we believe that thou camest forth from God.

31 Jesus answered them, Do ye now believe?

32 Behold, the hour cometh, yea, is now come, that ye shall be scattered, every man to his own, and shall leave me alone: and yet I am not alone, because the Father is with me.

33 These things I have spoken unto you, that in me ye might have peace. In the world ye shall have tribulation: but be of good cheer; I have overcome the world.

B. *The Promise (16:20–33)*. In their confused and hurting state, these bewildered disciples needed encouragement. Jesus reminded them not only of the promised Comforter and His ministry (16:7–15), but also promised their sorrow would turn to joy (16:20–22), that they would have power in prayer (16:23–24), and held out the prospect of a victorious peace (16:25–33). In our times of sorrow, these are the promises of the Lord to His disciples. (*See* Chart 55.)

The departure of Jesus would make the disciples sorrowful, but this sorrow would be followed by the joy of His reappearance. Jesus explained, "Your sorrow shall be turned into joy" (16:20). The very thing that was causing their sorrow (His death) would give birth to their joy. Further, no

Chart 55

WHEN IT HURTS TOO MUCH TO CRY	
1. Remember the Comforter (the Holy Spirit) has come.	(16:7–15)
2. Be assured that God will ultimately turn your sorrow into joy.	(16:20–22)
3. Take advantage of your tremendous power.	(16:23,24)
4. Claim the victorious peace of Christ in every battle.	(16:25–33)

one would be able to take the joy that derived from His death from them (16:22). This was a difficult concept for the disciples to grasp. Jesus used the double verily formula (verily, verily, 16:20) in its customary way, to assure those who were in doubt.

Jesus used a common Old Testament illustration of childbirth to help the disciples understand how their deep sorrow could result in lasting joy (see Isaiah 21:3; 26:17; 66:7; Hosea 13:13; Micah 4:9,10). The intense pain of labor is overwhelmed by floods of joy when a mother hears the cry of her newborn baby. The word *thlipseos*, here translated "anguish" (16:21), is the usual word for tribulation in the New Testament (see 16:33). Just as the tribulation of a pregnant woman (labor pains) results in an overwhelming sense of joy in the birth of a child, so Jesus promised His disciples their sorrow and tribulation in the world would also be turned to joy.

For the seventh and final time in this Upper Room Discourse, Jesus uses the formula "verily, verily" (16:23), this time with reference to prayer. The difficulty that the disciples had in believing this statement was not so much because of its content but because of their state. This promise of answered prayer was made earlier in the evening (14:13,14), but when people are hurting deeply, often they do not feel like praying. Our times of sorrow are not times to quit praying but rather to grow spiritually in every area including our prayer life.

Often believers find themselves questioning God rather than making requests of Him. John uses two different verbs both translated "'ask'" in verse twenty-three. The first verb, *erotesete*, literally means "to ask" in the sense of questioning. The second verb, *aitesete*, means "to ask" in the sense of making a request or demand for something. Jesus was telling them, "In that day after my death, you will not inquire of me with questions, but you will ask me in prayer, and my Father will give it to you." The tense of *ask* in verse twenty-four suggests a continuous asking. In our time of sorrow, our response should be to continually pray to the Father rather than questioning Him. If we do that asking, Jesus will do whatever questioning is necessary (16:26).

In verse twenty-five, Jesus acknowledges His use of proverbs to illustrate spiritual truth—shepherd and his sheep (10:1–6), the vine and the branches (15:1–8), the woman in

Chart 56

THREE FACTS OF PRAYER IN JOHN 16:23
1. Prayer is asking (*see* Matthew 7:7).   2. Pray in Jesus' name.   3. The Father answers prayer.

labor (16:21). But the time is coming when these dark sayings will become plain to them. This actually happened after the coming of the Holy Spirit. One point, however, He does make plain even now—His having come from the Father into the world, and His soon leaving the world to return to His Father (16:28). The word *parresiai* (16:25) means "plainly" in the sense of without reserve (10:24; 11:14) or without fear (11:54). In declaring His relationship with the Father, Jesus uses the preposition *para*, literally meaning "from beside" the Father (16:27). That part of His eternal existence falling between His incarnation and ascension formed a brief parenthesis in His intimate position with the Father.

As a result of Jesus' speaking plainly to His disciples rather than in proverbs, they affirmed their knowledge and belief that Jesus came from God (16:30). Even in this affirmation, there are hints that it may not be what it at first appears. The word *oidamen* (know) describes the disciples' view of Jesus' knowledge. Earlier they failed to understand the meaning of Jesus' statements, but now they knew. In this sense this verb marks the spiritual progress of the disciples. Still, their present knowledge falls short of Jesus' *ginosko* knowledge. Also, their statement of faith is called into question. Commenting on Jesus' question, "Do ye now believe?" (16:31), A. T. Robertson notes, "Their belief in Christ was genuine *as far as it went,* but perils await them of which they are ignorant. They are too self-confident as their despair at Christ's death shows."[46] Jesus warns them not to boast because they will soon forsake Him, leaving Him alone with His Father (16:32; *see* Proverbs 18:24). The word John uses here to describe the scattering of the disciples is *skorpisthete* (shall be scattered), the normal word used to describe the scampering of the sheep when the flock is attacked by the wolf (10:12).

As the life of Christ began with a declaration of peace (Luke 2:14), so Jesus concludes His final message to His

Chart 57

LIVING IN TWO WORLDS	
Twofold Life	In Me
	In the World
Twofold Experience	Peace
	Tribulation
Twofold Secret	I Have Overcome
	Good Cheer

disciples before the cross with a message of peace (16:33). He speaks of His triumph as already an accomplished fact and, by implication, the spiritual victory of His disciples is also guaranteed. John uses the word *tharseite*, translated "be of good cheer" (16:33). This is the only occurrence of the word in John's writings, but from its use elsewhere it is evident that this was normally a verb calling for courage in the face of perceived danger (*see* Matthew 9:2,22; Mark 10:49). The reason we can have this courage is found in the victory of Christ. The word *nenikeka* (overcome) means "to be victorious" or "to conquer," and in the New Testament always refers to spiritual victory. Jesus emphatically states here, "*I have overcome the world*" (16:33). Just as a mortally wounded animal continues to fight, so the attacks of the enemy on Christians are simply the death agonies of a conquered foe.

The Christian life is significant in that it involves living in two worlds (*see* Chart 57). It is only in Christ that we can find true peace (14:27). It is in the world that we are tested and tempted. No matter how much the world promises peace, all it can really offer us is tribulation.

NINETEEN

CHRIST—
THE INTERCESSOR
JOHN 17:1–26

After His death and ascension to heaven, one of the chief ministries of Christ on behalf of the believer is His intercession (Hebrews 7:25). While on earth, Jesus often prayed for Himself and others, but we do not know what He prayed nor how He addressed His request. This chapter alone records an extended prayer of Jesus to the Father. It reveals the heart of Christ and the heart of the Father. Because of this, John 17 has been called "the holy of holies in the New Testament." While Jesus on two occasions gave His disciples a model prayer, which has become known as "the Lord's Prayer," He never prayed it for Himself. Technically it is "the Believer's Prayer," for it includes requests for fallen man living in this world. For instance it asks, "Forgive us our sins." But there was never a need for Jesus to pray for forgiveness. In reality, the prayer recorded in John 17 could be called "the Lord's Prayer," because it deals with the personal desires and needs of Jesus Christ.

Because of the unique nature of this chapter, some commentators have been overwhelmed by its contents. Bishop J. C. Ryle described it as, "one of the most wonderful chapters in the Bible—wonderful as a specimen of the communication between the Father and the Son, wonderful as a pattern of His present intercessory work as our great High Priest, wonderful too as an example of the sort of things believers should mention in prayer."[47] Bengel notes, "This chapter is the simplest in language, the profoundest in meaning, in all the Scriptures. . . ."[48] Another writer has observed the relationship between this prayer and the preceding sermon of Christ to His disciples and suggested, "The best and fullest sermon ever preached was followed by the best of prayers."[49]

In this chapter Christ begins His high priestly intercession by first centering on the sacrifice, praying for those for whom the sacrifice is offered. In the Old Testament the high priest bore the names of the twelve tribes on his breast as he approached God on the annual Day of Atonement. Here, as Jesus prepares to fulfill this type once and for all, our great High Priest enters the presence of God thinking not only of those who followed Him on earth during His public ministry, but also those who follow Him today. He has us upon His heart. His prayer concerns redemption, and many of the great redemptive words are included in this chapter: salvation (17:2), manifestation (17:6), representation (17:9), preservation (17:12), sanctification (17:17–19), identification (17:21), and glorification (17:22).

This prayer is also intimate. Here we get an opportunity to go behind the veil and listen to a private conversation between the Son and the Father. The following day the veil will be ripped from top to bottom to symbolically open the way into the presence of God. The prayer by Jesus during the previous evening was Christ's presalvation ministry that made possible the opening of the way.

Darby suggests the key word in this prayer is the title, "Father." Jesus used this title exclusively when speaking to or about God.[50] The name Father (*Pater*) expresses the spirit of the whole prayer—it is not someone begging for mercy, but it reflects a son speaking to his father. This spirit is predictive of the Christian's prayer life when he is led and governed by the Holy Spirit (Romans 8:15).

In this prayer Jesus prays first for Himself, then for His disciples, and finally for those who will be numbered among His followers in the years to come. Some have objected to the authenticity of this prayer suggesting it is the composition of a disciple and not the actual words of Jesus. Actually, it is highly improbable that any disciple could enter into such intimacy with God as this prayer suggests. How did these private words get recorded by John? An ancient writer suggests that the record of this prayer is the result of "the tenacious memory of an old man recalling the greatest days of his life."[51] Actually, the Holy Spirit by revelation could have given John the contents so that he could write by inspiration; without having access to the words, John could have accurately written them for our benefit.

There is a difference of opinion as to the location where Christ offered this prayer. Scholars such as John Calvin, A. C. Gaebelein, and Henry Alford believe that all the events of John 13–17 took place in the upper room. Others, such as C. I. Scofield, H. A. Ironside, Merrill Tenney, J. C. Ryle, and G. Campbell Morgan, believe that while John 13–14 took place in the upper room, the events of John 15–17 occurred on the way to Gethsemane. The main reason for this difference of opinion results from the interpretation of the phrase, "Arise, let us go hence" (14:31).

I. JESUS' PRAYER FOR HIMSELF (17:1–5)

These words spake Jesus, and lifted up his eyes to heaven, and said, Father, the hour is come; glorify thy Son, that thy Son also may glorify thee:

2 As thou hast given him power over all flesh, that he should give eternal life to as many as thou hast given him.

3 And this is life eternal, that they might know thee the only true God, and Jesus Christ whom thou hast sent.

4 I have glorified thee on the earth: I have finished the work which thou gavest me to do.

5 And now, O Father, glorify thou me with thine own self with the glory which I had with thee before the world was.

In this prayer Jesus makes seven specific requests: first, He prays for the glorification of the Son (17:1); second, for the restoration of His original glory (17:5); third, for the protection of His disciples and future believers (17:11,15); fourth, for sanctification (17:17); fifth, for unification (17:21–23); sixth, for glorification (17:24); and seventh, for the salvation of the world (17:21). In a total of twenty-six verses, Jesus spent only five praying for Himself. Even when He prayed for Himself, it was with a view of accomplishing something for others. Intercession is prayer on behalf of others. Jesus' request for personal glory was with a view to glorify God and give eternal life to His followers.

Jesus began this prayer reminding His Father, "The hour is come" (17:1). As seen before, the term *hour* does not mean an exact time of day but refers to the time of messianic fulfillment. John clearly emphasizes the importance of this hour as the time of messianic revelation. Now the hour had come in which Christ would complete His work by His voluntary sacrifice. This was the motivation of His prayer. He knew that His greatest crisis was at hand. The crucial point of eternity was now before Him—the cross. Also, in making this prayer before offering the final sacrifice for sin, Jesus was following the example of the high priest who first dedicated a sacrifice to God before offering it as an atonement for the sins of the nation.

The word *glorify* (*doxason*) is an aorist active imperative of *doxazo* and is the only personal petition made in this prayer by Jesus. Earlier He had used this term as He instructed His disciples about His death (13:31,32). This was not a prayer for dying grace, for strength to endure the cross, but rather a prayer that the Father would be glorified in His death. The sacrificial death of Christ was the means whereby God and man were reconciled and, therefore, the Father was glorified (*see* 2 Corinthians 5:19).

God had already given Jesus the "power [literally "authority," *exousian*] over all flesh." In acknowledging this truth,

Chart 58

PRAYER FOR HIMSELF (17:1–5)	
Key Word:	Glorify
Purpose:	For Christ's former glory
Basis:	Because I have power over all flesh (17:2)
	Because I have finished my work (17:4)
	Because I had glory in eternity past (17:5)

Jesus was drawing a contrast between the weakness of mankind and the majesty of God. The expression *pares sarkos* (all flesh) was a Hebrew idiom denoting the whole of humanity in its imperfection (*see* Genesis 6:12; Psalms 65:2; Isaiah 40:5; Jeremiah 32:27). In making this claim, Christ was placing Himself above the realm of humanity. Jesus had made similar claims concerning His authority during His public ministry (*see* Matthew 11:27; Luke 10:22).

Eight times in seven verses Jesus speaks of Christians as given to Him by the Father (17:2,6,9,11,12,24). As Jesus is the Father's gift of love to the world (3:16; 1 John 3:1), so believers are the Father's gift of love to Christ. In this prayer, Jesus committed believers to the Father for safekeeping (17:11). The security of the believer, therefore, rests upon the Father's faithfulness to answer the prayers of His Son.

Not only are believers the gift of the Father to the Son, they are also themselves recipients of certain benefits from Christ. The Scriptures identify at least one hundred and thirty-one immediate benefits of salvation that may be claimed the moment an individual trusts Christ. In addition to these, the Apostle Paul suggests God will "freely give us all things" (Romans 8:32). In this chapter, Jesus emphasizes five of these many benefits. They include eternal life (17:2), the Father's name (17:6,26), the Father's words (17:8,14), His own joy (17:13), and His own glory (17:22).

Jesus defines eternal life in terms of knowing God. All men will live forever, although only believers will experience an eternal life of joy with God (Matthew 25:46). The word *ginoskosin*, here translated "they might know" (17:3), is a present active subjunctive verb and might better be expressed "they should keep on knowing" or "they should progressively perceive." The knowledge of God is a continually growing experience. It begins when one comes to the Father by way of the Son (14:6), but even for a great Christian like the Apostle Paul, that knowledge was only in part (1 Corinthians 13:9). After a lifetime of study, Paul cries out, "That I may know Him" (Philippians 3:10).

Jesus mentions two specific things that believers should know as a part of this eternal life. First, they should know God as "the only true God" (17:3). The word *alethinon* means "true," not as the opposite of wrong but rather as the opposite of false. Believers recognize first that God alone is genuine. The knowledge of the only genuine God is through Jesus Christ (14:6–9).

The second thing believers know is that Jesus is the Messiah sent by God. The title "Jesus Christ" occurs only twice in John's Gospel (1:17; 17:3). In this context it seems highly unlikely Jesus would refer to himself as "Jesus Christ." Probably, the title *Christon* should be regarded as a predicate accusative. In that case, the latter part of verse three would be translated, "and Jesus whom thou sent, as the Christ." The verb *apesteilas* (sent) is in an aorist tense, emphasizing the historic fact of Christ's mission.

Jesus had glorified the One who sent Him in that He finished the task He was sent to accomplish. Now He called upon His Father to glorify Him "with thine own self" (17:5) with the glory that was His previously. The expression *para seautoi* is a Greek idiom meaning "at thy side" or "in thy own presence." John begins his gospel observing, "The Word was with God" (1:1), and, "the Word was made flesh, . . . and we beheld his glory" (1:14). While on earth the earthly tabernacle was Christ's glory. Now the Word is prepared to return to His proper place.

Jesus speaks of His prior glory in terms of that "which I had with thee before the world was" (17:5). Paul suggests the humiliation of Christ (when He laid aside His glory) was specifically linked to His becoming a man (Philippians 2:7,8). Jesus did not have to become a man in order to receive glory. Rather, He had to set aside His glory, emptying Himself, in order that He might become a man and receive even greater glory as the God-man.

II. JESUS' PRAYER FOR THE ELEVEN (17:6–19)

6 I have manifested thy name unto the men which thou gavest me out of the world: thine they were, and thou gavest them me; and they have kept thy word.

7 Now they have known that all things whatsoever thou hast given me are of thee.

8 For I have given unto them the words which thou gavest me; and they have received them, and have known surely that I came out from thee, and they have believed that thou didst send me.

9 I pray for them: I pray not for the world, but for them which thou hast given me; for they are thine.

10 And all mine are thine, and thine are mine; and I am glorified in them.

After prayer concerning Himself, Jesus turned His attention directly to the eleven (*see* Chart 59). After verifying the faithfulness of both His disciples and Himself to the Father, He makes three requests for His followers. First, He prays for security, "Keep through thine own name those whom thou hast given me" (17:11). Second, He prays for deliverance, "Keep them from the evil" (17:15). Finally, He prays for sanctification, "Sanctify them through thy truth: thy word is truth" (17:17). All three of Christ's requests were not only answered regarding the eleven, but have been and are continually being answered in the experience of believers today.

Jesus begins this second part of His high priestly prayer noting, "I have manifested thy name unto the men which thou gavest me" (17:6). The name of God in Scripture is more than merely a title for the person of God. His name was one of the means by which He revealed His very nature and attributes. Jesus was here claiming He had fully manifested the nature and attributes of God to His disciples. This claim had already been verified by one of those disciples in this gospel. John wrote, "We beheld his glory, the glory as of the only begotten of the Father" (1:14), and "The only begotten Son, which is in the bosom of the Father, he hath declared him" (1:18).

Chart 59

PRAYER FOR HIS ELEVEN DISCIPLES (17:6–19)	
Key Word:	Keep
Purpose:	That the disciples have unity (17:11)
	That the disciples have joy (17:13)
Basis:	You gave them to Me (17:6,7)
	I gave them Thy Word (17:8,14)
	All Mine are Thine (17:10)

Jesus said of the eleven, "They have kept thy word" (17:6). This is not suggesting absolute obedience on the part of the disciples to the Word of God, but rather it is a general observation. Jesus summarized their development in terms of spiritual perception. First, there was an intellectual recognition of Jesus as the representative of God (17:7). This then led them to receive God's message which Jesus gave them (17:8). Third, their willingness to hear and heed His words resulted in a settled conviction concerning the deity of Christ (17:8). Finally, their faith in Christ resulted in a commitment of their lives to Him as the One sent by God (17:8).

The statement, "I pray not for the world" (17:9), should be understood within its context. It would be wrong to say Jesus never prayed for the world, because only a few hours later He does pray for the world (Luke 23:34). At this point He is simply limiting His present request. But even in this prayer, He expresses the concern "that the world may believe" (17:21). When Jesus prays for the world, He prays that individuals may believe.

Jesus closely integrates the prayer for His glorification with His request for the security, deliverance, and sanctification of His disciples. When prayer is answered for them, Jesus could say, "I am glorified in them" (17:10). When Jesus asked the Father to glorify the Son, He was specifically asking the Father to accept His redemptive sacrifice (17:1), restore Him to His rightful place of fellowship with the Father (17:5), and grant both faithfulness (17:11) and fruitfulness (17:20) to the eleven.

11 And now I am no more in the world, but these are in the world, and I come to thee. Holy Father, keep through thine own name those whom thou hast given me, that they may be one, as we are.

12 While I was with them in the world, I kept them in thy name: those that thou gavest me I have kept, and none of them is lost, but the son of perdition; that the scripture might be fulfilled.

13 And now come I to thee; and these things I speak in the world, that they might have my joy fulfilled in themselves.

A. A Prayer for Security (17:11–13). Jesus' prayer for the security of the eleven was based upon the revelation of God

as the "Holy Father" (17:11). This is the only occurrence of
this title for God in the Scriptures. Darby suggests Jesus here
uses this name because He desired the Father "to keep them
with the affection of a Father, and according to His holiness
of His nature." God's holiness is the guarantee that He will
keep the saints from the evil of the world.

The reasonableness of Jesus' request that God keep the
eleven is evidenced in that Jesus Himself had kept them
while He was in the world with them. Two different Greek
words are used in verse twelve for the word *kept*. The first is
eteroun from the verb *tereo* meaning "I keep" or "I preserve."
The second verb, *ephulaxa*, means "I guarded" and emphasizes the ministry of Christ as a sentinel over the souls of the
eleven. Jesus reminds the Father, "While I was in the world,
I guarded them as a means to their preservation. Now I am
no more in the world, and I come to thee; preserve them in
Thy name" (17:11,12, author's paraphrase).

Jesus claimed He had successfully kept all the Father had
given Him with the exception of one whom He identified as
"the son of perdition" (17:12). The Hebraism *son of* means
"similar in nature and moral character." This expression is
used elsewhere in the Scriptures only of the Antichrist
(2 Thessalonians 2:3), leaving some to conclude the future
Antichrist may be a reappearance of Judas Iscariot. There is
an apparent play on words between this title of Judas and
the word *apoleto*, translated "lost." Jesus is saying "None of
them perished except the son of perishing" (*apoleias*). The
loss of Judas was in keeping with the prophetic Scripture
concerning Jesus' betrayal by a friend (Psalms 41:9).

> 14 I have given them thy word; and the world hath
> hated them, because they are not of the world, even as I
> am not of the world.
> 15 I pray not that thou shouldest take them out of the
> world, but that thou shouldest keep them from the evil.
> 16 They are not of the world, even as I am not of the
> world.

B. A Prayer for Deliverance (17:14–16). Twice Jesus reminds the Father, "They are not of the world, even as I am
not of the world" (17:14,16). Throughout this gospel, John
has constantly portrayed the uniqueness of Jesus in opposi-

tion to the world. The world (*kosmos*) in this gospel represents the created physical world and sum total of created beings which belong to it. While God loves the world (3:16), the world chose to reject Christ in ignorance (1:10,11). In this sense the world represents all those who stand against Christ and reject Him with Satan who is called "the prince of this world" (12:31). The world is under judgment (9:39) but has been overcome by Christ (16:33).

His prayer for deliverance is that God "shouldest keep them from the evil" (17:15). The verb *areis*, translated "shouldest keep," more accurately means "should take." The construction *ek tou ponerou* involving the ablative case can mean "from the evil man" (Satan), or "from the evil deed." This same construction appears in the model prayer Jesus gave His disciples (Matthew 6:13). In both cases, *tou ponerou* should probably be taken as a title of the devil. As Satan is the prince of this world, the Father's deliverance of the eleven and of all believers in some sense involves keeping them from Satan.

17 Sanctify them through thy truth: thy word is truth.

18 As thou hast sent me into the world, even so have I also sent them into the world.

19 And for their sakes I sanctify myself, that they also might be sanctified through the truth.

C. *A Prayer for Sanctification (17:17–19)*. The third request Jesus makes for the eleven relates to their sanctification. The verb *sanctify* (*hagiazo*) means "to consecrate or set apart a person or thing to God." It involved a consecration of the whole life of that person or thing to the service of God. In the Old

Chart 60

THE BELIEVER AND THE WORLD IN JOHN 17
Given to Christ out of the world (17:6)
Left in the world (17:11–15)
Not of the world (17:14)
Hated by the world (17:14)
Kept from the world (17:15)
Sent into the world (17:18)
To preach Christ in the world (17:20)

Testament it usually conveyed the idea of making someone or something sacred, usually by the burning of a sacrifice. It does not mean to purify as to purify from sin. Jesus sanctified Himself even though He had no sin (17:19) by setting Himself apart as the sacrificial offering to God in order that His followers might also be sanctified.

III. JESUS' PRAYER FOR ALL BELIEVERS (17:20–26)

In the third major section of this high priestly prayer, Jesus prays for all believers. (*See* Chart 61.) He identifies this group with the participle *pisteuonton*, literally "believing ones." The present tense of this verb suggests the future body of believers is conceived as actually existing. He makes two specific requests: (1) "that they all may be one" (17:20–23), and (2) "that they may behold my glory"—be with Me in heaven (17:24–26). The first is a prayer for unity; the second a prayer for union.

> 20 Neither pray I for these alone, but for them also which shall believe on me through their word;
> 21 That they all may be one; as thou, Father, art in me, and I in thee, that they also may be one in us: that the world may believe that thou hast sent me.
> 22 And the glory which thou gavest me I have given them; that they may be one, even as we are one:
> 23 I in them, and thou in me, that they may be made perfect in one; and that the world may know that thou hast sent me, and hast loved them, as thou hast loved me.

Chart 61

PRAYER FOR ALL BELIEVERS IN JOHN 17:20–26	
Key Word:	One
Purpose:	That the world may believe (17:21,26)
	To show the love of God (17:26)
Basis:	Because we are one (17:21–23)

A. A Prayer for Unity (17:20–23). The expression "that they may be one" occurs five times in this chapter, once in the prayer for the eleven (17:11) and four times in the prayer for all believers (17:21–23). The repetition of this phrase in the high priestly prayer of Christ has often been misinterpreted to mean the reunification of the church (Protestants and Roman Catholics) and interchurch cooperations and unions (the ecumenical movement). Actually, Christ did not request the union of believers but rather a spirit of unity among believers. Four times the expression is *hina osin hen,* "that they may keep on being one" (17:11,21,22). Even though the expression changes slightly in verse twenty-three, "one" is still *hen,* a neuter singular. Christ's prayer for His disciples and all believers was for a oneness of will and spirit and not physical union which would require the masculine *heis.* In the immediate context of the prayer, the disciples were a union but lacked this spirit of unity (Luke 22:24). The only way to develop unity among believers is for all of them to first find unity with God in Christ (17:21). When this spirit of unity is achieved, a major stumbling block to faith is removed in the hope that the world may believe and know (17:21,23).

> 24 Father, I will that they also, whom thou hast given me, be with me where I am; that they may behold my glory, which thou hast given me: for thou lovedst me before the foundation of the world.
>
> 25 O righteous Father, the world hath not known thee: but I have known thee, and these have known that thou hast sent me.
>
> 26 And I have declared unto them thy name, and will declare it: that the love wherewith thou hast loved me may be in them, and I in them.

B. A Prayer for Union (17:24–26). The second request in this final section of the prayer, "that they also, whom thou hast given me, be with me where I am," is literally fulfilled every time a soul goes to heaven. This is the heart of the heavenly bridegroom. He would have His people with Him to share His glory and the Father's love. In the midst of this request, Jesus appeals to His Father as "righteous Father" (17:25). The Father's righteousness forbids Him to abandon His saints to the evil of the world. While someday all believ-

Chart 62

THE SIGNIFICANCE OF THE WORD *AS* IN JOHN 17
The believer has the same life as Christ (17:2). The believer has the same security as Christ (17:11). The believer has the same separation as Christ (17:14). The believer has the same sending into the world as Christ (17:18). The believer has the same union as Christ (17:21). The believer has the same glory as Christ (17:22). The believer has the same love as Christ (17:23).

ers will be in perfect union with Christ in heaven, the New Testament also recognizes a present spiritual union of Christ and the believer. This is implied in this chapter by the word *as*, which is used to relate the believer to Christ as shown in Chart 62.

TWENTY

CHRIST—
THE FAITHFUL ONE
OR THE FREE PRISONER
JOHN 18:1–40

After His high priestly prayer Jesus entered into the Garden of Gethsemane. It was here He was betrayed and arrested. This chapter records the arrest in the garden, the Jewish and Roman trials, and Peter's three denials of Christ. In the past few chapters John has been using the journalistic technique of discourse to communicate his message. In this chapter he returns to narrative. As in earlier narrative portions, the marks of an eyewitness are abundantly evident.

John begins this narrative with the expression, "he went forth" (18:1), but it is not clear where the disciples were when Jesus led them over Kidron Brook (TEV). Some commentators believe all of the events in John 13–17 took place in the upper room, but others argue Jesus had earlier left that place (see 14:31). Even if the disciples had remained in the upper room until the end of the high priestly prayer, they may have gone to the temple before leaving the city. It was customary for the priests to open the gates of the temple at midnight and for pilgrims to gather there at that time. The temple was on the east side of Jerusalem not far from Kidron and the Garden of Gethsemane. Westcott and others believe all the events of John 15—17 took place in the courts of the temple.

Jesus, knowing all things (18:4), led His disciples over Kidron to Gethsemane. Kidron is described by John with the word *cheimarrou*. This is a compound word meaning "flowing in winter." It was an intermittent stream or wadi that was only a brook during the winter or rainy season. Only John mentions Kidron, which is a Hebrew word meaning "black." Perhaps he identified crossing this dark and dry brook with the passing from the Holy of Holies (17:1–26) to the place where sin in all its darkness appeared to enjoy a momentary triumph.

When Jesus had spoken these words he went forth with his disciples over the brook Cedron, where was a garden, into the which he entered, and his disciples.

2 And Judas also, which betrayed him, knew the place: for Jesus ofttimes resorted thither with his disciples.

3 Judas then, having received a band of men and officers from the chief priests and Pharisees, cometh thither with lanterns and torches and weapons.

4 Jesus therefore, knowing all things that should come upon him, went forth, and said unto them, Whom seek ye?

5 They answered him, Jesus of Nazareth. Jesus saith unto them, I am he. And Judas also, which betrayed him, stood with them.

6 As soon then as he had said unto them, I am he, they went backward, and fell to the ground.

7 Then asked he them again, Whom seek ye? And they said, Jesus of Nazareth.

8 Jesus answered, I have told you that I am he: if therefore ye seek me, let these go their way:

9 That the saying might be fulfilled, which he spake, Of them which thou gavest me have I lost none.

10 Then Simon Peter having a sword drew it, and smote the high priest's servant, and cut off his right ear. The servant's name was Malchus.

11 Then said Jesus unto Peter, Put up thy sword into the sheath: the cup which my Father hath given me, shall I not drink it?

12 Then the band and the captain and officers of the Jews took Jesus, and bound him.

13 And led him away to Annas first; for he was father in law to Caiaphas, which was the high priest that same year.

14 Now Caiaphas was he, which gave counsel to the Jews, that it was expedient that one man should die for the people.

A. The Betrayal and Arrest of Jesus (18:1–14). The place where Jesus was betrayed was a garden in which Jesus and His disciples had often met. Godet is convinced Gethsemane was owned privately by friends of Jesus and made available to Him as a retreat from the crowds of Jerusalem whenever Jesus and His disciples were in that city. While the synoptic gospels portray Gethsemane as a place of sorrow and agony, John makes no mention at all of these events in his gospel. Perhaps he realized they were well known and wanted to emphasize to his readers that even now, in Gethsemane, Jesus was revealing Himself to all who had eyes to see. The early church often compared this garden with the Garden of Eden. In one garden, the human race was plunged into the bondage of sin. In the other garden, the sin bearer who liberates the slaves of sin was Himself bound.

When Judas came to betray Jesus, he was accompanied by enough support to get the job done. The expression *ten speiran*, here translated "a band" (18:3), normally referred to a military cohort and in this context could refer to as many as six hundred Roman soldiers stationed at the Tower of Antonia. Although many commentators argue it is unlikely that a full detachment would be sent to arrest Jesus, John uses the term *chiliarchos* (18:12), identifying the formal title of the chief captain of this detachment and suggests he was present at the arrest. If a small detachment had been sent, it is more likely that a centurion would have been the highest ranking officer present. In addition to the Roman soldiers, the temple police were also present. The Jews had earlier sent these officers to arrest Jesus, but they had at that time failed in their task (7:44,45).

Only John mentions the presence of lanterns. Perhaps the soldiers feared Jesus would hide in the shadows of the olive trees. The night in question may have been extremely cloudy (*see* 13:30). The fact these men came armed suggests they anticipated some degree of resistance on the part of Jesus. John, however, records the willing surrender of Jesus, even going out to meet His arrestors.

Jesus confronted this company with the question, "Whom seek ye?" (18:4). When they responded "Jesus of Nazareth," Jesus responded in a momentary revelation of His divine glory. Jesus used the familiar title "I am" (*ego eimi*, 18:5), identifying Himself with the Old Testament name of Jehovah. When He said, "I am," the power of God caused His arrestors to faint backward, being driven to the ground. John alone records this event which manifested the supernatural power of Christ. Throughout this chapter, John emphasizes the deity of Jesus, referring to His divine knowledge (18:4), His divine power (18:6), and His divine protection (18:8,9).

Twice in this chapter John uses the familiar expression, "That the saying might be fulfilled" (18:9,32). But unlike John's normal meaning when using this formula, he is not referring to a particular Old Testament Scripture, but rather to an earlier statement of Jesus made in this gospel (12:32,33; 17:12). In doing this, John treats the statements of Jesus on a par with the Old Testament Scriptures. As this gospel was written at a time when the New Testament was being collected at Ephesus, John may also be placing his gospel on a par with Old Testament Scripture.

Although it was contrary to Jewish law to carry a weapon on a feast day, there were two swords among the disciples when Jesus was arrested (Luke 22:38). This law was also being violated by those who arrested Jesus. Though all the Gospels record the cutting off of a servant's ear by a disciple, only John specifically identifies the servant as Malchus, and the disciple who did it as Peter (18:10). It may have been that John, who was known by the high priest (18:15), may have known this servant personally.

The sword Peter was carrying on this occasion was probably eighteen inches long and weighed about five pounds. The blade was thick and heavy and not necessarily sharp. When used in battle, one would raise this sword and bring it down on the head of the enemy hoping to find a weak place in the helmet and split his head. Some think this may have been Peter's intent but that his aim was slightly off. As a result, only the ear of Malchus was damaged. The verb *apekopsen*, here translated "cut off," literally means "to tear" or "to rip," not to slice. Peter cut off the right ear of the servant, but the Lord put it back on (Luke 22:51).

Peter seems to have been always doing the right things at the wrong time. Here Jesus rebuked Peter, reminding him that the Father had prepared a cup for Him to drink (18:11). Although John does not mention the agonizing prayer in Gethsemane as the other gospels do, he does make it clear that Jesus was resigned to doing the will of the Father and intended to drink of that bitter cup of judgment.

Treated as a dangerous criminal, Jesus was "bound" to prevent escape or rescue (18:12). According to the normal custom, this would simply involve tying the prisoner's hands behind his back. Still, this was an unusual procedure in this context as there was still no formal charge against Jesus. Also, under Jewish law it was unlawful to bind a prisoner before condemnation.

Chart 63

THE TRIALS OF JESUS
I. The Jewish trials
A. Before Annas (18:12–14)
B. Before Caiaphas (18:19–24)
C. Before the Sanhedrin (Matthew 27:1,2)
II. The Roman trials
A. Before Pilate (18:28–38)
B. Before Herod (Luke 23:6–11)
C. Before Pilate (18:39—19:16)

Jesus was first taken to Annas, whom John identifies as the father-in-law of Caiaphas, the high priest (18:13). Annas had himself served as high priest from A.D. 6 to 15 when he was deposed by Pilate's predecessor, Valerius Gratus. Though deposed, he was not without influence. He served as vice-president of the Sanhedrin and the patriarch of a family that held the office of the high priest as late as A.D. 62. These included five sons and a son-in-law. Also, there was some question among the Jews whether a Roman officer possessed the authority to depose a high priest, so that many Jews still looked to him as the high priest. While Annas may not have possessed the office of the high priest at this time, he was apparently the real power behind the office that night. Jesus' hearing before Annas was the first of three Jewish trials. John recorded the first two, both of which were illegal.

From a legal standpoint, the trial of Jesus was a farce. The very ones who laid great claims to upholding the law were guilty of its grossest violation. Some have suggested as many as forty-three specific illegalities in the proceedings. The requirements of Jewish law were very specific. A few of these violations are listed below:

1. The binding of a prisoner before he was condemned was unlawful unless resistance was offered or expected. Jesus certainly offered no resistance (18:12,24).
2. It was illegal for judges to participate in the arrest of the accused (18:3).
3. No legal transactions, including a trial, could be conducted at night (18:28).
4. The arrest was effected through the agency of an informer and traitor (18:5; *see* Exodus 23:6–8).
5. While an acquittal could be pronounced the same day, any other verdict required a majority of two and had to come on a subsequent day (Matthew 26:65,66).
6. No prisoner could be convicted on his own evidence (Matthew 26:63–65).
7. It was the duty of a judge to see that the interest of the accused was fully protected (18:14).
8. Preliminary hearings before a magistrate were completely foreign to the Jewish legal system (18:13).
9. It was illegal to carry weapons on the feast day (18:3).
10. The use of violence during the trial was apparently unopposed by the judges (18:22,23).
11. The judges sought false witnesses against Jesus (Matthew 26:59; Mark 14:56).
12. In a Jewish court the accused was to be assumed innocent until proved guilty by two or more witnesses (11:53).
13. The Jews failed to find two witnesses agreeing against Jesus (Mark 14:59).
14. When the witnesses first disagreed, the prisoner should have been released (Mark 14:56–59).
15. No witness was ever called for the defense.

16. The trial under Caiaphas took place in his home rather than the council chamber where it should have been held (18:13–16).
17. This court lacked the civil authority to condemn a man to death (18:31).
18. It was illegal to conduct a session of the court on a feast day (18:28).
19. A guilty verdict was rendered without evidence (18:30).
20. The balloting was illegal. It should have been by roll with the youngest voting first. Here the balloting is simultaneous (Matthew 26:66).
21. The sentence is finally passed in the palace of the high priest, but the law demanded it be pronounced in the temple, in the hall of hewn stone (18:28).
22. The high priest rends his garment (Matthew 26:65; see Leviticus 21:10). He was never permitted to tear his official robe. But if he did not have on his priestly robe, he couldn't put Christ under oath.

15 And Simon Peter followed Jesus, and so did another disciple: that disciple was known unto the high priest, and went in with Jesus into the palace of the high priest.

16 But Peter stood at the door without. Then went out that other disciple, which was known unto the high priest, and spake unto her that kept the door, and brought in Peter.

17 Then saith the damsel that kept the door unto Peter, Art not thou also one of this man's disciples? He saith, I am not.

18 And the servants and officers stood there, who had made a fire of coals; for it was cold: and they warmed themselves: and Peter stood with them, and warmed himself.

19 The high priest then asked Jesus of his disciples, and of his doctrine.

20 Jesus answered him, I spake openly to the world; I ever taught in the synagogue, and in the temple, whither the Jews always resort; and in secret have I said nothing.

21 Why askest thou me? ask them which heard me, what I have said unto them: behold, they know what I said.

22 And when he had thus spoken, one of the officers

which stood by struck Jesus with the palm of his hand, saying, Answerest thou the high priest so?

23 Jesus answered him, If I have spoken evil, bear witness of the evil: but if well, why smitest thou me?

24 Now Annas had sent him bound unto Caiaphas the high priest.

25 And Simon Peter stood and warmed himself. They said therefore unto him, Art not thou also one of his disciples? He denied it, and said, I am not.

26 One of the servants of the high priest, being his kinsman whose ear Peter cut off, saith, Did not I see thee in the garden with him?

27 Peter then denied again: and immediately the cock crew.

B. The Denial of Peter (18:15–27). In John's account of the Jewish trials, he intersperses a record of Peter's denial of Christ. The denials of Peter represent a major problem in that all the Gospels record three denials, but the context in which these denials occur are not the same. One proposed solution of this problem involves a literal interpretation of Jesus' predictions of the denial. According to Matthew, Luke, and John, Jesus said the cock would not crow until Peter had denied him three times (13:38; Matthew 26:34; Luke 22:34). Mark adds that there would be three denials before the cock crowed twice (Mark 14:30). If Peter had, in fact, denied Christ more than three times, it would only be necessary that three of these denials be recorded by each writer. That each writer recorded some denials differing from the others (*see* Chart 64) suggests there may have been other unrecorded denials.

When Jesus was arrested in the garden, all His disciples ran (Matthew 26:56). Later, John and Peter followed Jesus to the judgment hall. As John was known by the high priest, he was able to secure entrance to the home of the high priest for both Peter and himself. Although John remained faithful to Jesus being the only disciple present at the crucifixion (19:26), it was in the high priest's official residence that Peter denied Christ.

The denials of Peter began as soon as he entered the court of the high priest. It was a common Hebrew custom to have a female doorkeeper (*see* Acts 12:13). The expression *he paidiske he thuroros,* here translated "the damsel that kept the door" (18:17), designates the servant with this particular re-

Chart 64

THE RECORD OF PETER'S DENIAL OF CHRIST
1. When confronted by the maid at the door of the high priest's court (18:17).
2. When confronted by another maid near the fire in the court of the high priest (Matthew 26:70; Mark 14:66–68; Luke 22:55–57).
3. When asked by the group near the fire in the court of the high priest (18:25).
"And the cock crew" (Mark 14:68).
4. When confronted by the second maid a second time on the porch (Mark 14:69,70).
5. When confronted by a third maid on the porch (Matthew 26:71).
6. When confronted by another unidentified person (Luke 22:58).
7. When recognized by a kinsman of Malchus as being present in the garden with Jesus (18:26,27).
8. About an hour after number six above, when he is identified as a Galilean (Matthew 26:73,74; Luke 22:59,60).
9. When confronted by a group on account of his Galilean dialect (Mark 14:70,71).
"And the second time the cock crew" (Mark 14:72).

sponsibility. Her question was put to Peter anticipating a negative answer, "You are not also one of this man's disciples, are you?" (18:17, literal translation). The expression *tou anthropou toutou* (this man's) implied scorn and contempt. Probably the intent of the maid was to ridicule rather than expose Peter. She no doubt knew John was a disciple of Jesus and apparently did not make any further attempt to expose Peter publicly. Of all of Peter's confrontations that evening, this would have been the easiest place to confess Christ. Instead, he began a series of denials at the door.

While Peter was denying Christ in the outer court, the second illegal Jewish trial of Jesus was being conducted before Caiaphas. Though known popularly as Caiaphas, his real name was Joseph, and he held the office of the high priest from A.D. 18 to 36. According to Josephus and the later rabbinic writings, he had a reputation for intrigue, bribery, and the love of money. John has already twice revealed the decision of Caiaphas that Jesus should die for the people even before Jesus had been formally examined (11:49,50; 18:14). This was hardly the impartial attitude that should have characterized a judge.

Caiaphas began his questioning by asking about Jesus' disciples (18:19). Men would gather disciples either as a rabbi or Messiah. This was probably the first of many attempts that evening to secure from Jesus some statement that could be construed as blasphemous. Jesus responded to the high priest's questioning by reminding him that all of His teaching had been done publicly in the temple and in the synagogues of the Jews. In essence He was reminding Caiaphas of his duty to call witnesses and assuring him there were many witnesses who could be called. Mark records the lack of success the Sanhedrin experienced when they attempted to call their false witnesses (Mark 14:56,59).

One of the officers near Jesus struck Him (18:22). The verb *rapisma* occurs only three times in the New Testament (18:22; 19:3; Mark 14:65) and may mean "to strike with the hand or with a rod." The verb is etymologically related to the noun *rapis*, meaning "a rod." Another form of this verb is used in Matthew 26:67, where it means "to strike with a rod" in contrast with another verb meaning "to hit with the fist." It is not possible to be certain whether Jesus was here hit with the hand or rod of the officer. In either case, Jesus was bound and could not defend Himself from such attack. Also, the use of violence in a trial was strictly forbidden under Jewish law and should have been rebuked immediately by the high priest. Instead, it is Jesus who challenges the actions of this officer.

As Jesus was being tried by Caiaphas, Peter continued to deny Christ. The second denial recorded by John occurred when a group of the servants of this high priest and officers of the temple questioned him (18:25). The third recorded denial came when a kinsman of the man Peter had attacked in the garden questioned him (18:26,27). This would have been Peter's easiest denial. After denying Christ at least twice and then being confronted by one who might have been seeking revenge, it would have been very difficult for Peter to now change his story. If there had been any kind of family resemblance between Malchus and this servant, it would only have added to Peter's sense of fear and guilt. This third denial was followed by the crowing of a cock. This normally occurred about the third watch of the night, that is, 3:00 A.M. (*see* Mark 13:35).

Jesus was condemned by the Sanhedrin for blasphemy, which under Jewish law was punishable by stoning. Not all of the Pharisees were necessarily involved in this kangaroo court. John had earlier in this gospel suggested the support of Nicodemus (7:50,51) and carefully distinguishes between the Pharisees and that group within the Pharisees hostile toward Jesus known as "the Jews" (9:16,22). According to Jewish law, the quorum of the council was twenty-three, and a man could only be condemned by a majority of at least two. This means as few as thirteen men may have been responsible for the condemnation of Jesus. While it is likely that the hostile Jews numbered far more than this minimum, it is also possible that those Pharisees sympathetic to Jesus were absent, perhaps not even informed of the proceedings.

28 Then led they Jesus from Caiaphas unto the hall of judgment: and it was early; and they themselves went not into the judgment hall, lest they should be defiled; but that they might eat the passover.

29 Pilate then went out unto them, and said, What accusation bring ye against this man?

30 They answered and said unto him, If he were not a malefactor, we would not have delivered him up unto thee.

31 Then said Pilate unto them, Take ye him, and judge him according to your law. The Jews therefore said unto him, It is not lawful for us to put any man to death:

32 That the saying of Jesus might be fulfilled, which he spake, signifying what death he should die.

33 Then Pilate entered unto the judgment hall again, and called Jesus, and said unto him, Art thou the King of the Jews?

34 Jesus answered him, Sayest thou this thing of thyself, or did others tell it thee of me?

35 Pilate answered, Am I a Jew? Thine own nation and

the chief priests have delivered thee unto me: what hast thou done?

36 Jesus answered, My kingdom is not of this world: if my kingdom were of this world, then would my servants fight, that I should not be delivered to the Jews: but now is my kingdom not from hence.

37 Pilate therefore said unto him, Art thou a king then? Jesus answered, Thou sayest that I am a king. To this end was I born, and for this cause came I into the world, that I should bear witness unto the truth. Every one that is of the truth heareth my voice.

38 Pilate saith unto him, What is truth? And when he had said this, he went out again unto the Jews, and saith unto them, I find in him no fault at all.

39 But ye have a custom, that I should release unto you one at the passover: will ye therefore that I release unto you the King of the Jews?

40 Then cried they all again, saying, Not this man, but Barabbas. Now Barabbas was a robber.

C. *The Trial of Jesus Before Pilate (18:28–40).* According to John, Jesus was led from Caiaphas to the hall of judgment. The word *praitorion,* used here to describe the place, is derived from the Latin word *praetorium,* which was the name of the official residence of a Roman governor. Commentators are divided as to the location of Pilate's residence. Probably it was the palace built by Herod the Great in the western part of Jerusalem, although some also argue for the Castle of Antonia located just north of the temple. The trial before Pilate was very early. The word *proi,* here translated "early" was technically the fourth watch of the evening, 3:00–6:00 A.M. If the formal meeting of the Sanhedrin followed the denial of Peter and the cock crowing (3:00 A.M.), it must have been a rather brief gathering. By the end of the fourth watch, Jesus was delivered to be crucified (19:14).

When the Jews arrived at the judgment hall, they were careful not to enter. They had as yet not eaten the Passover and believed a Jew would be defiled if he entered a Gentile home. It is interesting to note their devotion to the law at this point having so blatantly violated it in the trial of Jesus. Commenting on the hypocrisy of the Jews during this particular Passover season, Darby observes, "Conscience did not prevent the Jews buying the blood of Jesus for thirty pieces of silver; but a scruple forbade their putting it into the temple of God, the money rejected by Judas, because it was the price of blood."[52] To this Hoskyns adds, "They who pretend so great devotion are in fact guilty of gross superstition, for the execution of the Messiah becomes the preparation for their solemn festival."[53]

Pontius Pilate was the procurator of Judea from A.D. 26 to 36. In A.D. 36 he was deposed by Vitellius and sent to Rome where he was tried and probably executed under Caligula. During his administration, he ruled Judea in a rather reckless and arbitrary fashion. According to Josephus, Pilate used funds in the temple treasury to build an aqueduct. When the people protested, they were beaten by Roman soldiers. Tenney believes the funds may have been given to Pilate by the priests in exchange for political favors. If this were the situation, it may explain the attitude of the Sanhedrin when they first approached Pilate. Initially, they apparently hoped Pilate would simply take their word that Jesus was guilty and crucify Him (18:30). Only after this failed did they present formal charges.

A Roman trial normally began with the statement, "What accusation bring ye against this man?" (18:29). When the charge was revealed, any evidence for both sides was presented and a verdict rendered. The Roman governor had the option to judge in the trial of a non-Roman citizen or to delegate his authority to another officer or court. When Pilate found that Jesus had violated some Jewish law, he apparently opted to authorize the Sanhedrin to try Him and carry out the prescribed sentence under Jewish law (18:31). This was the first of six attempts on the part of Pilate to release Jesus (see Chart 65).

The Jews declined the right to try Jesus claiming, "It is not lawful for us to put any man to death" (18:31). This statement has been interpreted various ways. Some suggest the Jews were merely acknowledging they did not have the civil authority to condemn a man to death. The problem with this interpretation is that Pilate's statement in effect authorized the Jews to inflict the necessary penalty for blasphemy—stoning. These Jews were apparently ready to inflict capital punishment earlier in Jesus' ministry (8:3–5, 59) and did in fact stone Stephen without first seeking Roman approval

Chart 65

HOW DID PILATE TRY TO RELEASE CHRIST?
1. You judge Him (18:31).
2. He is innocent (18:38).
3. Jews substitute Barabbas (18:39).
4. Partial punishment (19:1).
5. Play on pity (19:5).
6. Behold your King (19:14).

(Acts 7:58). This statement could also mean they were unable to kill Jesus because of the Passover. They were careful not to defile themselves by entering Pilate's hall and may have been just as careful not to defile themselves by physically participating in the actual execution of Jesus.

The phrase *ouk exestin* (it is not lawful) occurs only twice in John's Gospel (5:10; 18:31), although it commonly occurs in the other Gospels. On each occasion the phrase refers not to civil authority but rather the law of God. John himself seems to interpret this statement not so much concerning the fact of Jesus' death as the means whereby He is executed (18:32). Apparently the Jews had decided Jesus should be crucified, but the law of God forbade the shedding of human blood. As a result, they were dependent upon the Romans to carry out the sentence.

The accusation of Jesus before the Sanhedrin was for the sin of blasphemy (Mark 14:61–64). However, blasphemy was not considered a crime by the Romans and certainly not an act worthy of death. According to Luke, at least four other charges were laid against Jesus under Roman law (Luke 23:2,5). While Pilate apparently ignored three of these charges, he could not ignore the charge of treason. It was a crime to which Tiberius Caesar was particularly sensitive, and every suggestion that treason existed was carefully investigated and severely punished. Because the Jews would not enter the praetorium, the trials of Jesus before Pilate alternated between his outside meetings with the Jews and his inside meetings with Jesus as shown in Chart 66.

In His defense before Pilate, Jesus stated, "My kingdom is not of this world" (18:36). Some have erroneously taken this statement to mean Jesus was denying the future existence of

Chart 66

PILATE'S VACILLATION		
Out	Heard their non-indictment	18:28–32
In	Are you a king?	18:33–37
Out	I find no fault	18:38–40
In	Scourged Jesus	19:1–3
Out	Behold the Man	19:4–8
In	Pilate sought to release Him	19:9–12
Out	Behold your King	19:13–16

a literal kingdom on earth (the millennium). When understood within its context, this interpretation is not likely. Jesus was simply affirming, as He later did with His disciples, that this was not the time His kingdom would be established (see Acts 1:6–11). He reminds Pilate that had that been the case, there would have been some sort of armed insurrection against the Romans.

The phrase translated "Art thou a king then?" (18:37) is an interesting statement which could be translated as a question or as a declaration whose force is affirmative—"So then, you are a king!" Even if it is a question, the grammar is such that it assumes a positive response. John suggests Pilate recognizes the kingship of Jesus. One of the credal statements of the early church spoke of Jesus witnessing a good confession before Pilate (see 1 Timothy 6:13). During the Middle Ages several traditions arose suggesting Pilate was finally converted to Christ before his death, but these are apparently without historical verification. If Pilate had begun to recognize Jesus as a king, he had not yet recognized Him as his King. When he finally sent Jesus out to be crucified, his accusation read "Jesus of Nazareth the King of the Jews" (19:19).

After his initial interrogation of Jesus, Pilate arrived at the verdict, "I find in him no fault at all" (18:38). Until this point, Pilate had closely adhered to Roman law. With the pronouncement of a not-guilty verdict, the prisoner should immediately have been released. Under Roman law, everything in the trial of Jesus following this verdict was clearly illegal.

This chapter closes with an account of Pilate's attempt to release Jesus and the crowd's choice of Barabbas. Outside of the Gospels, this custom of releasing a prisoner is completely unknown. The name *Barabbas* is Aramaic meaning "a son of a father." It has been suggested that his release symbolically illustrates that Jesus died for every son of every father, for all men. It is an interesting irony that the mob chose Barabbas, a son of a father, over Jesus, whom John identified in a later epistle as "the son of the Father" (2 John 3).

TWENTY-ONE

CHRIST—
THE LAMB OF GOD
JOHN 19:1–42

Jesus was brought to trial six times before He was crucified. The first three of those trials were Jewish—before Annas (18:12–14), before the high priest (18:19–24), and before the Sanhedrin (Matthew 27:1,2). The last three were handled by the Romans. First, Jesus was brought before Pilate, the governor of Judea (18:28–38). After an intensive interrogation of Christ, Pilate concluded, "I find in him no fault at all" (18:38). Although John's record of the trials before Pilate appears as a continuation of the same trial, we know Christ was delivered to Herod in between verses thirty-eight and thirty-nine (Luke 23:4–12). The third Roman trial (the second before Pilate) begins in John 18:39 and ends in Jesus' crucifixion.

Why was the trial of Pilate interrupted and Jesus delivered to Herod? In an emotional outburst the people claimed Christ began His ministry in Galilee (Luke 23:5). When Pilate learned Jesus was a Galilean, he delivered Him to Herod, the governor of Galilee (Luke 23:6,7). Pilate had attempted in several ways to dispose of Jesus' case without rendering a verdict. Sending Jesus to Herod was another of those ways. Before Herod, Jesus refused to answer any questions, while the chief priests and scribes "vehemently accused him." After treating Him with contempt and mocking Him, Herod's soldiers threw around Him a beautiful robe, then returned Him to Pilate (Luke 23:8–12).

I. CHRIST BEFORE PILATE (19:1–15)

Pilate is the classic example of a vacillating individual with great authority and yet no willpower. Although he had great power at his command, he seems to have possessed neither courage nor self-determination. Convinced of Jesus' innocence, Pilate lacked the strength of character to oppose the threats and pressures of the Jews. He proves the adage, "Power in the hands of a little man is a dangerous thing." In the sentencing of Jesus, Pilate represents the principle of government by expediency.

> Then Pilate therefore took Jesus, and scourged him.
> 2 And the soldiers platted a crown of thorns, and put it on his head, and they put on him a purple robe.
> 3 And said, Hail, King of the Jews! and they smote him with their hands.

A. Inside the Praetorium (19:1–3). Initially unwilling to go the length of committing a judicial murder, Pilate scourged Jesus without cause, hoping thereby to satisfy the Jews. In this scourging the prisoner was stripped of his clothing and was bound to a low pillar or stake. Normally scourging was preliminary to a crucifixion, but this illegal act was performed before sentencing. The Roman whip consisted of a short handle to which were attached leather thongs. Some of these had metal stones or a lead ball attached to the end; some were only leather with knotted ends. The lashes broke the skin, and many times the flesh was broken or the entire back side was a mass of torn, bleeding tissue. Although the Jews had a limit of thirty-nine lashes in punishing prisoners, the Romans had no such limit. The severity of Christ's beating is probably evidenced in His inability to bear His cross (see Luke 23:26).

Pilate also allowed the cruel mockery by the soldiers and their continual slapping of Jesus. A comparison of the accounts of that night suggests Jesus may have been crowned with thorns several times, both before and after sentencing

(Matthew 27:27–30; Mark 15:16–19). Probably because Jesus had been accused of treason, the soldiers addressed Him with the greeting one would normally use in greeting Caesar, *chaire* (hail, 19:3). The tense of the verb *edidosan* suggests the emphasis "they kept on giving him slaps with their hands" (19:3).

> 4 Pilate therefore went forth again, and saith unto them, Behold, I bring him forth to you, that ye may know that I find no fault in him.
> 5 Then came Jesus forth, wearing the crown of thorns, and the purple robe. And Pilate saith unto them, Behold the man!
> 6 When the chief priests therefore and officers saw him, they cried out, saying, Crucify him, crucify him. Pilate saith unto them, Take ye him, and crucify him: for I find no fault in him.
> 7 The Jews answered him, We have a law, and by our law he ought to die, because he made himself the Son of God.

B. Outside the Praetorium (19:4–7) The Jews would not enter the praetorium because they would have been defiled, and the following day was the Passover. Because they would not enter before Pilate's judgment seat, the charges against Jesus should have been dismissed. The fact that Pilate went *out* to them is incredible. He did not have to go out, and by doing so, Pilate was honoring their wishes.

Pilate unsuccessfully appealed to the Jews in the hope that they would either agree to or ignore the release of Jesus. After declaring that Jesus was innocent, he brought Jesus out

Chart 67

THE FIVE INSULTS HEAPED UPON CHRIST BY THE ROMANS (19:1–3)
1. They scourged Him without cause.
2. They crowned Him with thorns.
3. They threw a royal robe on His bleeding back.
4. They mocked Him saying, "Hail, King of the Jews."
5. They slapped Him with their open hands.

to the crowd and presented Him to the Jews dressed in a purple robe and wearing a crown of thorns. In his appeal, Pilate urged "Behold the man!" (19:5). Perhaps he was hoping the sight of a severely beaten and abused man would touch a chord of humanity in them, but from the heart of the chief priests and their officers came the chant "Crucify him, crucify him." The verb *stauroson* (crucify, 19:6) is an aorist imperative with no stated object. Probably these leaders simply continued to chant the word *crucify* until others began to join in, the way fans in a stadium might follow the lead of cheerleaders. It was probably in a state of frustration that Pilate finally conceded and told the Jews to take Him and crucify Him, even though he still held to Jesus' innocence (19:6).

There were two charges brought against Christ by the Jews. The first charge was treason—that He claimed to be "the King of the Jews" (18:33,37). Finally, when Pilate did not take this charge seriously, the Jews threatened to blackmail him, "If thou let this man go, thou art not Caesar's friend: whosoever maketh himself a king speaketh against Caesar" (19:12). The second charge was blasphemy, "because he made himself the Son of God" (19:7). This was the real reason the Jews wanted to kill Jesus Christ, but it was not the legal charge against Him. Pilate set on His cross, "THIS IS JESUS THE KING OF THE JEWS" (Matthew 27:37).

The Jews revealed their real motive in wanting Him dead, "because he made himself the Son of God" (19:7). To the Jews, this was unheard-of blasphemy which demanded severe punishment. To a pagan leader like Pilate, a God-man was a real possibility that required careful investigation. Greek and Roman mythology are filled with accounts of the gods living among men. This was the third warning Pilate had received concerning his involvement in this case, and he became even more fearful (19:8, *see* Chart 68).

Chart 68

PILATE'S THREE WARNINGS
1. Dream of his wife (Matthew 27:19)
2. Good witness of Christ (1 Timothy 6:13)
3. Real motive of Sanhedrin revealed (John 19:7)

8 When Pilate therefore heard that saying, he was the more afraid;

9 And went again into the judgment hall, and saith unto Jesus, Whence art thou? But Jesus gave him no answer.

10 Then saith Pilate unto him, Speakest thou not unto me? knowest thou not that I have power to crucify thee, and have power to release thee?

11 Jesus answered, Thou couldest have no power at all against me, except it were given thee from above: therefore he that delivered me unto thee hath the greater sin.

C. *Inside the Praetorium (19:8–11).* Due to Pilate's fear, he returned to the judgment hall and asked Jesus, "Where are you from?" (19:9 RSV). When Jesus refused to answer him, Pilate reminded Him of his authority to either release or crucify Him. Pilate, a pagan, would not have understood the answer to his question, but he could understand the fact of the supremacy and ultimate authority of the deity. Pilate's sin was great, but that of the Sanhedrin was greater (19:11).

12 And from thenceforth Pilate sought to release him: but the Jews cried out, saying, If thou let this man go, thou art not Caesar's friend: whosoever maketh himself a king speaketh against Caesar.

13 When Pilate therefore heard that saying, he brought Jesus forth, and sat down in the judgment seat in a place that is called the Pavement, but in the Hebrew, Gabbatha.

14 And it was the preparation of the passover, and about the sixth hour: and he saith unto the Jews, Behold your King!

15 But they cried out, Away with him, away with him, crucify him. Pilate saith unto them, Shall I crucify your King? The chief priests answered, We have no king but Caesar.

D. *Outside the Praetorium (19:12–15).* Pilate sought by every means to release Jesus, not because he had a passion for justice, but for the sake of self-interest. For the same reason, he ordered the crucifixion of Jesus, driven by the fear of losing his position (19:12) and perhaps his life, if he should allow a man considered a dangerous rebel such as Jesus to go free. At all costs Pilate sought to retain Caesar's favor.

The expression "Caesar's friend" (19:12) was a formal title of honor used by the Romans, perhaps even one with which

Pilate had at times been addressed. But the intent of the Jews
in using this charge related not to title but to his personal
loyalty to Caesar. The reigning Caesar was particularly concerned over charges of treason, and such a rumor could result in Pilate's recall to Rome to stand trial. It was also a false
charge of treason that resulted in Pilate's initial willingness
to hear the case against Jesus.

Pilate's final attempt to release Jesus occurred about 6:00
A.M. on the day before the Passover, Friday (19:14). He presented Jesus noting, "Behold your King!" Perhaps for the
first and only time in their lives, the chief priests volunteered
the affirmation, "We have no king but Caesar" (19:15). On
any other occasion they would have resented being forced to
make such a statement.

Some writers have accused John of inaccuracy in recording
the time of these events. According to both Matthew and
Mark, Jesus was on the cross at the sixth hour (Matthew
27:45; Mark 15:33). The resolution to this problem is in recognizing the two different kinds of time used in the Gospels.
Matthew and Mark both use Jewish time, which began
counting the hours of the day at sunrise, 6:00 A.M. John,
however, uses Roman time in this occasion, which began
counting the hours at midnight. Therefore, the act of crucifixion began about dawn—the sixth hour, Jewish time.

II. THE CRUCIFIXION OF CHRIST (19:16–30)

16 Then delivered he him therefore unto them to be
crucified. And they took Jesus, and led him away.

17 And he bearing his cross went forth into a place
called the place of a skull, which is called in the Hebrew
Golgotha:

18 Where they crucified him, and two other with him,
on either side one, and Jesus in the midst.

19 And Pilate wrote a title, and put it on the cross. And
the writing was, JESUS OF NAZARETH THE KING OF
THE JEWS.

20 This title then read many of the Jews: for the place
where Jesus was crucified was nigh to the city: and it was
written in Hebrew, and Greek, and Latin.

21 Then said the chief priests of the Jews to Pilate, Write
not, The King of the Jews; but that he said, I am King of the
Jews.

22 Pilate answered, What I have written I have written.

23 Then the soldiers, when they had crucified Jesus, took his garments, and made four parts, to every soldier a part; and also his coat: now the coat was without seam, woven from the top throughout.

24 They said therefore among themselves, Let us not rend it, but cast lots for it, whose it shall be: that the scripture might be fulfilled, which saith, They parted my raiment among them, and for my vesture they did cast lots. These things therefore the soldiers did.

25 Now there stood by the cross of Jesus his mother, and his mother's sister, Mary the wife of Cleophas, and Mary Magdalene.

26 When Jesus therefore saw his mother, and the disciple standing by, whom he loved, he saith unto his mother, Woman, behold thy son!

27 Then saith he to the disciple, Behold thy mother! And from that hour that disciple took her unto his own home.

28 After this, Jesus knowing that all things were now accomplished, that the scripture might be fulfilled, saith, I thirst.

29 Now there was set a vessel full of vinegar: and they filled a spunge with vinegar, and put it upon hyssop, and put it to his mouth.

30 When Jesus therefore had received the vinegar, he said, It is finished: and he bowed his head, and gave up the ghost.

The most significant event in human history was now

Chart 69

WHAT KIND OF DEATH DID JESUS DIE? (19:14–37)	
It was a death of:	
1. Humiliation	19:17,18
2. Mourning	19:25–27
3. Suffering	19:28
4. Completing the Passover	19:14; Matthew 27:51
5. Fulfilling prophecy	19:36,37

about to be accomplished. Pilate delivered Jesus to the Jews knowing their intent was to crucify Him. The state of confusion that must have existed that day is evidenced in that it appears there was no formal sentencing of Jesus. John uses the verb *paredoken* (delivered), meaning "to give over to the side," to describe Pilate's act of surrendering Jesus to the Sanhedrin (19:16). This is the same verb used of the Sanhedrin's giving of Jesus to Pilate (18:30). In this gospel, John lays a great deal of emphasis on the involvement of the Jews in the crucifixion.

Because of its significance in Christian theology, each Gospel records an account of the crucifixion, emphasizing particular details not mentioned by the other writers. These accounts are not contradictory but complementary. When compared and studied together, we have a fuller outline of the details surrounding the crucifixion (*see* Chart 70).

Chart 70

THE EVENTS OF CALVARY		
1.	Carrying His cross.	John 19:17
2.	Simon substituted.	Luke 23:26
3.	Offer of stupefying drink.	Matthew 27:34
4.	Nailed between two thieves.	John 19:18–24
*5.	"Father, forgive them."	Luke 23:34
6.	Jews mock Jesus.	Matthew 27:39–43
7.	One thief rails at Jesus, the other receives salvation.	Luke 23:39–43
*8.	"To day shalt thou be with me."	Luke 23:43
*9.	"Woman, behold thy son!"	John 19:26,27
10.	Darkness.	Matthew 27:45
*11.	"My God, . . . why hast thou forsaken me?"	Matthew 27:46
*12.	"I thirst."	John 19:28
*13.	"It is finished."	John 19:30
*14.	"Father, into thy hands I commend my spirit."	Luke 23:46
15.	Our Lord dismisses His spirit.	John 19:30
* The seven sayings of Christ on the cross.		

Jesus was led to a place of execution outside the city and crucified between two robbers who, like Barabbas, may have been guilty of sedition and treason. He was "numbered with the transgressors," as prophesied in Isaiah 53:12. It was customary for a condemned criminal to carry his own cross to the place of execution. Jesus began bearing His cross, but after He stumbled under its weight, the Romans selected Simon of Cyrene and forced him to carry the cross (Luke 23:26). Probably Simon was selected at random from the crowd.

John, like Matthew and Mark, identifies the hill where Jesus was crucified as Golgotha, using the Hebrew name for that place. Luke uses the Greek name *Kranion* (Latin, *Calvaria*) for the same place (Luke 23:33). It was popularly known as "the place of a skull" (19:17) probably because the relief of that hill resembles a skull in appearance when viewed from a distance. Conservative scholars generally identify this place with Gordon's Calvary just outside the city of Jerusalem. It was there that they crucified Jesus. The hill was close to the city wall (19:20).

Crucifixion was a form of execution generally used by Rome to punish those guilty of capital offenses. It involved tying or nailing an individual to a cross in such a way as to suspend the body by the arms, resulting in a slow suffocation of the prisoner. Often the crucified man would use his legs for support, thus slowing the process of death. There are records of men who hung on the cross for up to nine days awaiting inevitable death. When the soldiers wanted the condemned to die faster, they would break his legs with a heavy mallet, making it impossible for the prisoner to support himself. This was the intent behind the request of the Jews (19:31).

It was customary to publish a title consisting of the name of the accused and the crime for which he was being crucified, and to post it on his cross. Only John records the detail that the title for Jesus' cross was actually written by Pilate himself (19:19). John uses the technical Latin word *titlon* to identify this board bearing the name and legal crime. This word was used widely for any official publication such as a bill, notice of sale, or even the title page of a book. This name and charge against Jesus was published in three languages: Hebrew, being the national language; Latin, the official lan-

guage of the empire; and Greek, a common language in that
area. Many writers have noted a second meaning to these
languages. Christ was not only the real center of religious
society (Hebrew), He is also the real center of the world's
intellectual community (Greek) and its legal and material
civilization (Latin). Comparing the Gospels, the full title of
Christ on the cross read, "This is Jesus of Nazareth the King
of the Jews" (19:19; Matthew 27:37).

When the title of Christ was published, the chief priests
appealed to Pilate to have it changed to include the prefix
"he said" (19:21). John here uses the unique expression "the
chief priests of the Jews," probably to emphasize a contrast
between them and the King of the Jews. The two words they
wanted added were *ekeinos eipen*, an emphatic expression
emphasizing the *he* in "he said." Even as Jesus hung on the
cross, they were concerned about minimizing the significance of His claims and feared the title might suggest the
Roman authorities took His claim seriously. While the title
"King of the Jews" was treasonous to the Romans, it was
messianic to the Jews. In a sudden fit of stubbornness, Pilate
refused this request.

Plummer calls attention to the contrast between the two
groups represented at the cross noting, "On the one hand,
the four plundering soldiers with the centurion; on the other,
the four ministering women with the beloved disciple."[54]
Even in the midst of the four soldiers gambling over the robe
of Christ (19:23,24), Scripture was being fulfilled (Psalms
22:18). The four women at the cross were Mary Magdalene,
Mary, the wife of Cleophas, Mary the mother of Jesus, and
Jesus' aunt (His mother's sister). These, along with John,
"the disciple . . . whom he loved" (19:26), were evidently

Chart 71

CHRIST SUFFERED FOR US	
1. Suffering anticipated	Leviticus 16:15
2. Suffering predicted	Isaiah 53:3–7
3. Suffering known by Jesus	Matthew 16:21
4. Suffering endured	John 19:28
5. Suffering finished	John 19:30

gathered to mourn and were the only sympathetic witnesses to the crucifixion of our Lord.

This gospel alone records the detail concerning Jesus, His mother, and the Apostle John (19:26,27). Note that Mary was assigned to be cared for by John, not John and the rest of the disciples cared for by Mary, as has been erroneously taught. Under the law, it was the responsibility of the firstborn to care for his aging parents. Here Jesus transfers that responsibility to His beloved disciple. His concern and provision for Mary, even in the midst of His agony, is an example of His shepherd's heart for all who rest under His spiritual responsibility.

As the end approached, Jesus was alert enough to know what was being accomplished spiritually in His death. His fifth cry from the cross was "I thirst" (19:28). Thirst was a common sensation experienced by a crucified man. While this expression may reflect a dimension of the passion of Christ, it had a greater significance in that it resulted in the fulfillment of Scripture. The fulfillment was not in the cry of Christ, but rather in the response of those around the cross who gave Him vinegar to drink (see Psalms 69:21). Their use of a hyssop reed (19:29) gives a hint as to the height of the cross, as the longest reed would not be more than three or four feet.

Although Jesus had earlier refused the offer of drugged vinegar, He did accept this offer. When He had done so, He made the next cry from the cross, "It is finished" (19:30; see Chart 73). This is John's last recorded statement of Jesus from the cross. He had finished the work He had come to accomplish and had now provided for the salvation of the world. The moment of His death was the moment of our salvation (see Romans 6:3; Galatians 2:20).

When Jesus "bowed his head, and gave up the ghost" (19:30), it literally means that Christ delivered up His own

Chart 72

JOHN'S VIEW OF JESUS ON THE CROSS
1. Behold the Lamb of God (1:29,36).
2. Behold the man (19:5).
3. Behold your King (19:14).

Chart 73

IT IS FINISHED
1. His physical suffering was over. 2. The last Old Testament lamb was sacrificed. 3. He made propitiation for the sins of the world. 4. He died physically. 5. The plan of salvation was complete.

spirit. Death had no power over Christ until by His own choice He surrendered to it, dismissing His spirit. Jesus predicted that He would lay down His life voluntarily and would raise it up again. "No man taketh it from me, but I lay it down of myself. I have power to lay it down, and I have power to take it again" (10:18). In order to accomplish redemption as the Lamb of God, He willingly and deliberately surrendered His life.

III. THE BURIAL OF JESUS (19:31–42)

31 The Jews therefore, because it was the preparation, that the bodies should not remain upon the cross on the sabbath day, (for that sabbath day was an high day,) besought Pilate that their legs might be broken, and that they might be taken away.

32 Then came the soldiers, and brake the legs of the first, and of the other which was crucified with him.

33 But when they came to Jesus, and saw that he was dead already, they brake not his legs:

34 But one of the soldiers with a spear pierced his side, and forthwith came there out blood and water.

35 And he that saw it bare record, and his record is true: and he knoweth that he saith true, that ye might believe.

36 For these things were done, that the scripture should be fulfilled, A bone of him shall not be broken.

37 And again another scripture saith, They shall look on him whom they pierced.

38 And after this Joseph of Arimathaea, being a disciple of Jesus, but secretly for fear of the Jews, besought Pilate that he might take away the body of Jesus: and Pilate gave

him leave. He came therefore, and took the body of Jesus.

39 And there came also Nicodemus, which at the first came to Jesus by night, and brought a mixture of myrrh and aloes, about an hundred pound weight.

40 Then took they the body of Jesus, and wound it in linen clothes with the spices, as the manner of the Jews is to bury.

41 Now in the place where he was crucified there was a garden; and in the garden a new sepulchre, wherein was never man yet laid.

42 There laid they Jesus therefore because of the Jews' preparation day; for the sepulchre was nigh at hand.

Because of the approaching Passover, the Jews requested that the legs of the men on the cross be broken, thus speeding their death. Although they had just committed judicial murder, they were concerned about observing the ritual law and did not want the bodies on the cross on the Sabbath. The breaking of the legs would hasten death and make possible the removal of the bodies before the beginning of the Passover Sabbath. But Jesus was already dead. To make certain, His side was pierced "and forthwith came there out blood and water" (19:34). Many writers argue from this account that the spear pierced the side of Jesus near the heart. The description of the blood and water separating suggests the physical cause of Jesus' death was a ruptured or broken heart. Whatever this may signify, the whole circumstance made a profound impression on the beloved disciple. (*See* Chart 74.)

Chart 74

WHAT REALITIES WERE INVOLVED IN THE PIERCING OF JESUS' SIDE?
1. Reality of Christ's *humanity*, for there was a flow of blood.
2. Reality of Christ's *deity*, for there was something unexpected, unusual, noteworthy—"blood and water"—something more than human.
3. Reality of Christ's *death* and, therefore, His resurrection.
4. Reality of clear and unexpected *fulfillment* of two messianic prophecies (19:36,37).

Not only was the piercing of His side significant, but also the fact that His bones were not broken. Had they been broken, it would have violated both scriptural requirements and prophecy. Exodus 12:46 reveals that in the Passover, the bones of the lamb could not be broken. Psalms 34:20 predicts that, "He keepeth all his bones: not one of them is broken." The prophet Zechariah had spoken concerning His pierced side (Zechariah 12:10).

In contrast to the hostile petition of the Jews, we have the friendly petition of Joseph of Arimathea. He, together with Nicodemus, courageously came forward to give the sacred body a fitting and dignified burial. The thoughts of Joseph and Nicodemus are not revealed; God only records the good deed they performed. But as they removed the body of Jesus from the cross, prepared it with perfumes and spices, and laid it in the burial chamber, they must have wondered if their reluctance as members of the Sanhedrin (3:1; Luke 23:50,51) to confess openly their support of Christ had contributed to His death. Nicodemus and Joseph were required by circumstances to reveal the testimony they had long kept secret.

While the synoptic gospels mention the role of Joseph in the burial of Christ, only John notes the involvement of Nicodemus. Nicodemus provided one hundred pounds of spices to anoint the body of Jesus. Even recognizing the Roman pound was only twelve ounces, this was still a lot of spices. Probably the men covered the entire body of Jesus before wrapping it for burial. The word translated "spices" (19:40) is *aromaton*, derived from the word for fumes. The men anointed the body of Christ and wrapped it in linen cloths

Chart 75

WHAT FACTS DO WE KNOW ABOUT THE TOMB WHERE JESUS WAS BURIED?
The tomb: 1. belonged to a rich man (19:38; Matthew 27:59,60). 2. was near the crucifixion spot (19:41). 3. had never been used before (19:41). 4. was hewn out of a rock (Mark 15:46). 5. had a stone rolled over the door (Mark 15:46).

Chart 76

HOW WAS THE BODY OF JESUS BURIED? (19:38–42)
1. By loving hands (19:38,39). 2. Wound in linen cloths (19:40). 3. Buried as a Jew (19:40). 4. Immediately (Luke 23:54). 5. Covered with one hundred pounds of spices (19:39). 6. Observed by the women (Mark 15:47).

(RSV). Both John and Luke use the word *othoniois* to identify these cloths which were also used by Greeks for ships' sails. The spices on the body were probably applied so liberally that there were none to anoint the linens. As Meyer observes, "Extraordinary reverence in its sorrowful excitement does not easily satisfy itself."[55] Still the fumes of the spices penetrated the linens to some degree. According to Luke, the women who witnessed this burial returned home to prepare spices and ointments to finish the burial procedure later (Luke 23:56).

This tomb was identified as belonging to Joseph (Matthew 27:59,60). According to John, it was located in a garden within the vicinity of the crucifixion. Since the sepulcher was in a familiar place to the women and the disciples, the women taking careful notice of where Jesus was placed in the tomb (Luke 23:55), it was impossible for the women to go to the wrong tomb on the resurrection day as some theological liberals proclaim. Not only were the death and burial of Jesus valid, but so also was His resurrection.

TWENTY-TWO

CHRIST—
THE VICTORIOUS ONE
JOHN 20:1–31

Fundamental to everything a Christian believes is the miracle of the physical resurrection of Christ from the dead. B.B. Warfield called it "the cardinal doctrine of our system: on it all other doctrines hang."[56] The pages of Acts record a constant emphasis in the preaching of the apostles concerning the resurrection of Christ. The Apostle Paul went so far in emphasis as to argue that if there is no resurrection, there is no Gospel (*see* 1 Corinthians 15). It is not surprising then that John gives extensive details about the resurrection and that his purpose for writing the book grows out of an understanding of the resurrection (20:31). The resurrection is the basis of eternal life that is promised to all who believe in Jesus Christ.

Unlike the philosophies and doctrines of other religious movements, the resurrection is more than an idea; it is an event in history. Thomas Arnold once wrote, "I know of no one fact in the history of mankind which is proved by better and fuller evidence of every sort, to the understanding of a fair inquirer, than the great sign which God hath given us that Christ died and rose again from the dead."[57] This chapter tells about the resurrection, which is described as Christianity's most certain event.

340

John, like Matthew, Mark, Luke, and Paul, tells an independent story of the resurrection, but no one contradicts the other; each gives different events that make up the complete narrative. Any seeming disagreements are due to the fact that each writer wrote what he witnessed or was told. John was the only writer to be an eyewitness of the empty tomb; therefore, his is a firsthand report.

I. THE PROOF OF THE EMPTY TOMB (20:1–10)

The first day of the week cometh Mary Magdalene early, when it was yet dark, unto the sepulchre, and seeth the stone taken away from the sepulchre.

2 Then she runneth, and cometh to Simon Peter, and to the other disciple, whom Jesus loved, and saith unto them, They have taken away the Lord out of the sepulchre, and we know not where they have laid him.

A. *Mary's Witness* (20:1,2). The first one to discover the empty tomb was Mary Magdalene. This was the same Mary out of whom Jesus cast seven demons (Mark 16:9). The tradition that she had been an immoral woman before following Jesus is without any biblical support. The name Magdalene literally means "from Magdala" and may refer to her home town. The village of Magdala was on the Sea of Galilee about five miles north of the town of Tiberias. Because of the great deliverance she had received from Christ, she had great devotion for Him.

Mary Magdalene came early to the tomb. Although John mentions her alone, she was not the only one at the tomb. The other gospels refer to three other women—Mary, the mother of James; Salome; and Joanna (Mark 16:1; Luke 24:10). John evidently referred to Mary Magdalene alone because she was the apparent leader of the group. Not only was she mentioned first in each Gospel account, but according to John she arrived earlier than the rest. Perhaps she left them a little ways to the rear or went ahead to survey the scene.

While all the Gospel writers agree the women found the tomb empty that Sunday morning, there is misunderstanding concerning the time. The synoptic gospels generally agree that these things occurred very early after sunrise. John here says, "when it was yet dark" (20:1). It may be that Mary made her way from her home even before dawn, but by the time the angels appeared to the women the sun had risen. A second possible explanation is in keeping with John's metaphorical use of *skotia*. At other times John has commented on the darkness of the hour, implying not just physical darkness but also spiritual darkness. In that case, Mary would have also arrived at the tomb "when it was yet dark"—still in a state of darkness because she had not yet seen the resurrected Light of the World.

Apparently Mary did not wait with the other women to inspect the tomb and see the angels. When she saw the stone was removed from the tomb, perhaps even before coming to the tomb itself, she concluded the body of Jesus had been stolen or removed. Her immediate reaction was to go to Peter and John and report this unusual situation (20:2). Some feel she returned to Jerusalem by a different path, hence she missed the other women who came to the tomb a few minutes later.

The conclusion that some group had removed the body of Jesus might not have been Mary's alone. The verb *oidamen* (we know, 20:2) is plural, implying this might have also been the initial conclusion of the other women. Therefore, others believe that while the three women remained to investigate further, Mary alone had gone for help. Who the women thought had taken the body is never suggested in the text. Probably no one was specifically suspected of this action. The women had found an empty tomb, and in a moment of confusion they concluded the body had been removed by someone or, more likely, some group. It had been an emotionally draining weekend for the followers of Jesus, so that this line of argument was not as illogical as it might seem to future generations of Christians.

> 3 Peter therefore went forth, and that other disciple, and came to the sepulchre.
>
> 4 So they ran both together: and the other disciple did outrun Peter, and came first to the sepulchre.
>
> 5 And he stooping down, and looking in, saw the linen clothes lying; yet went he not in.

B. The Disciples' Witness (20:3–5). Upon Mary's report of the empty tomb, Peter and John immediately began to race toward the tomb. Though they began running together, John, the younger, outran Peter and arrived first at the tomb. When he arrived, he did not enter into the tomb. Again, John's youth might have restrained him. But Peter's boldness is evident in that he ran impulsively into the tomb. John looked in where he "saw the linen clothes lying" (20:5). Only after Peter entered the tomb did John enter and realize the truth of the resurrection.

When Hebrews were buried, the body was not embalmed. Their Jewish custom prohibited them from handling blood. Instead a person was buried quickly, with linen cloths wrapped around the body. The cloths were anointed with a sweet gumlike ointment of spices, and the body was wrapped like a cocoon in which the body was mummified up to the head. Then the napkin was placed over the skull. When John saw the linen cloths from the door of the tomb, he was looking at an empty shell because the body had come out of the cocoon. The stone was rolled away to let the people in, not to let the Lord out.

> 6 Then cometh Simon Peter following him, and went into the sepulchre, and seeth the linen clothes lie.
>
> 7 And the napkin, that was about his head, not lying with the linen clothes, but wrapped together in a place by itself.
>
> 8 Then went in also that other disciple, which came first to the sepulchre, and he saw, and believed.
>
> 9 For as yet they knew not the scripture, that he must rise again from the dead.
>
> 10 Then the disciples went away again unto their own home.

C. *The Disciples' Investigation* (20:6–10). John uses three different Greek words in this chapter that are translated with the verb *to see*. The first of these verbs is *blepei* (20:5). When John looked into the tomb and saw the linen cloth, the verb used there refers to a quick glance. When Peter entered the tomb and saw not only the linen cloth but also the face cloth by itself, the verb used by John is *theorei*. This verb implies a greater intensity in the act of seeing, such as examining. It was a verb most likely to be used of a spectator watching a sports event or a child watching a parade.

The third verb translated by the English word *see* is *eiden* (20:8). Here the verb implies not only the physical act of seeing but also the idea of understanding or insight. When John arrived at the tomb, he noticed the linen cloth. Later when Peter entered the tomb, he examined the linen cloth and face cloth which had been set aside. Finally, John also entered the tomb and began to understand the meaning of what he had seen.

When Peter entered the tomb, he saw more than was visible from the door. The most notable thing he found was the face cloth set aside from the rest of the grave clothes. This face cloth was sometimes the size of a small hand towel. At other times it was like a small pillowcase folded several times, thick and large enough to pull down over the head and cover the face. John uses the verb *entetuligmenon* (20:7) describing the condition of this cloth. The verb means "to wrap or roll up." The presence of a neatly rolled face cloth set apart from the other grave clothes emphasizes the absence of haste and confusion in removing the body. Had Mary's theory of a stolen body been accurate, the grave would no doubt have been in a greater state of disorder.

When the disciples left the tomb that morning, Peter left still wondering (Luke 24:12). John, however, had become the first to believe that Jesus had risen from the dead. When confronted with the evidence of an empty tomb, there was no other reasonable conclusion for John than that Jesus was alive. John's testimony of faith was important in this context. At the time of writing, John was ministering to people who had been born after Jesus walked this earth. Certainly some must have felt they could have greater faith if only they too had seen the resurrected Lord (*see* 20:29). Here John, the last of the apostles, reminds the reader that he was the first who had come to faith in Christ, and that he had this faith before the angels told him what had happened. The evidence of the empty tomb was enough to convince John that "Jesus is the Christ, the Son of God" (20:31).

Despite the constant emphasis on the cross and resurrection in the later teaching of Jesus, the only ones who apparently took Him seriously were the chief priests and Pharisees (Matthew 27:62–66); they had posted guards at the tomb. Even on that resurrection morning, the followers of Christ arrived at the tomb expecting to find a dead body. When the body was missing, they concluded that it was stolen. John explains they "knew not the scripture" (20:9), probably referring specifically to Psalms 16:10, a passage quoted by Peter on the day of Pentecost (Acts 2:27). Even when confronted with the irrefutable evidence of the resurrection of Christ, people come to saving faith only when nurtured by the Scriptures (*see* Romans 10:17).

II. THE PROOF OF THE APPEARANCES (20:11–23)

The Bible records a number of postresurrection appearances of Christ, most of which occurred during the forty days following His passion (Acts 1:3). Several appearances occurred that very first Sunday. Darby and others have argued that every postresurrection appearance of Christ occurred on a Sunday which, therefore, became known to Christians as the Lord's Day (*see* Revelation 1:10). No place in Scripture lists all the postresurrection appearances of Christ. John lists only three in his gospel. In the Old Testament, only two or three witnesses were necessary to verify a fact (*see* Numbers 35:30; Deuteronomy 17:6). As illustrated in Chart 77, there were more than enough witnesses to verify Christ's resurrection.

> 11 But Mary stood without at the sepulchre weeping: and as she wept, she stooped down, and looked into the sepulchre,
>
> 12 And seeth two angels in white sitting, the one at the head, and the other at the feet, where the body of Jesus had lain.
>
> 13 And they say unto her, Woman, why weepest thou? She saith unto them, Because they have taken away my Lord, and I know not where they have laid him.
>
> 14 And when she had thus said, she turned herself back, and saw Jesus standing, and knew not that it was Jesus.
>
> 15 Jesus saith unto her, Woman, why weepest thou? whom seekest thou? She, supposing him to be the gardener, saith unto him, Sir, if thou have borne him hence, tell me where thou hast laid him, and I will take him away.

Chart 77

THE POSTRESURRECTION APPEARANCES OF CHRIST
1. To Mary Magdalene (20:11–18; Mark 16:9–11)
2. To women returning from the tomb (Matthew 28:8–10)
3. To Cleopas and a friend on the Emmaus Road (Mark 16:12; Luke 24:13–35)
4. To Peter (1 Corinthians 15:5)
5. To ten disciples in Jerusalem (20:19–25; Luke 24:36–49; Acts 1:3–5)
6. To eleven disciples (20:26–31; 1 Corinthians 15:5)
7. To seven disciples in Galilee (21:1–25)
8. To the apostles and more than five hundred brethren (Matthew 28:16–20; 1 Corinthians 15:6)
9. To James (1 Corinthians 15:7)
10. To the apostles on the Mount of Olives (Acts 1:6–12; 1 Corinthians 15:7)
11. To Stephen at his stoning (Acts 7:55–60)
12. To Paul at his conversion (Acts 9:3–8,17; 22:6–15; 26:12–19; 1 Corinthians 9:1; 15:8)
13. To Paul at Corinth (Acts 18:9,10)
14. To Paul in the temple (Acts 22:17–21)
15. To Paul later in Jerusalem (Acts 23:11)
16. To Paul in another vision (2 Corinthians 12:1–4)
17. To John on Patmos (Revelation)

16 Jesus saith unto her, Mary. She turned herself, and saith unto him, Rabboni; which is to say, Master.

17 Jesus saith unto her, Touch me not; for I am not yet ascended to my Father: but go to my brethren, and say unto them, I ascend unto my Father, and your Father; and to my God, and your God.

18 Mary Magdalene came and told the disciples that she had seen the Lord, and that he had spoken these things unto her.

A. Appearance to Mary (20:11–18). Mary Magdalene deeply loved the Lord because of what He had done for her. The cross had no doubt been hard on her emotionally. With others, she had seen His body, hastily prepared for burial before the Sabbath began. That first Easter morning she rose even before the sun to complete the task. Apparently she returned to the tomb after Peter and John came to investigate. The other women had already gone. She remained at the tomb weeping and wondering where she might find the body of Jesus.

When she stooped down and looked (*parekupsen*, literally "peeped") into the tomb, she saw two angels (20:11,12). Comparing the various accounts of this resurrection day, it is interesting to note angels appeared to the women, never to the men. As angels are spiritual beings, they had to take on some physical forms when appearing. Normally, they appeared as men dressed in white. The appearance of these two angels to Mary is the only physical manifestation of angels in the Gospel of John.

First, the angels asked her, "Woman, why weepest thou?" (20:13). This was the same question Jesus would ask a few minutes later. Her response to the angels is revealing. Normally when people saw angels in Scripture, they were terrified. So overwhelmed by grief and her love for the Lord, she continued to talk as though conversing with human beings. Though her response is similar to her initial comments to Peter and John, it differs significantly in two places. "Because they have taken away *my Lord,* and *I know* not where they have laid him" (20:13, *italics added*). The problem earlier had been the women did not know where to find the Lord. Now, later in the day, that problem had become more personal; Mary did not know where to find her Lord.

Some critics of the Bible have proposed what is known as the vision theory to explain the postresurrection appearances of Christ. According to this explanation, the disciples were so obsessed with the idea that Jesus would rise from the dead that, as a result of autosuggestion, one after the other had a vision of the resurrected Lord. Of course an examination of the biblical record shows how erroneous this theory is. The disciples apparently did not believe that Jesus would rise, and here, when Mary becomes the first to see the resurrected Lord, she fails to recognize Him.

Why did Mary not recognize Jesus in the garden? Several reasons might be suggested. First, it must be remembered she still thought Jesus was dead. Also, the man standing in the garden might have looked different from her last view of

Christ. She had last seen Jesus in His intense suffering on the cross. Then she had seen the mangled body of a crucified Saviour removed from the cross and placed in the tomb (*see* Isaiah 53:2,3). Now that body had been "raised in glory" (1 Corinthians 15:43). John suggests Mary thought Jesus was the gardener, which would have been a natural assumption. Gardeners normally worked in the gardens in the early morning hours. Also, she did not have a good look at the One speaking with her. Even while she was talking to Him, she probably turned back to look at the tomb. When Jesus called her by name, "she turned herself" (20:16) back toward Christ. What she had seen, she saw through tear-filled eyes and in a state of unbelief and spiritual blindness.

Nothing sounds sweeter than the sound of one's own name. This was never truer than at the moment Jesus said, "Mary" (20:16). Some of the early texts here insert the Aramaic form of her name, *Mariam*, whereas all texts agree in other places using the Greek *Maria*. Perhaps there was something in the way Jesus spoke her name that caused her to remember and realize that once again she was with Jesus.

Now that she knew whom she was addressing, her first word to Him was *rabboni* (20:16). John here translates this term "master" for the benefit of readers unfamiliar with Hebrew. While closely related to the term *rabbi*, there is a significant difference. Though used in older Jewish literature, it was never applied to a man as was *rabbi* but was reserved exclusively for God. "Rabboni" then was Mary's expression of faith, her way of declaring "Jesus is the Christ, the Son of God" (20:31).

When the women later saw Jesus after His resurrection, they "held him by the feet, and worshipped him" (Matthew 28:9). But here Jesus said to Mary, "Touch me not" (20:17). At least three explanations have been proposed concerning this apparent inconsistency on the part of Jesus. The first suggests she must release Him because He had not yet ascended into heaven. He had to go cleanse the heavenly places with his blood (Hebrews 9:12,23). The verb *anabebeka*, here translated "ascended" (20:17), is a perfect active indicative suggesting Jesus was in the process of active ascending when He appeared to Mary. Those who hold this view argue Jesus ascended to the Father in some sense between His appearance to Mary and His later appearance to the other women.

A second explanation focuses upon Mary's still limited understanding of the meaning of the resurrection. Mary had only known Jesus in the flesh. Her allegiance and love was to the physical Jesus. Three times this morning she had expressed concern over not being able to find the body of Jesus and had at least once declared her intent to remove the physical body of Christ (20:15). Perhaps what Jesus was trying to tell Mary was that she must move beyond the physical and enter into a spiritual relationship. He may have been saying, "It is not the physical you must love; it is the real Me, now that I am in My resurrection body. You must love Me for what I am."

A third possibility emphasizes the immediate context of the statement. The verb *haptou*, here translated "touch," primarily means "to fasten or cling to." In this case, it was not necessarily a prohibition against touching the body of Jesus, but rather a request to "quit hanging onto me." This was the first of at least four appearances He would make that day. Jesus wanted Mary to report her discovery to the disciples. Both of them had things to do, and Mary's cleaving to the Lord was detaining them both. Mary was, therefore, being asked to go to the disciples while Jesus made His way to the Father. Mary's devotion to Jesus would have detained Him; therefore, He very gently indicated that His relation to His disciples must be henceforth merely spiritual. Mary now became not only the herald of the empty tomb but also of the risen Christ. In obedience to Jesus, she reported her meeting to the disciples. According to the synoptic gospels, the disciples had a great deal of difficulty believing the early reports of the resurrection.

19 Then the same day at evening, being the first day of the week, when the doors were shut where the disciples were assembled for fear of the Jews, came Jesus and stood in the midst, and saith unto them, Peace be unto you.

20 And when he had so said, he shewed unto them his hands and his side. Then were the disciples glad, when they saw the Lord.

21 Then said Jesus to them again, Peace be unto you: as my Father hath sent me, even so send I you.

22 And when he had said this, he breathed on them, and
saith unto them, Receive ye the Holy Ghost:
23 Whose soever sins ye remit, they are remitted unto
them; and whose soever sins ye retain, they are retained.

B. *Appearance to the Disciples* (*20:19–23*). When John relates the first appearance of Jesus to His disciples, he describes the time of that appearance with the words *opsias tei
hemerai* (evening of the day, 20:19). This expression referred
technically to the hours from 6:00 to 9:00 P.M. That John here
says, "The same day at evening," is an evidence of Roman
time. The Jews always spoke of the evening as *preceding* the
day (*see* Genesis 1:5,8,13,19,23,31).

John is emphatic in declaring that Christ's first manifestation to His disciples occurred on Sunday evening, the same
day as the resurrection. He is also emphatic in declaring "the
doors were shut" (20:19), indicating the miraculous character of our Lord's appearance. The word *thuron* (doors) suggests the entrance to the room was through a double door
rather than that the room had several entrances. How then
did Jesus enter the room? Calvin suggested the doors were
miraculously opened, and Jesus merely passed through an
unbarricaded doorway (*see* Acts 12:10). Others have suggested the body of Christ materialized within the room. More
likely is the suggestion that Jesus, in His resurrection body,
simply passed through the locked door. Christ's resurrection
body, though a true body, was not subject to the limitations
of ordinary conditions of material bodies. That indeed it was
a true body—His crucified body risen—He assured His disciples by showing them His hands and His side, thus exhib-
iting the marks of His crucifixion.

In the Old Testament, the fear of man is mentioned as a
barrier to the fear of the Lord or saving faith (Proverbs 29:25).
Throughout this gospel, John speaks of the fear of the Jews
as a hindrance to faith. Because of the fear of the Jews, the
parents of the healed blind man would not verify that miracle (9:22). Because of the fear of the Jews, no one would
speak openly of Jesus at the Feast of Tabernacles (7:13). Because of the fear of the Jews, even some of the rulers of the
Jews who had begun to believe would not confess Christ
publicly (12:42). Now, this same fear of the Jews had the
very apostles of Christ hiding behind locked doors (20:19). In

this context, Jesus appeared before them offering a faith that would conquer fear (see Acts 4:13).

Jesus' first words to His disciples in this meeting were words of peace. The expression, "Peace be unto you" (20:19), was the common Jewish greeting. But in this context, His words were very uncommon. The last official words of Christ to His disciples before His death were words of peace (16:33). The peace here spoken of must be understood in terms of the doctrine of reconciliation. Because of what Jesus did on the cross, it was now possible that men could receive peace from God (Ephesians 2:17) and have peace with God (Romans 5:1). No wonder the disciples were glad when they saw the Lord.

John here records his version of the Great Commission (20:21). There are two words in this verse translated "sent" or "send" emphasizing the distinction between the Father's sending of Christ and His sending of us. The first word John uses is *apestalken*, from which the word *apostle* is derived. Jesus was sent as an apostle from God to us (Hebrews 3:1). This verb implies a commissioning with the authority similar to that of an embassy representing a foreign government. Jesus now has sent His disciples to report the success of that mission and preach the message of reconciliation. Jesus was sent into this world with a unique authority to accomplish a specific task for His Father—the reconciliation of the world to God (2 Corinthians 5:19).

After commissioning His disciples, Jesus empowered them to do the job. To equip His disciples for this work, Christ bestowed upon them the gift of the Holy Spirit, an anticipation and earnest of the Pentecostal blessing. Jesus did this by breathing on them. Throughout the Old Testament, the coming of the Holy Spirit is portrayed through the act of God breathing upon the ones receiving the Spirit (see Ezekiel 37:5). He is preparing them to live for the next fifty days until the day of Pentecost, when the Holy Spirit would be more fully received. Here they received the Holy Spirit to the degree that men received the Holy Spirit in the Old Testament, but it did not involve the baptism, fullness, or outpouring of the Holy Spirit which came at Pentecost and is classified as New Testament reality.

This appearance of Christ to His disciples ends with His giving them an awesome authority (20:23). On two other occasions Jesus had told His disciples they had authority to bind or loose sinners (Matthew 16:19; 18:18). Here, Jesus commissioned His disciples to preach the Gospel and reminded them of the eternal consequences of their actions. When they led others to Christ, they were remitting sin in that the new convert was being forgiven in heaven. When they failed to obey this commission, they were retaining sin because others were not given the opportunity to trust Christ as Saviour. Obviously, this passage did not give the disciples the authority to actually forgive sin. Only God can forgive sins (Mark 2:7). But even today Christians engage in the practice of remitting or retaining sin depending upon their response to the Great Commission.

III. THE PROOF OF THE NAIL PRINTS (20:24-29)

When Jesus first appeared to His disciples, Thomas was not present. He refused to accept the testimony of others concerning the resurrection. He had to see for himself. Eight days later the Lord appeared again in the midst of the disciples. On this second occasion, Thomas was present. Finally convinced, Thomas immediately confessed Christ as his Lord and God. Thus John ends his gospel as it begins, with a declaration of the deity of Christ.

24 But Thomas, one of the twelve, called Didymus, was not with them when Jesus came.

25 The other disciples therefore said unto him, We have seen the Lord. But he said unto them, Except I shall see in his hands the print of the nails, and put my finger into the print of the nails, and thrust my hand into his side, I will not believe.

A. *The Unbelief of Thomas* (20:24,25). On the basis of this account in the life of Thomas, he has been branded by Christians as "doubting Thomas." Perhaps in fairness to this disciple it should be remembered that only John appears to have believed in the resurrection before seeing the resurrected Lord. One of the first things Jesus did when He appeared to His disciples was upbraid them for their unbelief (Mark 16:14). Apparently Thomas was typical of the disciples in refusing to believe until he saw.

John has drawn attention to Thomas on three occasions. When Jesus turned to go to Jerusalem, it was Thomas who led the disciples to follow Him knowing something of the consequences (11:16). Later it was Thomas who interrupted Jesus in the upper room asking the way to the Father (14:5). Apparently Thomas was prepared even then to follow Jesus to the Father. John portrays Thomas as a man of extremes. In this passage Thomas is both emphatic in his unbelief and his faith.

Thomas claimed he would not believe until he had put his finger into the print of the nails, and thrust his hand into His side (20:25). The Greek verb translated "put" and "thrust" in this statement is *balo*. The emphatic nature of this verb could be emphasized in both cases with the translation "throw into." Further, in emphasizing his unwillingness to believe, Thomas used a double negative. Knox brings out this emphasis by translating the last part of Thomas's statement, "You will never make me believe" (20:25, KNOX).

> 26 And after eight days again his disciples were within, and Thomas with them: then came Jesus, the doors being shut, and stood in the midst, and said, Peace be unto you.
> 27 Then saith he to Thomas, Reach hither thy finger, and behold my hands; and reach hither thy hand, and thrust it into my side: and be not faithless, but believing.
> 28 And Thomas answered and said unto him, My Lord and my God.
> 29 Jesus saith unto him, Thomas, because thou hast seen me, thou hast believed: blessed are they that have not seen, and yet have believed.

B. *The Convincing of Thomas* (20:26–29). Jesus' second appearance to His disciples was similar to His first. This time Thomas was also present. The major purpose of Jesus' second visit was to bring Thomas from doubt to faith. He did this by inviting Thomas to inspect the marks of the crucifixion using the very language Thomas had earlier used in affirming his unbelief. He concludes with the statement, "and be not faithless, but believing" (20:27). In the Greek text John uses two closely related words translated "faithless" and "believing." The relationship between the words *apistos* (faithless) and *pistos* (believing) is similar to the English words *unbelieving* and *believing*. Chart 78 illustrates several layers of faith revealed in the Scripture.

Chart 78

THE PATHOLOGY OF FAITH		
Nonsaving Faith		
Vain faith	1 Corinthians 15:14–17	Faith in wrong doctrine
Dead faith	James 2:19,20	Faith in orthodox doctrine without personal belief in Christ
Saving Faith		
Unbelief	Mark 16:11–14	Believers in Christ who will not accept His work
Little faith	Matthew 14:31	Faith and unbelief mixed
Weak faith	Romans 14:1	Believers who have a legalistic expression of faith
Strong faith	Romans 4:20	Faith in the promises of God

The experience of Thomas is the third record of an individual conversion to the resurrected Christ in this chapter. Thomas's response to the presence of Jesus was to confess, "My Lord and my God" (20:28). This is the apex of the Gospel because it gives the strongest or highest expression of Old Testament deity (2 Samuel 7:28; 1 Kings 18:39; Psalms 30:2; 35:24; 86:15; 88:1; Jeremiah 38:17; Hosea 2:23). Thomas identified Jesus with both *Jehovah*, the Old Testament "I am," and *Elohim*, the Creator-God. This was Thomas's way of expressing that "Jesus is the Christ, the Son of God" (20:31).

In the last verse of this section, Jesus declares what Westcott calls "this last and greatest of the beatitudes."[58] Mary, Thomas, and the disciples did not believe in the resurrection until they had seen the resurrected Lord. Here Jesus pronounced a special state of blessedness on those who like John would believe having never seen the resurrection. This is one biblical promise that can be claimed by Christians today which could not be claimed by the early apostles.

IV. THE PURPOSE OF THE GOSPEL (20:30,31)

30 And many other signs truly did Jesus in the presence of his disciples, which are not written in this book:
31 But these are written, that ye might believe that Jesus is the Christ, the Son of God; and that believing ye might have life through his name.

John had set out to write a Gospel, not a biography. He does not tell all he knows but only enough to inculcate faith in Jesus as the long-promised Messiah and Son of God. Even John admits there are many miracles of Christ that are not recorded in his book (20:30). What is recorded is done so in keeping with John's major purpose. The language John uses to express this twofold purpose is vivid.

Chart 79

THREE INDIVIDUAL EXAMPLES OF SAVING FAITH IN JOHN 20			
Individual	Type of Conversion	Expression of Faith	Impact of Resurrection
John	Intellectual	He believed the Scripture concerning the resurrection.	Believed before seeing the resurrected Lord.
Mary	Emotional	"Rabboni."	Did not produce immediate faith—she thought He was a gardener.
Thomas	Volitional	"My Lord and my God."	Resulted in an immediate expression of faith.

The phrase "that ye might believe" (*hina pisteuete*) suggests John wrote this Gospel to the end that the reader would not only come to faith in Christ but that he might keep on believing. As the reader is continuing to believe, he will keep on having life. John uses the verb *eschete* (you may have), emphasizing that the Christian life is a continuing adventure in faith. For John life is more than mere existence. Among other things, life includes the knowledge of God (17:3) and belief "that Jesus is the Christ, the Son of God" (20:31).

Sometimes Christians wonder if another person is really saved or truly believes because his experience differs from their own. In this chapter John has told the story of three different people who came to faith in Christ, each in their own way (*see* Chart 79). Because of their different personalities, their type of conversion, expression of faith, and response to the resurrection were all different. Yet all believed. John is not so much concerned how people express their faith so long as they come to believe. If we, like John, are to be effective evangelists of the Gospel, we must be prepared to bring people to faith in Christ, understanding that their expression of faith may sometimes differ from the way we express it.

TWENTY-THREE

CHRIST—
THE GREAT SHEPHERD
(PART 1)
JOHN 21:1–14

The central thesis of the Gospel of John reaches its apex when Thomas confesses, "My Lord and my God" (20:28). Out of this statement, John naturally summarizes the purpose: first that people might believe in the deity of Christ, and second, that they may experience eternal life (20:31). This final chapter appears to be an afterthought or a postscript because it comes after the natural conclusion to the book. This does not suggest that it is not inspired, for it is. But more importantly, this chapter includes the third postresurrection appearance of Christ to the disciples as a group so that they gain important insight into the nature and mission of Christ.

I. RESIGNATION (20:1–5)

After these things Jesus shewed himself again to the disciples at the sea of Tiberias; and on this wise shewed he himself.

2 There were together Simon Peter, and Thomas called Didymus, and Nathanael of Cana in Galilee, and the sons of Zebedee, and two other of his disciples.

A. The Revelation of the Saviour (21:1,2). During the forty days following His passion, Christ appeared often to His followers and instructed them concerning the kingdom of God (Acts 1:3). Ten of these postresurrection appearances are recorded by the four evangelists. When placed in chronological order, this third meeting with His disciples is the seventh recorded appearance. (Other appearances were to individuals or a group of women.)

John begins this account with the familiar expression *meta tauta* (after these things). This is not to suggest the events of this chapter immediately followed those of the previous chapter, but rather that they occurred at some later and unspecified time. That some time must have passed is also seen in the change of setting. In the previous chapter, the disciples were still in Jerusalem, but here they are at the Sea of Galilee, probably in obedience to Jesus' instructions telling them to meet Him in Galilee (Matthew 28:7,10).

The word *ephanerosen* (showed) occurs twice in the first verse reemphasizing the reality of the resurrection. It is the first aorist active indicative of *phaneroo*, a verb used by John to show how others not only saw but understood Christ's earthly life (1:31; 2:11), the works of Christ (3:5), the second coming (1 John 2:28), and Christ in glory (1 John 3:2). It relates to the idea of shining forth and is often translated "manifested." Christ is the self-revealing God who uses the events on the lake shore to instruct His disciples.

John identifies some but not all of the seven disciples who had been fishing all night. The obvious are Simon Peter, Thomas (Didymus), Nathanael, James, and John. The two unidentified disciples are generally thought to be Andrew and Philip because Andrew probably would have gone with his brother Peter, and Philip is usually identified with Nathanael. Godet, who does not believe Nathanael was one of the twelve, argues the two unnamed disciples were also not from among the apostles but rather the larger group of disciples or followers of Christ. (Most commentators, however, believe Nathanael was also called Bartholomew, one of the twelve.) This is the first mention of Nathanael in the gospel since chapter one.

3 Simon Peter saith unto them, I go a fishing. They say unto him, We also go with thee. They went forth, and

entered into a ship immediately; and that night they caught nothing.

4 But when the morning was now come, Jesus stood on the shore: but the disciples knew not that it was Jesus.

5 Then Jesus saith unto them, Children, have ye any meat? They answered him, No.

B. The Blindness of the Disciples (21:3–5). Peter announced his decision, "I go fishing" (*hupago halieuein*, 21:3). Since he was the leader, the others went with him. There is some disagreement among Bible teachers what Peter meant. Those who think he was backslidden give at least three reasons. First, he was returning to his old occupation, fishing. Second, they see in the words *I go* a statement of self-determination, or an egotistical statement of pride. It does not appear that this simple statement was Peter's formal announcement that he was breaking his relationship with Christ as a disciple or that he was abandoning his preaching commission. That may be too much to read into his statement. It appears to be the statement of one who was not giving Christ first priority in his life. In the third place, some see the fact that he caught nothing shows that God would not bless him because he was backslidden.

Others, however, are less severe on Peter. First, they emphasize that Peter was in the place where God wanted him, Galilee (Matthew 28:7,10), although there is admittedly a difference between the appointed mountain and the Sea of Galilee. Second, they argue that Peter might be fishing to provide food and help for his family or for the seven disciples. When Jesus was with them, He had provided for the disciples through the purse, or by individuals inviting Jesus and the disciples for a meal, or through miraculous provision of food. These sources were no longer available and so Peter did what he could—fish. Peter may have recalled that Jesus had actually sent him fishing on one occasion to provide for a need (Matthew 17:27).

Whatever one decides concerning Peter's spiritual state should be applied to the other six disciples. With Peter's announcement, the others were ready with little hesitation. "They went forth, and entered into a ship immediately" (21:3). But despite the fact that several of the disciples were (1) fishermen by profession, (2) familiar with the region, and

(3) fishing at the best time (night) they came back empty-handed. The verb translated *ginomenes* (was now come, 21:4) indicates the sun had just risen or was just about to rise. As the disciples returned early the following morning, they failed to recognize Jesus standing on the shore.

Some see the fact that they did not recognize Jesus as a further evidence of their lack of spiritual perception. However, several factors should be kept in mind. They were still about one hundred yards from shore, and visibility was probably low. Even if the sun had begun to rise, a morning mist might have been on the Sea of Galilee preventing them from recognizing the man on the shore. Also, the disciples would be tired and were certainly not expecting to see Jesus on the shore.

As Jesus shouted to His disciples, He called them *paidia* (children, 21:5). Some have mistakenly thought the King James Version had mistranslated this word because it implies the disciples were like children. But this is what Jesus said. It is a diminutive of the word for child. He did not call them young men or the respectful name—men. This is the only occasion Jesus used this word in reference to His disciples. The term can be translated, "boys still under instruction." Perhaps with this word Jesus was reminding them (1) they needed instruction about who He was; (2) they were childish in their doubt and unbelief; and (3) He was prepared to teach them. Even in the face of this evidence, some suggest the term *children* was used more as a colloquial expression referring to one who is younger, or the natural word used by an old retired fisherman calling out from shore to younger, active fishermen.

The questions Jesus asked implied a negative answer. One translator expresses the thought, "Lads, you have no fish, have you?" (WILLIAMS). The word *prosphagion* (meat) is a compound word derived from the root *phag* from *esthio*, meaning "to eat," and *pros*, meaning "with" or "in addition to." It was broadly used to identify any form of relish to be eaten with food; therefore, in this context the reference is to fish. The disciples might have thought the man on the shore was asking the disciples if he could buy some fresh fish for breakfast. Or they might have thought the stranger was just inquisitive, as are many who watch fishermen and ask, "How many have you caught?"

II. RECOVERY (20:6–14)

> 6   And he said unto them, Cast the net on the right side of the ship, and ye shall find. They cast therefore, and now they were not able to draw it for the multitude of fishes.

A.   Command (21:6). Technically the miracle takes place in this verse—there is a multitude of fish. There are three possible sources for the fish. First, Christ could have used His *creative* power to create the fish. Second, He could have used His *omnipotent* power to guide the fish from some other place in the lake into their net. Third, He could have used His *omniscience* and, seeing the fish coming, called for the disciples to cast the net on the other side of the boat where the fish were swimming. Those who deny the miraculous claim Jesus was following a Galilean custom of stationing a man on the shore to spot the fish, telling those in the boat where to cast the net.

The immediate result of their obedience was "they were not able to draw" the net on account of the large catch (21:6). The word John uses here to describe this scene is an imperfect active picturing the disciples tugging at the net. It is almost incredible that these seven who had failed so miserably all night to catch a single fish should now be unable to haul in those that God supplied.

> 7   Therefore that disciple whom Jesus loved saith unto Peter, It is the Lord. Now when Simon Peter heard that it was the Lord, he girt his fisher's coat unto him, (for he was naked,) and did cast himself into the sea.
> 8   And the other disciples came in a little ship; (for they were not far from land, but as it were two hundred cubits,) dragging the net with fishes.
> 9   As soon then as they were come to land, they saw a fire of coals there, and fish laid thereon, and bread.

B.   Conviction (21:7–9). There are many similarities between this miracle and an earlier experience in the life of some of these same disciples (*see* Luke 5:1–11). Perhaps this was the reason John now has the spiritual perception to recognize the Lord. While John was the first to announce the identity of the man on the shore, Peter was first to act. Just as Peter was quick to act in past days, so he was quick to respond to Christ. He grabbbed his fisherman's coat and began to swim toward shore.

The term *gumnos* (naked, 21:7) does not denote nudity, but rather being stripped for work such as a fisherman might do. A businessman who normally wears a three-piece suit would remove his tie, jacket, and vest if he had to make a minor repair under the hood of his car. Peter had removed his bulky tunic but was not immodest; he probably was as clothed as any fisherman. This is also the description of John the Baptist.

Peter put on his fisher's coat (ependuten) before jumping in the water. This is the only place this word appears in the New Testament, and there is some discussion as to what is involved. Some believe the *ependuten* was a lined blouse, and others identify it as a heavier outer garment. Regardless of what it was, it would certainly have made it more difficult for Peter to swim to shore. Why then did Peter put on this additional garment? There are at least three interpretations. First, according to Jewish custom, to offer a greeting to someone was a religious act, and to carry out any religious act a man had to be fully clothed. That Peter reached for his coat before jumping into the water clearly shows his intent to be the first to greet the Lord. Second, some think Peter might have again tried to walk on the water (Matthew 14:29). However, the word *ebalen* (cast, 21:7) implies diving into the sea, not stepping out onto water. The third reason why he put his coat on is psychological. Peter was impetuous, and there were many other occasions when Peter acted without thinking; this was another of those occasions.

10   Jesus saith unto them, Bring of the fish which ye have now caught.

11   Simon Peter went up, and drew the net to land full of great fishes, an hundred and fifty and three: and for all there were so many, yet was not the net broken.

12   Jesus saith unto them, Come and dine. And none of the disciples durst ask him, Who art thou? knowing that it was the Lord.

13   Jesus then cometh, and taketh bread, and giveth them, and fish likewise.

14   This is now the third time that Jesus shewed himself to his disciples, after that he was risen from the dead.

C. *Compassion (21:10–14)*. When the disciples arrived at the shore, Jesus had already prepared broiled fish and toasted bread. The single fish implies Christ had provided for Himself. This does not mean He was not concerned for them. His fish was little, theirs were large. He provided for Himself; He also provided for them. But the law of the division of labor applies here. Christ tells us what to do, and if we do not obey, He does not do our job for us. The disciples were to cast their net on the other side of the boat; if they had not obeyed, employing their fishing skills, they would have been without fish.

Although they had forsaken Him, He was prepared to minister to them. Jesus instructed them to bring the fish they had just caught. Peter drew the net to land and apparently counted the catch. It is noted that there were 153 fish and that all the fish were large. Another unusual feature noted is that the net was not broken. Actually, there could be five miracles in this passage rather than one, which is the usual designation. First, there was the miraculous provision of 153 fish. Second, the net which should have broken was not broken. John a fisherman had the background to observe, "Yet was not the net broken" (21:11). Third, the seven disciples in the boat could not haul in the net, and now Peter apparently does it by himself (21:6,11). The fourth miracle was the fire on the beach. Perhaps it was left over from the previous night, but the Son of God who walked the clouds of eternity and created the sun in the heaven could just as easily have walked that Galilean beach and created a fire to cook the fish. The fifth miracle is the fish and bread on the fire. Surely Jesus would not have purchased or asked for the food from someone on the shore. In His postresurrection body, that would have been counted as an appearance (1 Corinthians 15:5–8). He who created fish and bread for the five thousand, could also do it for the seven disciples.

The number of 153 fish recorded in verse eleven has been the subject of much comment through the years. There are at least four explanations as to why the number 153 appears. Cyril of Alexander saw the number as representing God and the church. According to this early church leader, one hundred was the number of the fullness of the Gentiles (Matthew 18:12), fifty represented the remnant of Israel, and three signified the Trinity to whose glory all things were

done. In a somewhat more creative vein, Augustine interpreted this number in light of ten, the number of the law,
and seven, the number of grace. Ten plus seven equals seventeen, and the sum of all the numbers from one through
seventeen inclusive totals 153. Therefore, argued Augustine,
153 stands for all who by law or grace have been moved to
come to Jesus. Jerome and other early church leaders saw the
significance of this number in the ancient belief that there
were 153 basic kinds of fish in the sea. They argued, therefore, that the miraculous catch included every kind of fish.
Someday, all men of all nations will be gathered together to
Christ. A fourth suggestion is that 153 appears in the text
because that happened to be the exact number of fish caught
in the net at that time. Other than being an accurate count,
there is no hidden spiritual meaning in the number.

Also, some who see a special significance in the number-
ing of the fish usually interpret the net as a type of the
church. If that is so, it is interesting to note the net was not
eschisthe (broken). John's verb here is a form of the word
schizo from which we get the English word *schism*.

Jesus invited His disciples to *aristesate* (dine) with Him.
The Greek verb *aristesate* originally meant "to break a fast"
and then later came to refer to a more substantial meal. Some
have suggested this was Sunday when Jesus appeared to the
disciples. The disciples had fasted on the traditional Sabbath,
gone fishing when the Sabbath was over (at sundown), and
now they were having Sunday breakfast with Christ. Those
who suggest Sunday also imply that Jesus appeared to His
disciples only on Sunday to reinforce it as the new day of
worship (20:19,26; Revelation 1:10).

By the time the disciples were gathered on the beach eating fish and bread with Jesus, no one had to ask who He
was. The purpose of the miracle was for Jesus to reveal Himself (*phaneroo*, 21:1), which is more than just an appearance
so that they could see Him. This appearance was for them to
see and understand the resurrection. What He revealed in
the previous appearance they apparently did not fully understand. The first Sunday they still had doubts (20:25; Mark
16:11–13). The second Sunday they were upbraided for their
unbelief (Mark 16:14). Also when the eleven disciples met
Him on a mountain in Galilee "some doubted" (Matthew
28:17). This revelation of Christ is so extensive that none of

the disciples have to ask anything, "knowing that it was the Lord" (21:12).

This lesson concludes with John mentioning this as the third postresurrection appearance of Christ to His disciples as a group. Some believe it is significant that John records three meetings with His disciples. Darby suggests these three appearances illustrate the Church. The first appearance (20:19–23) is said to represent the Church immediately following Pentecost. The second appearance to the disciples including Thomas (20:26–29) represents the Church at the rapture, complete. According to Darby, this third appearance represents the Church in the millennium.

Chart 80

THE THREE POSTRESURRECTION APPEARANCES OF CHRIST TO HIS DISCIPLES IN JOHN
1. Sunday night, the day of His resurrection, in Jerusalem (20:19–23).
2. Sunday night, eight days after His resurrection, in Jerusalem (20:26–29).
3. Later, at the Sea of Tiberias/Galilee (21:1–23).

TWENTY-FOUR

CHRIST—
THE GREAT SHEPHERD
(PART 2)
JOHN 21:15–25

After Jesus shared breakfast with the seven disciples, His attention was focused upon one in particular—Simon Peter. This brief encounter pictures the restoration of Peter into full fellowship with his Lord. Here also Peter received his *commission* for future service and was told of his *cross* that was predictive of his death.

III.   RESTORATION (21:15–19)

15 So when they had dined, Jesus saith to Simon Peter, Simon, son of Jonas, lovest thou me more than these? He saith unto him, Yea, Lord; thou knowest that I love thee. He saith unto him, Feed my lambs.

16 He saith to him again the second time, Simon, son of Jonas, lovest thou me? He saith unto him, Yea, Lord; thou knowest that I love thee. He saith unto him, Feed my sheep.

17 He saith unto him the third time, Simon, son of Jonas, lovest thou me? Peter was grieved because he said unto him the third time, Lovest thou me? And he said unto him,

Lord, thou knowest all things; thou knowest that I love thee. Jesus saith unto him, Feed my sheep.

A. The Restoration (21:15–17). There is no indication in the text that Peter speaks until spoken to by the Lord. Peter was the disciple never lacking for words, but he said nothing when John said in the boat, "It is the Lord" (21:7). Neither is he recorded as saying anything while he was drawing in the fish or eating breakfast with Jesus and the other disciples. Why do these pages of inspiration record the silence of the never-silent Peter? Several answers may be suggested. Peter may have been ashamed of his denial of the Lord, now he had been caught leading other disciples in a denial of their commission. (Those who fall into sin usually try to drag someone along.) Also, Peter may not have known where he stood with Christ at this point; therefore, until Christ asked him a question, he had nothing to say. A third possible reason for this silence may relate to an earlier appearance of Christ to Peter alone (Luke 24:34; 1 Corinthians 15:5). While the Scriptures record this appearance, what was communicated at that time is not recorded. Perhaps that earlier meeting was preparatory for this meeting on the beach, and Peter was waiting for an appropriate time to begin a follow-up conversation. The fourth suggestion is that previously Jesus had appeared to the disciples, hence they saw and experienced Him but did not understand all they should have because they were blinded by selfish desires and doubts. This time Jesus revealed Himself (*phaneroo*), and they understood. Whereas some conviction comes when a person sees his sin, here Peter was convicted when he saw and understood Jesus. Hence he could say nothing.

Jesus addressed Peter not as Cephas, the name He had earlier given him (1:42), but rather as Simon, son of Jonas (21:15). This was his original name before he began following Jesus. Evidently, Jesus recognized him as truer to his natural state than to his God-given name, *Petros*, which meant "stone," a symbol of solidity or steadfastness. Jesus' repeated use of this name for his disciple (21:15,16,17) may have humbled Peter, reminding him of what he was before he met Christ. In the same way a Mother may sternly call "Charles" when her son has done something wrong, whereas she usually calls him "Charlie," a term of affection.

In this meeting, Jesus is evaluating to see how much of the old Simon remains in the new Peter.

The English translation of the conversation between Jesus and Peter suggests Jesus three times asked the same question, Peter responded with the same answer, and Jesus assigned the same task. Actually there was no repetition of the same words. A closer look reveals that each question, each response, and each task is a little different from the previous one (*see* Chart 81). This difference is significant in that it reveals something of the spiritual progress of this disciple.

The first question asked by Jesus is, "Lovest thou me more than these?" (21:15). Jesus uses the ablative case of comparison *touton* (these) following *pleon* (many, much, more). At least four suggestions have been made as to what is meant by the question. It could be interpreted to mean, (1) "Do you love Me more than you love these disciples?" or (2) "Do you love Me more than you love these fish?" or (3) "Do you love Me more than you love fishing?"—the boats, nets, Peter's means of livelihood—or (4) "Do you love Me more than these other disciples love Me?" While all four of the above questions are possible interpretations, it is most likely that the fourth represents the emphasis of Jesus' question. Earlier, Peter had boasted of his superior love for Christ, suggesting that he loved Christ more than the other disciples (Matthew 26:33; Mark 14:29).

Peter's response indicates a higher level of spiritual maturity than he has previously displayed. He simply states, "Thou knowest that I love thee" (21:15). Peter completely avoids the apparent invitation to compare the superiority of his love. If he had boasted that he loved Christ more than the other disciples, he would have been guilty of a childish ex-

Chart 81

Jesus	Simon	Jesus
1. Do you love Me (*agapao*)?	I am fond of You (*phileo*).	Feed My little lambs.
2. Do you love Me (*agapao*)?	I am fond of You (*phileo*).	Shepherd My sheep.
3. Do you love Me (*phileo*)?	I am fond of You (*phileo*).	Feed My sheep.

aggeration, not a mature disciple of Christ. Hence when Peter says he loves (*phileo*) Christ, he is saying "I have affection for you." Peter realizes he has failed the Lord, even in the face of his exaggeration (13:37). He is honest when he says he only has shallow affection for Christ.

Jesus then gives Peter his first task, "Feed my lambs" (21:15). The Greek word translated "feed" (*boske*) is a present active imperative meaning "keep on feeding." The verb was used of the herdsman with the responsibility of feeding the flocks. Also, the word *arnia* (lambs) is really a diminutive of *arnos*, the usual word for lambs. The task then given to Peter is literally, "Keep on feeding My little lambs"—young converts to the faith. Peter's first confession of honesty leads to a restoration of his commission but only a small amount of responsibility. Some have suggested Peter is restored to discipleship but not yet to his previous leadership among the disciples.

In Jesus' second question there are no more comparisons with others. He simply asks, "Lovest thou me?" (21:16). Peter would no doubt have here understood the difference between what Jesus was asking and how he was answering. Two words for *love* are used in the dialogue between Jesus and Peter. In these first two questions, Jesus uses the verb *agapeo*, meaning "the deep sacrificing love that has its source in God." In his responses, Peter used the verb *phileo*, meaning "brotherly affection." Comparing the two words, *phileo* is the term for liking or being fond of someone, whereas *agapao* is the term of deeper love.

Peter's response to this second question again indicates his honesty. The normal response in this kind of situation might be to upgrade one's statement of love, but Peter knew his heart. After earlier expressing his willingness to die for Christ, he saw his sinful heart when he denied Christ. He honestly can only express affection, *phileo*.

The second command Peter receives from Christ is, "Feed my sheep" (21:16). The word here translated "feed" is the Greek term *poimaine*, literally meaning "shepherd." This is a higher responsibility, probably because Jesus had tested him and realized he was spiritually ready for a greater sphere of ministry. *Poimaine* comes from the same word as *pastor*. He is now ready to pastor a flock of sheep. *Poimaine* is a present active imperative implying a command to be continuously performed. The word for sheep here is *probatia*, a diminutive of *probata*, the usual word for sheep. These are more mature than the lambs in the previous commission. Peter's task then was to continue to shepherd sheep for Christ.

Jesus uses *agapao* in His first two questions but changes the verb to *phileo* the third time He questions Peter's love. Here he is further testing the degree of love that the restored Peter has already twice affirmed. The question is to determine if Peter is ready to be lifted to full responsibility. Also, perhaps this third question was designed to remind Peter of his third denial of Christ.

Peter's emotional and verbal response to this third question demonstrates the honesty and humility of Peter. This third question "grieved" Peter (21:17). The term *elupethe* is an aorist passive form of the verb *lupeo* (I grieve). The degree of grief felt by Peter is perhaps best understood when it is realized John at another place used a form of this verb to describe the sorrow of a woman giving birth (16:21). As childbirth seemingly takes a woman to the point of death, Jesus' third question causes Peter to die to self. He responds "Thou knowest all things; thou knowest that I love thee" (21:17).

There are two Greek words for knowledge, and in verse seventeen Peter uses both. *Ginoskein* means "to acquire knowledge" or "to learn by experience," whereas *eidenai* means "[to possess] innate knowledge about something," but not necessarily to learn it. Peter's response to this third question is, "Lord, Thou knowest (*eidenai*) all things by Your nature; Thou knowest (*ginoskein*) by Your experience that I am fond of You (*phileo*)."

As a result of Peter's honesty, the Lord gives him his third task, "Feed (*boske*) My sheep (*probata*)." Here the term for sheep is the usual word referring to more mature sheep. As Jesus progressively gives Peter a larger responsibility, He teaches him that faithfulness in a small matter leads to a larger responsibility.

> 18 Verily, verily, I say unto thee, When thou wast young, thou girdedst thyself, and walkedst whither thou wouldest: but when thou shalt be old, thou shalt stretch forth thy hands, and another shall gird thee, and carry thee whither thou wouldest not.
>
> 19 This spake he, signifying by what death he should

Chart 82

THE CONVERSATION OF JESUS AND PETER (21: 15–17)
Jesus: Do you love (*agapao*) Me more than these? Peter: I am fond of You (*phileo*). Jesus: Keep on feeding My little lambs.
Jesus: Do you love (*agapao*) Me? Peter: I am fond of You (*phileo*). Jesus: Keep on shepherding My little sheep.
Jesus: Are you fond of Me (*phileo*)? Peter: You know all things by Your nature (*eidenai*). You know by Your experience (*ginoskein*) that I am fond of You (*phileo*). Jesus: Keep on feeding My sheep.

glorify God. And when he had spoken this, he saith unto him, Follow me.

B. The Commission and the Cross (21:18,19). At this breakfast with Jesus, Peter received a twofold blessing. He received both a commission and a cross. As noted in Chart 82, Peter received a threefold challenge concerning the care of the flock of God. In each case, Jesus used the preposition *my*, reminding Peter that though he had a responsibility to the flock, the flock still belonged to Christ. Hence Jesus is the shepherd and pastors are the undershepherds of a flock. It was not a lesson Peter would soon forget. Years later he would challenge other pastors to "feed the flock of God which is among you" (1 Peter 5:2).

Actually, the progressive commission of Christ is an outline of the future ministry of Peter (*see* Chart 83). In the early years of the church, Peter was one of those principally responsible for leading people to Christ and feeding them (little lambs). Second, Peter was a pastor of the Jerusalem flock, and when controversy arose concerning the relation of the law to Gentile converts, Peter was one of those at the Jerusalem conference who helped solve the problem (shepherd My sheep). Finally, his ministry in the epistles illustrates his

Chart 83

THE COMMISSION AND MINISTRY OF PETER	
Commission	**Ministry**
Feeding the little lambs (21:15)	Pentecost, Cornelius's household (Acts 1—10)
Shepherding the little sheep (21:16)	Controversy over Gentile conversions (Acts 10—15)
Feeding the mature sheep (21:17)	Later ministry in epistles (1 Peter, 2 Peter)

ultimate responsibility of communicating truth to coming generations (feed My sheep).

Most commentators see a prediction of Peter's martyrdom by crucifixion in John 21:18,19. The night before the crucifixion of Christ, Peter offered to lay down his life (13:37). But that night he denied Christ. Jesus here tells Peter he will someday die in the same way as his Saviour. Tradition concerning his death states Peter was crucified by the Romans in Nero's circus in A.D. 67 and that at his own request he was crucified upside down. What he volunteered to do was eventually carried out. This was the death by which Peter would glorify God. By the time John recorded these verses, Peter had been dead more than twenty years.

IV.   REALIZATION (21:20–25)

20   Then Peter, turning about, seeth the disciple whom Jesus loved following; which also leaned on his breast at supper, and said, Lord, which is he that betrayeth thee?

21 Peter seeing him saith to Jesus, Lord, and what shall this man do?

22 Jesus saith unto him, If I will that he tarry till I come, what is that to thee? follow thou me.

23 Then went this saying abroad among the brethren, that that disciple should not die: yet Jesus said not unto him, He shall not die; but, If I will that he tarry till I come, what is that to thee?

A.   *What Is That to Thee? (21:20–23).* After Jesus finished His conversation with Peter, He commanded him,

"Follow me" (20:19). As he began following, Peter turned to see John following also. Peter turned back to Jesus and asked, "What shall this man do?" (21:21). Actually, Peter's question is not really that coherent. Remember, he had just been informed his life would end on a cross. When he then turned and saw his lifelong friend, he asked, *"Houtos de ti"* (literally, "But this one . . . what?"). With the new knowledge of his crucifixion followed by the sight of a dear friend, Peter is again at a loss for words.

It was natural for John to follow Peter as he followed Christ. Likewise, it was natural for Peter to be concerned about John. However, Jesus let Peter know that he was to obey Jesus regardless of what happened to John. Therefore, He told him the second time, "Follow thou me." Note the first time Jesus told Peter, "Follow me"; now He adds the word *thou* or *you*. The construction of the sentence in the original language makes it emphatic—"*You* follow Me." No Christian should keep his eyes on another Christian but should look unto Jesus (*see* Hebrews 12:1,2).

The whole intention of Christ's reference to John was that Jesus deals with each Christian individually in ways that other believers may not understand and about which they should not ask questions. He was not affirming that John would live until Christ returned but only rebuking Peter's curiosity.

Peter and John would follow Christ together in the future, just as they had been together in the past. Even before Christ called them, Peter, Andrew, James, and John were partners in the fishing business, lived in the same town (Bethsaida), and possibly grew up together. Jesus called these four to follow Him at the same time. As the disciples multiplied, Jesus chose Peter and John, along with James, to be in His inner circle. These were to be the recipients of special revelations and teachings as shown in Chart 84.

Because Jesus emphasized going out two by two, Peter and John gradually paired off. First, the two of them were sent by Christ to prepare the Passover (Luke 22:8). They were sitting next to each other at the Lord's Supper (13:22–25). When Mary Magdalene found the empty tomb, she ran to tell Peter and John, and they were the first two disciples to enter the tomb (20:1–8). When they were fishing with five other disciples and the Lord was on the shore, John was the

Chart 84

THE FOUR EVENTS WITNESSED EXCLUSIVELY BY THE INNER CIRCLE
1. The raising to life of the daughter of Jairus (Mark 5:37; Luke 8:51)
2. The transfiguration (Matthew 17:1; Mark 9:2; Luke 9:28).
3. The Olivet discourse (Andrew was there also) Matthew 24; Mark 13:3; Luke 21).
4. The withdrawal in the Garden of Gethsemane for special prayer before the betrayal (Matthew 26:37; Mark 14:33).

one who told Peter, his close partner, "It is the Lord" (21:7). We also find Peter and John working together after Pentecost (Acts 3:1; 4:1–3,13,19,20; 8:14–17; Galatians 2:9).

24 This is the disciple which testifieth of these things, and wrote these things: and we know that his testimony is true.

25 And there are also many other things which Jesus did, the which, if they should be written every one, I suppose that even the world itself could not contain the books that should be written. Amen.

B. *What Am I to Thee? (21:24,25).* Some have suggested that John 20:31 is the purpose and conclusion to John. But no conservative scholar questions whether the twenty-first chapter should be included in the book. True, John 20:31 is the aim and apparent conclusion to the book, but the events of chapter twenty-one personify the aim—that people believe in Christ's deity and come to enjoy eternal life. John is identified as the writer (21:20–24) who testifies (*marturia*, eyewitness) to the events in the book, including the events in chapter twenty-one.

Because of the appearance of *I* and *we* in verses twenty-four and twenty-five, and that the writer of John is described objectively, not personally, in this verse, many interpreters think verse twenty-four was written by some other hand than John's. Based upon Clement of Alexandria's statement that John wrote at the urging of his friends in Ephesus, it is believed this verse is a declaration of the veracity of the contents of the gospel made by an Ephesian elder. By the time

John wrote this gospel, the church at Ephesus had already begun to collect the inspired writings of Paul and others. Certainly no more credibility could be given to John's writings than is found in verse twenty-four. Because someone wrote it does not make it less inspired than the case where Moses wrote Deuteronomy, yet another described his death (Deuteronomy 34:5–12).

This gospel concludes acknowledging, "There are also many other things which Jesus did" (21:25). This entire gospel records the events of only twenty days in a period of over three years. For the first and only time in this gospel, the text speaks directly to the reader concluding, "If they [the unrecorded teachings and miracles] should be written every one, I suppose that even the world itself could not contain the books that should be written. Amen" (21:25).

As we hear Jesus ask, "Lovest thou Me?" we need to evaluate ourselves. Any study of a book such as the Gospel of John should serve the ultimate purpose of drawing us nearer to Christ. If Christ is not nearer and more precious to you as a result of studying His Word, then you have missed the aim of John.

SOURCE NOTES

1. E. W. Bullinger, *The Companion Bible* (Grand Rapids, Mich.: Zondervan Bible Publishers, 1974), 1515.
2. John Calvin, cited by Fredrick Godet, *Commentary on the Gospel of John with an Historical and Critical Introduction*, trans. Timothy Dwight, vol. 1 (New York: Funk & Wagnalls, 1886), 345.
3. Henry Allan Ironside, *Addresses on the Gospel of John* (Neptune, N.J.: Loizeaux Brothers, 1974), 76.
4. William Barclay, *The Daily Study Bible: The Gospel of John*, vol. 1 (Philadelphia: The Westminster Press, 1956), 83.
5. Godet, *Commentary*, vol. 1, 356.
6. Cited by Barclay, *Gospel of John*, vol. 1, 155.
7. Cited by Godet, *Commentary*, vol. 1, 433, and Barclay, *Gospel of John*, vol. 1, 155.
8. Cited by Barclay, *Gospel of John*, vol. 1, 176.
9. Brooke Foss Westcott, *Commentary on the Gospel of John: Speaker's Commentary*, cited by Marvin R. Vincent, *Word Studies in the New Testament*, vol. 2 (Grand Rapids, Mich.: Wm. B. Eerdmans Publishing Co., 1965), 134.
10. Barclay, *Gospel of John*, vol. 1, 197.
11. Arthur W. Pink, *Expositions of the Gospel of John*, vol. 1 (Swengel, Penn.: Bible Truth Depot, 1945), 325.
12. Barclay, *Gospel of John*, vol. 1, 201.
13. Cited by Barclay, *Gospel of John*, vol. 1, 217.
14. Cited by Godet, *Commentary*, vol. 2, 21, and Barclay, *Gospel of John*, vol. 1, 220.
15. Martin Luther, cited by Vincent, *Word Studies*, 151f.
16. Aurelius Augustine, *The Works of Aurelius Augustine, Bishop of Hippo: Lectures or Tractates on the Gospel According to St. John* (Edinburgh: T. & T. Clark, 1873), 379.

17. Archibald Thomas Robertson, *Word Pictures in the New Testament*, vol. 5 (New York: Harper & Brothers Publishers, 1932), 139.
18. Vincent, *Word Studies*, 169f.
19. Westcott, cited by Vincent, *Word Studies*, 170.
20. Vincent, *Word Studies*, 171.
21. Barclay, *Gospel of John*, vol. 2, 37.
22. Oswald J. Smith, as reported in a student missionary convention in Toronto, February, 1977.
23. Pliny, cited by Barclay, *Gospel of John*, vol. 2, 49.
24. Robertson, *Word Pictures*, 177.
25. Vincent, *Word Studies*, 190.
26. Alfred Edersheim, *The Life and Times of Jesus the Messiah*, vol. 1 (New York: Longmans, Green, and Co., 1896), 555.
27. Vincent, *Word Studies*, 200.
28. Westcott, cited by Vincent, *Word Studies*, 201.
29. Richard Chenevix Trench, *Synonyms of the New Testament* (New York: Blakeman & Mason, 1859), 197.
30. Godet, *Commentary*, vol. 2, 180.
31. Robertson, *Word Pictures*, 203.
32. Godet, *Commentary*, 185.
33. Lewis Sperry Chafer, *Systematic Theology*, Ed. John F. Walvoord, Donald K. Campbell and Roy B. Zuck, vol. 2 (Wheaton, Illinois: Victor Books, 1988), 367, 484, 485.
34. Alfred Edersheim, *The Temple, Its Ministry and Services, as They Were at the Time of Jesus Christ* (New York: James Pott & Co., 1874), 205.
35. Martin Luther's complete translation of John 13:24 reads, "Dem winkte Simon Petrus und sprach zu ihm: Sag, wer ist's, von dem er redet!"
36. Edwyn Clement Hoskyns, *The Fourth Gospel*, ed. Francis Noel Davey (London: Faber and Faber Ltd., 1947), 443.
37. Godet, *Commentary*, 263.
38. Lucian, cited by Godet, *Commentary*, vol. 2, 266.
39. Tertullian, *Apologetical Works*, 39, cited by G. H. C. MacGregor, *The Gospel of John* (London: Hodder and Stoughton, 1928), 35.
40. Jerome, *Commentary on Galatians*, 6, 10, cited by Barclay, *The Master's Men* (Nashville, Tenn.: Abingdon, 1980), 39.
41. Barclay, *Gospel of John*, vol. 2, 176.
42. Westcott, cited by Vincent, *Word Studies*, 246.
43. C. I. Scofield, *The New Scofield Reference Bible* (New York: Oxford University Press, 1967), footnote 1 on John 16:12, 1149.

44. Henry Alford, *The Greek New Testament*, vol. 1 (London: Rivingtons, 1863), 849.

45. Robertson, *Word Pictures*, 266.

46. Robertson, *Word Pictures*, 272.

47. J. C. Ryle, *Expository Thoughts on the Gospels for Family and Private Use: St. John*, vol. 3 (New York: Fleming H. Revell Co., 1873), 167.

48. John Albert Bengel, *Gnomon of the New Testament*, vol. 2, trans. Andrew R. Fausset (Edinburgh: T. & T. Clark, 1860), 460.

49. Matthew Henry, cited by Pink, *Exposition*, vol. 4, 68.

50. John Nelson Darby, *Notes on the Gospel of John* (London: G. Morrish, n.d.), 236.

51. Darby, *Notes*, 250.

52. Darby, *Notes*, 266.

53. Hoskyns, *Fourth Gospel*, 518.

54. A. Plummer, *The Gospel According to S. John* (Cambridge: University Press, 1882), 330.

55. Heinrich A. W. Meyer, *Critical and Exegetical Handbook to the Gospel of John*, cited by Vincent, *Word Studies*, 289.

56. Benjamin B. Warfield, *The Person and Work of Christ*, 537.

57. Thomas Arnold, *Sermons on the Christian Life—Its Hopes, Its Fears, and Its Close*, 6th ed. (London: 1859), 324.

58. Brooke Foss Westcott, *The Gospel According to St. John: The Authorised Version with Introduction and Notes* (London: John Murray, 1890), 297.